THE
Fall River Tragedy

A HISTORY OF THE
BORDEN MURDERS

BY EDWIN H. PORTER

A facsimile of the 1893 book with a foreword
by Robert A. Flynn

King Philip Publishing Co., Portland, Maine

1985

The Fall River Tragedy—A History of the Borden Murders by Edwin H. Porter was published by Geo. R. H. Buffinton in 1893 at the press of J. D. Munroe in Fall River, Massachusetts. Entered according to an act of Congress in the year 1893 by Geo. R. H. Buffinton in the Office of the Librarian of Congress at Washington, D.C.

This First Facsimile of that edition is published by King Philip Publishing Co., 466 Ocean Avenue, Portland, Maine 04103 in the year 1985.

Library of Congress Catalog Card Number: 85–70910

International Standard Book Number: 0–9614811–0–2

© 1985 by Robert A. Flynn, King Philip Publishing Co.

This edition is limited to one thousand copies.

Printed in the United States of America.

Composition of new text by The Anthoensen Press, Portland, Maine.

Reprinting and binding by Edwards Brothers, Inc., Ann Arbor, Michigan.

FOREWORD

IT HAS BEEN ninety-two years since Edwin H. Porter wrote his history of the Borden murders and very few people have ever read the book. Lizzie Borden prevented its circulation by buying out and destroying the entire edition.

Just how many copies survived the book's suppression in 1893 is as much a mystery as the Borden case itself.

The copy I obtained recently in Fall River (my birthplace) after a forty-year search is one of the rare copies that have surfaced in recent years.

Victoria Lincoln (*A Private Disgrace*, G. P. Putnam's Sons, 1967) and Robert Sullivan (*Goodbye Lizzie Borden*, The Stephen Greene Press, 1974) both indicated in their books that only three copies existed. Williams, Smithburn, and Peterson (*Lizzie Borden: A Case Book of Family and Crime in the 1890s*, T. I. S. Publications Division, Indiana University, 1980) believed only two copies existed. Most other books on the subject make reference to the book's suppression and its extreme rarity.

So, in effect, by reproducing this book I am making it available to the public for the first time.

I have made every effort to print the book in as exact a reproduction of the original size, shape, binding color, and design as is possible despite the poor quality of paper and photographs in the initial printing.

ROBERT A. FLYNN

THE

Fall River Tragedy.

A HISTORY OF THE

BORDEN MURDERS.

A PLAIN STATEMENT OF THE MATERIAL FACTS PERTAINING TO THE

MOST FAMOUS CRIME OF THE CENTURY, INCLUDING THE STORY OF

THE ARREST AND PRELIMINARY TRIAL OF MISS LIZZIE A.

BORDEN AND A FULL REPORT OF THE SUPERIOR COURT

TRIAL, WITH A HITHERTO UNPUBLISHED ACCOUNT

OF THE RENOWNED TRICKEY-McHENRY AFFAIR

COMPILED FROM OFFICIAL SOURCES AND

PROFUSELY ILLUSTRATED WITH

ORIGINAL ENGRAVINGS.

BY EDWIN H. PORTER,

POLICE REPORTER OF THE FALL RIVER GLOBE.

GEO. R. H. BUFFINTON, PUBLISHER.

FALL RIVER.
PRESS OF J. D. MUNROE.
1893.

PREFACE.

When the assassination of Andrew J. Borden and Abbie D. Borden, his wife, was announced, not only the people of Fall River and of Massachusetts, but the public throughout the country manifested the deepest interest in the affair. The murders soon became the theme of universal comment, both in public and private, and every newspaper reference to the affair was read with eagerness, digested and commented upon in a manner unprecedented. The crimes stand out in bold relief as the most atrocious, and at the same time, the most mystifying which the American public had ever before been called upon to discuss. They had about them that fascination of uncertainty, horrible though they were, which fixes the attention and holds it continually. Miss Lizzie A. Borden, a daughter of the murdered man, was arrested and charged with the killing. She was a young woman of hitherto spotless reputation and character, and more than that she was educated, refined and prominently connected with the work of the christian church in Fall River. Her arrest added more and more to the interest which the public had taken in the matter. She was tried before the Superior Court of Massachusetts and a jury of her peers and found not guilty of the crimes. This event settled beyond question the probability of her guilt, and yet the case lost none of its absorbing interest. The author of this book therefore, has for a purpose the desire to give the reading public a connected story of the whole case, commencing with the day of the tragedy and ending with the day that Miss Borden was set free. Persons believing implicitly in the correctness of the findings of the jury at New Bedford will see much wrong done in those chapters which treat of the police work. But that the grand jury indicted the young lady is no fault of the author, and the story of what brought that indictment about is important, therefore it is given without prejudice. Harsh words were said of Miss Borden, but they came from those who had a sworn duty to perform, and they alone are responsible. Her defense is given as freely as the case of the prosecution, and with it the history is made as complete as was possible. The facts discussed came from official sources and are dependent upon the testimony submitted at the court trials.

EDWIN H. PORTER.

CHAPTER I.

Discovery of the Murders.

A T high noon on Thursday the fourth day of August, 1892, the
cry of murder swept through the city of Fall River like a
typhoon on the smooth surface of an eastern sea.   It was caught up
by a thousand tongues and repeated at every street corner until it
reached the utmost confines of the municipality.   A double murder,
the most atrocious of crimes, committed under the very glare of the
mid-day sun within three minutes walk of the City Hall was the way

THE BORDEN RESIDENCE.

the story went and it was true in every particular.   Andrew J. Borden and his wife Abbie D. Borden had been assassinated in their home
at 92 Second street.   The manner in which the deed was done seemed
so brutal, so mysterious, and the tragedy itself so unprecedented that
people stared with open-mouthed amazement as they listened to the
story passing from tongue to tongue.   In the excitement of the

moment the murderer had slipped away unobserved, and bloody as his crime had been he left no trace behind, nor clue to his identity. He had wielded an axe or some similar instrument with the skill of a headsman and had butchered in the most horrible manner the bodies of his defenseless victims.

When discovered, the remains of Mr. Borden lay stretched at full length upon the sofa in the sitting room of his home; the head literally hacked into fragments and the fresh blood trickling from every wound. Up stairs in the guest chamber lay the body of Mrs. Borden similarly mangled and butchered with the head reeking in a crimson pool. She had been murdered while in the act of making the bed and her husband had died as he lay taking his morning nap.

In the house was Miss Lizzie A. Borden, youngest daughter of the slain couple, and Bridget Sullivan, the only servant. They and they alone had been within calling distance of the victims as the fiend or fiends struck the fatal blows. The servant was in the attic, and the daughter was in the barn not more than thirty feet from the back door of the house. This was the condition of things on the premises when the cry went forth which shocked the city and startled the entire country. Neighbors, friends, physicians, police officers and newspaper reporters gathered at the scene in an incredibly short space of time. It was soon learned that the daughter Lizzie had been the first to make the horrible discovery. She said that not many minutes before, she had spoken to her father upon his return from the city; and that after seeing him comfortably seated on the sofa she had gone out to the barn to remain a very short time. Upon returning she saw his dead body and gave the alarm which brought the servant from the attic. Without thinking of Mrs. Borden the daughter sent Bridget for help. Mrs. Adelaide B. Churchill the nearest neighbor, Dr. S. W. Bowen and Miss Alice Russell were among the first to respond. Shortly afterward the dead body of Mrs. Borden was discovered and the unparalleled monstrosity of the crime became apparent. There had been murder most foul, and so far as the developments of the moment indicated, without a motive or a cause. The street in front of the house soon became blocked with a surging mass of humanity, and the excitement grew more and more intense as the meager details of the assassination were learned. Men with blanched faces hurried back and forth through the yard ; police officers stood in groups for a moment and talked mysteriously; physicians consulted among themselves and kind friends ministered to the bereaved daughter and offered her consolation.

Inside the house where the bodies lay the rooms were in perfect order. Mrs. Borden had smoothed out the last fold in the snow white counterpane, and placed the pillows on the bed with the utmost care of a tidy housewife. Every piece of furniture stood in its accustomed place and every book and paper was laid away with rigid exactness. Only the blood as it had dashed in isolated spots against the walls and door jams, and the reeking bodies themselves showed that death in its most violent form had stalked through the unpretentious home and left nothing but its bloody work to tell the tale. No one dared go so far as to suggest a motive for the crime. The house had not been robbed and the friends of the dead had never heard of such a thing as an enemy possessed of hatred enough to commit so monstrous a deed. As the hours passed a veil of deepest mystery closed around the scene and the most strenuous efforts of the authorities to clear the mystery away seemed more and more futile as their work progressed. Men with cool heads, and with cunning and experience sought in vain to unearth some facts to indicate who the criminal might be, but their skill was unavailing, they were baffled at every turn. The author of that hideous slaughter had come and gone as gently as the south wind, but had fulfilled his mission as terrifically as a cyclone. No more cunning plan had ever been hatched in a madman's brain, and no more thorough work was ever done by the guillotine. Mystery sombre and absolute hung in impenetrable folds over the Borden house, and not one ray of light existed to penetrate its blackness.

Mr. Borden and his wife were spending their declining years, highly respected residents, with wealth enough to enjoy all the comforts and luxuries of modern life. Mr. Borden by years of genuine New England thrift and energy had gathered a fortune, and his exemplary life had served to add credit to a family name which had been identified with the development and prosperity of his native state for two hundred years, and which has been known to public and private life since the time of William the Conqueror. His family had the *open sesame* to the best society. The contentment which wealth, influence and high social standing could bring was possible to his family, if its members chose to have it. But he and his wife had been murdered and there was no one who cared to come forward and explain why death had so ruthlessly overtaken them. One thing was manifest ; an iron will and a heart of flint had directed the arm which struck those unoffending people down in a manner exceeding the savage cruelty of the most blood-thirsty creature—man or beast.

The police officers invaded the house and searched in vain for some evidence to assist them in hunting down the murderer. They learned nothing tangible, but they laid the foundation for their future work by carefully scrutinizing the home and its surroundings as well as the bodies. A hint was sent out that a mysterious man had been seen on the doorsteps arguing with Mr. Borden only a few days before. Had *he* done the deed? To those who stopped to contemplate the circumstances surrounding the double murder, it was marvelous to reflect how fortune had favored the assassin. Not once in a million times would fate have paved such a way for him. He had to deal with a family of six persons in an unpretentious two-and-a-half story house, the rooms of which were all connected and in which it would have been a difficult matter to stifle sound. He must catch Mr. Borden alone and either asleep, or off his guard, and kill him with one fell blow. The faintest outcry would have sounded an alarm. He must also encounter Mrs. Borden alone and fell her, a heavy woman, noiselessly. To do this he must either make his way from the sitting room on the ground floor to the spare bed room above the parlor and avoid five persons in the passage, or he must conceal himself in one of the rooms up stairs and make the descent under the same conditions. The murdered woman must not lisp a syllable at the first attack, and her fall must not attract attention. He must then conceal the dripping implement of death and depart in broad daylight by a much frequented street. In order to accomplish this he must take a time when Miss Emma L. Borden, the elder daughter of the murdered man, was on a visit to relatives out of the city; Miss Lizzie A. Borden, the other daughter, must be in the barn and remain there twenty minutes. A less time than that would not suffice. Bridget Sullivan, the servant, must be in the attic asleep on her own bed. Her presence in the pantry or kitchen or any room on the first or second floors would have frustrated the fiend's designs, unless he also killed her so that she would die without a murmur. In making his escape there must be no blood stains upon his clothing ; for such tell-tale marks might have betrayed him. And so, if the assailant of the aged couple was not familiar with the premises, his luck favored him exactly as described. He made no false move. He could not have proceeded more swiftly nor surely had he lived in the modest edifice for years. At the most he had just twenty minutes in which to complete his work. He must go into the house after Miss Lizzie entered the barn and he must disappear before she returned. More than that, the sixth member of the family, John V. Morse, must vanish from the house while the work was being done. He could not have been counted on by any criminal, however shrewd, who had planned the tragedy ahead. Mr. Morse came and went at the Borden homestead. He was not engaged in business in Fall River and there were no stated times when the wretch who did the slaughtering could depend upon his absence. Mr. Morse must not loiter about the house or yard after breakfast as was his custom; he must take a car to some other part of the city and he must not return until his host and hostess have been stretched lifeless. The slightest hitch in these conditions and the murderer would have been balked or detected red handed upon the spot. Had Miss Emma remained at home she would have been a stumbling block; had Miss Lizzie left the stable a few moments earlier she would have seen the murderer as he ran out the side door; had Bridget Sullivan short-ened her nap and descended the stairs she would have heard her mistress drop, as the axe fell on her head; had Mr. Morse cut short his visit to friends by as much as ten minutes the butcher would have dashed into his arms as he ran out at the front gate; had Mr. Borden returned earlier from his morning visit to the post office he would have caught the assassin murdering his aged wife, or had he uttered a scream at the time he himself was cut down, at least two persons would have rushed to his assistance.

CITY MARSHAL RUFUS B. HILLIARD.

It was a wonderful chain of circumstances which conspired to clear the way for the murderer; so wonderful that its links baffled men's understanding.

City Marshal Rufus B. Hilliard received the first intimation that a murder had been committed by telephone message. He was sitting in his office at the Central police station when John Cunningham entered a store half a block from the Borden house and gave notice of the affair. He immediately sent officer George Allen to the scene and then by signal informed each member of his force who was on duty at the time. This was at 11.15 in the forenoon. Officer Allen was the first policeman to visit the house and he saw the horribly muti-

lated body of Mr. Borden, as it lay on the sofa. One glance was
sufficient to cause the policeman to stand almost rooted to the floor,
for he had come unprepared to witness such a sight. Without delay he hurried to the Marshal's office and made a personal
report of what he had seen.

Almost all of the night patrolmen and many of the day men were
absent from the city on the day of the killing, on the annual excursion
of the Fall River Police Association to Rocky Point, a shore resort
near Providence, R. I., and this unusual condition served greatly
to handicap the efforts of Marshal Hilliard in his attempt to get
possession of a tangible clue to the perpetration of the crimes. The
city was but poorly protected by members of the day force, who were
doing double duty.

However, within half an hour after the general alarm had been
sent out a half dozen officers from the central part of the city had

JOHN CUNNINGHAM.

arrived at the Borden house. They were
instructed to make a careful search of the
premises. Officer Allen before he returned
to the police station, had stationed Charles
S. Sawyer at the door on the north side of
the house, and had instructed him to allow
no one except policemen and physicians to
enter the building. Mr. Sawyer was
besieged by hundreds of citizens, but stood
firmly at his post during the entire day,
and it was a time of intense excitement and
pressing demands for admittance. The street in front of the house
was blocked before noon with wagons, teams and pedestrians, and the
people stood for hours in the hot sunshine of an exceptionally warm
midsummer day and speculated and theorized as to what possible
motive any one could have had in so heartlessly butchering
the aged man and woman. Inside the yard and house, ·policemen in
uniform and in citizen's garb, hurried to and fro with an air of mystery
which was becoming them, for to all appearances the assassin had
vanished as completely as if the earth had opened and swallowed him.

The Borden house, a plain two-and-a-half story frame structure,
stands on the east side of Second street and is numbered 92. It is
but one block away from the main thoroughfare of the busy city of
Fall River. Hundreds of vehicles and numberless people pass and
repass before the building daily and yet no person could be found
who saw a suspicious move or heard an unaccustomed sound on

that fatal forenoon, until Miss Lizzie told how she had called Mrs. Churchill, and informed her that a murder had been committed. Mrs. Churchill had been to market and was returning home at about 11 o'clock. She saw Bridget Sullivan, who was also familiarly called "Maggie," running across the street to the residence of Dr. S. W. Bowen, the family physician. The girl told her that "something awful" had happened, and then Mrs. Churchill went into her own house and in a very short time appeared at the kitchen window, which commands a view of the side door of the Borden residence. She saw Miss Lizzie sitting on the back doorsteps, with her face buried in her hands and seemingly in great distress. Mrs. Churchill crossed the yard and offered Miss Lizzie a few words of consolation.

Bridget Sullivan, the only living person who admits that she was in the house at the time of the killing, was the first to give the alarm, by notifying Mrs. Dr. Bowen. Bridget was in her own room in the attic where she had gone to wash the windows; and after completing the work had lain down on the bed to rest. While there she heard Miss Lizzie call and from the tone of her voice knew that something was wrong. Bridget came down quickly and Miss Lizzie said to her, "Father is dead, go for Dr. Bowen." Bridget obeyed. The physician was not at home and she returned. Then Miss Lizzie

GEORGE W. ALLEN.

sent her for Miss Alice Russell, who lived two blocks away, and who was an intimate friend of the family. Briefly this is what had taken place before the arrival of officer Allen; and up to that time no one except the assassin knew that the body of Mrs. Abbie D. Borden lay weltering in its own blood, in the guest chamber on the second floor. To those who early visited the house, the vision of Mr. Borden's body as it lay on the sofa, with the life blood still warm, and flowing from a dozen gaping wounds was a horror so dreadful that they had no thought of Mrs. Borden. It remained for the neighbor, Mrs. Churchill, and the servant Bridget, to make this awful discovery. Dr. Bowen, who had arrived shortly after Bridget's visit to his house, in response to her call, asked for a sheet with which to cover the body of Mr. Borden. Bridget brought one from one of the back bedrooms on the upper floor. About this time Miss Lizzie asked for her mother. It is related that this request for some one to go and find

Mrs. Borden was the second made by Miss Lizzie. Suddenly it dawned upon those present that in the midst of the excitement of the moment, Mrs. Borden had been forgotten. Of all persons in the world, she would have been more deeply interested in the death of her husband and possibly she could give some explanation of his tragic taking off.

Bridget was unwilling to go alone in search of Mrs. Borden and so Mrs. Churchill volunteered to bear her company. The two women passed through the front hall and ascended the stairs in the front entry. Reaching a landing half way up where their eyes were on a level with the floor, they looked across the hall, through an open door, under the bed, and saw the prostrate form of the dead woman. It lay full on the face and the arms were folded underneath. Mrs. Churchill turned and retraced her steps to the kitchen. She sighed audibly as she took a chair and Miss Russell

JOHN J. MANNING.

said to her, "What, another?" The reply was, "Yes, Mrs. Borden is killed too." Bridget had followed back to the kitchen.

Special police officer Patrick H. Doherty was the second policeman to reach the house, and he was soon followed by Assistant Marshal John Fleet and officers Michael Mullaly, John Devine and William H. Medley. Before noon several other policemen, friends of the family and local newspaper men, had been admitted to the house. Also Medical Examiner Dr. William A. Dolan and a number of other physicians.

The Medical Examiner arrived at 11.45 and encountered Dr. Bowen and Bridget on his way into the sitting room. He then made a hasty view of the bodies and the house, and commenced immediately to make preparations for holding an autopsy.

John Vinnicum Morse, brother of Andrew J. Borden's first wife and uncle of Misses Lizzie and Emma, arrived at the house shortly before noon. He entered the north gate and went directly to a pear tree in the back yard, where he ate two pears and then returned to the side door and entered; then Miss Lizzie told him that Mr. and Mrs. Borden had been murdered. Mr. Morse had slept in the guest chamber, where Mrs. Borden's body was found, on the previous night and had after eating his breakfast that morning, left the house to visit a relative who resided on Weybosset street, in Fall River, about a mile from the Borden House.   It was remembered that Mr. Borden fastened the screen on the side door after Mr. Morse passed out at 9.20 o'clock in the morning, and bade his guest return in time for dinner.   Mr. Morse had come to the house on the afternoon before the tragedy and had spent a few hours with Mr. Borden and then had driven to the Borden summer residence and farm which are situated about six miles from the city, in the town of Somerset.   He returned in time for supper and spent the night in the house.

Miss Lizzie sat at the foot of the back stairs and near the side door, when Mrs. Churchill arrived.   She had called her neighbor and informed her that Mr. Borden had been "stabbed or killed." Then she went into the kitchen and remained a few minutes.   Here she was seen by a number of policemen, physicians and others who had been admitted to the house before noon.   She told Mrs. Churchill that she had been absent from the sitting room a few minutes and that she spent the time in the barn, where she had gone to get a piece of iron.

About noon she went upstairs to her own bedroom in company with Miss Alice Russell, and the two sat alone for sometime.   While in the upper part of the house she was approached by Assistant Marshal John Fleet who made numerous inquiries concerning the condition of things in the house previous to the murders. She told him as she had told others, that Mrs. Borden had received a note delivered by a boy, early in the morning, asking her to come and visit a friend who was sick.   She did not know who sent the message nor who delivered it, except that the bearer was a small boy.   Her father she said had had angry words with an unknown man on the front steps a few days before the murder.   She thought the man was a farm laborer.   The daughter also gave the police information that the entire family had been sick a few days before and that she feared that an enemy had attempted to poison them.   The sickness had followed after drinking milk, and this fact was enough to cause Miss Lizzie to suspect that the milk had been tampered with.   The information given by the daughter was carried to Marshal Hilliard and he ordered several policeman to guard the main roads leading out of the city.   A squad was also sent to Taunton River Bridge, over which the assassin, if he was a farm laborer, would pass on his way to the country.   The police questioned Bridget closely and she corroborated what Miss Lizzie had said about the sickness in the family.

So confused was the servant girl that she could tell no coherent story of the condition of things about the house during the forenoon. She did say that during the morning, Mrs. Borden had instructed her to wash the windows from the outside of the house. This she had done. After receiving this order from her mistress, Bridget did not see her alive again. She finished her work before 10 o'clock, and while in the sitting room heard Mr. Borden trying to get in at the front door. He had returned from the city. She opened the front door and let Mr. Borden in and then went up stairs. This was the last she saw of him until Miss Lizzie called her when the body was found.

When the police officers arrived they began to search the house for the weapon, and Bridget showed them into the cellar. Here they found four hatchets, one of which had the appearance of having been washed after recent use. At this time little attention was paid to this particular hatchet, but all the hatchets were taken to the police station.

Shortly after 12 o'clock special officer Philip Harrington arrived at the house, as had other policemen. He joined in the search for evidence which would lead to the arrest of the murderer or to the discovery of the weapon. After viewing the bodies he went to Miss Lizzie, who was in her own room talking with Miss Alice Russell. He asked her if she knew anything about the crime, and she replied " No." It was then that she detailed to him the story of her visit to the barn, and he cautioned her to be careful, and to give him all the information in her possession.

" Perhaps tomorrow," said the officer, " you will have a clearer frame of mind." No sir," responded Miss Lizzie with a gentle courtesy, " I can tell you all I know now just as well as at any other time."

The conversation was prolonged and during the entire time Miss Lizzie controlled her emotions wonderfully for a young lady who had so recently been called upon to witness the blood of her father and step-mother flowing from dozens of hideous wounds. When the officer left her he went to the City Marshal and related his experience. The public was not informed that then and there suspicions were aroused in the minds of the police that the daughter knew more of the circumstances of the tragedy then she cared to tell, but nevertheless this was true.

All through that eventful day the police searched the house, cellar, yard and barn but found nothing to confirm any suspicions which they might have entertained as to who was guilty of the crimes.

Hon. John W. Coughlin, mayor of the city, who is a physician, was among the first at the house and he took an active interest in the search for evidence. From cellar to attic the police and physicians delved into every nook and corner; every particle of hay in the barn loft and every blade of grass in the yard was turned over; and when the day was done the harvest had been nothing, except the discovery of the double murder of a peaceful old man and his harmless wife, struck down in their home like an ox in the stall. There was no assassin, no weapon, no motive; just the crime and veil of mystery surrounding which apparently time alone could lift.

They found the house in perfect order. The front and cellar doors were locked ; and every window sash was down. Even the victims as they lay showed no signs of a struggle and the blood which spurted as the weapon fell had not bespattered the rooms and furniture as it generally does under circumstances such as these which surrounded the butchery of the Bordens. They found two persons in the house living and two dead; and the living could throw no light upon the darkness which clouded the stark forms of the dead. A sturdy old man, rich in this world's goods, highly esteemed, retired from active life, without a known enemy, and his equally unoffending wife were cut down in their own house, in the broad daylight; and the assassin had left absolutely no trace of himself. No man had seen him enter the house and no one had witnessed his departure. The city was excited as it never was before; thousands of people hurried from their places of business, from the workshop and the mill, and gathered in the street in front of the house. Newspaper men from the principal cities of New York and New England, to which the telegraph had communicated the news of the astounding crime, arrived on the afternoon trains ; and as the day wore on, the dark mystery grew darker and the task of fastening the crime on the guilty party took on the semblance of an impossibility.

Medical Examiner Dolan and a corps of physicians held an autopsy on the bodies in the afternoon and found that thirteen blows had rained upon the head of the unsuspecting Mr. Borden, and that no less than eighteen had descended upon the skull of Mrs. Borden. The cuts were deep and long and any one of them would have produced instant death.

Could any but a maniac have inflicted those pitiless wounds; or could any but a madman have struck so ruthlessly and unerringly and watched the effect as the weapon sped on its mission of death, time and time again? These were questions which suggested themselves to the public, but they were unanswered and seemingly unanswerable.

This was the baffling condition of things which beset Marshal Hilliard and his officers after the scene had been hurriedly gone over. Out of this chaos of bloody crime and bewildering uncertainty, the police were expected to bring light and order. It was a herculean task yet they went to work with an energy prompted by duty, and spurred to greater efforts by the public demand that justice overtake the author of the foul deeds.

CHAPTER II.

POLICE SEARCHING THE PREMISES.

LET us go back to the Borden house on the afternoon following the time of the massacre. Medical Examiner Dolan and his associates are found at work on the partial autopsy. The bodies had been removed to the sitting room. The physicians found thirteen wounds on the head of Mr. Borden, which were clean cut and evidently made by some very sharp instrument. The largest was four and a half inches long and two inches wide. Many of them penetrated the skull and one severed the eye-ball and jaw bone. In Dr. Dolan's own words the "sight was the most ghastly" he had ever witnessed. Mrs. Borden's body was even more severely dealt with. The head was chopped into ribbons of flesh and the skull broken in several places. A deep wound was discovered between the shoulder blades, and had the appearance of having been made by a hatchet, the blade penetrating full three inches deep. The stomachs of the victims were taken out, sealed up and sent to Prof. E. S. Wood, an eminent chemist of Harvard University, for analysis.

CHARLES S. SAWYER.

It was desirable to know if their contents would reveal the fact as to whether or not the milk which was used, had been poisoned. Then again there was a difference of opinion as to which of the two persons had been killed first. Only the condition of the blood at the time of the discovery, and the contents of the stomachs could detemine that question. The pool of blood in which Mrs. Borden's head lay was coagulated, while the life-giving element of Mr. Borden's body was fresh and oozing from the wounds. It was evident that the woman had been dead two hours before the assassin slaughtered the old man. Yet this must be established beyond a doubt, and in order to do so, Prof. Wood must determine to what stage digestion had passed. The autopsy was partially finished and the bodies delivered into the hands of undertaker Winward, who prepared them for burial.

The police were more than ever active during the afternoon. City Marshal Hilliard and State Detective George Seaver of Taunton, visited the house and made personal inquiry of the inmates, and viewed the bodies and their surroundings. The search for evidence was continued until night with little or no satisfactory result, so far as the public knew. Dr. Bowen, who was the first physician to enter the house, told the writer the following story of the condition of things as he found them.

"When I reached my home, and before I entered it, my wife said to me, ' you are wanted at the Borden's, something terrible has happened.' Without waiting to learn what the trouble was, I hurried across the street, and entered the house by the side door, which leads

DR. S. W. BOWEN.

to the kitchen, there I was confronted by Mrs. Churchill, who lives next door to the Bordens, and by Miss Alice Russell and Miss Lizzie Borden. Miss Russell was sitting by Miss Lizzie's side, rubbing her forehead and hands and otherwise comforting her. I asked what the trouble was and they told me that Mr. Borden had been killed. I asked how long since it had happened, and they replied that it was only a few minutes. By conservative calculation, I believe that I was present at Mr. Borden's side not over twenty minutes after the fatal blows had been inflicted. Alone I walked into the sitting room and there I saw the body of Mr. Borden on a lounge. I determined to make a thorough investigation without delay and proceeded. The sofa upon which the dead man reclined was of mahogany with hair cloth covering, such as was commonly manufactured for high class parlor furniture forty years ago. Mr. Borden lay partly on his right side, with his coat thrown over the arm of the sofa at its head. He wore a dressing gown and his feet rested on the carpet. It was his custom to lie in that way. His position was perfectly natural and he appeared as if he had just lain down to sleep. I was impressed at this.

point with the manifest absence of any sign of a struggle. Mr. Borden's hands were not clinched; no piece of furniture was overturned; there was no contraction of the muscles or indications of pain, such as we expect to find under similiar circumstances. I am satisfied that he was asleep when he received the first blow, which was necessarily fatal. I approached the body and felt for the pulse. It had ceased to beat. Then I examined the body to note its condition and the extent of the wounds. Mr. Borden's clothing was not disarranged, and his pockets had apparently not been touched. The blows were delivered on the left side of the head, which was more exposed than the other, by reason of the dead man's position. I do not believe he moved a muscle after being struck. The cuts extended from the eye and nose around the ear. In a small space there were at least eleven distinct cuts of about the same depth and general appearance. In my opinion, any one of them would have proved fatal almost instantly. Physician that I am and accustomed to all kinds of horrible sights, it sickened me to look upon the dead man's face. I am inclined to think that an axe was the instrument used. The cuts were about four and a half inches in length and one of them had severed the eye-ball and socket. There was some blood on the floor and spatters on the wall, but nothing to indicate the slaughter that had taken place. I calculated that nearly all the blows were delivered from behind with great rapidity. At this point I returned to the kitchen and inquired for Mrs. Borden. Miss Lizzie replied that she did not know where her mother was. She said that she (Lizzie) had been out to the barn and that the servant was on the third floor. Mrs. Churchill suggested that I go up stairs, which I did, entering the front room. I was informed that Mr. John Morse had occupied it the night before. As I passed within I was horrified to see the body of Mrs. Borden on the floor between the bed and dressing-case in the northeast corner. I walked over and realized that she was dead, but at that moment I was not sure she had been murdered. I thought she might have fainted. The sad truth was discovered too soon. Mrs. Borden had also been murdered. I think she must have been engaged in making the bed when the murderer appeared with an axe or hatchet and made a slash at her. After that she turned, and the fiend chopped her head as if it had been a cake of ice. One blow killed the woman but the murderer kept on hacking at her until he was well satisfied that she was dead. It is a mystery to me how he could have done so much savage work in so short a time and made no noise. The weapon must have been a sharp one for the cuts were as clean as if made by a razor. There were, however, no signs of a struggle in the surroundings. There was a large pool of blood under the dead woman's head as she lay with her hands under her. I easily made out eleven distinct gashes of apparently the same size as those on her husband's face. Some of these blows had been delivered from the rear and two or three from the front. One glance blow cut off nearly two square inches of flesh from the side of the head. In my judgment, the dead woman did not struggle. She was rendered unconscious by the first blow. Not a chair was displaced and not a towel disturbed on the rack near by. I visited the dead in company with the police officers, but made no further observations at that time. I afterwards talked with Miss Lizzie, but she was in a highly nervous state. She said that her father left the house about 9 o'clock and went to the bank and the post-office. He returned about 10.30, as near as she could remember, and took off his coat to put on his dressing gown. She asked him about the mail, and also if he was feeling any better, as he had been sick the day before. She said he replied to her, ' I feel no better now, no worse,' and then went into the sitting room. Shortly afterward the daughter went out to the barn. She told me that she didn't think that she was gone more than fifteen or twenty minutes, and then came back and discovered the murdered bodies of her father and her step-mother.

"Members of the family had been sick recently. Mrs. Borden came to me Wednesday morning and said that she was very much frightened, for she thought she had been poisoned. She and Mr. Borden had vomited all night and she feared the poison had been from the baker's bread or the milk. Miss Lizzie and Bridget had been sick with the same symptoms, and it was their belief that an enemy had attempted to kill the whole family."

The police upon investigation found that Dr. Bowen's story that the Borden's had been ill was true in every particular and they naturally went to work in order to find, if possible, the person who administered the poison. Special officers Harrington and Doherty were assigned to this task and before midnight they had made a startling discovery. So astounding in fact, that they hardly believed their senses. They started out late in the afternoon, to visit the various drug stores of the city and to make inquiry as to who bought or offered to buy poison. They worked without success until they came to D. R. Smith's pharmacy, at the corner of South Main and Columbia streets. Eli Bence, the clerk, informed them that on Wednesday before the murder, a young woman had come into his store and asked to buy a small bottle of hydrocyanic acid.

Suspicions are cruel, and if unfounded, they burn like hot iron ; but in a murder mystery, where every link may strengthen the chain, they rise up at a thousand points and cannot be ignored. She wanted poison to kill the moths which were eating her seal skin cloak. If a person wished to kill and avoid detection, and that person were wise, hydrocyanic acid would be first choice among all deadly drugs. It is a diluted form of prussic acid and it does its work surely. It is not necessary to use it in bulk, homeopathic doses are all sufficient. It is absorbed by the nervous system and leaves no traces, and it produces none of the anti-mortem symptoms peculiar to most violent poisons. There is no vomiting, no spasm or convulsions, no contraction of the muscles—hydrocyanic acid simply takes hold of the

THE BORDEN HOMESTEAD, FERRY STREET.

heart and stops its beating. It may not have been used in this case, and at this time the detectives did not claim that it was. Mr. Bence told her that he did not sell so deadly a poison except upon a doctor's certificate and she went away empty handed. This woman, Mr. Bence and others positively identified as Miss Lizzie Borden. When the clerk told his story to the officers they took him to the Borden house. This was about 10 o'clock on the night following the murder. He was placed in a position to see Miss Lizzie and when he came out was more certain than before that she was the lady who called for the prussic acid. This then was a possible clue and the first and only one which the police had secured. The *Fall River Daily Globe* published the particulars of this incident the next day. But almost every newspaper in the country failed to accept it as authentic, and while it served to point the police toward a possible solution of the great murder mystery, it also brought down upon them the vituperation of many a bucolic newspaper man who knew not of what he wrote, or knowing cared little for justice and truth. From the day after the killing, newspapers throughout the country questioned the ability of the officers of the Fall River police department and some of them went so far as to criticise sharply the work done. An act of injustice unless the author of the criticism knew as much of the case as the police themselves, which was hardly to be expected. However, the work went on, yet with this slight clue the mystery seemed dark as ever.

More bewildering in fact, for there arose countless suggestions during the afternoon which the police were called upon to consider. John V. Morse developed into a seemingly very important factor before the day had passed, and special officer Medley was detailed to look up the facts concerning his whereabouts during that day. Mr. Morse had told the newspaper reporters of his visit in the morning to the house of a relative, Mrs. Emery at No. 4 Weybosset street. Thither went the policeman accompanied by the writer to investigate. The Emery's were found at home and Mrs. Emery said that Mr. Morse had visited her house that morning, arriving there before 10 o'clock and remaining until 11.20. A niece of Mr. Morse was present and she also declared that her uncle had left the house at the time stated. The testimony of these two witnesses would set at rest forever the theory that John V. Morse was within a mile of the Borden house when the old people were done to death. But these facts were not then generally known and there were many persons who believed that he knew more concerning the killing than he cared to relate.

The City Marshal sent a detail of police to guard the Borden house soon after the murder was reported and instructions were given out that every member of the household be shadowed. Officer John Devine was designated to keep Mr. Morse in sight and every movement which he made was carefully watched. He was allowed to come and go at will, but whenever he appeared on the street a great crowd gathered. On one evening in particular when the excitement was at the highest tension Mr. Morse set out for the post office. Before he had completed his journey a mob numbering a thousand people was at his heels and fears were entertained less he would be roughly handled. Officer Devine was in the shadow of Mr. Morse and saw him safely back to the Borden house.

CHAPTER III.

The Borden Family.

ANDREW J. BORDEN was numbered among the wealthy and influential men of Fall River. He was one of the family of Bordens whose name has always been identified with the growth and business enterprises of the city and vicinity. No one knows how much money he was worth, but persons who are as well acquainted with his affairs as he would allow them to be, do not hesitate to say that his estate was worth $300,000. He was a thrifty Yankee in every sense of the word, and nothing that represented money was ever wasted by him. No other man knew the worth of a dollar better than he, and none were more thoroughly convinced that a dollar properly invested would bring its returns many times over. Upon the death of his father Abraham Borden he came into possession of a small estate but his fortune was of his own creation. Abraham Borden sold fish in the streets of Fall River when the place was but a village and thus by patient and plodding economy accumulated enough money to purchase a house on Ferry street and some other real estate. But the murdered man was never too busy counting his money to stop and do a day's work. He owned farms across the Taunton river in Somerset and took the greatest interest in superintending the work thereon. There was nothing like style around him, and no one wondered why he did not make a show of his money. He had devoted his entire life to its accumulation, spending but little and it was not expected of him to change his manner of life in old age, although many a man would have pursued a different course in his declining years. Other matters besides those of the farm occupied the old man's attention for he was a prominent figure in financial circles. He was president of the Union Savings Bank, a member of its Board of Trustees and investment, a director of the Merchants Manufacturing Company, the B. M. C. Durfee Safe Deposit and Trust Company, the Globe Yarn Mills, the Troy Cotton and Woolen Manufactory and other manufacturing concerns. In each of these he had large sums of money invested and the returns were undoubtedly large. In early life

Mr. Borden was for many years engaged in the undertaking business with William M. Almy and Theodore D. W. Wood and it was his boast that during his active business life he never borrowed a cent or gave a promisory note. He was always conservative in his investments of money; a man of excellent judgment, and he was often called upon to act as appraiser on land values. Two years before his death he erected one of the finest business blocks in the city located at the corner of South Main and Anawan streets. His mode of living was simple and unostentatious, and he was a pattern of old

MRS. ABBIE D. BORDEN.

time New England industry, thrift, economy and good citizenship. He was twice married, his first wife being Sarah A. Morse, daughter of Anthony Morse. His second was Abbie D. Gray, daughter of Oliver Gray, whom he married on June 6, 1865. He lived with his two daughters Emma L. and Lizzie A., who were issues of his first marriage. At the time of his death he was seventy years of age and his wife was sixty-seven.

Miss Lizzie Andrew Borden was thirty-two years old at the time of her father's death. Her mother died when she was two years of age, and she was cared for in her early childhood by her elder sister. A few years before the murder she joined the Central Congregational church and was ofttimes an active member of that society. She was reared under conditions which could have made life a luxury had she and her parents turned their attention to society. The most aristocratic drawing rooms of the city would have welcomed the daughters of Andrew J. Borden. But Miss Lizzie seemed to care but little for society. She preferred to move in a limited circle of friends and never sought to enlarge the number of her acquaintances. She avoided strangers and persons with whom she was not familiar. She was born in the old Borden homestead on Ferry street in Fall River and received her education in the public schools, graduating from the high school early in life. Her classmates say that she was rather eccentric in her manner of life, and of a retiring disposition. She never attended college although her father was amply able to give her the best education that the schools of the country could furnish. At the mission of the Central church on Pleasant street, Fall River, she taught a class of young people, and there formed the acquaintance of the Rev. Edwin A. Buck who was her constant companion and spiritual adviser during the great affliction which came to her in after life. Besides her active church work she was a member of the Fruit and Flower Mission and other charitable organizations as well as the Woman's Christian Temperance Union. In all of these she was considered a valuable and conscientious worker. In the summer of 1890 she joined a party of young ladies who made the tour of Europe, but aside from this she never traveled extensively.

Miss Emma L. Borden was the eldest child, being thirty-seven at the time of her father's murder. She had been less active in church matters than Miss Lizzie and had not traveled outside the bounds of New England. Her education, disposition and manner of life were somewhat similar to those of her sister. At the time of the murders she was visiting friends in Fairhaven, Mass., and arrived home on the evening of August 4, in response to a telegram sent by Dr. Bowen.

John V. Morse was sixty-nine years of age at the time of the murders. He is a native of New England, his early home being at Dartmouth, Mass. At the age of twenty-five he went west and located at Hastings, Iowa, where he engaged in farming, and built up a comfortable fortune. For tweny years he was separated from his friends in Massachusetts and during that time, by honesty and frugality made himself a respected and influential citizen of his adopted state. Besides his farming interest he was engaged in other enterprises which brought in a goodly sum of money. After his years of work in the west he came back to New England, arriving at Warren, Rhode Island, in April, 1888. He remained a short time in Warren and then removed to Dartmouth, which place he called his permanent home. After his return he made frequent visits to the home of the Bordens in Fall River and was upon the most intimate terms with all the members of the family.

CHAPTER IV.

HIRAM C. HARRINGTON'S STORY.

HIRAM C. HARRINGTON a brother-in-law of Andrew J. Borden having married Mr. Borden's only sister, Luanna, and a blacksmith by trade, threw some light upon the manner in which the Borden's lived which was highly interesting and important for the police to know.   He said in an inteview the day after the murder :

"I have become acquainted with a good deal of the family history during years past.   Mr. Borden was an exceedingly hard man concerning money matters, determined and stubborn, and when once he gets an idea nothing could change him.   As the motive for this crime it was money, unquestionably money.   If Mr. Borden died he would have left something over $500,000 and in my opinion that estate furnishes the only motive, and a sufficient one for the double murder.   Last evening I had a long interview with Miss Lizzie, who has refused to see anyone else.   I questioned her carefully as to her story of the crime.   She was very composed, showed no signs of any emotion, nor were there any traces of grief upon her countenance. That did not surprise me, as she is not naturally emotional.   I asked her what she knew of her father's death and after telling of the unimportant events of the early morning she said her father came home at 10:30 o'clock.   She was in the kitchen at the time, she said, but went into the sitting room when her father arrived.   She was very solicitous concerning him and assisted to remove his coat and put on his dressing gown and inquired about his health.   She told me that she helped him to get a comfortable reclining place upon the sofa, and asked him if he did not wish the blinds closed to keep out the sun so that he could have a nice nap.   She pressed him to allow her to place an afghan over his body, but he said he did not need it.   Then she asked him tenderly several times if he was perfectly comfortable, if there was anything she could do for him and upon receiving assurance to the negative she withdrew.

"I then questioned her very carefully as to the time she left the house, and she told me positively that it was about 10:45.   She said she saw her father on the lounge as she passed out. On leaving the house, she says she went directly to the barn to obtain some lead. She informed me that it was her intention to go to Marion on a vacation, and she wanted the lead in the barn loft to make some sinkers. She was a very enthusiastic angler. I went over the ground several times and she repeated the same story. She told me that it was hard to place the exact time she was in the barn, as she was cutting the lead into sizable sinkers, but thought she was absent about twenty minutes. Then she thought again, and said it might have been thirty minutes. She entered the house and went directly to the sitting room, as she says she was anxious concerning her father's health. 'I discovered him dead,' she said, 'and cried for Bridget, who was upstairs in her room.' 'Did you go and look for your stepmother?' I asked. 'Who found her?' But she did not reply. I pressed her for some idea of the motive and the author of the act, and after she had thought a moment she said, calmly: 'A year ago last spring our house was broken into while father and mother were at Swansea, and a large amount of money stolen, together with diamonds. You never heard of it because father did not want it mentioned, so as to give the detectives a chance to recover the property. That may have some connection with the murder. Then I have seen strange men around the house. A few months ago I was coming through the back yard, and as I approached the side door I saw a man there examining the door and premises. I did not mention it to any one. The other day I saw the same man hanging about the house, evidently watching us. I became frightened and told my parents about it. I also wrote to my sister at Fairhaven about it.'

Miss Borden then gave it as her opinion that the strange man had a direct connection with the murder, but she could not see why the house was not robbed, and did not know of any one who would desire revenge upon her father.

" Yes, there were family dissentions although it has been always kept very quiet. For nearly ten years there have been constant disputes between the daughters and their father and stepmother. It arose, of course with regard to the stepmother. Mr. Borden gave her some bank stock, and the girls thought they ought to be treated as evenly as the mother. I guess Mr. Borden did try to do it, for he deeded to the daughters, Emma L. and Lizzie A., the homestead on Ferry street, an estate of 120 rods of land, with a house and barn, all valued at $3000. This was in 1887. The trouble about money matters did not diminish, nor the acerbity of the family ruptures

lessen, and Mr. Borden gave each girl ten shares in the Crystal Spring
Bleachery Company, which he paid $100 a share for. They sold them
soon after for less than $40 a share. He also gave them some bank
stock at various times, allowing them of course, the entire income
from them. In addition to this he gave them a weekly stipend,
amounting to $200 a year. In spite of all this the dispute about their
not being allowed enough went on with equal bitterness. Lizzie did
most of the demonstrative contention, as Emma is very quiet and
unassuming, and would feel very deeply any disparaging or angry
word from her father. Lizzie on the contrary, was haughty and
domineering with the stubborn will of her father and bound to contest
for her rights. There were many animated interviews between father
and daughter on this point. Lizzie is of a repellant disposition, and,
after an unsuccessful passage with her father, would become sulky
and refuse to speak to him for days at a time. She moved in the best
society in Fall River, was a member of the Congregational church,
and is a brilliant conversationalist. She thought she ought to entertain as others did, and felt that with her father's wealth she was
expected to hold her end up with others of her set. Her father's
constant refusal to allow her to entertain lavishly angered her. I
have heard many bitter things she has said of her father, and know
she was deeply resentful of her father's maintained stand in this
matter. This house on Ferry street was an old one, and was in constant need of repairs. There were two tenants paying $16.50 and $14
a month, but with taxes and repairs there was very little income from
the property. It was a great deal of trouble for the girls to keep the
house in repair, and a month or two ago they got disgusted and
deeded the house back to their father. I am positive that Emma
knows nothing of the murder.''

CHAPTER V.

The Search of the House.

FRIDAY morning came and with it little but mystery to add to the awful tragedy. The police had guarded the house all night. Marshal Hilliard had been active to an unusual degree, but the solution of the great murder mystery seemed to be as far distant as at any time since the discovery of the bodies. It was stated early Friday morning that arrests would be made during the day, but they were not. Miss Lizzie Borden was suspected but there was no evidence against her. It would have been a serious matter to arrest a person for such a terrible crime as this double murder, especially when it is considered that the one suspected occupied a high social position in the community. Besides, she had a spotless reputation, not one word of criticism had passed upon her before this time; and, furthermore, she was an heiress to a fortune of not less than $300,000. The officers of the law must have more evidence, and with this idea in view they again visited the house for the

ASST. MARSHAL JOHN FLEET.

purpose of a more thorough search. On the afternoon before the report had gone out that Miss Lizzie had refused the officers permission to search her room. This was promptly denied. However, they were not satisfied, and the ground was carefully gone over again. Five officers spent over three hours ransacking rooms, bureaus, beds, boxes, trunks and everything else where it was thought that anything which they would like to find might be hidden.

Not a thing was discovered which afforded the slightest clue to the perpetrator of the bold and blood curdling crimes.

The searching party consisted of Marshal Hilliard, Assistant Marshal Fleet, State Detective Seaver, Medical Examiner Dolan and Capt. Desmond. They went to the house shortly after 3 o'clock, and did not leave until nearly 6 o'clock. There were a number of people in the house beside the two daughters, the servant and John V. Morse. Among them were Mrs. Holmes and Miss Russell, friends of the family, who had been sent for by the Misses Borden to keep them company.

The squad of police surrounding the house were given instructions not to let any one enter or leave while the search was in progress, and they obeyed their orders to the letter.

Attorney Andrew J. Jennings of Fall River, was also present. He had been retained by the Misses Borden to look after their interests, but made no attempt to interfere in any way with the searching party. Mr. Morse offered his services to the officers, but they were declined with thanks. The police were satisfied after an hour's work on the first floor and cellar, and then they passed to the second floor. Miss Lizzie was in her room when they approached the door. She opened her trunk and said "Is there anything I can do or show you, gentlemen?" She was told that nothing further was expected of her. They spent another hour ransacking the rooms on this floor but their efforts were unrewarded. Then the yard and barn were again searched but with the same result. Nothing was found and nothing was taken from the premises, if the words of a policeman at the time were to be depended upon. After the party left one of the officers in conversation dwelt particularly upon the demeanor of Miss Lizzie at the time of the search. He said :—" I was surprised at the way she carried herself and I must say that I admire her nerve. I did not think that a woman could have so much. She did not appear to be in the least bit excited or worried. I have wondered why she did not faint upon her discovery of the dead body of her father. Most women would have done so, for a more horrible sight I never saw, and I have walked over a battle-field where thousands lay mangled and dead. She is a woman of remarkable nerve and self control and her sister Emma is very much of the same disposition, although not so strong.

After so thorough a search of the house it was expected that some startling developments would be made, but the public was doomed to disappointment. Contrary to the expectations of all it was announced that absolutely nothing had been discovered which would lead to a clue or assist in any way in clearing up the great mystery.

There was one thing of importance which the police did accomplish on the second day after the murder. The time of the taking off of Mr. Borden was fixed at between 10:50 and 11:03 o'clock, and it was assumed that Mrs. Borden was killed before that time.

They arrive at their decision regarding the old gentleman by the following facts:

It was known that Mr. Borden was talking to Mr. Charles M. Horton at 10:30 o'clock, as they were seen together by persons on the Chace Mill car that leaves City Hall for Bedford and Quarry streets at 10:30. The car was standing in front of the building. After leaving Mr. Horton Mr.

BRIDGET SULLIVAN.

Borden walked up South Main street, stopping for a minute or two at this block and then going through Borden street to Second and to his home. Bridget Sullivan was positive that she admitted him at the front door between 10:45 and 10:50; it was before 11 and after 10:45. Marshal Hilliard made special inquiries of the persons in the office with him concerning the time that he received the telephone message, and it has been fixed at within a minute of 11:15. Officer Allen was sent to investigate, and positively asserts that he was at the house at 10:20. A man who heard the alarm on the street says that at the time there was no one in sight except the person who informed him. He was able to fix the time to within a minute of 10:45 by attending circumstances that he can recall clearly. The clock at Dr. Bowen's had struck 11 just before Miss Lizzie came to the door for the doctor, and Dr. Bowen reached Mr. Borden's house at 11:30.

The murder was reported within fifteen minutes from the time that Mr. Borden is known to have been alive.

With this detail were involved many issues. It practically broke down any theories that a mysterious assassin slyly entered the house, sneaked into the rooms and then killed his victims. The intervening space of time was too brief. It became perfectly apparent to the police that the body of Mrs. Borden lay for an hour or more, in the room where Mr. Morse slept, brutally hacked, the work of a murderer, showing beyond all question and cavil that the blows were administered, not in a frenzy at the sight of blood, but with one all absorbing purpose—immediate death. There was evidence of fiendish brutality in the work, shown not alone in the manner in which it was done, but in the apparent sole desire of the guilty one to complete the crime so that the victim could not by any chance escape from the fate intended. They became more and more convinced that the body of Mrs. Borden could not have lain in the room for one or two hours, without having been discovered by some one in the house. In the minds of the police the proposition resolved itself into this form. Could there have been a dead body and an assassin in the house for nearly two hours unknown to and undiscovered by Miss Lizzie or the servant?

CHAPTER VI.

THE FUNERAL.

THE funeral of the murdered people took place on the morning of August 6th. Crowds of people numbering between 3000 and 4000 appeared on Second street in front of the house, and about twenty policemen stood around and maintained a clear passage. Rev. Dr. Adams of the First Congregational Church and City Missionary Buck soon arrived and entered the house. The bodies were laid in two black cloth-covered caskets in the sitting room, where Mr. Borden was killed. An ivy wreath was placed on Mr. Borden's bier and a boquet of white roses and fern leaves, tied with a white satin ribbon, was placed over Mrs. Borden. There were about 75 persons present at the funeral services in the house. The services consisted of reading from the scriptures and prayer. There were no singing and no remarks.

The bodies of the victims were laid in the caskets with the mutilated portions of the head turned down, so that the cuts could not be noticed. The caskets were open and the faces of both looked wonderfully peaceful.

The mourners who were present were Mrs. Oliver Gray, the stepmother of the deceased woman ; G. F. Fish and wife of Hartford, Ct., the latter a sister of Mrs. Borden ; Dr. Bowen and wife, Southard H. Miller and a very few of the neighbors who had been invited to attend the services in the house.

The funeral was private—that is, only a very few of the immediate friends were asked to accompany the remains to the cemetery. But from 11 o'clock until 11:30, when the funeral procession of eleven hacks and two hearses started on its way, there were immense crowds of people lining every sidewalk. There was a detachment of police at the cemetery and another posse accompanied the remains on their way through Borden and Rock streets to the northern end of the city, where the cemetery is located.

The pallbearers were : For Mr. Borden—Abram G. Hart, cashier of the Union Savings Bank ; George W. Dean, a retired capitalist ;

Jerome C. Borden, a relative of the deceased; Richard B. Borden, treasurer of the Troy mills, in which Mr. Borden was a director ; James M. Osborn an associate of the deceased in several mills; Andrew Borden, treasurer of the Merchants' mill, in which Mr. Borden was a large owner.   For Mrs. Borden—James C. Eddy, Henry S. Buffington, Frank L. Almy, J. Henry Wells, Simeon B. Chase, John H. Boone, all of them gentlemen in the highest local social and business circles.

As the procession wended its way along North Main street many old associates of Mr. Borden were seen to raise their hats.   They forgot all knowledge of the curiosity seekers who stood gaping beside them.

Miss Lizzie and Miss Emma Borden were, of course, the principal mourners.   Miss Lizzie went out of the house first, leaning on Undertaker Winward's arm.

Miss Emma was calm and she walked quickly, and took her seat without hardly glancing at the crowds staring at her.

Both ladies were without veils.

The last person to leave the house was Mr. Morse, who went into a carriage with Rev. Mr. Buck and Dr. Adams.

The procession arrived at the cemetery. about 12:23 o'clock, when several hundred people stood about the grounds awaiting the burial.   The crowd was kept back by a dozen policemen under direction of Sergt. John Brocklehurst.   No one left any of the carriages during the ceremonies except the officiating clergy, the bearers and Mr. Morse.

Rev. E. A. Buck began the funeral exercises by reading New Testament passages introduced with '' I am the resurrection and the life. ''   He was followed by Rev. Dr. Adams, who prayed for the spiritual guidance of all and the inclination of all to submit to divine control, besought that justice should overtake the wrong that had been done, also that those who are seeking to serve the ends of justice might

MRS. CHURCHILL.

be delivered from mistake, be helped to possess all mercifulness, as well as all righteousness, and in conclusion prayed that all might be delivered from the dominion of evil.

There was a pause of perhaps five minutes, during which the carriages kept their places and no one stirred toward the grave except an elderly lady in plain dress, who hastened to the casket of Mrs. Borden, and was about to kneel in reverence before it, when she was moved away by an officer, and went to the fence around the ground, where, with back to the crowd, she buried her head in tears. It was whispered that she had been employed long ago by the Bordens.

The bodies were not interred in the graves, as a telegraphic order had been received from Boston instructing that they should not be buried. Both caskets were returned to the hearses and were deposited in a receiving tomb.

CHAPTER VII.

A Reward Offered.

ON the morning after the tragedy the following notice was sent to the newspapers:

" Five thousand dollars reward. The above reward will be paid to any one who may secure the arrest and conviction of the person or persons, who occasioned the death of Andrew J. Borden and his wife.
Signed, Emma L. Borden and Lizzie A. Borden.''

Here was an incentive calculated to invigorate the work of those who were bent on solving the great mystery. But the police officers did not stop to read this announcement. It was as plain as a pike staff that they were not devoting their entire time and energies toward hunting up farm hands, mysterious Portuguese and Westport horse traders. Yet it is an unquestionable fact that City Marshal Hilliard left no stone unturned to follow every clue of this kind to its end. They all ended in smoke.

The hatchets which had been found in the cellar had been sent to Prof. Wood for critical examination, and the public awaited with almost breathless anxiety the making of his report. Upon it depended much which would assist in clearing up the case. After the bodies had been placed in the receiving vault at Oak Grove, Mr. Morse concluded to bury the clothing which the victims wore at the time of death. He employed men to do the work. Under orders the clothing was interred in the yard back of the barn. Just after this incident, Mr. Morse locked the barn door with two Boston reporters on the inside, and when they demanded their release he found considerable fault with the liberties people were taking on the premises. He was reminded that a reward of $5,000 had been offered, and that therefore everybody was intensely interested.

On the same afternoon Andrew J. Jennings, an astute lawyer and a conservative man, who had been employed by the Misses Borden, as before stated, was questioned about the case. He had no particular desire to talk about the family affairs of the Borden's, but he admitted that as far as he knew, the murdered man left no will. The estate would as a matter of course, go to the daughters. As to the crime itself, Mr. Jennings said:

"I have read many cases in books, in newspapers and in fiction—in novels—and I never heard of a case as remarkable as this. A most outrageous, brutal crime, perpetrated in mid-day in an open house on a prominent thoroughfare, and absolutely motiveless. The theory advanced—these quarrels about wages and about the possession of stores and that sort of thing—are simply ridiculous. They do not offer a motive. If it was shown that the thing was done during even such a quarrel, in the heat of passion, it would be different; but to suppose that for such a matter a man will lie in wait or steal upon his victim while asleep and hack him to death is preposterous. Even with revenge in his heart, the sight of his victim asleep would disarm most any man. Then for a man to enter, commit the deed and escape without being discovered, would be a remarkable combination of circumstances."

In answer to a question as to what he thought about the possibility of the murder being committed by a member of the family, he replied:

"Well, there are but two women of the household and this man Morse. He accounts so satisfactorily for every hour of that morning, showing him to be out of the house, that there seems to be no ground to base a reasonable suspicion. Further than that, he appeared on the scene almost immediately after the discovery, from the outside, and in the same clothes that he had worn in the morning. Now it is almost impossible that this frightful work could have been done without the clothes of the person who did it being bespattered with blood. Then came Lizzie Borden, dressed in the same clothes she wore before the killing. This, together with the improbability that any woman could do such a piece of work, makes the suspicion seem altogether irrational."

Complication after complication arose as the facts in the case slowly came to light. Not a scream nor a groan was heard coming from the Borden house that morning; neither did the family living in the Buffington house which stands next north of the Borden house, see anybody coming out on that morning except Mr. Borden himself. He left his home, as has been stated, about 9 o'clock. Mrs. Churchill, who lives with her mother, Mrs. E. P. Buffington, across the yard, watched Mr. Borden go out. There is a fence between the two houses, and Mrs. Buffington's kitchen windows look over the fence into the Borden yard, directly opposite the side door, and not twenty-eight feet from the Borden house. The barn is but twenty feet behind

the house, and the distance from the east end of the house to the east
end of the barn is not more than fifty feet.   Behind the barn is a
fence eight feet high, protected by barbed wire.   This fence divides
the Borden estate from that of Dr. J. B. Chagnon, whose house
fronts on Third street.   On the rear of Dr. Chagnon's place are
half a dozen apple and pear trees that stand up against the fence
which partitions the Borden estate from that of Dr. Chagnon.

On the south side of the Borden house is Dr. Kelly's residence.
A low fence stands between.

Miss Addie Cheetham lives with her mother and Mrs. Churchill
with Mrs. Buffington.   All these persons were about their own houses
all of Thursday morning.   Miss Cheetham sat writing a letter at 10
o'clock and at 10: 55 went to the postoffice.   She saw no one come
out of the Borden house during the time she sat near the window
fronting on the Borden lawn.   She could hear the side door bang if it

opened at all, but it did not, she
says.   Mrs. Churchill was about
the house until 10:15, when she
went to the market to secure
dinner.   She returned about
10:50, and it was perhaps twenty-five minutes later when she
had occasion to go into the
kitchen.   She looked out of the
window and just at that moment
Lizzie Borden pushed open the
side door of her own house.

Mrs. Churchill ran over to
Mrs. Borden's, and just at that
minute Bridget, who had been
sent to summon Dr. Bowen, returned, saying that she could

CAPTAIN PATRICK H. DOHERTY.   not find the doctor.   Mrs.

Churchill then went over to Lew Hall's sail loft, where her hired
man, Tom Bolles, was talking and asked him to run for Dr. Chagnon.
Bolles ran around the square to find the Chagnon house locked up.
The family had that day gone to Pawtucket and the hired girl was
down street from 10: 30 until nearly 12 o'clock.

Bolles came back and while running up Second street saw Dr.
Bowen driving in front of his office, and then it was that the family
physician was notified.

Bolles saw Bridget cleaning windows on the north and west side of the house early in the forenoon, but she was not in sight at 11:20. All the members of the Buffington household agreed that if there had been any scream from inside the Borden house it would certainly have been heard by them.

In Dr. Kelly's yard some men were working, and if the assassin proceeding on the theory that a man attempted to scale the fence at that place, he would perhaps have been seen by the laborers. He would also have to pass the barn where Lizzie was, provided, of course, he got out of the house between 10:55 and 11:20. If he jumped over the Buffington fence, he might have been seen by the inmates of the house, and to try to escape by cutting his way over the Kelly fence would have been to fall into the hands of the laborers. It would have been dangerous for him to go out by the Second street entrance, for there are always passers by on this thoroughfare, as well as on Third street.

Clues are absolutely indispensable adjuncts to all criminal operations and in the Borden case they were omnipresent. Everybody seemed to have a suggestion to offer. Around the police headquarters there congregated all kinds of men, including a number of cranks. Those of the latter class who could not report in form, sent in their contributions by mail until Marshal Hilliard's desk was piled high with curious and original documents. But the police themselves worked night and day and kept their doings as secret as possible, under the circumstances. Before two days passed the press all over the country began to assail the work of the officers, and it was kept up with a vigor worthy a better cause. Undoubtedly this criticism was brought about by the fact that the twenty-five or more newspaper men who interviewed the Marshal daily, or said they did, gleaned the fact that he harbored the suspicion that a member of the family had committed the crimes. But it was clear to all who wished to see it, that he paid as much attention to hunting down "outside clues" as he did in pursuing his inquiries in the other direction. The more plausible clues were diligently followed.

A theory which gave promise of good results was as follows:

On Tuesday before the murder, about 9 o'clock in the morning, a horse and buggy turned into Second street out of Spring street, and came to a halt in front of the Borden House. A young man who was employed near by sat in his buggy which stood opposite the house and was facing south. He took the trouble to watch closely the two men who occupied the buggy. One of them got out and rang the door bell. Mr. Borden answered the call and the stranger was admitted. In about ten minutes he came out and resumed his seat in the buggy and the pair drove off in the direction of Pleasant street. This circumstance was considered of importance, when it became known that the police had information of another person who had seen a strange man about the premises. A boy named Kierouack, aged twelve, who resided on Central street, told the authorities that he was passing the house at about 11 o'clock that morning and that he saw a man scale the fence which separates the Borden and Chagnon estates. Young Kierouack was put to the most rigid examination by the police and he stuck to his story. This clue was effectually disposed of by the authorities who found another person who was with Kierouack at the time of his trip down Second street. This man gave a particular story of his movements that morning and denied that young Kierouack had seen a suspicious character. Adjoining the yard of the Borden place is the house occupied by Dr. Chagnon. On the evening in question the physician was unexpectedly summoned away and asked Dr. Collet, if, as a favor, he would allow the latter's little son to attend to the telephone during Dr. Chagnon's absence. The boy was absent, and Dr. Collet sent his daughter to Dr. Chagnon's residence, but upon her arrival the doctor had departed and the office was locked. The little girl decided to await the arrival of some one and sat down in the yard for that purpose. Soon the man who had driven the doctor away returned, and the office was opened. Miss Chagnon remained in the yard adjoining the Borden place. She was there at the time it was alleged the unknown man jumped the fence, and she declares that she saw no one attempt anything of the kind, but the fact that there was a considerable extent of barbed wire along its top was submitted in answer. Barbed wire necessitates careful handling, and it was argued in support of the truth of the girl's statement and the falsity of the other story that the passage of a man over such a barrier would require such time as to render detection possible.

Notwithstanding the fact that Mr. Morse had clearly established an alibi there were those who insisted that he knew more of the murder than he had made public. Proceeding on this theory the officers took up the task of investigating Mr. Morse. Officer Medley was given the work, and in company with Inspector Hathaway of the New Bedford police, he discovered that Mr. Morse had lived, as before stated, in Dartmouth.

There was at that time a camp of itinerant horse traders in the town of Westport. It was related that Mr. Morse had had dealings with these men and the sensational press soon coupled his name with a possible hired assassin, a member of the gang of traders. This story was given color by the then unexploded story of young Kierouack, especially when it became known that officer Medley had discovered a man who seemed to fit the description of the stranger alleged to have been seen around the premises. This suspect was the head trader in the Westport Camp and when accosted he readily consented to come to Fall River and surrender himself. He succeeded in showing beyond a reasonable doubt that he was in the city of New Bedford at the time of the Borden murders.

Within a few hours after the murder was reported a detail of police was sent to guard the house. This policy was kept up for more than a week and as early as Friday morning the officers on guard had instructions to keep the Misses Borden, John V. Morse and Bridget Sullivan under the strictest surveillance and not allow either of them to leave the city. If they left the premises they were followed. The Medical Examiner, the Marshal and the officers at work on the case were constantly coming and going about the house, and while it may have appeared to them that the problem was in a fair way of solution, the public was getting more and more hopelessly involved in the mass of stories which were circulated from day to day.

The letter which was alleged to have been received by Mrs. Borden on the morning of the tragedy, continued to excite public interest. "*Once a Week*," the New York journal, offered a reward of $500 for the writer of the note, and the *Fall River News* implored its readers to unite in one effort in the cause of justice, and if possible, find the note and deliver it into the editor's hands. The missive, however, was not found. Miss Lizzie A.

MEDICAL EXAMINER DR. W. A. DOLAN.

Borden seemingly put an end to that theory when she told Dr. Dolan that she had attempted to find the note and being unsuccessful, she feared it had been burned in the kitchen stove. Not one of the household seemed to be able to give more than a general idea of the contents of the note. It was from a friend who was ill, but as neither the friend nor the note could be found by the united efforts of the police and members of the family, the matter was dropped early in the investigation.

CHAPTER VIII.

A SERMON ON THE MURDERS.

O N Saturday the case took on an unexpected phaze. Superintendent O. M. Hanscom of the Boston office of the Pinkerton Detective Agency appeared on the scene. He was not employed by the Mayor of Fall River nor the Marshal of Police and it soon became noised abroad that he was present in the interests of the Misses Borden with the avowed intention of clearing up the mystery. In company with Mr. Jennings he visited the Borden house and was in consultation with members of the family for about two hours. Detective Hanscom remained in Fall River nearly two days and then disappeared as mysteriously as he came. It was the univĕrsal opinion at the time that the Pinkertons would unearth the assassin in a short while, but the public was never informed as to the reasons why they withdrew from the case. It was believed, however, that there was a rupture between Marshal Hilliard's men and the Pinkertons. This may or may not have been the cause of their sudden disappearance.

Sunday morning the Central Church worshippers met with the First Church congregation in the stone church on Main street. All of the pews were filled, many being in their seats some half hour before the service began. It was supposed that the Rev. W. Walker Jubb, who occupied the pulpit, would make some allusion to the awful experiences through which one family in his charge had been compelled to pass during the week, and the supposition was correct. Mr. Jubb read for the morning lesson a portion of Matthew, containing the significant words which imply that what is concealed shall be revealed. In his prayer, Mr. Jubb evoked the divine blessing on the community, rendering thanks for the blessings bestowed on many, and, pausing, referred to the murder of two innocent persons. He prayed fervently that right might prevail, and that in good time the terrible mystery might be cleared away ; that the people of the city might do everything in their power to assist the authorities, and asked for divine guidance for the police, that they might prosecute unflinch-

ingly and unceasingly the search for the murderer.   Mr. Jubb prayed
that their hands might be strengthened, that their movements might
be characterized by discretion, and that wisdom and great power of
discernment might be given to them in their work.   "And while we
hope," he continued, "for the triumph of justice, let our acts be
tempered with mercy.   Help us to refrain from giving voice to those
insinuations and innuendoes which we have no right to utter.   Save
us from blasting a life, innocent and blameless; keep us from taking
the sweetness from a future by our ill-advised words, and let us be
charitable as we remember the poor, grief-stricken family and minister
unto them."

The clergyman asked that those who were writing of the crime
might be careful of the reputations of the living, which could so
easily be undermined.

For his text, Mr. Jubb took the first chapter of Ecclesiastes, ninth
verse : "The thing that hath been is that which shall be ; and that
which is done is that which shall be done ; and there is no new thing
under the sun."   The speaker considered the monotonies of life, and
expatiated on the causes of indifference in persons who would be
nothing if not geniuses, drawing lessons from successes in humble
sphere.   At the end of the sermon Mr. Jubb stepped to the side of the
pulpit and said slowly and impressively :

"I cannot close my sermon this morning without speaking of the
horrible crime that has startled our beloved city this week, ruthlessly
taking from our church household two respected and esteemed members.   I cannot close without referring to my pain and surprise at the
atrocity of the outrage.   A more brutal, cunning, daring and fiendish
murder I never heard of in all my life.   What must have been the
person who could have been guilty of such a revolting crime ?   One to
commit such a murder must have been without heart, without soul, a
fiend incarnate, the very vilest of degraded and depraved humanity,
or he must have been a maniac.   The circumstances, execution and
all the surroundings cover it with mystery profound.   Explanations
and evidence as to both perpetrator and motive are shrouded in a
mystery that is almost inexplicable.   That such a crime could have
been committed during the busy hours of the day, right in the heart
of a populous city, is passing comprehension.   As we ponder, we ex-
claim in our perplexity, why was the deed done ?   What could have
induced anybody to engage in such a butchery ?   Where is the motive ?
When men resort to crime it is for plunder, for gain, from enmity, in
sudden anger or for revenge. Strangely, nothing of this nature enters

into this case, and again I ask—what was the motive? I believe, and am only voicing your feelings fully when I say that I hope the criminal will be speedily brought to justice. This city cannot afford to have in its midst such an inhuman brute as the murderer of Andrew J. Borden and his wife. Why, a man who could conceive and execute such a murder as that would not hesitate to burn the city.

" I trust that the police may do their duty and lose no opportunity which might lead to the capture of the criminal. I would impress upon them that they should not say too much and thus unconsciously assist in defeating the ends of justice. I also trust that the press (and I say this because I recognize its influence and power), I trust that it will use discretion in disseminating its theories and conclusions, and that pens may be guided by consideration and charity. I would wish the papers to remember that by casting a groundless or undeserved insinuation that they may blacken and blast a life forever, like a tree smitten by a bolt of lightning ; a life which has always commanded respect, whose acts and motives have always been pure and holy. Let us ourselves curb our tongues and preserve a blameless life from undeserved suspicions. I think I have the right to ask for the prayers of this church and of my own congregation. The murdered husband and wife were members of this church, and a daughter now stands in the same relation to each one of you, as you, as church members, do to each other. God help and comfort her. Poor stricken girls, may they both be comforted, and may they both realize how fully God is their refuge. ''

Marshal Hilliard and his officers after two days and two nights work concluded that the case was of so much importance that it was advisable to call District Attorney Hosea M. Knowlton, of New Bedford, Mass., into their counsels, and accordingly he arrived from his home in New Bedford, on Saturday morning. A short consultation was held at police headquarters and then adjourned until the afternoon. The District Attorney, Marshal Hilliard, State Officer Seaver, Mayor Coughlin and Dr. Dolan met according to agreement in one of the parlors of the Mellen House.

The Marshal took all the evidence which he had collected in the shape of notes, papers, etc., together with other documents bearing on the case, into the room where the five men were closeted and they commenced at the beginning. At the close of the conference held earlier in the afternoon, the District Attorney had advised the officers to proceed with the utmost caution, and was extremely conservative in the conclusions which he found. At that time he

had not been made acquainted with all the details. At the
Mellen House consultation the same caution was observed.
The quintet were working on one of the most remarkable
criminal records in history, and were obliged to proceed slowly.
The Marshal began at the beginning and continued to the
end. He was assisted in his explanation by the Mayor and
the Medical Examiner. Mr. Seaver listened. There were details
almost without end, and all of them were picked to pieces and viewed
in every conceivable light. Considerable new evidence was introduced,
and then the testimony of officers not present was submitted, which
showed that Miss Lizzie Borden might have been mistaken in one
important particular. The Marshal informed the District Attorney
that the murder had occurred between ten minutes of 11 o'clock and
thirteen minutes after 11 on Thursday morning. The time was as
accurate as they could get it, and they had spared no pains to fix it.

The alarm had been given by Miss Lizzie Borden, the daughter
of the murdered man, when she returned from the barn. At the
moment of the discovery she did not know that her stepmother was
also dead, though she explained afterwards that she thought her
mother had left the house. It was but a short distance from the barn
to the house. Nobody had been found who had seen anybody
leaving the yard of the Borden house or entering it, although a
number of people, who were named, were sitting by their windows
close by. It was also true that nobody had seen Miss Borden enter
or leave the barn. She had explained that she went to the stable to
procure some lead for a fish line, which she was going to use at
Warren. Here there was a stumbling block which puzzled the
District Attorney and his assistants. On the day of the murder
Miss Lizzie had explained that she went to the loft of the barn for
the lead, and an officer who was examining the premises also went to
the loft. It was covered with dust and there were no tracks to prove
that any person had been there for weeks. He took particular notice
of the fact, and reported back that he had walked about on the dust-
covered floor on purpose to discover whether or not his own feet left
any tracks. He said that they did and thought it singular that
anybody could have visited the floor a short time before him and
make no impression on the dust. The lower floor of the stable told
no such tale, as it was evident that it had been used more frequently
and the dust had not accumulated there. The conclusion reached
was that in the excitement incident to the awful discovery, Miss
Borden had forgotten just where she went for the lead. When she

found her father lying on the lounge, she ran to the stairs and ascended three or four steps to call Maggie. Maggie is the name by which Bridget Sullivan was called by members of the family. She did not call for her stepmother, because, as she stated afterward, she did not think she was in. Then came the history of the mysterious letter. Miss Lizzie had said that on the morning of the tragedy her stepmother received a letter asking her to visit a sick friend. She knew that at about 9 o'clock her stepmother went upstairs to put shams on the pillows, and she did not see her again. It was that letter which led her to believe that her stepmother had gone out. Here was stumbling block number two. The officers had searched all over the house for that letter, the Marshal said, but had failed to find any trace of it. Miss Lizzie had feared that it had been burned in the kitchen stove.

The Marshal's men had found other letters and fragments of letters in the waste paper basket and had put them together piece by piece. The one letter that was wanted had not been found. It was considered singular that, with all the furore that has been raised over this note, the woman who wrote it has not come forward before this and cleared up the mystery. It is also strange that the boy who delivered the note has not made himself known. It was believed that every boy in town old enough to do an errand had visited the house since the tragedy, but the particular boy has kept in the background.

It was presumed that Mrs. Borden's correspondent feared the notoriety which would come to her if she disclosed her identity, but it was unfortunate that she should allow any such scruples to overcome what ought to be a desire to assist in every way possible in unravelling the knot.

The Marshal, Medical Examiner and Mayor then carefully rehearsed, step by step, the summoning of Dr. Bowen, who was not at home when the murder was committed, and his ghastly discovery on the second floor. No theory other than that Mrs. Borden was murdered first was entertained. Miss Lizzie Borden's demeanor during the many interviews which the police had with her was described at length, and the story of John V. Morse's whereabouts was retold.

Thorough investigation of theories advanced upon the strength of Bridget Sullivan's statement that the crime was committed by the Portuguese employed upon the farm of Andrew Borden in Somerset, resulted in placing them with the other numerous opinions and possibilities which have been exploded by the authorities. In the excitement attending the discovery of the bodies of the murdered couple, inquiries directed to the domestic, elicted answers to the effect that the Portuguese must have done it. The individual referred to was a Swede laborer, and Marshal Hilliard thereupon drove to the Somerset farm. The investigation there was necessarily brief in its character, but such as it was, satisfied the Marshal that the laborer, whom the Sullivan woman designated as the Portuguese, was far removed from the house on Second street at the time the murders were committed. In their persistent following of every possible clue the authorities deemed it advisable to make an exhaustive examination regarding the whereabouts of the Swedish laborer, at the time of the tragedy, and with this end in view another trip had been made to Somerset. The result confirmed the opinion of Marshal Hilliard. The man established a thoroughly satisfactory alibi, and the officials were forced to acquit him of the possibility of any knowledge or of complicity in the affair.

Some time before Andrew Borden had purchased some property located across the river. This property was owned by a number of persons, heirs of a former owner, and among them was one who was strangely disinclined to part with the place, at least at the figures satisfactory to the other owners. His dissatisfaction was made manifest to such an extent that among the stories circulated regarding the affair was one which suggested the possibility of this dissatisfied individual having some knowledge of the ones responsible for the tragedy. This story, although without reliable foundation, it was deemed best to investigate also, and accordingly the person referred to received a visit from the Government officials. The desired knowledge was easily secured, and the fact readily established that the party in question had no connection whatever with the murder of the aged couple.

After this extended conference of the highest authorities in the county it was given out that the District Attorney was much pleased with the work of the police and that an inquest would be held immediately, before Judge Josiah C. Blaisdell of the Second District Court of Bristol, which is the Fall River local Court.

CHAPTER IX.

Theories Advanced.

BY Monday morning following the tragedy, the fact that some member of the Borden family was suspected of the crime by the police, became a matter of public comment. But withal there was nothing to substantiate this suspicion, except that the officers kept up their daily and nightly watch of the house and its surroundings. Public sentiment began to be divided. The police had a large following who believed implicitly in their ability to ferret out the crimes, and it soon became noised about that no less a person than the District Attorney himself was in hearty co-operation with the officers and shared with them the fear that some member of the household was the author of the crime. Whether this rumor was based upon fact or not will be decided by those who follow the course of subsequent events. Friends of the Borden household became mightily aroused to the trend of public opinion and to the now undisguised work of the police. Four days had passed and the officers of the law seemed to find no other clue than that which kept them inside the Borden yard. Those people who found that it was beyond the pale of human conception to suspect that the crime could have been committed by a member of the household, began to rally to the support of the suspected parties; and their influence was felt in certain quarters; yet it did not disarm the frightful suspicion, cruel and groundless though it might have been.

The public had been led to suspect that arrests would be made on or before Saturday night. People became confirmed in the view that there never would be a conviction and sentence of the guilty party. Up to this time, absolutely nothing but circumstantial evidence, had been discovered, and for the most part it was fair to suppose that no evidence of any other nature had been gathered. This was an unpleasant conclusion to reach and men did not arrive at it cheerfully, but they were forced to accept it, nevertheless. They saw but one bright spot in the murky horizon, and that was a tiny one. The government might sooner or later strike a clue which would put them on the right track of the assassin, who, whether male or female, might break down and confess. But if the assassin had no confederates and kept his own counsel, he was safe. Such was the course of reasoning pursued on Monday, and it seemed to be logical.

The police had been terribly in earnest in their work and they had pursued it efficiently and effectively. They had been severely criticised as they undoubtedly expected to be, but perhaps that was unjust. At the start they were caught at a disadvantage, they were the victims of circumstances which could entangle them but one day in the year, and perhaps a mistake was made when they did not take absolute and immediate possession of the house, barn and yard and place a guard in every room. Yet had this been done the well meaning public would perhaps have been more caustic in criticism. If they did make a mistake it was a matter which no human being could sit in judgment upon. They had to deal with a horror calculated to stagger any detective force in the world whatever its training, skill or experience. An unparalelled horror it may be, but one without an equal in the annals of New England crime. That a false step was taken during the first hour of the commotion was not surprising.

INSPECTOR WM. H. MEDLEY.

Among the many theories which were advanced as to who was responsible for the crime, that of Mr. John Beattie, then an Alderman of Fall River, will suffice to show how deeply the people had thought upon the subject. Mr. Beattie said in a published interview: "My theory —and it is mine alone—is one formed from the circumstances of the case. The brain which devised this crime was cunning enough to devise beforehand, the means to escape detention. Supposing it was a woman, she was cunning enough to wear a loose wrapper which would have covered her clothes, and gloves which would have protected her hands from the stains of blood. If so there was time to burn both wrapper and gloves in the hot fire, which was known to have been burning in the kitchen stove at the time of the tragedy. '' The Alderman's theory is simply given here to show the trend of public opinion, and while it was perhaps his cwn, there were many conservative people who shared it with him.

On Sunday two '' outside clues '' came up for consideration of the authorities. Special officers, Harrington and Doherty, were sent out to find one Thomas Walker and succeeded. The man was taken to task concerning his whereabouts on Thursday and he told his story. He was a tailor and worked for Thomas Carey on Main street, had been recently married and moved into a tenement belonging to Andrew J. Borden, which was located on Fourth street. The rumor had been that Walker had experienced domestic troubles and after a long period of temperance had taken some intoxicants. Three weeks before the tragedy Mr. Borden called at Carey's shop and had a talk with Walker. The rent was due and Mr. Borden wanted it paid or else he wanted Walker to move out. After some argument the tenant concluded to move and did so. It was rumored that unpleasant words had passed between the two men and the police deemed it advisable to give Walker a chance to make an explanation. Mr. Walker told so straight and clear a story of his wherabouts on that day that it was taken for truth and especially so when Mr. Carey, his employer, corroborated every statement which he had made.

The other clue was to the effect that a Portuguese had been seen burying a bloody hatchet on the Borden farm in Swansea. Officer Medley visited the farm and searched in vain where the axe was alleged to have been buried. He found a Portuguese laborer who had been on the farm all day Thursday and who had killed some chickens for market.

Another clue which showed a strong point in support of Miss Borden's story of having been in the barn was that told by one Hyman Lubinsky. He said that while driving on Second street at 10:30 a. m., on Thursday, he saw a woman in the Borden yard; noticed her walk from the barn to the side door on the north and enter. The description which he gave of the woman fitted that of Miss Lizzie and it appeared to verify her story of having been in the barn as before stated. This man was not introduced by the defense at the preliminary trial.

But there was a clue which caused no end of comment, both personal and in the press. Information reached the police that Officer Joseph Hyde had seen a suspicious looking stranger in the vicinity of Second street on that morning. On the following Tuesday, Dr. B. J. Handy, one of the best known physicians in the city, made public the fact that he also saw a very strange appearing man on Second street on the morning of the murder between 10:25 and 10:45 o'clock.

The doctor took some notice of this man and in the afternoon while in conversation with his wife he became more and more impressed with the idea that the stranger had some connection with the awful crime. This theory became a matter of much importance and Dr. Handy did not at this time know that Officer Hyde was reported to have seen a similar person. Dr. Handy's statement was that at some time within fifteen minutes of 10:30 o'clock that morning he was driving down Second street. When as he was passing the residence of Dr. Kelly,—which is the next house south of the Borden premises, —his attention was attracted to a pedestrian walking slowly along the sidewalk near the Borden house. Ordinarily the face of a stranger would not excite much interest in the mind of Dr. Handy, inasmuch as he was continually passing the streets of the city on his professional calls. In this case, however, he looked twice at the passerby, and even turned in his carriage to inspect him more closely. Just what caused him to do this the doctor did not definitely explain. There was a peculiarity about the man which he could not exactly describe. The individual was about 30 years of age, five feet five inches in height, weight perhaps about 125 or 130 pounds. His clothes were of light gray of just what cut and texture the doctor could not positively state ; nor could he tell whether the man's hat was of felt or straw. It was not the dress which attracted Dr. Handy, it was the man's features, which he saw. He was pale, almost white ; not with the ghastly pallor of a sick man, but rather the whitish appearance of a man whose face had not been touched by the sun's rays ; who might have been in confinement, or whose work was of such a nature as to keep him constantly in a cellar. There was something beyond this paleness which aroused the doctor particularly to observe him, and that was that he appeared to be in a state of intense nervousness.

Within an hour after Dr. Handy had heard of the terrible tragedy and within three hours after he had seen the queer looking stranger he had in his own mind decided that the unknown knew something of the murders. He communicated his suspicions to the police and gave a complete description of the man. More unfavorable comment was directed at the authorities because they failed to find this man as readily as they did other suspects than was apparently absolutely necessary. Column after column of the leading newspapers were devoted to the discussion of this stranger until he became known as " Dr. Handy's Wild Eyed Man, " and while the police were accused of neglecting this seemingly important clue there are trustworthy men who know and can show beyond contradiction that he was sought after in the most diligent manner. So faithfully in fact did the officers search for the stranger, all the while neglecting, if it may be called by that name, to follow more plausible clues; many of them finally said they were forced to the conclusion that the wild eyed man was a myth, and that with all due respect to Dr. Handy's opinions and conclusions. But myth or reality some of the friends of Miss Lizzie insisted that he be materialized if the former, or produced if the latter. There was a man known to the police as "Mike the Soldier" and he in a measure seemed to fit the description of the "Wild Eyed." Pursuing the plan which Marshal Hilliard did from the beginning, of following every clue no matter how trivial or unimportant, his men were sent in every direction to hunt the curious stranger. "Mike the Soldier" was discovered, as will be seen later.

Mr. Andrew J. Borden.

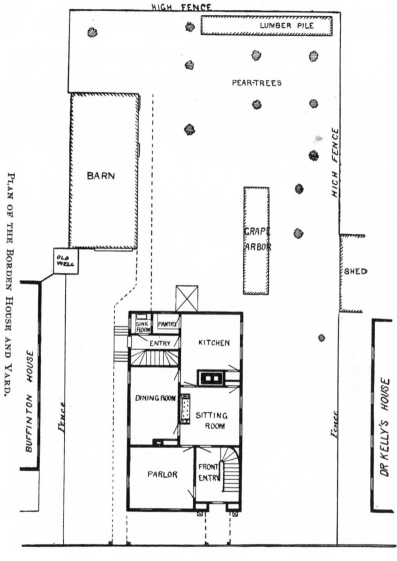

PLAN OF THE BORDEN HOUSE AND YARD.

HIGH FENCE

LUMBER PILE

PEAR-TREES

BARN

HIGH FENCE

OLD WELL

GRAPE ARBOR

SHED

BUFFINTON HOUSE

Fence

SINK ROOM

PANTRY

ENTRY

KITCHEN

DINING ROOM

SITTING ROOM

PARLOR

FRONT ENTRY

Fence

DR KELLY'S HOUSE

SECOND STREET

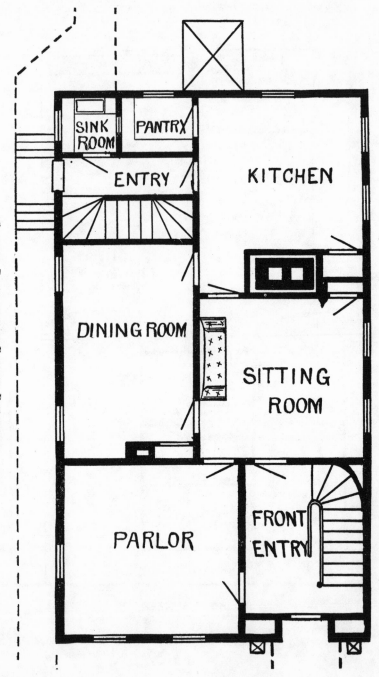

SINK ROOM

PANTRY

ENTRY

KITCHEN

DINING ROOM

SITTING ROOM

PARLOR

FRONT ENTRY

GROUND PLAN OF THE BORDEN RESIDENCE.

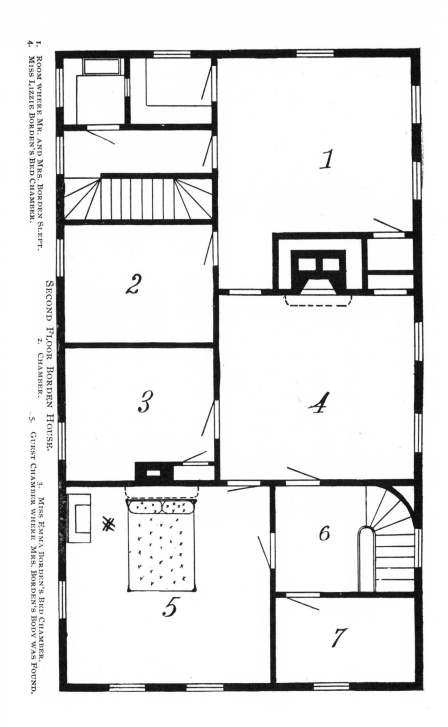

SECOND FLOOR BORDEN HOUSE.

1. ROOM WHERE MR. AND MRS. BORDEN SLEPT.   2. CHAMBER.   3. MISS EMMA BORDEN'S BED CHAMBER.
4. MISS LIZZIE BORDEN'S BED CHAMBER.   5. GUEST CHAMBER WHERE MRS. BORDEN'S BODY WAS FOUND.

CHAPTER X.

THERE was intense excitement in Fall River the day the murder was reported. It grew hourly and showed no signs of abatement, but rather continued on the increase, until on Tuesday following it was at fever heat. Men no longer gathered in knots on the sidewalks. On some of the streets, and particularly the thoroughfares in the vicinity of the police station, people were scattered along the curbing for blocks. The report that an inquest was to be held in the Second District Court before Judge J. C. Blaisdell, was sufficient to draw the crowds. Everything was in readiness by 10 o'clock and when a hack started for the Borden house to convey Miss Lizzie and a friend to the police station where the inquest was to be held, the news spread with great rapidity. Business was partially suspended in the center of the city as it had been on Thursday noon, when the story of the tragedy was first made known. The report went out that a hack, containing Marshal Hilliard and Officer Harrington had gone to the Borden house. Groups of men found time to rush to Court Square, and to the streets approaching and await developments. Others still more curious ran after the carriage, and others more on the alert, to jump toward Main street in case the driver took that route. Hundreds who were not so well informed were content to join the groups mentioned, and to stand still without asking questions. What was there to see? A hack drawn by two horses, with two ladies on the back seat and two officers in the front seat, dressed in citizen's clothes. Men on wagons saw the vehicle coming and they drove post haste for the police station. Men, women and children joined in a wild scramble for the narrow alleyway, and Court Square was choked in a twinkling. The crowd would have waited complacently all the afternoon, rather than have missed one brief glance at the carriage and its occupants. The driver saw what was going to happen and he laid the whip on his horses, but to no purpose. The sightseers would not be outdone and they arrived ahead of time. Windows were thrown open, heads were thrust out, crowds pushed through the streets and for ten minutes it seemed as if the whole town within a stone's throw of police headquarters was vibrating. It was not strange that the tension tightened. The community had reached a point when it felt that it must clear up the mystery or go insane. Men complained that they went to bed with murder on the brain, and that the same grim phantom was visible the moment they opened their eyes in the morning. It is the pace that tells, and for five days the pace had been furious. The human mind will not cease to work. Its possessor has no control over it when it takes hold of such a subject as this. It demands an assassin caught red-handed with the dripping axe concealed beneath his coat. It asks that the evidence of his guilt be made conclusive. It wants no guess work. Then it attempts to rid itself of the horrible theory on which it had been feeding for one hundred and twenty hours and travels off in another direction. It conceals a maniac in the upper part of the Borden house, watches him kill the woman, follows him as he descends the stairs and slays Mr. Borden, sees him pass out unobserved and takes him off and sets him down a thousand miles from the scene of his work, safe from capture. This would be a relief to the mind if it were more than temporary; but the mind does all this in the twinkling of an eye, and in the next moment asks why the maniac could not be appeased with one

JUDGE JOSIAH C. BLAISDELL.

slaughter, and is back again at the beginning, asking questions and hunting clues. This is not overstating the mental condition of the populace during the first few weeks subsequent to the killing.

Up to the time of opening the inquest there had been nothing but circumstantial evidence found whereon to base a suspicion of guilt, and the fact that District Attorney Knowlton and Attorney General Albert E. Pillsbury, a distinguished and acute lawyer, had been called into the case, showed that the authorities needed the wise counsel of the foremost legal talent in Massachusetts, before taking the all important step of making an arrest. If, after a thorough sifting of this circumstantial evidence, it was discovered that the theory of the state was wrong, then the guard would be called away from the Borden house, and the authorities would be compelled to start on a new trail. The police were free to admit that there was but one theory, one clue, and if it proved unsuccessful, they had no other to take its place.

Officer Doherty was sent to the Borden house to bring Bridget Sullivan to the police station to appear as the first witness at the inquest. He had some difficulty at the house because the impression had gone forth that he intended to arrest the servant girl. For a time there were tears and lamentation, but finally the officer made it understood that the only intention was to have the young woman talk to the District Attorney. On the way to the station Miss Sullivan's tears came forth again. She told the office that she had given all information in her power to the police, and that she knew nothing more than what she had stated. Talking about the family relations, she remarked that things didn't go in the house as they should, and that she wanted to leave and had threatened to do so several times in the past two years. " But Mrs. Borden," she declared, " was a lovely woman, and I remained there because she wanted me to. Now that she is gone, however, I will stay there no longer than I have to, and will leave just as soon as the police will allow me. " Bridget also said that the strain of remaining in the place was intense. All the women there who were members of the household—the Borden girls and Miss Sullivan—were almost ready to give way to nervous prostration. Awaiting her presence were District Attorney Knowlton, State Officer Seaver, Marshal Hilliard and Medical Examiner Dolan, and soon after they were joined by Mayor Coughlin. A report that an inquest was under way quickly spread, but received prompt denial by the Marshal. When asked the meaning of the gathering he said it was an inquiry and the officers were searching for information. The domestic was in the presence of the officials for several hours and was subject to a searching cross examination, every detail of the tragedy being gone over exhaustively. After this informed conference in the Marshal's office the party adjourned to the District Court room which is situated on the second floor in the building. There were present Judge Blaisdell, District Attorney Knowlton, City Marshal Hilliard, District Officers Seaver and Rhodes, Medical Examiner Dolan, the District Attorney's stenographer, Miss Annie White, and a couple of police officials, who were among the first called to the house of the Bordens. Bridget Sullivan was in deep distress, and, if she had not already cried her eyes out, would probably have been very much agitated. On the contrary, while tremulous in voice and now and then crying a little, she was calm enough to receive the interrogatories without exhibiting much emotion and answered them comprehensively. The first question put to her was in regard to her whereabouts all through the morning of Thursday up to the time of the murder. She answered that she had been doing her regular work in the kitchen on the first floor. She had washed the breakfast dishes. She saw Miss Lizzie pass through the kitchen after breakfast time and the young lady might have passed through again. Bridget continued that she had finished up her work down-stairs and resumed window washing on the third floor, which had been begun the preceding day. She might have seen Mrs. Borden as she went up-stairs. She could hardly remember. Mr. Borden had already left the house.

The witness went up into the third floor, and while washing windows talked down to the sidewalk with a friend. She went on with the windows and might have made considerable noise as she raised and lowered them. She heard no noise inside the house in the meantime. By-and-by she heard Miss Lizzie call her. She answered at once, and went down stairs to the first floor, not thinking of looking about on the second floor, where Mrs. Borden was found dead shortly afterwards, because there was nothing to make her look around as she obeyed Miss Lizzie's call. She found Mr. Borden dead and Lizzie at the door of the room. The last point touched was the letter sent to Mrs. Borden warning her that she might be poisoned. Bridget said she knew nothing about this matter at all. Bridget finished her testimony shortly after noon and then returned to the matron's apartments. City Marshal Hilliard had served the summons on Miss Lizzie at the house and she arrived at the station about 2 o'clock. About this time Attorney Andrew J. Jennings appeared at the City Marshal's office and applied for permission to be present at the inquest in order to look after the interests of the witnesses, but he was refused. The Counsel argued at length against being excluded, but the Court would not yield and he was compelled to withdraw. All the afternoon Miss Lizzie was kept on the witness stand and testified to what she knew of the killing of her father and stepmother ; and at the close of the day District Attorney Knowlton gave out a bulletin stating that two witnesses had been examined. As the inquest was held behind doors closed and doubly guarded by the police, there was no way of finding out what had transpired within. Although the inquest was held in secret, the day was marked by numerous happenings which lent interest to the already famous case. The Attorney General who had been in consultation with the local authorities left the city in the afternoon, but before going he took occasion to say to an assembly of newspaper men that the case was not so mysterious as had been reported, and bantered them concerning their clues. Perhaps his conversation was a bit of sarcasm. He was informed that the murder was mysterious enough to baffle the police, and that five days had elapsed and that there had been no arrest. Somebody took the pains further to inform him that the evidence was purely circumstantial. "You newspaper men know, or ought to know," said Mr. Pillsbury, "that you may not be in a position to pronounce on the case. There may besome things which you have not heard of and which may have an important bearing." The reply was to the effect that the head men who had been working on the case, had conceded at noon that day, that they had no other evidence, and that they ought to be pretty good authority. " Police officers do not always tell what they know," was the parting shot of the Attorney General as he withdrew.

At 5 o'clock Bridget Sullivan left the police station in company with Officer Doherty and passed down Court Square. She was dressed in a green gown with hat to match and appeared to be nervous and excited. Nobody knew her, however, and she attracted no attention whatever. She went to the Borden house for a bundle and, still accompanied by Officer Doherty, walked to No. 95 Division street, where her cousin, Patrick Harrington lives, and where she passed the night. She was allowed to go on her own recognizance and seemed to be much relieved to get away from the Borden house. The Government impressed her with the necessity of saying nothing about the proceedings at the inquest and she was warned not to talk with anybody regarding her testimony. Bridget Sullivan is one of fourteen children. She came to this country six years ago. For three years she worked for a number of families in this city and the police reported that she bore an excellent reputation. For three years she had lived with the Borden family and for some time had been threatening to return to Ireland. She said that Mrs. Borden was a very kind mistress and that she was very much attached to her. Mrs. Borden used to talk to her about going home to Ireland, and used to tell her that she would be lonely without her. Accordingly, the girl said that she did not have the heart to leave, but she never expected to be in such an awful perdicament. She had been terrified ever since the tragedy. Prof. Wood, of Cambridge, arrived on the 4 o'clock train Monday afternoon, but was not called to testify at the inquest on Tuesday. He was questioned regarding the nature of his visit, and stated that he had come to Fall River to see what there was for him to do. "Have you examined any axe, Professor?" was asked. Prof. Wood hesitated a moment, and said : " I have seen an axe." "Will you make an examination down here?" was the next question. " I do not expect to, " was the reply. " I could not very well bring down my laboratory. " At 6 o'clock Miss Lizzie Borden, accompanied by her friend, Mrs. George Brigham, and Marshal Hilliard, entered a carriage and drove to Miss Borden's home. The excitement was not over for the day, but the District Attorney's bulletin made it plain that the authorities would make no further move that night. When the inquest adjourned, the situation in a nutshell was this : The authorities were evidently convinced that they could rely on Bridget Sullivan, and she was released from custody. She had been in custody since Thursday noon. Miss Lizzie Borden had been partially examined, and the police had completed their work on the case, so far as the collection of evidence was concerned.

There was almost as much mystery about the scenes incidental to the inquest as there was about the murder. In the first place the authorities seemed to want it understood that there was no inquest. Some of them intimated that the Government was simply conducting an informal examination with a view to drawing from the witnesses their last stories and making a comparison of them. In fact, that was the impression which prevailed up to noon, and it was reported that the oath was not administered. Nevertheless, the great pains which all connected with the proceedings took to keep information from the public made it plain that the officials were attempting to conclude the case. It was common talk around the police station Tuesday evening that there was something very significant in the fact that Bridget Sullivan, the only government witness, with the exception of Miss Lizzie Borden, and a person on whom the prosecution must rely to explain certain occurrences before and after the tragedy, was allowed to go upon her own recognizance ; and the bearing of the officials who had worked up the case indicated that they were in possession of information which they considered very valuable and which they had before been unable to secure.

At a meeting of the Board of Aldermen held that evening the following order was adopted: " Inasmuch as a terrible crime has been committed in this city requiring an unusually large number of men to do police duty, it is hereby ordered that the City Marshal be and he is hereby directed to employ such extra constables as he may deem necessary for the detection of the criminals, the expense to be charged to the appropriation for police." Up to this time, for all the public knew, the police had been unsuccessful in the hunt for the weapon. That was still one of the missing links in the chain of evidence which was claimed. In the afternoon, a story became circulated that Peleg Brightman, a paper-hanger, had been at work in South Somerset, near the two farms owned by the late Mr. Borden in that region. The story went that a bloody hatchet had been found on one of the Brayton Farms, the implement being wrapped up in a piece of newspaper and hidden in a laborer's house. As the story circulated a great breeze of inquiry and excitement arose. Several vehicles containing newspaper reporters, started immediately for the scene of the alleged discovery. Officer Harrington was also dispatched to the farm by the Marshal. The several parties reached the place about 4:30 o'clock and found a Portuguese woman in charge of the house. The woman was frightened by her visitors, and being unable to understand English well, there was no little excitement. She called her husband from the fields and he understood. He said he knew nothing about the finding of such a hatchet as had been described, but gave the squad of investigators leave to search the house. They looked it all over. The only weapon with an edge which they found was a hatchet lying on the kitchen shelf. It had no blood stains upon it. The police returned to the city in the evening, but some of the newspaper men continued their search to the two Borden farms and did not return till late. After the issuance of the official bulletin, with its practical announcement that there would be no further developments before the continuation of the inquest on Wednesday morning, there was a decided lull in the feeling of general anticipation which had existed for the past few days. This brief lull and the authoritative knowledge that nothing of importance would develop until the renewal of the inquest and the re-appearance of Bridget Sullivan and Lizzie Borden before the authorities came as a great relief, temporary though its character was, and confident in the assurance, the wearied people and the weary workers retired from the streets and at midnight the city was asleep.

As was natural, the newspapers throughout the country began at about this stage of the proceedings to take sides upon the question of the wisdom exhibited by the police. The editorial quoted below is from the *Springfield Republican* and is a fair sample of the opinions of those who saw the investigation from a distance. It read:

"All through the investigations carried on by the Fall River police, a lack of ability has been shown seldom equalled, and causes they assign for connecting the daughter with the murder are on a par with their other exhibitions of lack of wisdom. Because some one, unknown to them and too smart for them to catch, butchered two people in the daytime on a principal street of the city, using brute force, far in excess of that possessed by this girl, they conclude that there is probable reason to believe that she is the murderess. Because they found no one walking along the street with his hands and clothes reeking with blood, they conclude that it is probable, after swinging the axe with the precision and effect of a butcher, she washed the blood from her hands and clothes."

Wednesday morning the inquest was resumed. At its close the District Attorney issued the following bulletin:

"Inquest continued at 10 to-day. Witnesses examined were Lizzie Borden, Dr. S. W. Bowen, Adelaide B. Churchill, Hiram C. Harrington, John V. Morse and Emma Borden. Nothing developed for publication."

Among those present, in addition to the prosecuting officials, was Prof. Wood of Harvard, to whom the stomachs of the murdered couple had been sent for analysis. After an hour's stay in the Police Station a carriage was ordered by the Marshal, and, upon its arrival, Prof. Wood entered. Next a trunk was brought out under the charge of Medical Examiner Dolan and placed upon the carriage. The latter bade Prof. Wood good-bye and the Cambridge man was driven to the station. It was promptly presumed that included in the contents of the trunk were the axe and articles requiring analysis, and an inquiry covering these points was directed to Dr. Dolan. He declined to affirm or deny anything, and informed the newspaper representatives in a jocular vein that all the clues and secrets of the case were carefully secreted in the trunk. All this time public interest was centred in the fact of Miss Lizzie's presence in the court room, and it was felt that the most important hours of the investigation were dragging along. If the young woman, toward whom such suspicion had been directed, should come forth and retire to her home, but little more could be expected in this direction. Certainly, after the searching examination, which all knew she was undergoing, any further questioning could but be useless, and there were those in the gathered crowds in the vicinity of Court Square who openly proclaimed their earnest convictions that with the exit of Lizzie Borden from the station house the cloud of suspicions which had hovered about her must be dispelled, with the accompanying practical admission by the authorities that they were unable to connect her with the commission of the crime. This statement was based upon the wide-spread knowledge that the police had been moving with the greatest caution in their investigation upon the thoroughly understood line.

The members of the Borden family held a high position, their wealth was great, and, apart from the fact that their interests were being guarded by one of the ablest attorneys in the city, it was known that influential friends of the family had deemed it wise to request the Marshal to move with the utmost care before taking active steps toward the arrest of any member of that household. Perhaps the accusation that, had certain suspected persons been possessed of less wealth and influence, they would long ere this have been apprehended was unjust to the hard-working police, but the fact was patent to everybody that the extreme care in this particular case reached far beyond the usual, particularly as all the time every movement of the Borden girls was only made under the surveillance of a police officer. During the afternoon carpenter Maurice Daly, the Marshal and Officer Harrington appeared at the Borden house. The first mentioned had a kit of carpenter's tools in his hand and the three men entered the house. After half an hour they came out and were noticed carrying three bundles. These contained parts of the woodwork about the doors and windows which showed blood spots. Marshal Hilliard, previous to the opening of the inquest, had employed Detective Edwin D. McHenry of Providence, R. I., to assist his men in running down clues. Mr. McHenry was destined to form an important factor in the case and its subsequent developments, as will be seen farther on. His first work, so far as the police knew, was in connection with Officer Medley in following the clue given to the police by Dr. Handy. It was at a cottage at Marion, owned by Dr. Handy, that Miss Lizzie Borden intended to spend her vacation, and this, coupled with the prominence of the physician, made the authorities feel particularly anxious to ascertain the personality of this "wild eyed man," confident though they were that he was entirely innocent of any complicity in the tragedy at the Borden house. The chase was not a difficult one, and the individual was located promptly by the officers. He was Michael Graham, better known as "Mike, the Soldier," a weaver employed in Border City Mill No. 2, and for some days previous to Thursday he had been drinking freely. The officers learned that Graham was in the vicinity of the Borden house just before 10 o'clock on the morning of the murder and that his physical condition, as a result of his excesses, was such as to render his countenance almost ghastly in its color. He reached the mills where he is employed shortly after 10 o'clock, and his condition was at once apparent, and the men in charge there declined to allow him to go to work.

The officers found the saloons in which Graham spent Wednesday night, and learned there that he drank immoderately, and was feeling badly as a result. The description of Graham corresponded in every particular with that given by Officer Hyde, who furnished more details as to the clothing of the man than could be advanced by Dr. Handy. His trousers were of a peculiar texture and hue, and were rendered extremely noticeable on this account. This, in itself, was believed to be sufficient identification, but in all other particulars there was an unmistaken similarity, and the authorities arrived at once at the conclusion that the man was identical with the person described by Dr. Handy and the police officer. The explosion of this theory afforded much satisfaction to the authorities. Yet there appeared many weeks afterward reasons known to the Marshal alone which caused him to start Officer Medley in search of " Mike the Soldier" again. The search ended in a day and the suspect was again located. Superintendent Hanscom of the Pinkerton Agency, was in Fall River for several days about the time of the inquest. He declined to be interviewed about his work and as the public observed, made numerous visits to the law office of Mr. Jennings. The conclusion of some police officers, perhaps erroneous, was that he was present to protect the members of the household. He talked very little but was credited with saying with a smile, that Marshal Hilliard was doing good work. The local authorities, however, expressed themselves in very strong terms regarding the doubts which the Pinkerton man cast upon the reliability of a portion of their accumulated wisdom.

CHAPTER XI.

Miss Lizzie Borden Arrested.

THURSDAY was the last day of the inquest, and in its evening hours a veritable sensation was produced. The same impenetrable secrecy was maintained all day long, and no one knew what progress was being made behind the grim stone walls of the Central Police Station wherein Judge Blaisdell and the chosen few sat in solemn conclave. The scenes of the day before were enacted in the guard room and the streets about the building. Crowds surged about the doors and a double guard of patrolmen were doing duty in the hallways. The forenoon session developed nothing so far as the public was concerned. In the afternoon, Eli Bence, the drug clerk, Fred Hart, another clerk, and Frank Kilroy, who saw Mr. Borden on the morning of the tragedy, strolled into the guard room and were shown upstairs. Later, Bridget Sullivan, escorted by two officers, walked up the alley. She attracted no attention and appeared to be at her ease. The fact that Bridget walked from her temporary residence at 95 Division street to the police station, a distance of more than a mile in the heat of an August day, while other women witnesses rode in a hack from the Borden house, a distance of less than an eighth of a mile, caused some comment. About 3 o'clock in the afternoon the closed carriage which had become almost as familiar a sight as the police patrol, rattled over the rough pavement. Half a dozen men were in sight, and in a twinkling two hundred men, women and children swarmed around the coach. The City Marshal gave an order, Steward Geagan cracked a whip, officers hustled the crowd back and Mrs. George S. Brigham alighted. She was followed by Misses Emma and Lizzie Borden. Then Officer Doherty disappeared with the hack and returned with another witness. The same crowd collected but no one tried to drive it back. The excitement subsided. It was growing tiresome in Fall River.

The reaction had set in, the community was losing its patience. For two days it had been informed that the end was near and that the die was about to be cast; but at 3 o'clock the bulletin boards announced that no action had been taken and no verdict had been rendered, and the crowds muttered and grumbled. They wanted something done; their interest in clues and theories and suspicious characters had about died out. More than that, they were no longer satisfied with reports of the proceedings at the inquest detailed step by step. They demanded the grand finale which would bring the drama to a close or ring the curtain up on a new scene; but it seemed as if the grand finale had been indefinitely postponed. The hour dragged along and the gray walls of the Court House in the Square kept their secrets, if they had any to keep. It was the same story over and over again. Witnesses known to be connected with the case appeared and disappeared; officers were sent hither and thither and various rumors were afloat regarding the probable outcome.

From the time that the carriage rolled up to the entrance to the Central Police Station at 4:30 o'clock and Lizzie Borden, Emma Borden and Mrs. George Brigham dismounted under the watchful eye of Marshal Hilliard, people commenced to congregate about the streets contiguous to the station house. By that intuitive perception by which the general public becomes aware of all important proceedings looking towards the capture or apprehension of criminals in noted cases, it was recognized that the most important movements of the long investigation had been entered upon; and that their passing were fraught with the greatest import to all directly concerned in the case as well as the public, restless under the week's delay in clearing the way for the arrest of the murderer.

LIEUT. JOHN DEVINE.

There was nothing remarkable in the appearance of the party, Miss Emma Borden being evidently the most agitated. The excitement grew as the hour passed, and there was no movement from the court room. In the meanwhile information arrived that an expert safe opener had arrived from Boston, and had been driven hurriedly to the Borden house on Second street. Investigation showed the truth of this story, and the further fact that he had commenced work upon the safe in which Andrew J. Borden kept his books and papers. This safe was found locked at the time of the tragedy, and the secret of the combination died with the murdered man. The expert believed he could easily open the safe, but he found the combination most intricate, and he worked away without apparent result.

At 5 o'clock Marshal Hilliard and District Attorney Knowlton came from the court room and entered a carriage. Soon the Marshal returned, but the District Attorney was absent for nearly an hour, and it was reported that he had visited the Borden house and had learned that the safe opener had not completed his work. Outside the court room the stalwart officers kept guard, and at the foot of the stairs in the station house the large force of newspaper representatives were on guard. The subordinate officers who had been working upon the case expressed their convictions that the long delayed arrest was about to be made, and that Lizzie Borden would not depart from the station with the remaining members of the household. Soon Bridget Sullivan emerged, and escorted by a police officer walked slowly down the street. The gravity of the situation was apparent, for the natural sternness of some of the officials, including the Marshal, was increased to such an extent as to warrant the inference that something of importance in connection with the case was about to happen. Soon the inquisition was apparently ended, and then Lizzie Borden, her sister and Mrs. Brigham were escorted across the entry from the court room to the matron's room, which is situated upon the same floor. An officer came out and soon returned with supper for the party. Miss Lizzie Borden threw herself upon the lounge in the room, and the repast was disturbed but little.

Across the room there was grave work, and the decision of the authorities to arrest Lizzie Borden was arrived at after a consultation lasting but ten minutes. The services of Clerk were called into requisition. The warrant was quickly drawn, and the result of the long examinations and the week's work of the Government was in the hands of the police force of Fall River. At this time the news was among the reporters, but none were certain enough of the fact to dispatch the intelligence to the journals they represented. The excitement became general, and men, women and children stood about the street and waited. Soon Marshal Hilliard came out accompanied by Mr. Knowlton, and as they entered a carriage a telephone message informed Andrew J. Jennings, attorney for the family, that the two men were about to pay him a visit at his residence. This information obtained but little publicity, and not a few in the assembled crowds believed that Mr. Knowlton was being driven to the Boston train. The Marshal and the District Attorney proceeded to Mr. Jenning's residence and informed that gentleman that the Government had decided upon the arrest of Lizzie Borden, and, recognizing that his presence at the station would be desirable, had deemed it wise to notify him of the decision arrived at and the contemplated action. The officials returned to the court room and were followed in a few moments by the attorney. George Brigham also came to the station and entered the presence of the women in the matron's quarters.

There was a moment's preparation, and then Lizzie Borden was informed that she was held by the Government on the charge of having murdered her father. Marshal Hilliard and Detective Seaver entered the room, the former holding in his hand a sheet of paper—the warrant for Lizzie Borden's arrest—and, after requesting Mrs. Brightman to leave the room, addressing the prostrate woman in the gentlest possible manner, said : " I have here a warrant for your arrest—issued by the judge of the District Court. I shall read it to you if you desire, but you have the right to waive the reading of it ?" He looked at Lawyer Jennings as he completed the latter part of the statement, and that gentleman turned toward Lizzie and said : " Waive the reading." The first and only time during the scene that the accused woman uttered a word was in response to the direction of her attorney. Turning slightly in her position, she flashed a look at the Marshal, one of those queer glances which nobody has attempt-'ed to describe, except by saying that they are a part and parcel of Lizzie Borden, and replied : " You need not read it." The information had a most depressing effect upon all the others present, particularly upon Miss Emma Borden, who was greatly affected. Upon the face of the prisoner there was a pallor, and while her eyes were moist with tears there was little evidence of emotion in the almost stolid countenance. The remaining members of the party then prepared to depart, and the effects of the arrest became apparent upon the prisoner. She still displayed all the characteristics of her peculiarly unemotional nature, and though almost prostrated, she did not shed a tear. A carriage was ordered and Miss Emma Borden and Mr. and Mrs. Brigham prepared to leave. As they emerged from the station into the view of the curious crowds, the women, particularly Miss Emma, looked about with almost a pathetic glance. The people crowded forward and the police pushed them back. Miss Borden appeared to be suffering intensely, and all the external evidences of agitation were visible upon her countenance. Mrs. Brigham was more composed, but was evidently deeply concerned. The party entered the carriage and were driven rapidly towards Second street.

Lizzie A. Borden was accused of the murder of her father, Andrew J. Borden. The warrant made no reference to the killing of Abbie D. Borden. That night the prisoner was overcome by the great mental strain to which she had been subjected for nearly a week and when all had departed, except the kindly matron, the burden proved heavier than she could bear. She gave way to her feelings and sobbed as if her heart would break. Then she gave up to a violent fit of vomiting and the efforts of the matrons to stop it were unavailing. Dr. Bowen was sent for and he succeeded in relieving her physical sufferings. The prisoner was not confined in a cell room of the lock-up down stairs.

Judge Blaisdell, District Attorney Knowlton and Marshal Hilliard are men of experience, good sense and reliable judgment, and no other three men on earth regretted the step they had taken more than they. But from their point of view it was duty, not sentiment which guided their actions. No other prisoner arrested in Bristol county had been accorded the delicate and patient consideration which Marshal Hilliard bestowed upon Miss Lizzie Borden. No cell doors closed upon her until after an open, fair and impartial trial before a competent judge, and defended by her chosen legal counsel, she was adjudged " probably guilty."

During the afternoon Medical Examiner Dolan, Drs. Cone, Leary and Medical Examiner Draper of Boston, held another autopsy on the bodies of the murdered people at receiving vault in Oak Grove Cemetery. They discovered a wound in Mrs. Borden back, between the shoulder blades. It was a frightful cut and was made by an axe or hatchet which entered the flesh and bone clear up to the helve. It alone would have produced instant death. In addition to this the doctors severed the poor, mutilated heads from both the bodies, and Dr. Dolan took possession of the ghastly objects. They were taken to a suitable place and the flesh and blood removed from the bones. The glaring white skulls with great rents, where the murderous axe had crushed, then were added to Dr. Dolan's collection of evidence which could not properly be called " circumstantial." The skulls were photographed.

In view of the severe criticism which had been directed towards the police from many quarters and by newspapers from all parts of the country, a review of their conduct of this case might be interesting. City Marshal Hilliard, his position corresponding to that of the Chief of Police in other cities, was sitting in his office at 11 o'clock on Thursday, Aug. 4, when a telephone message from John Cunningham announced that a stabbing affray had occurred on Second street. Assistant Marshal Fleet was engaged in the Second District Court, and more than half the members of the police department were at

Rocky Point on their annual excursion. Officer George Allen was alone on duty at the station. The Marshal came from the office and sent Officer Allen to investigate the case. Allen ran to 92 Second street and was dumbfounded at the sight which met his gaze. He stopped long enough to see Andrew J. Borden's body lying on the sitting room sofa. The officer was back at the station in short order, and this action alone has caused the most severe criticism. The officer was, to put it mildly, taken considerably aback by the sight in the house, and, to put it not too strongly, was frightened out of his wits. He left no guard upon the house when he ran back to the station. A general alarm was sent out, and in half an hour every officer in the city had been notified and a dozen of them were at the scene. They invaded the house and searched the yard and barn for some evidence to assist them in starting the work. The cry went out from some source or other that a Swedish farm hand, dubbed "the Portuguese," had done the deed. This was the first clue, and it started half a dozen policemen and the City Marshal over the river to the Borden farm. The hunt ended the same afternoon and the clue was promptly exploded, for the farm hands were all in their accustomed places, and it was impossible to connect any of them with this crime.

Before morning six new clues, all more or less promising, had developed. Among them was one which pointed to the startling suspicion that some member of the family might have been a participant, directly or indirectly, in the awful crime. This was early, and naturally looked upon as the most important of all, and the officers worked day and night towards its solution. Others were not neglected, and all the different clues were investigated by officers especially detailed to do the work assisted by officers in neighboring cities and private detectives. A small boy reported that he had seen a man jump over the back fence. A Frenchman had helped the same man escape toward New Bedford, and it was stated that he was the chief of a gang of gypsy horse traders encamped at Westport. Two officers from Fall River and as many from New Bedford searched for this man and found Bearsley S. Cooper, who accurately answered the description. Cooper promptly proved an alibi. He was in New Bedford on the day of the murder selling a horse to a well-known citizen.

John V. Morse was at first suspected of having had something to do with these horse traders. Morse had told the officers a story of his whereabouts on that day, and a detail was sent out to verify his statement or find something to the contrary. Morse's movements were easily followed and it was soon well understood that he was not in the house at the time of the tragedy. During the time that had elapsed since the murder a police cordon had surrounded the house day and night. The night after the murder Officers Harrington and Doherty were detailed to search the drug stores of the city to see if any member of the family had endeavored to purchase poison, a hint to this effect having been received by the department. At the store of D. R. Smith they found that Lizzie had but recently endeavored to purchase ten cents worth of hydrocyanic acid. The clerk was taken that night before Miss Borden, and identified her. This was considered important. A report was received that a stranger had boarded the train at Mount Pleasant on the afternoon of the murder. He was said to have been covered with dust and his clothes showed spots of blood. Investigation showed that he was a respectable citizen of New Bedford, and was in no way connected with this affair. Dr. Handy reported that he had seen a man acting wildly and strangely on Second street that morning. The police ran down two men, one of them in Boston, who answered the description. One was a Fall River man, and he was doubtless intensely surprised at being chased by detectives and police officers who were imbued with the idea that he might in some way have been connected with the Borden murder. The Boston man was badly frightened at being seized as a suspect, and established an alibi without difficulty. Mrs. Chase said she saw a man on the back fence in the Borden yard at 11 o'clock. He was found and admitted, with some hesitation, that he was there, the hesitation being due to the fact that he had been engaged in the reprehensible occupation of stealing pears. A stonemason, who was working near by, saw him and informed the police of his whereabouts. On Saturday the police narrowed down to the theory to which all their efforts appeared to direct in spite of themselves, and searched the Borden house and premises. On Monday they made another search. Tuesday the house was again besieged by the officers. Monday night the bloody hatchet was found on the farm in South Somerset. It belonged to an old man named Sylvia. The only thing that it had killed was a chicken.

On Tuesday the District Attorney and Attorney General were called into the case, and an inquest was ordered by Judge Blaisdell. For three days it was in session, and all the evidence accumulated by the police was submitted. Medical Examiner Dolan, Prof. Wood of Harvard and Medical Examiner Draper held an autopsy on the bodies and worked in conjunction with the police. In addition to all this an endless number of minor clues were worked out, and they all resulted in failure to connect the parties alleged to have been concerned with the murder of Mr. and Mrs. Borden. While the detectives were running down clues, Marshal Hilliard and State Detective Seaver were giving their personal attention to everything that might establish the connection of any member of the Borden household with the crime. The conditions were such that haste would have availed nothing, for there was no possibility from the time that suspicion was first cast in that direction of any of the parties in question leaving the city.

Thursday the work of the police, as far as establishing in their minds beyond a reasonable doubt the identity of the murderer of the aged couple, was finished, and at 4:20 o'clock in the afternoon Lizzie Borden, daughter of the victim, was brought to the Central Police Station and retained there as a prisoner. This, in substance, comprised the labors of the police force of Fall River upon this celebrated case so far as the public was informed.

CHAPTER XII.

LIZZIE BORDEN PLEADS "NOT GUILTY."

MISS LIZZIE A. BORDEN was to be arraigned in the Second District Court, on Friday morning. By 9 o'clock a crowd of people thronged the streets and stood in a drenching rain to await the opening of the door of the room in which the court held its sittings. It was not a well-dressed crowd, nor was there anybody in it from the acquaintance circle of the Borden family in Fall River. Soon after 9 o'clock, a hack rolled up to the side door and Emma Borden and John V. Morse alighted and went up the stairs. They were not admitted at once to the matron's room. Rev. E. A. Buck was already present and was at the time, engaged in conversation with the prisoner. Judge Blaisdell passed up the stairs, while Miss Emma was waiting to see her sister, and entered the court room. Mr. Jennings, the counsel, also arrived. The District Attorney was already in the court room, and soon the Marshal brought in his large book of complaints, and took his seat at the desk. The door of the matron's room opened and Mr. Jennings, Miss Emma Borden and Mr. Morse met the prisoner. All retired within the room. A few moments later Mr. Jennings came out and entered the court room. He at once secured a blank sheet of legal cap and began to write. The City Marshal approached him, and Mr. Jennings nodded an assent to an inquiry if the prisoner could now be brought in.

Lizzie Borden entered the room immediately after on the arm of Rev. Mr. Buck. She was dressed in a dark blue suit and her hat was black with red flowers on the front. She was escorted to a chair. The prisoner was not crying, but her features were far from firm. She has a face and chin betokening strength of character, but a rather sensitive mouth, and on this occasion the sensitiveness of the lips especially betrayed itself. She was constantly moving her lips as she sat in the court room in a way to show that she was not altogether unemotional. Clerk Leonard called the case of the Commonwealth of Massachusetts against Lizzie Borden, on complaint of murder. Mr. Jennings, who was still writing, asked for a little more time. He soon arose and went over to the prisoner. He spoke to her, and then she arose and went to his desk. He read what he had been writing to her, and then gave her a pen. She signed the paper.

Mr. Jennings then addressed the court saying:

"Your Honor, before the prisoner pleads she wishes to present the following." He then read as follows:

"Bristol ss. Second District Court. Commonwealth vs. Lizzie A. Borden. Complaint for homicide. Defendant's plea.

"And now comes the defendant in the above entitled complaint and before pleading thereto says that the Hon. Josiah C. Blaisdell, the presiding Justice of the Second District Court of Bristol, before which said complaint is returnable, has been and believes is still engaged as the presiding magistrate at an inquest upon the death of said Andrew J. Borden, the person whom it is alleged in said complaint the defendant killed, and has received and heard and is still engaged in receiving and hearing evidence in relation to said killing and to said defendant's connection therewith which is not and has not been allowed to hear or know the report of, whereof she says that said Hon. Josiah C. Blaisdell is disqualified to hear this complaint, and she objects to his so doing, and all of this she is ready to verify.

Lizzie A. Borden, by her attorney, Andrew J. Jennings, (Her signature) Lizzie A. Borden. Sworn to this the 12th day of August, A. D., 1892, before me, Andrew J. Jennings, Justice of the peace."

When Mr. Jennings concluded the District Attorney arose and asked the Court if this paper was to delay the prisoner's plea. The Court said it was not to, and ordered the Clerk, to read the warrant.

"You needn't read it," said Mr. Jennings, " the prisoner pleads not guilty."

The text of the warrant however was as follows:

"Commonwealth of Massachusetts,

To Augustus B. Leonard, Clerk of the Second District Court of Bristol, in the county Bristol, and Justice of the Peace:

Rufus B. Hilliard, City Marshal of Fall River, in said county, in behalf of said Commonwealth, on oath, complains that Lizzie A. Borden of Fall River, in the county of Bristol, at Fall River, aforesaid, in the county aforesaid, on the fourth day of August, in the year of our Lord 1892, in and upon one Andrew J. Borden, feloniously, willfully and of her malice aforethought, did make assault and that the said Lizzie A. Borden, then and there with a certain weapon, to wit, a hatchet, in and upon the head of the said Andrew J. Borden, then and there feloniously, willfully and of her malice aforethought, did strike, giving unto the said Andrew J. Borden, then and there, with the hatchet aforesaid, by the stroke aforesaid, in manner aforesaid, in and upon the head of the said Andrew J. Borden, one mortal wound, of which said mortal wound the said Andrew J. Borden then and there instantly died. And so the complainant aforesaid, upon his oath aforesaid, further complains and says that the said Lizzie A. Borden, the said Andrew J. Borden, in manner and form aforesaid, then and there feloniously, wilfully and of her malice aforethought did kill and murder.

(Signed)   R. B. HILLIARD."

"The prisoner must plead in person," said Judge Blaisdell. At a sign from City Marshal Hilliard the prisoner arose in her seat.

"What is your plea?" asked the Clerk.

"Not guilty," said the girl, and then, having said this indistinctly and the clerk repeating his question, she answered the same thing in a louder voice and, with a very clearly cut emphasis on the word "Not."

Mr. Jennings now arose. "It seems to me," said he, "your Honor, that this proceeding is most extraordinary. This girl is called to plead to a complaint issued in the progress of an inquest now only in its early stages. The complaint has been brought in spite of the fact that she was not allowed to be represented by counsel in the hearing before the inquest. She has no knowledge of the evidence on which the complaint is made. I spoke to the District Attorney about this fact before she testified at the inquest, and I admitted that it might be legally done. But this has left the girl in this position, that she is charged with a crime in a complaint issued during the inquest, and I understand that inquest is still open. Your Honor sits here to hear this case, which is returnable before you, when you have already been sitting on the case in another capacity. We do not know what you have heard on this case in the inquest or of the purport of the testimony there. By all the laws of human nature you cannot help being prejudiced from the character of the evidence which has been submitted to you. You might look at things differently from what you do, if certain questions that may have been asked in the inquest had been excluded, or if you had been allowed to hear both sides, with counsel to ask for rulings upon the character of the interrogatories. So it seems to me that you are sitting in a double capacity to hear a charge against my client based upon evidence of which we know nothing, and for all that we know you may have formed opinions which make you incompetent to hear this complaint under the rules of law. The constitution does not allow a Judge to sit in such a double capacity and it guarantees a defendant from a prejudiced hearing.''

District Attorney Knowlton answered saying: '' The commonwealth demurs from the plea. My brother is entirely in error in stating that there is anything extraordinary in this proceeding. This is exactly the line laid down that has been followed in other cases that have excited less attention than this one. More than twenty times to my certain knowledge, has a similar thing been done, and I should not be doing my duty if this thing should not be done now. You have your duty at the inquest and you are also obliged by statute to hear cases of this kind. I must respectfully submit that it is not a compliment to your Honor's conception of your duty, to suggest that you cannot faithfully and impartially perform the duties that devolve upon you in this case. The inquest was against no one. It was to ascertain who committed these murders. The inquest is still proceeding, and the evidence before it has nothing to do with this case. It is your Honor's duty to hear this complaint and you ought not to be deterred.''

Mr. Jennings then said : '' I don't think that the District Attorney comprehended my point. The inquest is generally held early in a case of this kind, and you can see where suspicion falls. The difference between the custom and this case is, that after the police determined whom they thought the guilty person was, then, without holding an open trial at once, they settled on the guilty party and held an inquest to examine her, without anybody to defend her. That's what this inquest is, and because your Honor has been sitting here before the inquest you can't help being prejudiced. To illustrate: A person comes to your law office and states his case, and then after that you go into court to hear the case and pronounce judgment on it.''

Judge Blaisdell—'' I think Mr. Jennings is mistaken. The statutes make it my imperative duty to hold an inquest and upon the testimony introduced at that hearing, to direct the issuance of warrants. The motion is overruled and the demurred sustained.''

Mr. Jennings—'' Then, your Honor, we are ready for trial.''

Mr. Knowlton—'' The evidence in this case could not be completed at once. It could hardly all be gathered by next week.'' He moved a continuance till one week, Monday, August 22, at 2 o'clock, when the State hoped to be entirely ready with the case.

Mr. Jennings—''We are very anxious to proceed at once. We ask for a trial at the earliest possible moment.''

District Attorney Knowlton—"I didn't know but what you would waive examination here, so I am not ready now."

The two lawyers consulted for a moment, and then announced they had agreed on Monday, August 22, as the date of the preliminary hearing.

District Attorney Knowlton moved that the prisoner be committed till that date. Judge Blaisdell granted the motion, remarking that other procedure was impossible, the offence not being a bailable one.

Bridget Sullivan had entered the court room during the talk between the court and the lawyers. Mr. Morse had not entered the room. Neither had Miss Emma Borden. The District Attorney now addressed the Court again. He said the importance of Mr. Morse and Bridget Sullivan to the case of the State was so great that he wished to move that they be placed under bonds to guarantee their presence inside the Court's jurisdiction. Judge Blaisdell said he would grant the request, and asked how much the bonds should be.

MAYOR JOHN W. COUGHLIN.

Mr. Knowlton—"Three hundred dollars is the usual amount, but on account of the gravity of this case I suggest the amount be $500. Mr. Morse can procure bail, we suppose ; but we don't know about Bridget Sullivan. The servant girl was called from the corner where she sat, and Mr. Morse got up. Bridget was as pale as a ghost and her eyes plainly said she did not understand what was going on. The order of the Court was read to the man and woman, they standing side by side. They were then led across the room by the Marshal and given seats far away from the outside door. Mr. Jennings had two of the Notary Publics whom he keeps at his office in the court room, and he at once dispatched one of them down town for a bondsman or bondsmen. Lizzie Borden had in the interval left the room on the arm of Rev. Mr. Buck. She went back to the matron's room. Her sister and Mr. Buck remained with her for fifteen or twenty minutes. Then Mr. Morse, having obtained bail, came out. The elder sister soon after left the court building with Mr. Morse, being driven home in the same carriage they came in. The crowd about the carriage when the old man and his niece entered it was a large one. Messrs. Almy and Milne, proprietors of the *Fall River Daily News*, went bail for Mr. Morse. Bridget returned to her friend's residence on Division street. The prisoner remained in the matron's room to await transportation to the County Jail at Taunton.

For the first time in six days the strain was lifted from Fall River and people breathed and thought and transacted routine business more naturally. The suspense was temporarily over and everybody felt relieved. This would have been the result whatever the verdict reached Thursday evening. A decisive step had to be taken in one direction or another, and when the final announcement came, the mind of the community grew more settled. There was more or less excitement, of course, and the impulse to dart into Court Square whenever a coach or the patrol wagon made its appearance, was nearly as strong as ever, but on the whole, men talked and acted more rationally. They were anxious to learn what the breaking of the safe had revealed, how the prisoner passed the night, the particulars of the arraignment and other minor details, but when they were informed that the safe had hidden nothing which bore on the case, that Miss Borden had slept quietly and appeared to be self-contained and composed in her quarters in the matron's room, and that there were likely to be no further developments of importance for a week or more, the life of the town settled back into the old ruts. Rev. E. A. Buck called on the prisoner at noon and from the sidewalk near the station a bouquet could be seen in the windows of the matron's apartments. After the vigorous protest of Andrew J. Jennings, Esq., relative to the preliminary trial had electrified the court room audience, and his motion had been overruled, it was decided to take the prisoner to Taunton on the 3:40 train. Fall River has no house of detention and no quarters suitable for sheltering persons who are held on suspicion. Court Square was choked as usual with a crowd of sightseers. One carriage drew up at the main entrance and Miss Emma Borden and Andrew J. Jennings, Esq., entered it and were driven to the depot. Miss Lizzie Borden, the prisoner, stepped into a carriage which was in waiting at the side entrance and was also driven off. To all outward appearances, she was as calm as though she had been going for a visit to relatives. Rev. E. A. Buck, City Marshal Hilliard and

State Officer Seaver accompanied her. A small valise containing the prisoner's clothing was placed on the box.

The representatives of the press followed the carriage containing the prisoner in cabs, and at 3:30 Court Square was quiet. The newsboys, who had taken possession and held high revel in it for a week, had gone off with their bundles, the curious no longer loitered on the sidewalks, and no more rumors floated out from the guard room. On Thursday night when the finale was known, the friends of the Borden family were cool and philosophical. Friday they denounced the course pursued by the authorities from beginning to end. In partnership with her sister, Miss Emma Borden had offered a reward of $5000 for the conviction of the murderer of her father and stepmother, and had secured the services of a detective to track the butcher. On the Government side it was fair and natural to presume, that she, above any person on the face of the earth, desired to bring the wretch who had committed the deed to the gallows. The very fact that she was suspected, was of itself sufficient to warrant such a conclusion, all other considerations aside. The only surmise possible, therefore, was that she would assist the authorities to the best of her ability in unravelling the mystery and in freeing herself from the chain of circumstances, weak or strong, which surrounded her. It was to be supposed that she would not only answer every question cheerfully, but that she would volunteer every particle of information in her possession, and that the more searching the examination, the better she would be satisfied. She had everything to gain and nothing to lose by a full revelation of the truth. Anybody in his sober senses would have been slow to even suggest that District Attorney Knowlton, or any other prosecuting officer, was eager to convict the innocent, to embarrass witnesses, or to impose any unnecessary hardships upon them. At the inquest every person examined was a government witness; there was no defendant, and of course, no witnesses for the defense. Whether Miss Borden did assist the court and the authorities to clear up the grim problem which confronted them, was not known. If the government officers were possessed of the ordinary intelligence, they were aware that it was a terrible thing to swear out a warrant for the arrest of a young lady and charge her with killing her father. If, as it was openly alleged at the time, the government did so, because it did not appreciate the full significance of such a charge, it must be admitted their conduct was more extraordinary and inexplicable than any feature of the crime itself. The government authorities knew that once the warrant had been issued, Miss Borden's character, at the time of trial which had always been irreproachable, was blotted forever; it must have known that even if she left the Superior Court room acquitted, nothing that it could do could lift the blight from her life.

The route taken by the carriage containing Lizzie Borden, Marshal Hilliard, Officer Seaver and Rev. Mr Buck toward the Fall River railroad depot was most peculiar. It is a direct road from the Central Station to the depot. Along the main thoroughfare were people eager to catch a glimpse of the prisoner, and the Marshal, considerate of his charge, decided to disappoint the curiosity seekers. Accordingly, the journey was up hill and down dale, through side streets and along thoroughfares skirting the river. Following the carriage were others containing the representatives of the leading newspapers of the East, and these latter drew up at the depot a few seconds in advance of the official vehicle. A squad of officers was on duty there, and as the crowd surged they pushed it back. The train for Taunton was a few minutes late, and until its arrival Lizzie Borden and Mr. Buck remained in the carriage. As the clang of the engine bell was heard, the Marshal pulled up the carriage curtains and assisted Lizzie Borden to alight. She was prettily dressed and appeared quite prepossessing. She wore a blue dress of new design, and a short blue veil. At the realization that the moment for departure had arrived she seemed overcome by a momentary weakness and almost tottered. She was at once supported by the Marshal and Mr. Buck, and leaning upon the arms of these two she walked through the ladies' waiting room and out towards the cars. The eager crowd pushed and stared and gossipped as the party entered the rear car of the train. Rev. Mr. Buck carried a box containing a number of religious and other papers and magazines, and also some books. A telescope bag containing Miss Borden's apparel was placed in the cars. The prisoner sat near the window in a seat with Mr. Buck, and behind them was Mr. Hilliard. The blinds were drawn in order to prevent annoyance to Miss Borden by curious persons. Her glance was vacant and her thoughts were manifestly removed from her present surroundings. Not a word was exchanged between the members of the party, and the prisoner still remained in the same position, staring at nothing. In some manner the information that Miss Borden was upon the train spread, and at the few stations at which it stopped small knots of inquisitive people were gathered.

Taunton was reached at 4:20 o'clock. Awaiting her arrival was a gathering of hundreds, and they crowded about every car. Officer

Seaver in order to attract their attention, hurried to the north end of the station, and the throng hurried in that direction. At this time Mr. Hilliard and Mr. Buck escorted the prisoner from the south end of the station and into a carriage. Mr. Seaver joined them, and the crowd found itself disappointed. After the vehicle rolled the cabs of the newspaper men. Taunton Jail is not far removed from the centre of the city and is a picturesque looking stone structure. There is the main building and the keeper's residence, which is attached. On the outside of the structure ivy grows in profusion and the building does not resemble, except in the material of its construction, the generally accepted appearance of a place of confinement. It has accommodations for sixty-five prisoners, and the women's department is on the southeast side. In this portion of the building there are but nine cells, and before the arrival of Lizzie Borden but five of these were occupied. These were confined for offences of a minor nature, as it not customary for the officials of Bristol County to send many women to Taunton, the majority being committed to the jail at New Bedford, where there is employment for them. The matron is Mrs. Wright, wife of Sheriff Andrew J. Wright, keeper of the jail, and her personal attention is given to the female prisoners. The officers had been notified of the coming of Miss Borden, and her arrival was unattended by any unusual ceremony inside the jail. Her step was firmer than ever, as, unassisted, she walked up the three steps and into the office of the keeper. From there she was directed to the corridor which runs along the cells of the women's department, and here Mr. Hilliard left her. Returning to the office he handed the committing mittimus to Sheriff Wright, who examined it and found it correct.

In the meanwhile Lizzie Borden was alone with the clergyman. He spoke words of cheer to her and left her in the care of the matron. Mr. Buck said she was not shocked at the sight of the cells, and, knowing that she was innocent, accepted the situation with a calm resignation. He said her friends would call upon her from time to time, this being allowed by the institution.

The cell in which Lizzie Borden was confined is nine and one-half feet high and seven and one-half feet wide. Across the corridor, looking through the iron bars, her gaze will rest upon whitewashed walls. The furniture of the cell consists of a bedstead, chair and washbowl. At her personal request she saw none of the daily newspapers. Consequently she was not familiar with the comments of the papers regarding the case. Taken in charge by the matron, Lizzie Borden was escorted to the cell, and the iron doors clanged behind her. Perhaps no person in Taunton experienced a greater surprise and shock at the arrival of Lizzie Borden than Mrs. Wright, the matron, in whose care the prisoner was committed. Sheriff Wright was for years a resident of Fall River, and at one time held the position of Marshal of the city police, the place now occupied by Mr. Hilliard. Mr. and Mrs. Wright were well acquainted with the Borden family, but the first names of their acquaintances had slipped from their memory, and the Sheriff and his wife did not connect the Borden they formerly knew with the prominent actors in this tragedy. When Lizzie Borden entered the presence of the matron, the latter noticed something familiar in the countenance of the young woman, and after the retirement of Rev. Mr. Buck commenced to question her. Finally, after a number of questions, Mrs. Wright asked, '' Are you not the Lizzie Borden who used as a child to play with my daughter Isabel?'' The answer was an affirmative one, and the information touched Mrs. Wright to the quick. When she appeared in the keeper's office a few moments later her eyes were moist with tears.

CHAPTER XIII.

The Preliminary Hearing Adjourned.

ABOUT ten days elapsed between the date of Miss Borden's commitment to Taunton Jail and the date set for the preliminary trial. During this time there was no end of theories advanced by both sides as to the guilt or innocence of the accused. Meanwhile she remained in custody of Sheriff Wright and was apparently undisturbed by circumstances which surrounded her. The days went by in a quiet uneventful manner and those who predicted a collapse of her mental or physical system, while she was a temporary inmate of the jail were disappointed; as there was no outward evidence that the prisoner was at all alarmed at the gravity of her position. In many ways the consideration extended to her by the authorities was manifest. During her incarceration she was visited regularly by Rev. E. A. Buck, her sister Emma and her legal counsel. From all parts of the country came assurances that the prisoner had a host of devoted friends. Ministers of the gospel took occasion to proclaim her innocence from the pulpit. A sample of this friendliness can be seen from the following words of Rev. Dr. Mason of Bowden College Church, Brunswick, Me. He occupied the pulpit of the Central Church in Fall River and in the course of his sermon said "A great, dark cloud has settled down upon one of our families. But God is in that cloud. He is with that poor, tried tempest-tossed girl; he will give her strength and peace; he will make her glad. It is impossible for a wrong to be done in this world that eternity will not undo. Good is coming; good out of evil; light out of darkness. The father is over all. He will vindicate, and raise and glorify."

At a meeting of the Woman's Auxiliary of the Young Men's Christian Association of Fall River held about this time a prayer was offered for Miss Borden by Mrs. Hezekiah C. Brayton of Fall River, and the religious societies all over the country called upon the Divinity to assist the unfortunate woman. Throughout the whole proceeding against Miss Borden she was called "unfortunate," but no man or woman, good, bad, or indifferent was heard to say that the murdered man and woman were "unfortunate."

Judge Blaisdell, who presided at the inquest and who, being the Justice of the Second District Court, was to be the presiding justice in the coming preliminary trial came in for more than his share of criticism. He was a man of advanced years and remarkable vitality, had served in both branches of the State legislature and was one of the first mayors of the city of Fall River. He had presided as Justice of the Second District Court since its establishment about twenty years ago. He said that he thought he knew enough to attend to his duties no matter who sought to criticise him. A sample of the editorial attacks which were being made upon the Judge was shown to him. It related to the harsh words used in the complaint which

TAUNTON JAIL.

accused Lizzie A. Borden of murdering her father. The Judge said that he did not know before that such ignorance existed. The form of complaint was decided upon at least one hundred and fifty years before Miss Borden was born, and was adapted to fit capital crimes. Rev. W. W. Jubb, Miss Borden's pastor, characterized Judge Blaisdell's action in sitting on the bench while presiding at the inquest as indecent, outrageous and not to be tolerated in any civilized community. He proposed to use every means to have another Judge preside at the preliminary hearing. Rev. Mr. Jubb, formerly of Morsley, England, had at that time been a resident in America about twelve months. The act which he criticised was an American constitution nearly two hundred years old.

The preliminary trial of Miss Borden was assigned for Monday, August 22, and the prisoner was on the morning of that day taken trom Taunton Jail and brought by rail to Fall River, Clad in the same gown that she wore at the time of her departure from Fall River, and with her face partly concealed with the same blue veil, she stepped from the train in custody of Marshal Hilliard and Rev. Mr. Buck. As she was still possessed of all that wonderful nerve there was no indication in her manner nor bearing that she was a prisoner who had been taken from jail after several days confinement to face the mass of evidence which the State announced it had accumulated against her. And for aught that her appearance might indicate she was the same undemonstrative traveler returning to her home and quietly welcomed by her friends. The trip to Fall River had been made without incident, she sitting motionless in her seat and not even raising her eyes to see the passengers who walked through the car in ostensible search for seats, but really to satisfy their curiosity with a glance at the young woman. In Fall River it was common knowledge that she was to arrive just before 2 o'clock, and so the arrival of Miss Emma Borden and Mrs. Holmes at the police station at 10:30 attracted no attention. The police gave no sign, but after the arrival of Miss Emma, half a dozen of them sauntered slowly towards the depot. As the train from Taunton pulled up at 11 o'clock, Lizzie Borden and the others alighted. Some newspaper men were on the train and others were at the depot. The services of the police were not needed, for there was no crowd to keep back, and the carriage of the authorities drove away in an opposite direction to that of the police station. Then it wound around through alleys and back streets, and finally reached the police headquarters through a rear thoroughfare. As a result there were just five persons at the side entrance through which the party passed, and before the gathering had swelled to hundreds, which it did very promptly, Miss Borden was greeting her sister and friend in the room of the matron, adjoining the court room. Lunch was served there and preparations were made for facing the ordeal of the afternoon. Soon after noon the regular session of the Second District Court concluded. City Marshal Hilliard, acting under orders from the Judge, did not allow everybody to enter the court room. Only those persons who had good reasons for being present were to be at any sessons of the hearing. The scenes attendant upon the commencement of the hearing, which, in public estimation was to take more of the form of a trial, will long be remembered in Fall River. During the noon hour the crowds commenced to gather in Court Square. and the passageway through the centre of the narrow streets upon which the Central Police Station stands was rendered impassable. There are two entrances to the building on the side, and from each of these, lines strung out, formed at first of men in single file, aud then widening out until toward the end they formed large crowds. There they stood for hours and perspired while the police labored strenuously to keep them in order. In the meanwhile the little courtroom, with seating capacity for three hundred, was rapidly being occupied without the knowledge of the patient crowds who were waiting for the doors to open. The curious individuals were not confined to the males, for at 12: 30 o'clock all the seats in the large guard room of the station were occupied by women. Apparently none of them were from the lower walks of life and the majority were good looking and well dressed. In but a very few cases were they accompanied by escorts, and an hour before the announced time for the commencement of proceedings they were allowed to file up-stairs. Upon arriving in the court room they promptly occupied all the best seats and then spread out on the sides. After them prominent citizens of Fall River were admitted and these comprised a goodly number. Judge Carter, of the Haverhill Police Court, a friend of Judge Blaisdell, accompanied by his wife, were prominent figures in the centre of the room. Despite all the talk about limited accommodations for the press, tables and chairs in sufficient quantities were placed inside the railing. There were about forty newspaper representatives present. Many members of the Massachusetts bar came to the building and were admitted, and other professional men came into the court room. A peculiar feature was the presence of a large number of physicians, and they manifested a great curiosity in everything relating to the affair. As time passed the crowds outside the building received accessions and a few minutes before 2 o'clock the jam was almost frightful.

An immense delegation of mill girls had swelled the throngs at the entrances and had managed to get near the doors. There they waited while the hundreds in back pushed them about and created work for the officers. At the main entrance a large force of women had succeeded in getting into the guard room, and this compelled the placing of more officers at the stairway leading from there to the court room. At any of the doors it was worth one's life to attempt to enter or leave the building, and traffic in the vicinity was necessarily

abandoned. The seats on the left of the court room were reserved
for witnesses and those on the right for friends of the family. The
first person of consequence to enter was Bridget Sullivan, and she
grew white under the glances of the crowd and the buzz of conversation that her presence created among the women. She was followed by
Dr. S. W. Bowen, Mayor John W. Coughlin and others prominent in
the case, the advent of each adding excitement to the occasion. Five
minutes later the District Attorney entered. Inside the court room
the atmosphere was torrid. Judge Blaisdell entered the room at 2
o'clock and took his seat. All the witnesses were present. Half an
hour passed and there was no movement toward commencing the
proceedings. Attorney Jennings' books and documents were piled up
on his table, but he was nowhere to be seen. It was finally learned
that he was closeted with his client. The presence of Eli Bence, the
drug clerk, among the witnesses, caused general belief that one of the
theories upon which the State was placing dependence was that relating to the purchase and use of poison. Rev. Mr. Burnham, Andrew
J. Borden's former pastor, now occupying a pulpit in Springfield,
was also present. Mr. Jennings' consultation with his client lasted
but a few moments, and then he commenced a conference with
District Attorney Knowlton. Time passed slowly in the court room,
and the presiding Justice frequently glanced impatiently at his watch.
Everybody was offering surmises as to the cause of the delay, and it
was finally learned that there was a disagreement of opinion between
the attorneys representing the prosecution and defence regarding the
amount of testimony to be submitted by the Government. Mr.
Adams, associated with Mr. Jennings for the defence, was also present
at the conference, and the attorneys continued to argue as the
minutes dragged along. The Government desired to place in
evidence the reports of certain experts, and the attorneys for the
defence insisted that they should be furnished in evidence at the
hearing. It was understood that the report upon which there was a
disagreement was that of Professor Wood, of Harvard. Finally, at
2:50 o'clock, the attorneys entered the court room. A few minutes
conversation ensued between the lawyers, and then District Attorney
Knowlton addressing Judge Blaisdell said : '' Your Honor, some parts
of this case required the examination of various things belonging in
the house of the prisoner and attached to her person, and these
things are now in the hands of gentlemen who are experts in the
examination of such matters. We have not been able to get reports
of the examinations sufficiently extensive to allow the experts to be

called as witnesses. My learned friends both agree that this case cannot, therefore, be ready to-day, to-morrow or the next day, and we are thus forced to ask that the trial be adjourned till Thursday at 10 o'clock. I think my brother will agree to what I ask.''

Mr. Jennings arose and assented to what Mr. Knowlton had said, and Judge Blaisdell at once declared the hearing adjourned till Thursday the 25th, at ten o'clock, a. m. The prisoner remained in charge of the police matron and was not taken back to Taunton Jail.

The day before the preliminary hearing commenced, a scene was reported to have occurred in the matron's room between Misses Lizzie and Emma Borden which surprised the attendant, Matron Reagan. During the day, Miss Emma entered the matron's room and to her great surprise was greeted with this remark from Miss Lizzie:—" You gave me away, Emma, didn't you?'' Then said Emma ''I only told Mr. Jennings what I thought he ought to know. '' Miss Lizzie was apparently very much agitated at this and said to her sister, '' Remember, Emma, that I will never give in one inch, never.'' Mrs. Reagan was interviewed by the writer shortly after this incident and next day some of the leading newspapers published an account of the quarrel. The doubting Thomases stamped it as a '' fake '' and an effort to prejudice the public against the prisoner. Next day and after the court had adjourned Attorney Jennings made himself the object of much interest in and around the police station. He and his associate, Col. Melvin O. Adams, of Boston, with Rev. Mr. Buck and other staunch friends of the accused, attempted to show to the public that the story of a quarrel between the sisters was a lie, pure and simple. But the plan probably did not succeed as well as anticipated. Detective Edwin D. McHenry, of Providence, who had from the beginning been actively engaged under orders of Marshal Hilliard, happened to see the friends of Miss Borden in the act of drawing up a document which he learned was to be presented to Matron Reagan to sign. He promptly notified Assistant Marshal Fleet and the two officers awaited developments. The paper was drawn up and its contents set forth that Mrs. Reagan, the undersigned, never overheard a quarrel between the two women as related in the many papers of that day and that moreover she never told anybody that she had. It also set forth that she was to assert upon her oath that the story of a quarrel was false from beginning to end. This carefully prepared statement was placed in the hands of Mr. Buck and he was entrusted with the delicate mission of inducing Matron Reagan to affix her name thereunto. But Mrs. Reagan refused, saying that she would have to consult the marshal. Meanwhile the two officers mentioned had informed the Marshal of what was passing and he was prepared for the advent of Lawyer Jennings. This action on the part of the defense had taken place up stairs ; and upon the refusal of Mrs. Reagan to sign, lawyer Jennings carried the document to the Marshal' s office. The writer was present when the Marshal refused to allow Mrs. Reagan to sign the paper, even if she were willing to, and Mr. Hilliard's advice to Mrs. Reagan was that she remain silent until called upon to testify to what she had heard. To say that Mr. Jennings was excited would be putting it mildly. He left the Marshal's office in a state of rage and with the paper in his hand called loudly to the half hundred newspaper men in the guard room, saying: —" This is an outrage, the Marshal has refused to allow Mrs. Reagan to sign this denial of the quarrel story.'' The lawyer was informed that Mrs. Reagan had not agreed to sign it ; therefore the Marshal had nothing to do in the matter. An exciting scene followed in which there was animated talk

On the morning of August the 25th, the day set for the beginning of the trial, the same old scenes were enacted in and around the police station. At 8 o'clock crowds of men, women and children were upon the sidewalks, and half an hour later their numbers had been increased to such an extent that an extra detail of police was placed at the entrance in a vain endeavor to keep the roadways passable for vehicles. The ordinary session of the Court commenced at 9 o'clock, and at that very hour every seat outside the railing was occupied. As before, the gathering was composed almost exclusively of women, many of whom marched boldly into the court room swinging lunch baskets in their hands. There were fewer of these from the station of life occupied by the Borden family than on Monday, but those who were present listened eagerly while a man was tried and convicted of being a common drunkard ; craned their ears to listen to the testimony of wives who bore marks of their husband's brutality, and smiled at the children who were charged with violating the laws of the Commonwealth by refusing obedience to their parents.

In the room of the matron across the passageway Lizzie Borden awaited the commencement of the hearing. Her first visitor of the day was her sister, and soon after Rev. Mr. Buck arrived full of solicitude for the comfort of the prisoner. In the meanwhile the session of the court dragged on in the midst of considerable disorder. This was not occasioned by those in the spectators row, for they were fully occupied, and no more were admitted. Inside the railing however, the great body of newspaper correspondents labored vigorously while the court officers hurried in and out with chairs and tables in their efforts to accommodate the largely increased number of reporters These latter reached nearly fifty, and they touched elbows all around as they wrote. Attorneys from near-by cities were present, courtesy of admittance being extended to them. The Fall River bar and the medical profession were as before largely represented in that section of the room generally reserved for witnesses, and there were clergymen of all denominations scattered about in the place. The entrance of Bridget Sullivan at ten minutes before 10 o'clock transferred the interest of the spectators from the trial of a Sunday liquor seller to the most important government witness in the Borden case. Miss Sullivan stood the curious glances and loud whispers much better than on Monday, and, though evidently a trifle disconcerted, the pallor noticeable upon her countenance at her previous entrance to the court room was absent. She was accompanied by her attorney, James T. Cummings. The other witnesses commenced to arrive at this time and then Mr. Jennings entered the matron's room for a consultation with his client. At 10 o'clock the session of the ordinary court was still in progress, and the gathering was amusing itself by listening to the trial of an individual who declared that he had purchased many hogsheads of beer to celebrate the accession of Gladstone to power, and had no intention of selling the stuff. This concluded the minor cases and there was a great bustle of expectation as the numerous prisoners were taken from the room. Their places were quickly occupied, while outside the building the waiting hundreds stood patiently in the streets. The latter included many out of town people, who had come to the place in the hope that they might secure admission to the court room. So large was this influx of visitors that all the rooms in the hotel were engaged at an early hour of the morning. At 10: 15 o'clock Attorneys Jennings and Adams of the defence entered and took positions at the table, two green bags filled with books being brought after them. The excitement immediately increased, and the eyes of all the spectators were riveted on the door, awaiting the entrance of the prisoner. " Make way for the witnesses, " called out the court officer, and the remaining persons summoned filed into the room. Their number was a general surprise, for they extended in a long line around the room. Among them the figures of John V. Morse, Dr. Bowen and the drug clerk Bence were conspicuous and their presence heightened the interest. Conversation was brisk and loud for a few moments and then it lagged perceptibly and everybody fell to wondering why District Attorney Knowlton was not present, and when Lizzie Borden would come into the sight of the curious throng.   The District Attorney arrived at 10:30 o'clock, and a few minutes later Lizzie Borden entered. First came Emma Borden, escorted by Mr. Holmes. She was dressed in black, and appeared somewhat excited. Following her came Mrs. Holmes and Mrs. Brigham, and behind them was the prisoner, leaning on the arm of Rev. Mr. Buck. Lizzie Borden was dressed in the blue gown which she wore to Taunton, and at her entrance everybody grew so excited that nearly half of those present were on their feet almost unconsciously. The prisoner was composed, and beyond a slight twitching of the lips betrayed no excitement whatever.

At 10:31 o'clock District Attorney Knowlton arose and asked the Judge, "Is Your Honor all ready?" Judge Blaisdell answered that

ARRIVAL OF MISS LIZZIE BORDEN AT THE POLICE STATION.

he was. Then without other words of introduction he called on the Medical Examiner, Dr. William A. Dolan, to testify. Dr. Dolan testified as follows : " Have made a good many autopsies. First saw the bodies of Mr. and Mrs. Borden about a quarter of 12, Aug. 4. Saw the body of Andrew Borden first. It was lying on the north side of a lounge which was on the south side of the room. The head of the sofa was to the west. There was a Prince Albert coat on the top of the sofa cushion. On that rested Mr. Borden's head. His feet were on the floor, his head was toward the front door and the face was looking toward the sitting room windows. Examined the wounds sufficiently to make a view then, and removed and sealed up the contents of the stomach and sent same to an expert. Saw the body of Mrs. Borden a few moments after I saw Mr. Borden's body. She was lying face down on the floor. She was dressed in a calico dress. There was a silk handkerchief on the floor that might have been on her head. It was touching her head as she lay there. Can't say if it was cut. ''

At this moment Thomas Kieran, an architect, who had drawn plans, was sworn. He said he was at the house August 16, and described the plans in detail. Mr. Jennings and Mr. Knowlton looked over the plans together. Mr. Kieran said the length of the room where he had found the carpet taken up was fifteen feet and five inches, and that there was a space of two feet eleven inches. A board had been taken up in this room, and witness had seen a spot of blood on it when the Marshal showed it to him at the police station Sunday. Mr. Kieran said he had also drawn a map of the outside of the house, with measurements of the height of the fences and the character of the fences. Witness had seen a spot on the casing of the kitchen door leading to the sitting room, and one on the wall paper by the sofa. The witness was asked to designate the head of the sofa on which Mr. Borden's body was found, and said that it was towards the parlor. There was also a spot of blood on a picture in the sitting room hanging on the wall back of the sofa. After questions bringing out these replies the District Attorney inquired of Judge Blaisdell if he were familiar with the premises, and upon an affirmative response from the Judge the District Attorney said he would not bring out any further facts in relation to measurements.

Dr. Dolan was called back to the stand. He testified that when he removed the sheet that had been over Mr. Borden's head, he saw one of the most ghastly sights he had ever known. He was told to speak without generalizing and drew from his pocket a report of the autopsy taken one week after the murders. He proceeded to read a description of the wounds from his report. Mr. Jennings objected to the reading of these notes and Mr. Knowlton told him to put them away. Dr. Dolan put up his paper and gave a description of the wounds from memory. There were ten in all from four to an inch and a half long. The largest was four inches long and two and a half inches wide. There was no other cause of death. The body was warm when he got there, blood oozing from the wounds. **Mr.**

Borden, the witness thought, could not have been dead half an hour. There were in all eighty-eight blood spots behind Andrew Borden's head, dropping towards the east on the wall. These eighty-eight blood spots were in a cluster, beginning three or four inches from Mr. Borden's head. "I then found on the paper of the wall a spot of blood six feet, one inch and three-quarters from the floor. Another spot was near that one. These two were the highest spots of any except one found on the ceiling. They were the largest spots of blood found. They were about three-quarters of an inch in diameter. The blood spot on the picture was fifty-eight inches from the floor. I found spots on the moulding back of the lounge also. Had to move the lounge to find the spots. Also found seven blood spots on the upper two panels of the parlor door. There were two spots on the ceiling, but only one of them was human blood. I think an insect had been killed on the other spot. Another spot was on the west door jamb of

OFFICER A. E. CHACE.

the door leading to the dining room. It was not a spot, but a string, so to speak, of blood, two and one-half inches long, as it was drawn out. There were two spots on the kitchen door, one in the groove of the door and another on the edge of the casing. The spot I describe as a stain on the jamb of the door leading to the dining room, was such a mark that the murderer of Andrew J. Borden might have made. A hatchet or axe was, in my opinion, the weapon with which the murder was committed. A weapon weighing four or five pounds could easily have made the cuts."

"Couldn't see any part of Mrs. Borden's face, for the arms were thrown about it. As it lay there you could see there were a number of wounds. There were at least seven or eight blows which went through the skull into the brain. I turned the body up. Altogether there were eighteen distinct wounds on the head, and all but four of them were on the right side of the head. Imagine a line drawn from the nape of the neck around the ear. That would include fourteen of the wounds. They were from the left side back and downward to the right side. One of them was five inches in length. They were diagonally. Seven or eight of them went through the skull into the brain. Others took pieces of the skull out. The other four were on the left side, but none of them went through the skull. Those on the left were flat scalp wounds half an inch in depth. There was a contusion on the nose and two over the left eye. They were such as might be made by falling. I found one immediately over the spine some time later. It was two and one-half inches long and two and one-half inches deep. It was a conical wound. These were made by a sharp cutting instrument and might have been caused by a hatchet or small axe. Under her head and pretty well down on her breast she was lying in a pool of clotted blood. The front of the clothing was very much soaked and also the back. On the pillow sham there were three spots, on the rail of the bed were thirty or forty spots. Those on the sham were near the wall. The sham was eighteen inches from her head. The spots on the rail were lateral. On the drawers of the dressing case there were three or four spots on the first one and six or seven on the second, as if they had gone up in the air and come down. On the moulding of the east window there was a spot, and above that and about two feet there was a spot on the paper. These were six or seven feet from the head, on an angle.''

The witness saw Mrs. Borden's body immediately after viewing that of Mr. Borden and was asked by Mr. Knowlton if there was anything inconsistent in his opinion in the appearance of the body with the supposition that she had been dead for two hours?

Mr. Adams objected and Mr. Knowlton said he had asked a similar question in every murder case he had tried. Mr. Adams retorted that there were a number of bad habits the District Attorney had acquired which should be corrected. The Court thought the question could be allowed. Mr. Jennings thereupon objected and commenced to argue. Mr. Knowlton said the habit of arguing after a decision was not one of his bad ones, and Mr. Adams objected to Mr. Knowlton's hitting him over Mr. Jennings' shoulder.

Dr. Dolan said there was nothing inconsistent with the appearance of the body and the opinion that she had been dead for two hours. Mrs. Borden died from shock. He removed her stomach and forwarded it by express to Prof. Wood. ''I went down the cellar stairs and found four axes or hatchets resting against the cellar partition. One was a peculiar hatchet, the head being a hammer claw. There were three others, and all were lying six or eight feet from the cellar door. I examined two of them, which were brought to me by the officers. One of them looked as though it had been scraped on the blade. This had a cutting surface of five inches and would weigh from three to five pounds. The officer took it. Afterwards I examined it with a glass and found two hairs upon it and what appeared to be blood.   I could not swear it was blood.   I gave this hatchet and the axes to Prof. Wood, on all of them there was what appeared to be blood.   Took certain dresses also.   Told Mr. Jennings I wanted them and he got them of Miss Borden.   Sent them to Prof. Wood.''

The court then took a recess for dinner and Mr. Adams furnished for publication a copy of a letter received by Emma Borden.   He produced the original copy and the envelope, and according to the latter it was mailed in Waltham, Mass., August 18, at 11: 30 a. m., and received in Fall River on the same day at 4: 30 p. m.   The letter is as follows :

Waltham, Mass., Aug. 17, 1892.

Miss Emma Borden :

Dear Madam—You must excuse that I take the liberty in send-ing you these few lines.   I ought to have written to you before this, as I was unable to do so, as I was travelling every day.   My name is Samuel Robinsky.   I am a Jewish pedler.   When the fatal murder in Fall River occurred I was only a few miles from Fall River.   That day, while sitting on the roadside, towards New Bedford, I met a man who was covered with blood.   He told me that he worked on a farm and that he never could get his wages, so he had a fight with the farmer.   He said he ran away and did not get any money after all.   All he had was a five-dollar bill.   He bought from me four handkerchiefs, one looking glass, one necktie, collar and shoe black-ing.   His boots were covered with blood, and he put lots of blacking on them.   I helped him to fix up again and get cleaned, but by this time I did not know anything about the murder.   I felt sorry for him and thought only he gave the farmer a good licking.   I advised him to travel at night, which he said he would do, as he feared arrest during the day.   I gave him my lunch, and he gave me a quarter, and told me not to say anything that I met him.   He asked me what time the train left for Boston after 8 o'clock at night and I told him.   He had also a bundle with him which was about two feet thick or big; when I was peddling I did not read any papers only Sundays, as I am study-ing the English language.   When I was in Boston last Sunday a friend of mine told me about the Fall River murder. I told him about the stranger, and my friend said : '' And why did you not report this to the police ? ''   I told him I was afraid, as they would lock me up as a witness, and another thing, I did not have any license, so I was afraid.   I told my friend I would write to you, or Mr. Jennings, I read last Sunday's Boston *Globe*, and thought that I might have seen the murderer.   If I should see him in Boston, I am sure, yes, dead sure, I know him again.   He is of medium height, dark brown hair, reddish whiskers or moustache, weight about 135 pounds, a gray suit, brown derby hat.   His shoes were what they call Russian leather. No blacking on so-called summer shoes.   He put my blacking on to make them look black, so that people could not see the blood.   It was about 1 o'clock noon that day. I only heard about the murder at 6 or 7 o'clock that night. I kept quiet as I had no license and feared to be arrested. My stranger was very much afraid. He asked me a million times if he looked all right again, and I brushed him off with my shoe brush and told him to wait till dark. If I come again to Fall River next week I shall call on you, if you think it is necessary, but all I can swear he is the stranger which I have seen that afternoon. This is all; but if this man was the murderer I cannot say, but I shall find him out of fifteen thousand. Will close now. Will go to Fitchburg to-morrow morning and return to Boston Saturday night. Please do not say anything to the police. I would be arrested. If I had known about the murder the time I met my stranger it would have been different, as I would have followed him up and perhaps got the reward. I thought it was a poor farm hand and so took pity on him, as I know as a rule, farmers seldom pay their hands during summer. Hoping that my information may be of some use to you,

I remain very respectfully,

SAMUEL ROBINSKY.

P. S.--Please excuse paper and mistakes as I am a foreigner.

Immediately upon the receipt of this letter Mr. Jennings dispatched the following telegram :

"Aug. 19, 1892—To George L. Mayberry, Mayor, Waltham, Mass.—Does Samuel Robinsky, a Jewish peddler, live in Waltham ? Andrew J. Jennings."

The answer received from the Mayor of Waltham was as follows, dated Waltham, Mass., Aug., 20, 1892 :

To Andrew J. Jennings, Fall River. "Cannot find that he lives here. Am told that a peddler of that name is living in Boston, and sometimes comes out here. Signed, G. L. Mayberry."

This satisfied the attorneys for the defence that such a person as Robinsky existed and Mr. Adams assured the newspaper representatives that they were making strenuous efforts to find him. He said a search had been made around the vicinity of Manchester, and that they were now looking for the man. He appeared to' think that the publicity attendant upon publication of the letter might assist in locating the individual.

CHAPTER XIV.

DR. DOLAN CROSS-EXAMINED.

IN the afternoon Dr. Dolan was placed upon the stand and continued his testimony under the cross-examination of Col. Adams. He said: " It was about noonday when I got to Andrew J. Borden's house. First heard of the murder when I was in front of the Borden house. Was out driving to visit patients. It was in consequence of questions I asked when I saw the crowd before the house that I learned what had happened. I went into the hall or entry-way in the rear of the house. I met Bridget Sullivan and Dr. Bowen in the kitchen. I then went into the sitting room. Andrew Borden lay in such a way as to face me. There were two officers present. I looked at the body and inquired where Mrs. Borden was. I went up the stairs; they were winding stairs to a certain extent; there was a Brussels carpet on the floor; I had to turn to the left to enter the doorway. On my left side between me and the bureau was a bedstead; the bedstead was opposite the front of the house; can't remember if anybody was in the room when I entered it. Dr. Bowen gave me my information about Mrs. Borden; Dr. Tourtellot and Dr. Hartley were with me afterwards to examine the room; I looked across the bed when I got into the room and saw the body; the woman's arms were raised a circle above her jaw, and her head lay in the circle, the woman lying on her face; I pointed out three things to the architect or engineer when he was there. As nearly as I saw then, should say the distance between the bureau or dressing case and bed was more than two feet ten inches which the architect gave as the distance this morning. Mrs. Borden was a stout woman; her body did not fill up the space between the bureau and the bedstead; there was a foot of space left on either side of her. She was lying a little on her left side; it was diagonally on her left side; this left the right and a portion of the left side of her head fairly well exposed; it must have been 12 o'clock nearly before I went upstairs; the body had not been changed in position at that time; I was told by Dr. Bowen it had not been. I put my hands into the wounds of the old lady; am very confident no blood dropped from my hands when I drew them away; I got several spots of blood on me either upstairs or down stairs—I think down stairs. Cannot recollect if my hands touched Mr. Borden before I went up stairs: I think I touched Mrs. Borden first, when I saw her the second time.''

Col. Adams spent an hour in questioning the witness about irrelative matters and then the Medical Examiner continued saying: '' I took notes the second time I was in the room; after that I assisted Officers Mullaly and Doherty in searching the house. We searched the lower floor first, I think. Don't know where Miss Lizzie was at

CENTRAL POLICE STATION.

this time. She was up in her room, where I saw her last before the search. I think she was up in her room when we began the search; think she went upstairs by the front way; saw her in her room three or four times; wouldn't say I saw her in her room when I took the view; am not positive whether I made the examination of Mrs. Borden before or after the search; saw Miss Lizzie last at 1:30 o'clock. At the time of the examination of Mr. Borden others were also present. Mrs. Borden was dressed in a calico gown.'' The lawyers for the defence now both began to cut the strings of a bundle which had been placed on Mr. Jennings' desk. As they were doing it Judge Blaisdell asked Dr. Dolan if he wouldn't sit down. The doctor said not just yet, but Mr. Adams, looking up, asked if he was the one referred to. The Court said he wasn't, and Mr. Adams remarked that he wasn't quite ready yet. Out of the bundle which Messrs.

Jennings and Adams were opening there now rolled a doll about ten
inches in height, and the head of a record doll. Mr. Adams called
the doll a manikin in talking to the Court afterwards, but it was simply
a doll. As it was produced the crowd in the court room laughed.

Dr. Dolan testified that a pillow sham with spots of blood on it
was on the bed in the room where Mrs. Borden was. The piece of
door jamb was brought in and with it a piece of plastering. After
careful examination of the moulding Dr. Dolan indicated a tiny spot
on the paint. It was about the size of two pin heads. After Mr.
Adams had finished with the piece of moulding, Mr. Jennings took it
and showed it to Rev. Mr. Buck, who sat behind him, pointing out
the spots to the reverend gentleman. Rev. Mr. Buck smiled incred-
ulously and settled back in his chair. Mr. Brigham, whose wife was
the firm friend of the Borden girls, looked at the moulding and said
nothing. The relic was being passed along further when Mr.
Knowlton suggested it be returned to the desk and it was placed
there. Mr. Adams discussed the wounds of Mr. Borden next, and
had them carefully described to him with marks in the doll's head
and by measuring the extent of the blows on his own face.

Dr. Dolan continued: "Did not go to the house Friday; went
there Saturday and met Marshal Hilliard, Mr. Jennings, Assistant
Marshal Fleet and Mr. Seaver; took up and carried away a great
many things; took away a white underskirt; there was a spot of
blood on the meshes of this skirt; the spot was about a foot from the
ground. There was also a smooch found at the upper part of the
opening to a pocket in a dress. I saw this through a microscope.
All these things went to Prof. Wood. I think Mr. Jennings gave
them to me. There were in all a dress, a blouse waist and underskirt and a pair of shoes. The shoes were sent for afterward. We
had searched everywhere on Saturday and been afforded every
opportunity for looking around. There were two hairs on one of the
hatchets found in the cellar. They were gray hairs and one was
very short. The short one was three-quarters of an inch long and
was caught in the rough end surface of the handle. I looked at it
under a microscope. I do not know whether or not this was a human
hair, but it looked as if one end was broken; the other end was fine."

At this point the hearing was adjourned to Friday morning at
10 o'clock. District Attorney Knowlton stated that as his presence
at the hearing was purely voluntary, he would ask the Court to
question three or four witnesses who might be called before his
arrival in the morning. He said they would testify to the movements
of Mr. Borden while out doors on the morning of the tragedy.

CHAPTER XV.

Second Day of the Trial.

DR DOLAN was placed upon the stand again and dwelt at length upon the question of his opinion as to which of the Bordens was murdered first. He said: "I will say that the condition of the blood indicated that it had been out of the living tissues an hour and a half to two hours. Did not, the first time I was up-stairs, examine the edges of the wounds of Mrs. Borden. Formed my opinion of the time since Mrs. Borden's death when I first saw her. Think she must have been dead an hour and a half to two hours."

Abram G. Hart was then called to the stand. He is the Treasurer of the Union Savings Bank, of which the late Mr. Borden was President. He testified: "Saw Mr. Borden about 9:30 o'clock at the bank on the day of his death. He usually called at the bank at that time in the morning. The day before, at a quarterly meeting of the trustees, he was not present. He said on the morning of the day he died that he would have been present on the preceding day, but had been ill." The defence did not cross-examine the witness.

John T. Burrell, cashier of the National Union Bank, in which institution Mr. Borden was a depositor and stockholder, saw Mr. Borden come into his bank on the morning of Aug. 4, the day he died. Did not know if Mr. Borden came back to the bank again. The two banks are in the same building. The defence did not cross-examine.

Everett Cook, cashier of the First National Bank, of which Mr. Borden was a director, saw Mr. Borden at the bank Aug. 4. He came in about quarter of 10 and went out five minutes of 10. He did not come in again that day. He usually came in daily. Charles T. Cook, insurance agent, had charge of one of Mr. Borden's business blocks on the corner of Anawan and South Main streets. He had been in the habit of seeing Mr. Borden, but did not see him on the day of the murder. The last time the witness talked with Mr. Borden was on the Sunday before the murder. There was no talk with reference to a will. Three weeks before that he had told the witness he had no will, but said nothing about making one. The witness positively denied that he had spoken to Inspector Medley about the fact that Mr. Borden was making a will.

Mrs. Dr. Kelly who lives next door south of the Borden residence, testified that she was at home on the morning of August 4th and saw Mr. Borden walking around from the back door as if he had been trying to get into the house. He had a small white package in his hand at the time. This was at twenty-seven or twenty-eight minutes before 11 o'clock, and she fixed the time, by an appointment which she had with the dentist. Jonathan Clegg saw Mr. Borden in his store on the morning of the murder at 10:20 o'clock, and he left there exactly at 10:29 o'clock. On leaving the store Mr. Borden went south.

John Cunningham, a newsdealer, testified that he was in front of a house four houses north of the Borden place when he first heard of the murder. Saw Mrs. Churchill cross the street. Was told that Mrs. Churchill wanted a policeman and telephoned to the City Marshal by a clerk in the paint shop. It was ten minutes to 11. Cross-examined by Mr. Jennings—"When I telephoned I was going up towards the store. Mrs. Churchill I saw coming from her own house, I should think. Mrs. Churchill came over to some men. I passed them, and after I had gone three or four feet a boy told me Mrs. Churchill wanted me to telephone. Officer Allen then came along. He went in the house right off and came out. Charles Sawyer went into the house with Mr. Allen. Then I went down street, and when Mr. Allen came out I asked him what the matter was and went in. Found Mr. Manning and Mr. Stevens, two reporters, in the yard. Did not notice anybody go in the barn."

Mr. Jennings—"Did you notice the cellar door, Mr. Cunningham?" "I did particularly. I tried it and it was locked. I remained there about ten minutes more. Officers Doherty and Mullaly came."

Francis H. Wixon, a deputy sheriff, was in the Marshal's office when he heard of the murder. The Marshal was talking through the telephone. It was about ten or fifteen minutes past 11, as on his way to the office he heard the bell in the city hall strike 11. The witness went up five or six minutes after the message was received and arrived at about 11:30 o'clock. There were not many people in the house and the witness saw Dr. Bowen there upon his arrival. Officer Doherty overtook the speaker in the yard, and together they went in the house, and looked at the body of Mr. Borden. He knew nothing about Mrs. Borden's murder and had some consultation with Dr. Bowen. The result was that the witness removed Mr. Borden's watch. Saw nothing of Lizzie Borden. Dr. Bowen then went upstairs and the witness and the officer followed. He saw Dr. Dolan there before the witness left. Continuing, Mr. Wixon said, "I went out in the yard and looked south. There I saw a man in an open space, who was sawing wood. In the same lot I saw two other men at work. They had not heard of the murder and I told them."

At this point the court took a recess for dinner, and upon coming in again, John Shortsleeves testified to having seen Mr. Borden in a shop on South Main street at 10:30 or 10:40 o'clock. Then John V. Morse, a brother of Mr. Borden's first wife, was called, and said:

"I am 59 years old; live at present at the Borden house. My permanent home is Dartmouth. I used to live in Iowa, in the West. I returned from the West after living there 20 years, three years ago last April. I first lived in Warren and then in Dartmouth. My sister, the past Mrs. Borden, died about 1863. Heard of the marriage to the second wife before I came from the West. Have resided in Dartmouth the past year, coming to Fall River every month or two. In connection with the tragedy, left New Bedford to come here August 3 on 12:35 train. Saw Lizzie at the Borden house. Arrived there about 1:30 o'clock; dined there, stayed till after 3, then went over to Swansea; hired a horse and wagon, and got back about a quarter of 9. Visited Borden's farm and another place; went there on business relating to Mr. Borden; went there to see about cattle that day; invited Mr. Borden to go with me. I saw Mr. and Mrs. Borden on my return. Emma did not arrive until the night of the tragedy at about 6 o'clock. I did not see Lizzie until after the couple were killed. I heard her come in the night before and go up the front stairs. This was about 9:15. Her room was at the head of the front stairs, and I occupied the spare chamber. This room was not accessible at night from the stairs. Mr. and Mrs. Borden slept in the east room next to Lizzie's room. Miss Emma's room was just north of Lizzie's, just back of the spare room. Stairs lead from Miss Lizzie's room to the spare room. I did not hear Miss Lizzie's voice when she entered. I retired about 10 o'clock. Mrs. Borden retired first. I rose about 6 o'clock and came down stairs a few minutes afterwards. When I came down I found no one, and I first saw Mr. Borden. This was fifteen minutes after I came down. He entered the sitting room and Mrs. Borden appeared soon afterwards. I took breakfast with the family, Mr. and Mrs. Borden and myself. We ate breakfast at about 7 o'clock, and I then saw the servant. She waited upon the table, coming in when the bell was rung. There were bananas on the table. After breakfast we went into the sitting room and engaged in conversation. Mrs. Borden came in and out of the room, and was dusting. She had nothing on her head. I went away at a quarter before 9, and Miss Lizzie had not been down, to my knowledge. I went down to the post office and mailed a letter. Then I went up Pleasant to Weybosset street to visit a niece at the home of Daniel Emery. This is about a mile away."

District Attorney—" Where did you go when you went away from the house? I don't ask this for my own sake. The witness is no client of mine, but it's only fair in view of what has been said that he should tell his story."

" The last I saw of Mrs. Borden she was in the front entry. The last words Mr. Borden said were : ' John, come back to dinner.' I fix the time I left the Borden house at a quarter of 9 by having my watch with me. I saw Mrs. Borden go into the front hall before I left home. Can't say if she had a feather duster in her hand. It was the last time I saw her alive. It was Mr. Borden who let me out that morning. The letter I posted was, I think, to Mr. William Lincoln. I walked up to Emery's; left there at 11 :20 o'clock. The dinner hour at the Borden house was usually 12 o'clock. I çame back on the horse car down Pleasant street, and went right up Second street. At the door the servant girl told me of the affair. Inside the house were Mr. Sawyer, Dr.

CAPTAIN PHILIP H. HARRINGTON.

Bowen and two policemen. I did not see Dr. Dolan there. Then it was about a quarter of 12, I should estimate. After I had been in the house two or three minutes I saw Miss Lizzie in the dining room on the sofa. I spoke to her, but I do not remember what I said. I saw the bodies and then went down stairs and saw Lizzie. I did no searching. The last time I was at the house before this was in the middle of July. I did not see Miss Lizzie then. I was there in June and stayed a day and did not see Miss Lizzie at that time. I was on corresponding terms with Mr. Borden and Emma when I was West. I never had a letter from Lizzie in my life.''

Mr. Morse testified that Mr. Borden had told him that most of the family had been sick the day before. He was also questioned at length concerning the condition of things at the house when he arrived.

Bridget Sullivan was then called and said: '' My name is Bridget Sullivan, and I was known by the name of Maggie at the Borden house. I was employed there for two years and nine months. I swept the front hall every other week and had no duties in the bedrooms. At the time of the tragedy Miss Emma was not at home. She had been out of town for a week, and when she was gone the family consisted of Mr. and Mrs. Borden and Miss Lizzie. Miss Lizzie went with Miss Emma when she went away, but came back. I first saw Mr. Morse between 1:30 and 2 o'clock on the day he arrived. I saw him again walking out in the afternoon. I did not see him when he arrived home that night. I got up at 6:15 o'clock Thursday morning, and it was 10 o'clock the night before when I retired. I locked the screen door and the back wooden door before I went to bed. When I came down in the morning I found the doors exactly as I had left them, and I opened them. I went out for milk, and afterward hooked up the screen door. The back door remained open. Nobody else came in or out that I can remember, except members of the house. I did not go out of the house again until Mr. Borden went out. Nobody was up when I came down, and the first one I saw was Mrs. Borden. I saw her in the kitchen and on the back stairs at half past 6. Never knew anybody to go up the back way to the front part, or the front way to the back part; Mr. Borden came down about two minutes after Mrs. Borden; he went out doors before breakfast; he went into the barn and got some water; he emptied a pail from the house and came back; I was in the kitchen all the time; after Mr. Borden came in with his pail he washed up; he put his dressing coat on after washing up; think he put his necktie and collar on after breakfast; we had for breakfast cold mutton, soup, johnny cakes and coffee; breakfast, as nearly as I recollect, was at 7 :15; after breakfast they were in the sitting room ; Mr. Morse had come down to breakfast; he went out at quarter of 9, I should judge ; Mr. Borden let him out; Mrs. Borden, I expect, was in the sitting room when Mr. Morse went; I saw Mr. Borden there about 9 ; don't know when Mr. Morse went;

after Morse went, Mr. Borden went up the back stairs; did not see him when he came down or went out; don't know if he went out the front or back door; I went out in the back yard awhile; I was sick at my stomach and vomited; did not see Mrs. Borden when I came back; was out in the yard four or five minutes, and came back into the kitchen and washed dishes. Mrs. Borden told me she wanted the windows washed inside and outside all around the house. I did not see Mrs. Borden after that. She went into the kitchen. The next time I saw her she was dead. Lizzie was then through with her breakfast. She came down stairs before I went outside. She was then in the kitchen. When I came back I don't know where she was. I asked Lizzie what she wanted for breakfast and she said she didn't feel like eating anything. When I saw Mrs. Borden she had a dusting cloth and was dusting the dining room. I didn't know where Lizzie was. That was after both men had gone. I don't know whether or not I locked the screen door after I came in from vomiting. I then cleaned up the kitchen and straightened up and commenced to prepare to wash the windows. I went down cellar and got a pail, got a brush from the closet and went out to the barn to get a stick. Miss Lizzie then came into the back entry and asked where I was going. I told her I was going to wash windows and that she need not hook the door. I told her I'd get the water in the barn, and she said all right. The door was then hooked and I had to unhook it. I was down in the cellar earlier in the morning to get coal and wood. The next time I went down was when I got the pail. It was half an hour after Mrs. Borden told me to wash the windows before I commenced. During that time I did not see Miss Lizzie except when she came to the screen door. Where she was I don't know. I had not been doing any work in the spare room; Lizzie Borden never did work in the spare room when her friends had occupied it. After I went out to wash the windows I saw Lizzie; she had asked me as I went out if I was going to wash the windows; I told her yes, and that if she wanted to close the windows I would get water in the barn; five windows I had to wash; I shut three before I went out, and two others were already shut. I did not see Miss Lizzie after I got out; I had not seen anybody while I was in the barn after the dipper. When I went down stairs after the pail, I went down the kitchen stairs. We wash on Monday, and iron Tuesday, and on Monday and Tuesday the cellar door was open. I opened the door the day I hung my clothes out, and don't know if anybody else went in or out of it that week before the murder. I shut and locked the door Tuesday, myself.

I got through washing the windows at twenty minutes past 10, I think. Washed the sitting room side first and then the parlor and last the dining room. The windows were shut upstairs. I then went inside at the screen door, hooked it, and getting a hand basin washed the sitting room windows inside. Did not see Lizzie or Mr. Borden in the house while I was washing the sitting room windows. Didn't see anybody outside or in the house while I was washing windows. I heard Mr. Borden try to get in at the front door. Afterwards went to the front door and found the bolt and lock turned. Miss Lizzie was upstairs at that time. She might have been in the hall, for I heard her laugh upstairs as I let Mr. Borden in. I went to open the door and it was locked, and I made some exclamation when she laughed aloud. I did not see her until five or ten minutes afterwards. I was in the sitting room. Mr. Borden came in and sat down at the head of the lounge in the dining room. He was reading and I was in the sitting room washing windows. I did not see her when I let Mr. Borden in. I heard her tell her father that Mrs. Borden got a note and went out. Lizzie spoke very low. I don't know where Lizzie went then, and I don't know whether or not she stayed in her room. After I finished in the sitting room, Mr. Borden took the key from the sitting room shelf and started upstairs the back way. When he came down I was just going into the dining room. I did not see Miss Lizzie then. She was not in the dining room, sitting room or kitchen. Then Mr. Borden sat down near the window in the sitting room, with a book or paper in his hand. He brought the key back and put it on the shelf. He sat in an easy chair, and I had started to wash the first window in the dining room. I did not see Miss Lizzie, and only saw her when she came into the dining room, and then to the kitchen, and then back again to the dining room with an ironing board. She placed the ironing board on the dining room table. Where she came from I do not know. She put the ironing board on a corner of the table. It was about two feet long. She always ironed the handkerchiefs. I did not hear Mr. Borden leave the chair in which he was sitting. After I finished I came into the kitchen, and Miss Lizzie asked me if I was going out. I told her I didn't know, as I was feeling sick, and she said if I went out to be sure and lock the door, as "I may be out," and Mrs. Borden had got a note and gone out. I then went upstairs to my room, and Miss Lizzie was down stairs working at the ironing board. She came out and told me there was a sale of dry goods at Sargent's. If Mr. Borden changed his position to the sofa, I didn't know it. Soon after I got upstairs it struck 11 o'clock. I was then lying in bed, but I didn't take my clothes off. I thought I had time enough to get dinner at half past 11. I always went upstairs before dinner if I had time. Didn't look at the fire before I went upstairs. The dinner was to be soup to warm over and cold mutton. Had not put the soup on, and the potatoes were in the soup. A coal fire was started in the morning. I was going down stairs about 11:30. Had not gone out of the screen door again after I commenced to wash the windows inside. I next heard something when Lizzie called me. It might have been ten or fifteen minutes after I came upstairs. She hollored at me. I knew from the way she hollored something was the matter. She hollored loud ; she said her father was dead. She told me to run after Dr. Bowen. I wanted to run in ahead and see, but she told me to run quick and tell the doctor. I went and told Mrs. Bowen about it. Mrs. Bowen told me to tell Miss Russell about it and I went back and told Miss Lizzie. She told me to go after Miss Russell. When I got back from the Bowens, Miss Lizzie was still at the door. When I got back from Miss Russell's Dr. Bowen had just got out of his wagon, and I think Mrs. Churchill was there. Miss Lizzie was then in the kitchen. We talked, and Miss Lizzie said she'd like us to search for Mrs. Borden. I said I'd go upstairs, and Mrs. Churchill said she'd go with me. I went up and saw Mrs. Borden before I went in. When the house was searched that day a box of hatchets was behind the furnace. I don't know if the cellar door was open when the officers were searching the house the day of the murder. I asked Lizzie where she was, and she said she was out in the back yard. ''

''When was it she said that?'' '' After I got back from Mrs. Russell's.'' '' Do you know what dress she had on?'' ''I don't know.'' '' Had Mrs. Borden said anything to you about going out?'' ''No, sir.'' '' Was it her habit to notify you when she went out?'' Mr. Adams promptly objected to this and the Court excluded the question. ''Then the only thing you know about her going out was what Lizzie told you?'' Mr. Jennings objected to this question and said that while he did not object to the District Attorney asking leading questions on unimportant matters, this was altogether too serious a point to allow such queries. District Attorney Knowlton declined to take this view of the matter, and a discussion commenced, pending which an adjournment for the day was taken.

CHAPTER XVI.

Third and Fourth Days of the Trial.

MR. KNOWLTON called Bridget Sullivan to the stand and she continued her testimony—"Mrs. Borden came down stairs Wednesday morning, saying she and Mr. Borden had been sick that night. They looked pretty sick. Lizzie said she had been sick all night, too. I came down to start the fire. Miss Lizzie had been ironing eight or nine minutes when I went up stairs. There used to be a horse kept in the barn. Since the horse was kept there, I have seen Lizzie go to the barn. Miss Lizzie spoke about her mother going out and said her mother had received a note that morning."

Mr. Knowlton—"Did Lizzie say anything about hearing her mother groan?"

Bridget—"She said she heard her father groan."

Mr. Knowlton—"Did you at any time that day see Lizzie crying?"

Bridget—"No, not in all the day."

Mr. Adams conducted the cross-examination, and commenced by politely asking the witness if she would be seated. She declined a chair, and questions commenced rapidly. The counsel required her to review the history of her life and then commenced questioning her regarding her movements on the fatal day. She said—"I always carry a night key and lock the doors, as I pass in and out. The night before the murders I was out, but came home alone. Never had a man call on me at that house. When some one came it was not a Fall River man. Was out in the yard Wednesday morning and Lizzie told me she had been sick. That day had pork steak, 'johnny cakes' and coffee for breakfast. Had soup and mutton for dinner. Soup, bread, cake and tea for supper.

"Tuesday night, when they were taken sick, we had swordfish warmed over for dinner. Had baker's bread, too. Got the bread myself. Went of my own notion to get the bread, and when I got back Mrs. Borden gave me five cents. I didn't eat any of that bread. I was taken sick that night. Didn't see Lizzie Wednesday after breakfast.

They were all sick. Wednesday morning I went down stairs after coal and kindlings. Then opened the blinds in the dining room. I never rang a bell for breakfast. They all got up without calling. Didn't have anything particular to do in the dining room till breakfast. Mrs. Borden came down stairs and told me Mr. Morse was in the house. I asked her if he slept in the attic, and she said no, in the spare chamber. That Thursday morning Mr. Borden had brought in a basket of pears from the tree. He had brought in some a day or two before. They got rotten and he had dumped them under the barn. The only rooms I had been in Thursday morning up to breakfast time were the kitchen and dining room. Mrs. Borden often asked after breakfast what I had to do that day. The ice chest was in a closet opening from the entry. We went upstairs out of that entry-way. Never saw any clothes but my own on the nails in the entry. There was a shawl sometimes hanging there. It belonged to the house. Didn't see a felt hat that morning. In the closet were kept the bonnets and shawl of Mrs. Borden, that she would come and get and go out with any time. Sure I didn't go into any room except the dining room and kitchen the day of the murder. Think it was before 9 o'clock when Mrs. Borden said, ' What have you got to do to-day, Maggie?' She told me that I had better wash the windows outside and in. Lizzie took her breakfast in the kitchen. She took coffee. Am sure of that. Lizzie was in the dining room, I think, when her mother asked me what I had to do. Lizzie said, coming out into the kitchen, that she was going to have a cookie and coffee for breakfast. She sat down by the kitchen table. There were old magazines in the closet. Had seen Lizzie sit down in the kitchen sometimes and read the old magazines. When I went out into the back yard she was eating her breakfast. Didn't mean to say the first time I saw Lizzie was when I saw her at the screen door. First saw her coming out of the dining room door to the kitchen when I was at the sink. It was about an hour after she came down that she came to the screen door. During that hour I was washing up the dishes. I was out in the yard when she was at her breakfast. I felt sick that morning getting up. I drank some of the milk, but I didn't eat any of the bread. I don't know whether they drank milk before being taken sick or not. I had eaten some mutton soup and some of my own bread before being taken sick. I had not eaten any of the pears, for I'm no great lover of them. I came back in again and Lizzie had had her breakfast. I went to work washing windows, I didn't know where Lizzie was then, but she wasn't in the kitchen. Mr. Morse went away while I was washing the dishes, but I don't know whether this was before or after Lizzie had had her breakfast. When I was taken sick to my stomach and came back Mr. Morse had gone out. I went down stairs into the laundry, got a pail and brush and then went out into the barn to get a handle for the brush. I got it in one of the stalls. As I went out I spoke to Lizzie at one of the screen doors. Lizzie asked me if I was going to wash the windows, and I said yes. She followed me into the entry. Didn't say yesterday that I came back from the barn and then spoke to Lizzie at the screen door. When I told her she needn't fasten the screen door, she didn't do it. Must have got six or seven pails of water from the barn to wash the windows. The dipper I went in and got was an ordinary tin dipper. Got it in the kitchen. Mr. Borden was in the habit of going out the back door, but I didn't see him. Didn't see Mr. Borden go out before I washed the windows. Raised the sitting room windows to wash them from the inside. The window nearest the hall was open when I heard Mr. Borden at the front door. Can't say if the bell rang. Made a coal fire that morning. Didn't finish the dishes in the house. They always put the ironing board on the dining room table. Washed Monday, hanging out the clothes Tuesday and ironed Wednesday. Finished ironing that evening. Then I laid the clothes ironed out in piles and Mrs. Borden and the girls took them up stairs. I mean Lizzie took hers up instead of the girls took them up. They took the piles of clothes up Thursday morning, I separated the clothes before breakfast. The little ironing board was not quite as big as a large board. Sometimes in hot weather the girls ironed in the kitchen, but usually it was in the dining room. Can't say if Lizzie was in the dining room when I came in for the dipper.'' The court then adjourned until next morning, when the hearing was resumed.

Mrs. Adelaide B. Churchill, a neighbor and friend of the Bordens, was called to the witness stand as soon as Judge Blaisdell announced that he was ready. She said : '' The first that I knew about the tragedy was when I saw Bridget Sullivan going to Dr. Bowen's house. I was on Second street, coming from the City Hall. She was going in the direction of Dr. Bowen's house and appeared frightened. I went to my house, into the kitchen. The back door of my house is opposite the back door of the dining room. I looked out to the Borden house and saw Lizzie Borden standing inside the screen door. She looked distressed. She had her hand to her head. I asked her what was the matter. She said : '' Somebody has killed

father, come over.' I went over and went into the house. Lizzie
was sitting on the second stair inside the screen door. The stairway
is at the right as you come in. I put my hand on her arm and said,
' O, Lizzie, where is your father?' She said, ' In the sitting room.'
I said, ' Where were you?' She said, ' I went out to the barn to get
a piece of iron. I heard a distressing noise and came back and found
the screen door open.' I asked Lizzie where her mother was. She
said she had a note, inviting her to go visit some one who was sick.
She didn't know but she was killed, too, and wished we'd try and
find her, for she thought she had heard her come in. She said,
'Father must have an enemy, for we have all been sick.' She
thought they must have been poisoned. Then she said she must
have a doctor. I said I would get one, and went to find somebody.
There was no one in the sitting room I thought. I saw no one else
in the house or coming to it. I went down Second street to Hall's
stable to get a young man I thought I could find there. I went back
again, and in a few moments Dr. Bowen came. Lizzie told him to
go into the sitting room. We went, Bridget, Lizzie and I, to the
dining room door. Pretty soon Dr. Bowen came out and asked for a
sheet. Bridget did not want to go up stairs alone, so I went up with
her. Bridget got the sheets and gave one to Dr. Bowen. I think
Dr. Bowen went out then. Soon after Miss Russell came in Lizzie
said she wished somebody would hunt for her mother. Bridget would
not go up alone and I went with her. I went up the stairs and saw
on the far or north side of the bed the prostrate form. I didn't go
any further. I was half way up the stairs, and my eyes were about
on a level with the floor. I went right down. Miss Russell asked
if I made the noise, and asked me if I had found another. Dr.
Bowen was not there then. A gentleman named Allen came in next,
and then Charles Sawyer. I saw Mr. Borden in the yard about 9
o'clock, before he went down street. He stood by the screen door.
Afterwards saw him headed down street." In the cross-examination
concluded by Mr. Jennings the witness said that she saw one of the
windows open. It was opposite the screen door.

Miss Alice C. Russell was then called. She said she lived on Borden street, three hundred yards from the Borden house, and had known
Lizzie eleven years. She thought it was about 11:30, Bridget
Sullivan told her of the affair and she went right over. Lizzie was
there in the door. "Did you say anything to Lizzie or she to you?"
"I don't remember." "Was Dr. Bowen there?" "I didn't see
him.' "Did you go in and see the bodies?" "No, sir." "Do you

remember how Lizzie was dressed?'' ''No, I don't.'' ''Do you remember anything about it?'' ''Nothing very connected.'' ''Do you remember talking to Miss Lizzie after that?'' ''Yes, but I don't remember what was said. I remember she said she was out in the barn getting a piece of tin or iron with which to fit the screens. '' Do you recall when that was that she said that?'' ''I think it was up stairs.'' ''Were there many people there, and did you remain there, Miss Russell?'' ''There were people down stairs. I stayed four nights at the house.'' Mr. Knowlton—''Have you often visited the house, Miss Russell?'' ''Yes; have stayed there nights. Have been the guest of the girls. Made my quarters in the guest chamber with the girls. Went there as often as I had reason to go, sometimes twice or three times a week.'' ''Was there a bed in that chamber?'' ''Yes sir.'' Mr. Jennings—''When you went in where did you say Lizzie was?'' ''She was standing at the screen door, and asked me to sit down in the chair in the kitchen. Saw no blood on her dress. Saw her hands. Rubbed them. There was no blood on them. Rubbed her cheeks. There was no blood on them or her hair. Her hair, I think, was done up as usual. Her clothes had no blood on them. Don't know if she had on the same shoes I have seen her wear before.' ''Was she fainting from exertion?'' ''No, she wasn't fainting.'' ''Do you remember if Lizzie went upstairs before the officers did?'' ''No, she did not.'' ''How do you know?'' ''Because I

POLICE MATRON REAGAN.

remember they were all down talking to her.'' ''Do you know if an officer went up stairs?'' ''They went up stairs. I don't know if I went with them. I can't connect it with them, if I went too. I remember being up stairs.'' ''Did they go into Miss Lizzie's room before she went up?'' ''Yes; they tried to open Miss Lizzie's door and it was locked. They had to break it in and pull the hook out. I told them to let me look in first. I went in and they came in after I looked around. Do not know who the officers were. Did not know Officer Doherty by sight. Know him now. I was in the parlor with them down-stairs. Do recollect now one of the officers. It was Assistant Marshal. Fleet.'' ''Did the officers go up to Miss Lizzie's room when she was there?'' ''Yes; they went up then and afterwards. It seems to me they were coming all day. They asked her questions and she answered them freely.''

Miss Lucy Collette said that she was at Dr. Chagnon's house on August 4. She went there at ten minutes before 11 in answer to a telephone message from a clerk at Dr. Chagnon's. She was to take any telephone message, for Dr. Chagnon's family were away. All the doors were locked and so the witness sat on the piazza in front of the house. She was there up to 12 o'clock and saw nobody either in the yard or pass through. She could see the whole yard and there was nobody there during the time she sat on the piazza.

The calling of the next witness, in the judgment of many of the spectators in Court, produced evidence of uneasiness on the part of Lizzie Borden. He was Eli Bence, the drug clerk. He said he remembered the day of the tragedy and knew the defendant. She was in his store the day before the tragedy between 10 and 11 :30 o'clock. "She asked me for ten cents worth of prussic acid. I told her we didn't sell it without a doctor's prescription. She said she wanted to use it on a sealskin cape and I again told her we couldn't sell it without a prescription, and she said she had bought it before. Then she went out. "Is the defendant the person who tried to purchase this poison?" "She is," was the answer. "Who was there?" "Mr. Hart and Mr. Kilroy, the clerks." This was all that Mr. Bence was required to tell by Mr. Knowlton, but Mr. Adams cross-examined him at great length. His testimony was not shaken.

Frederick E. Hart, who worked for Smith the druggist, said he saw Miss Borden between 10 and 10 :30 Wednesday morning: "A woman came in and said she wanted ten cents worth of prussic acid to put around the edges of a seal skin sacque or cape. She did not speak to me, though she was very close to me." "Is the defendant the woman?" "Yes, sir."

Frank H. Kilroy was in Smith's drug store at the time. He said "I saw this lady come in. She went to the counter and asked for prussic acid. Mr. Bence said: "I can't sell prussic acid without a prescription." The only other thing I heard was the woman use the words, 'seal skin cape.' She left the store then. That was all I heard." Mr. Knowlton "Are you sure this is the woman?" "Yes, sir."

Assistant Marshal John Fleet testified as follows : "I was home when the news came from the Marshal, who had sent word to me by a man in a team. I drove down to the Borden house and arrived about ten minutes of 12. I saw officer Allen and Mr. Manning at the front door. Mr. Sawyer was at the rear door. Inside I found Bridget, Mr. Morse, Dr. Dolan, Dr. Bowen and Miss Lizzie. I went into the sitting room and saw Dr. Dolan standing over Mr. Borden. Then I went upstairs and saw Mrs. Borden. Soon after I went into Miss Lizzie's room and had a conversation with her. She was sitting in the room with Rev. Mr. Buck. I asked her if she knew anything about the man who killed her father and mother? She said it was not her mother, but her step-mother. Her mother was dead. I asked her if she had seen anyone around the premises, and she said she had not. Then she said she heard a man talking to her father at 9 or half-past 9, and she thought they were talking about some store. I asked her if this man would do her father any injury, and she said no. I asked her if she knew this man, and she said no. She said she did not know that any one had threatened her father or would do him harm. At this point Miss Russell said : ' Lizzie, tell him all about that man.' Then Lizzie said that two weeks ago a man had come to the front door and had held a long conversation with her father. The man seemed to be angry, and was talking about a store he wanted her father to let. She said she heard Mr. Borden say he wouldn't let it for that purpose. She said she thought the man was a stranger in Fall River. I asked her if Bridget was in the house during the morning, and she said she had been washing windows and came in after her father came and then went up stairs. She said she didn't think Bridget had anything to do with it. Lizzie said that when Bridget went up stairs she went up in the barn. ' Up in the barn?' I said, and she said ' Yes.' ' What do you mean by up?' I asked. ' Up stairs,' she said. I asked her how long she remained in the barn and she said half an hour. She said her father was lying upon a lounge in the sitting room when she went out, and when she came back she found him all cut up, lying in the same position as she had left him. She also said John V. Morse had been there, and I asked her if Mr. Morse had anything to do with it. She said it was impossible, for he went away at 9 o'clock in the morning and didn't come back. She didn't tell me what she was doing in the yard. Rev. Mr. Buck and Miss Russell were present during the conversation. I then started to search all the rooms I could go into.''

'' What did you find down in the cellar? ''

'' Found Mr. Mullaly, with a number of axes on the floor of the washroom. We reached the cellar, and found nothing other than the two axes and two hatchets. The two axes were dusty, or covered with ashes, and so was the little hatchet. The large hatchet was clean with the exception of a small rust spot. It was about four inches long from the head, to the edge six inches, and it had a claw handle. I tried the cellar door, and then went out to the barn. I satisfied myself there was nobody there to do this deed. Then I went into the house again and consulted with two of my officers and State Officer Dexter. I made another search and saw Lizzie again in the presence of two officers, Dr. Bowen was holding the door. I told him I wanted to search the room. He said something to her. He went in. He came out and asked me if I must search the room. I said I must examine the room to make my report. He let me in then. When I got in, Miss Borden said: " How long will it take you? " I said I didn't know, but that I had to search the room. She said: " I do hope you will get through soon. this is making me sick." I searched the room.

Mr. Knowlton—" Did you say anything more to Miss Borden? "

Assistant Marshal Fleet—" Yes, I said: ' You say, Miss Borden, that you went out to the barn, and that you were out there half an hour, while your father and mother were killed. You still say that?' She said: ' I do not. I say I was in the barn twenty minutes to half an hour.' Said I ' You told me this morning that you were out there

half an hour.' ' I don't say so now,' she said, ' It was twenty minutes to half an hour.' ' What makes you say twenty minutes to half an hour?' I asked her; ' Which is it now, twenty minutes or half an hour?' She said, ' It was twenty minutes to half an hour.' "

Mr. Knowlton—" Did you search the premises then? Did you have any more talk with her then? "

CAPTAIN PATRICK CONNORS.

Marshal Fleet—" I searched the room and bureau and then went behind Lizzie's door to another door. It was locked. I asked her what room that was. She said: ' That is father's room.' ' Is there another way to get into it?' I asked. She said there was, by going by way of the back stairs; that the door from her room was always locked. I started to go around, as there was no other way. When I got into the entry I asked her what was in the clothes press. She asked me if I must seach that. I told her I must. She said she had the key and would open it. She produced the key and opened it."

Mr. Knowlton—" Describe the room."

Marshal Fleet—" It was about five by eight; there was a window in it, but it had not been opened in some time. We took nothing, and then we searched the rest of the house. I tried the door of Mrs.

Borden's room, from Miss Lizzie's room. It was fastened by a bolt, I think, on the other side. Mr. Knowlton—"Did you go in there? What else did you say to Miss Borden?" Marshal Fleet—"When I went into Miss Borden's room, Miss Lizzie said there was no use going there, that she always locked her door, and there was no possible way for anybody to get into it. I asked her when she saw her mother last. She said about 9 o'clock, when she was going down stairs. Her mother was in the room where she was found murdered. Miss Lizzie also said that Mrs. Borden had received a note or letter from some one that morning. She thought it was from somebody of the house." Mr. Knowlton—"Was Lizzie in tears while in her room." Marshal Fleet—"No." The cross-examination of the witness brought out nothing of importance.

POSITION OF MRS. BORDEN'S BODY WHEN FOUND.

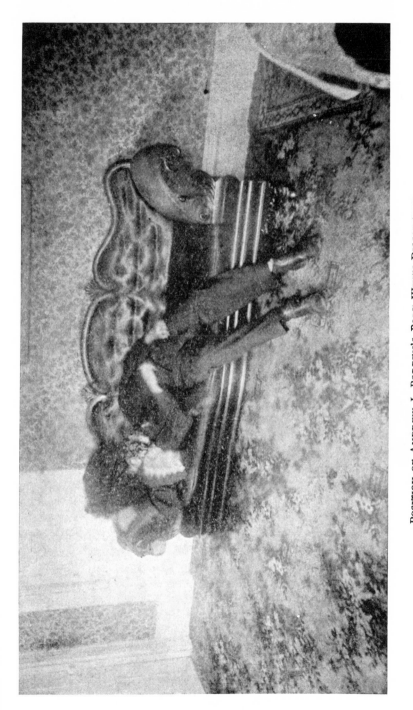

POSITION OF ANDREW J. BORDEN'S BODY WHEN DISCOVERED:

CHAPTER XVII.

FIFTH DAY OF THE TRIAL.

THERE was a deathly stillness in the little court room as Prof. Edward S. Wood of Harvard College, the expert in chemistry, upon whose evidence it was believed so much would depend, was called to the stand. Lizzie Borden did not look as strong as on preceding days, and the look which she concentrated upon the countenance of Prof. Wood was absolutely pitiful. Emma Borden's face wore a slight flush and the other members of the party did not stir a muscle. Every eye in the room was upon the witness and not a sound broke the silence except the startling testimony which the professor at once commenced to give.

He said: "I received a package containing two stomachs August 5. The package contained four jars. The first one was labelled "Milk of August 4,' the second was labelled ' Milk of August 5,' the third was labelled 'Stomach of Andrew J. Borden,' and the fourth, ' Stomach of Mrs. Andrew J. Borden.' I opened the packages, which bore their original seals, and found both stomachs perfectly natural in appearance. There was no evidence of any inflammation. I opened and examined the contents of the stomachs. The stomach of Mrs. Andrew J. Borden contained eleven ounces of semi-solid food, the rest being water. At least four-fifths and perhaps nine-tenths was solid food. The rest was water. It was partially digested. The solid food contained bread or rather wheat, starch and a good deal of fat. That is, the contents were chiefly bread, or similar food, meat and oil. It also contained many vegetable pulp cells; which might be potatoes, and also some vegetable tissue, which might be apple or onion skins. The digestion seemed to be advanced two or three hours. To the best of my opinion it had advanced two and one-half hours more or less. The stomach was immediately tested for prussic acid with negative results. There was no prussic acid in the stomach. I made a more complete analysis later with the same result. The stomach of Mr. Borden contained six ounces, mostly water. Nine-tenths was water and one-tenth solid material. In connection with Mrs. Borden's stomach there were many solid bits of meat. In Mr. Borden's stomach the food contained but small quantities of starch. The principal part of the solid food was vegetable pulp, and digestion in his stomach had advanced three and one-half to four hours. Digestion was very much further advanced than in the case of Mrs. Borden. There was about two and one-half hours difference. There were a few shreds of vegetable tissue in his stomach. I tested Mr. Borden's stomach for prussic acid with negative results. I did not test it for any other poison, but there was no evidence of irritation in either. I have not yet analyzed the milk.''

There was a pause as Prof. Wood concluded the sentences and a notable relaxation of the tension which prevailed through the room. It was but momentary, however, and in a second everybody was on edge again, as the District Attorney propounded the next inquiry.

'' Did you receive a trunk? '' he asked.

'' I did,'' answered the professor. ''I was in Fall River, August 9, and on August 10 I received from Dr. Dolan a trunk. In the trunk there was a hatchet and two axes, a blue dress skirt, a blue dress waist, a white starched skirt, a lounge cover and a large envelope which contained three small envelopes. One was marked, 'Hair taken from Andrew J. Borden,' a second, 'Hair taken from Mrs. Andrew J. Borden,' a third, 'Hair taken from the hatchet.' On Aug. 16, I received from Marshal Hilliard a box containing a pair of shoes and a pair of woman's black stockings. Of these I examined the hatchet. It contained quite a number of suspicious looking spots, which looked as if they might be blood spots. They were on the edge and handle. There were no blood spots, however, on the hatchet, as my examination showed. The same was true of the axes. Every spot that it seemed possible might be blood I tested, and found no blood whatever on the instruments. On the blue dress there was a stain near the pocket. It was a smirch and looked as if it might be a blood smooch, but it was not. There was a lower stain of similar appearance, but it was not blood. There was no spot whatever on the blue dress waist. The white skirt had one very small spot, which was plainer outside than on the inside of the garment. It was almost a foot and six inches from the bottom. It was one-sixteenth of an inch in diameter. That was a spot of blood, and there was no other spot on the skirt. The carpet was light Brussels and had two dried pools of blood. I recognized it as the sitting room carpet. The other carpet was saturated. It was from the spare room and was found under the body. There was a stain on the lounge cover, which looked like blood, but it was not. The envelope marked hair from Andrew J. Borden, contained a lock of white hair stained with blood. The envelope marked hair from Mrs. Andrew J. Borden, contained a lock of dark gray hair, stained with blood. The envelope marked hair from the hatchet, contained a hair of red brown color. The root and end were there and the hair was like that of a cow or some other animal. It was not a human hair. I next examined the pair of shoes. On the bottom of the right shoe there was a stain that looked like blood, but a careful testing showed that it came from the tanning. There was no spot on the shoe, and I found nothing on either of the other two axes."

Then pent-up excitement could be contained no longer, and

great sighs of relief from the strain were heard as the professor concluded the important portion of his testimony. The friends of Miss Borden looked greatly relieved and the prisoner herself appeared easier, but there was no change upon the placid countenance of the District Attorney. Mr. Knowlton then asked some questions regarding the stains on the hatchet. Professor Wood said the material that looked like blood was chiefly wood and other fibres. There was a little stain and a long narrow stain on the bended edge, and on the blade was a spatter of water and iron

CAPTAIN DENNIS DESMOND.

rust. "I examined the stains on the handle for blood spots with negative results." This ended Prof. Wood's testimony and Captain Philip Harrington was called. He said: "After hearing of the murders, I went to the house, and entered at the side door. Went into the sitting room and on the lounge was a body. It was very much mutilated. Went up stairs and saw Mrs. Borden's body. Came down and looking into a room saw Miss Lizzie and Miss Russell. I stepped into the room and asked Miss Lizzie if she knew anything about the crime, and she said ' No.' She was cool and collected, and said she could tell me nothing at all. I then asked her when she last saw her father. She said: ' When he returned from the Post Office.' She said Maggie was in the house and she was in the barn. I asked her how long she was there and she said, 'twenty minutes.' I asked her if she was sure it was fifteen minutes or half an hour, and she said, ' No, it was twenty minutes.' Then I told her she had better be careful what she said, and that to-morrow she might have a clearer frame of mind. She made a courtesy and said, 'No, sir, I can tell you all I know now, just as well as at any other time.' I asked her if she had seen anybody go by, and she said no. I said, ' The barn is not a great distance, and as the screen door would have made a noise if anybody had passed it, would she not have heard it.' She said she was up in the loft. She said she saw nobody in the yard or about. I asked her if she had any suspicion, and she told me about a man who had angry words with her father about a store. She heard her father say he would never let his store for that business. The man came again about two months ago, and there was another angry interview. Then she heard her father tell him the next time he was in town to call and see about it. I asked her if the man was from out of town, and she said yes, she should judge so. I said, ' Miss Borden, I would advise you not to submit to any further interviews. By to-morrow you may be able to recollect more about this man.' I asked her if she had heard her father say anything about this and she said no. I then went down stairs and Dr. Bowen was there. There was a small fire in the stove and what appeared to be the remains of some burned paper lay in the fire place of the stove. The fire was very low." Officer Harrington then detailed the story of the search of the barn. The hay, he said, was tossed about.

When he had finished, the District Attorney read the short-hand report of the testimony of Miss Lizzie Borden given at the inquest, and taken by Miss White, the official stenographer. It was as follows: " My father and stepmother were married twenty-seven years ago. I have no idea how much my father was worth and have never heard him form an opinion. I know something about what real estate my father owned." " How do you know? " Mr. Adams promptly objected. He said he did so on the ground of the admissibility of a statement, which was detrimental to her. Judge Blaisdell said he didn't know that any statement the defendant might make would not be competent. Mr. Adams argued in support of his objection. He said any statement that did not bear directly on the issue between the prosecution and the defence was not material.

Judge Blaisdell allowed the introduction of the question and the answer was "two farms in Swansea, the homestead, some property on North Main street, Borden Block, some land further south and some he had recently purchased." "Did you ever deed him any property?" "He gave us some land, but my father bought it back. Had no other transaction with him. He paid in five thousand dollars cash for this property. Never knew my father made a will, but heard so from Uncle Morse." "Did you know of anybody that your father had trouble with?" "There was a man who came there some weeks before, but I do not know who he was. He came to the house one day, and I heard them talk about a store. My father told him he could not have a store. The man said: 'I thought with your liking for money you would let anybody in.' I heard my father order him out of the house. Think he lived out of town, because he said he could go back and talk with father.' "Did your father and anybody else have bad feelings between them?" "Yes, Hiram C. Harrington. He married my father's only sister." "Nobody else?" "I have no reason to suppose that that man had seen my father before that day." "Did you ever have any trouble with your stepmother?" "No." "Within a year?" "No." "Within three years?" "No. About five years ago." "What was it about?" "About my stepmother's stepsister, Mrs. George Whitehead." "Was it a violent expression of feeling?" "It was simply a difference of opinion." "Were you always cordial with your stepmother?" "That depends upon one's idea of cordiality." "Was it cordial according to your ideas of cordiality?" "Yes." Continuing: "I did not regard her as my mother, though she came there when I was young. I decline to say whether my relations between her and myself were those of mother and daughter or not. I called her Mrs. Borden and sometimes mother. I stopped calling her mother after the affair regarding her sister-in-law." "Why did you leave off calling her mother?" "Because I wanted to." "Have you any other answer to give me?" "No, sir. I always went to my sister. She was older than I was. I don't know but that my father and stepmother were happily united. I never knew of any difficulty between them, and they seemed to be affectionate. The day they were killed I had on a blue dress. I changed it in the afternoon and put on a print dress. Mr. Morse came into our house whenever he wanted to. He has been here once since the river was frozen over. I don't know how often he came to spend the nights, because I had been away so much. I have not been away much during the year. He has been there very little during the past year.

I have been away a great deal in the daytime during the last year. I don't think I have been away much at night, except once when I was in New Bedford. I was abroad in 1890. I first saw Morse Thursday noon. Wednesday evening I was with Miss Russell at 9 o'clock, and I don't know whether the family were in or not. I went direct to my room. I locked the front door when I came in. Was in my room Wednesday, not feeling well all day. Did not go down to supper. Went out that evening and came in and locked the front door. Came down about 9 next morning. Did not inquire about Mr. Morse that morning. Did not go to Marion at that time, because they could go sooner than I. I had taken the Secretaryship of the Christian Endeavor Society and had to remain over till the 10th. There had been nobody else around there that week but the man I have spoken of. I did not say that he came a week before, but that week. Mr. Morse slept in the spare room Wednesday night. It was my habit to close my room door when I was in it. That Wednesday afternoon they made such a noise that I closed the door. First saw my father Thursday morning down stairs reading the *Providence Journal*. Saw my mother with a dust cloth in her hand. Maggie was putting a cloth into a mop. Don't know whether I ate cookies and tea that morning. Know the coffee pot was on the stove. My father went down town after 9 o'clock. I did not finish the handkerchiefs because the irons were not right. I was in the kitchen reading when he returned. I am not sure that I was in the kitchen when my father returned I stayed in my room long enough to sew a piece of lace on a garment. That was before he came back. I don't know where Maggie was. I think she let my father in, and that he rang the bell. I understood Maggie to say he said he had forgotten his key. I think I was up stairs when my father came in, and I think I was on the stairs when he entered. I don't know whether Maggie was washing windows or not when my father came in." At this point the District Attorney had called Miss Borden's attention to her conflicting statements regarding her position when her father came in, and her answer was: "You have asked me so many questions, I don't know what I have said." Later, she said she was reading in the kitchen and had gone into the other room for a copy of the *Providence Journal*. "I last saw my mother when I was down stairs. She was dusting the dining room. She said she had been up stairs and made the bed and was going up stairs to put on the pillow slips. She had some cotton cloth pillows up there, and she said she was going to work on them. If she had remained down stairs I should have

seen her.   She would have gone up the back way to go to her room.
If she had gone to the kitchen I would have seen her.   There is no
reason to suppose I would not have seen her when she was down
stairs or in her room, except when I went down stairs once for two or
three minutes.''   '' I ask you again what you suppose she was doing
from the time you saw her till 11 o'clock? ''   '' I don't know, unless
she was making her bed.''   '' She would have had to pass your room,
and you would have seen her, wouldn't you? ''   '' Yes, unless I was
in my room or down cellar.   I supposed she had gone away, because
she told me she was going, and we talked about the dinner.   Didn't
hear her go out or come back.   When I first came down stairs saw
Maggie coming in, and my mother asked me how I was feeling.   My
father was still there, still reading.   My mother used to go and do
the marketing.'' '' Now I call your attention to the fact you said twice
yesterday that you first saw your father after he came in when you were
standing on the stairs.''   '' I did not.   I was in the kitchen when he
came in, or in one of the three rooms, the
dining room, kitchen and sitting room.   It
would have been difficult for anybody to
pass through these rooms unless they passed
through while I was in the dining room.''
'' A portion of the time the girl was out of
doors, wasn't she? ''   '' Yes.''   '' So far as
I know, I was alone in the house the larger
part of the time while my father was away.
I was eating a pear when my father came

REV. E. A. BUCK.

in.   I had put a stick of wood into the fire
to see if I could start it.   I did no more ironing after my father came in.
I then went in to tell him.   I did not put away the ironing board.   I
don't know what time my father came in.   When I went out to the
barn I left him on the sofa.   The last thing I said was to ask him if
he wanted the window left that way.   Then I went to the barn to get
some lead for a sinker.   I went upstairs in the barn.   There was a
bench there which contained some lead.   I unhooked the screen door
when I went out.   I don't know when Bridget got through washing
the windows inside.   I knew she washed the windows outside.   I
knew she didn't wash the kitchen windows, but I don't know
whether she washed the sitting room windows or not.   I thought the
flats would be hot by the time I got back.   I had not fishing appara-
tus, but there was some at the farm.   It is five years since I used the

fish line. I don't think there was any sinker on my line. I don't think there were any fish lines suitable for use at the farm." "What! did you think you would find sinkers in the barn?" "My father once told me that there was some lead and nails in the barn." "How long do you think you occupied in looking for the sinkers?" "About fifteen or twenty minutes." "Did you do nothing besides look for sinkers in the twenty minutes?" "Yes, sir. I ate some pears." "Would it take you all that time to eat a few pears?" "I do not do things in a hurry." "Was Bridget not washing the dining room windows and the sitting room windows?" "I do not know. I did not see her." "Did you tell Bridget to wash the windows?" "No, sir." "Who did?" "My mother." "Did you see Bridget after your mother told her to wash the windows?" "Yes, sir." "What was she doing?" "She had got a long pole and was sticking it in a brush, and she had a pail of water." "About what time did you go out into the barn?" "About as near as I can recollect, 10 o'clock." "What did you go into the barn for?" "To find some sinkers." "How many pears did you eat in that twenty minutes?" "Three." "Is that all you did?" "No. I went over to the window and opened it". "Why did you do that?" "Because it was too hot." "I suppose that it is the hottest place on the premises?" "Yes sir." "Could you, while standing looking out of that window, see anybody enter the kitchen?" "No, sir. " I thought you said you could see people from the barn?" "Not after you pass a jog in the barn. It obstructs the view of the back door." "What kind of lead were you looking for, for sinkers? Hard lead?" "No, sir; soft lead." "Did you expect to find the sinkers already made?" "Well, no. I thought I might find one with a hole through it." "Was the lead referred to tea lead or lead that comes in tea chests?" "I don't know." "When were you going fishing?" "Monday." "The next Monday after the fatal day?" "Yes, sir." "Had you lines all ready?" "No, sir." "Did you have a line?" "Yes sir." "Where was your line?" "Down to the farm." "Do you know whether there were any sinkers on the line you left at the farm?" "I think there was none on the line." "Did you have any hooks?" "No, sir." "Then you were making all this preparation without either hook or line. Why did you go into the barn after sinkers?" "Because I was going down town to buy some hooks and line, and thought it would save me from buying them." "Now, to the barn again. Do you not think I could go into the barn and do the same as you in a few minutes.?" "I do not do things in a hurry." "Did you then think there were no sinkers at the barn?" "I thought there were no sinkers anywhere there. I had no idea of using my lines. I thought you understood that I wasn't going to use these lines at the farm, because they hadn't sinkers. I went upstairs to the kind of bench there. I had heard my father say there was lead there. Looked for lead in a box up there. There were nails and perhaps an old door knob. Did. not find any lead as thin as tea lead in the box. Did not look anywhere except on the bench. I ate some pears up there. I have now told you everything that took place up in the barn. It was the hottest place in the premises. I suppose I ate my pears when I first went up there. I stood looking out of the window. I was feeling well enough to eat pears, but don't know how to answer the question if I was feeling better than I was in the morning, because I was feeling better that morning. I picked the pears up from the ground. I was not in the rear of the barn. I was in the front of it. Don't see how anybody could leave the house then without my seeing them. I pulled over boards to look for the lead. That took me some time. I returned from the barn and put my hat in the dining room. I found my father and called to Maggie. I found the fire gone out. I went to the barn because the irons were not hot enough and the fire had gone out. I made no efforts to find my mother at all. Sent Maggie for Dr. Bowen. Didn't see or find anything after the murders to tell me my mother had been sewing in the spare room that morning. "What did your mother say when you saw her?" "She told me she had had a note and was going out. She said she would get the dinner." The District Attorney continued to read : "My mother did not tell when she was coming back. I did not know Mr. Morse was coming to dinner. I don't know whether I was at tea Wednesday night or not. I had no apron on Thursday ; that is, I don't think I had. I don't remember surely. I had no occasion to use the axe or hatchet. I knew there was an old axe down stairs and last time I saw it it was on the old chopping block. I don't know whether my father owned a hatchet or not. Assuming a hatchet was found in the cellar I don't know how it got there, and if there was blood on it I have no idea as to how it got there. My father killed some pigeons last May. When I found my father I did not think of Mrs. Borden, for I believed she was out. I remember asking Mrs. Churchill to look for my mother. I left the screen door closed when I left, and it was open when I came from the barn. I can give no idea of the time my father came home. I went right to the barn. I don't know whether he came to the sitting room at once or not. I don't remember his being in the sitting room or sitting down. I think I was in there when I asked him if there was any mail. I do not think he went upstairs. He had a letter in his hand. I did not help him to lie down and did not touch the sofa. He was taking medicine for some time. Mrs. Borden's father's house was for sale on Fourth street. My father bought Mrs. Borden's half sister's share and gave it to her. We thought what he did for her people he ought to do for his own and he then gave us grandfather's house. I always thought my stepmother induced him to purchase the interest. I don't know when the windows were last washed before that day. All day Tuesday I was at the table. I gave the officer the same skirt I wore that day, and if there was any blood on it I can give an explanation as to how it got there. If the blood came from the outside, I cannot say how it got there. I wore tie shoes that day and black stockings. I was under the pear trees four or five minutes. I came down the front stairs when I came down in the morning. The dress I wore that forenoon was a white and blue stripe of some sort. It is at home in the attic. I did not go to Smith's drug store to buy prussic acid. Did not go to the rooms where mother or father lay after the murder. Went through when I went up

STATE OFFICER GEORGE SEAVER.

stairs that day. I wore the shoes I gave to the officer all day Thursday and Friday." "I now ask you if you can furnish any other suspicion concerning any person who might have committed the crime?" "Yes; one night as I was coming home not long ago I saw the shadow of a man on the house at the east end. I thought it was a man because I could not see any skirts. I hurried in the front door. It was about 8 :45 o'clock ; not later than 9. I saw somebody run around the house last winter. The last time I saw anybody lately was since my sister went to Marion. I told Mr. Jennings, may have told Mr. Hanscom." " Who suggested the reward offered, you or your sister?" "I don't know. I may have." "Mr. Knowlton now stopped reading, and announced: "This is the case of the Commonwealth."

Col. Adams for the defence called Dr. Bowen who testified to the facts as related in the interview published before. City Marshal Rufus B. Hilliard was also called by the defence and gave his testimony which was not different from that of the other officers. The evidence was then concluded and the court adjourned for the day.

CHAPTER XVIII.

SIXTH DAY OF THE TRIAL.

THE proceedings opened by Judge Blaisdell announcing that he was ready to hear the arguments of counsel. Mr. Jennings arose and said: "May it please Your Honor, this complaint upon which you have to pass to-day, in substance, alleges that on the 4th of August last Andrew J. Borden was murdered by his daughter Lizzie. I must say I close this case with feelings entirely different from those I have ever experienced at the conclusion of any case. This man was not merely my client, he was my friend. I had known him from boyhood days, and if three short weeks ago any one had told me that I should stand here defending his youngest daughter from the charge of murdering him, I should have pronounced it beyond the realm of human credibility. But such is the fact, and upon the decision of Your Honor will rest the liberty and good name of this young woman. There are some things of which there is no doubt. There is no doubt that Andrew J. Borden was murdered in his house at the time given by Bridget Sullivan, Mr. Shortsleeves and Jonathan Clegg. All these give the time from the City Hall clock. Mr. Clegg sees Mr. Borden leave his store at 10 : 30 o'clock, a time he fixes by looking at the clock. As Mr. Borden entered his other store, one of the men working there saw it was twenty minutes before 11. It seems to me it is fixed almost beyond a peradventure that the last time Andrew J. Borden entered the house was between quarter and ten minutes before 11. Mrs. Kelly is wrong unless the others are wrong. Mr. Borden did not enter his home at twenty minutes before 11 unless Mr. Shortsleeves is wrong and Bridget Sullivan is wrong. The time between his entering the house and the giving of the alarm is from twenty-five minutes to half an hour. Now what took place after he got there? Bridget Sullivan says she left him in the sitting room reading the paper, and within this narrow limit of half an hour Andrew Borden has to talk with Lizzie, talk with Bridget, go up stairs, go down-stairs, compose himself in the chair and place himself upon the sofa. If the theory of the Government is correct, it certainly took five minutes or perhaps ten minutes from the time Miss Lizzie gave the alarm to the time information was received at the Central Station. Now, I claim that you must deduct ten minutes from the time at which he left the centre of the city to the time he was found dead. If you do that you limit the time of the committing of this crime to fifteen, to thirteen, or perhaps to not more than ten minutes. We have had a description of the injuries, and I suggest that even the learned District Attorney himself cannot imagine that any person could have committed that crime unless his heart was as black with hatred as hell itself.'' At this point, for the first time in public since the commission of the crime, Lizzie Borden almost broke down. Her form was convulsed, her lips were trembling, and she shaded her eyes with her hands in order to partially conceal the tears, which were freely flowing.

Mr. Jennings continued as follows: ''Blow after blow was showered upon them, cutting through blood, bone and flesh into the very brain. Not one, not two, but in the case of the woman, eighteen. I know it will be said that the person who did this wanted to make sure. There is an unnecessary brutality about this that suggests nothing but insanity or brutal hatred. There is another thing. Every blow showed that the person who wielded that hatchet was a person of experience with the instrument. Every blow shows its own line of demarcation and, taking with this the fact that all the blows were parallel, I venture to say that no hand could strike those blows that had not a powerful wrist and experience in handling a hatchet. But now, Your Honor, it is a maxim of law that better one hundred guilty persons should escape than one innocent man perish. But more of these wounds. Prof. Wood told you it was almost impossible for a person to commit these crimes without being almost covered with blood, from the waist upward in the case of Mr. Borden, and from the feet upward in the case of Mrs. Borden. Now, what takes place? It becomes the duty of the Commonwealth to investigate an atrocious crime like this with the greatest care. It is of the utmost importance that the guilty party should be found and not someone accused of it. The Commonwealth seems to have made up its mind that the crime was committed by some one in that house. All their labors have been directed with that view. It is perfectly evident to lawyers that this was one of the views the Commonwealth was taking in present-ing its case. They say no one could get out on the south because Mrs. Kelly is there, Crowe's yard is there, men are working there and there is the Chagnon house. You have Mrs. Churchill on the north and others on the west. The first thing they've got to do in order to draw the line around the people in the house is to isolate that house. Now, what is the fact? They know that the house has been burglarized and the barn broken into within a few months. Whether they know it or not, a person would say they ought to think that there was someone who knew that there was money in Mr. Borden's room. You know that Mrs. Manley saw a man standing at that gate. The police have had I don't know how many men in this case, but they never found this woman. They never found the man Dr. Handy saw. They can find the axes Lizzie Borden killed her father with, but they can not find this man. I don't say they haven't tried to, but the fact is they haven't. Certain men got over that back fence that day and Mrs. Churchill didn't see them, nor did Miss Collette. Miss Collette didn't see Frank Wixon get over that fence and walk on it before 12 o'clock that day. John Crowe's man didn't see him either. The District Attorney will tell you that Mrs. Chagnon and her daughter heard pounding. They described it as of some one getting over a fence. If Your Honor will think a minute, you will see that it was not pounding which was in their minds, but the thought of a man getting over a fence. We claim, Your Honor, that this shows an idea that nobody else could have got into that house and escaped. Mr. John Morse appears to have satisfactorily accounted for his time, and that brings us to two parties, Bridget Sullivan and Lizzie Borden. In the natural course of things who would be the party to be suspected? Whose clothing would be examined, and who would have to account for every movement of her time? Would it be the stranger, or would it be the one bound to the murdered man by ties of love? And right here, what does it mean when we say the youngest daughter? The last one whose baby fingers have been lovingly entwined about her father's head. Is there nothing in the ties of love and affection?" The words of Mr. Jennings about the youngest daughter caused the prisoner strong feelings. She bit her lips and then the tears began to shine in her eyes. She raised her hand to her eyes and then placed her handkerchief there. She did not cry, however, and as soon as Mr. Jennings left this line of talk she wiped her eyes and was as before, except that her eyes were now red as any woman's who lets tears get the best of her. " And I do not wish to be misunderstood. I do not believe that Bridget Sullivan committed that murder any more than I believe Lizzie Borden did. Why don't the District Attorney make Bridget Sullivan explain what she was doing during the twenty minutes which elapsed while she is supposed to be washing the upper sitting room windows? Does it take her twenty minutes to wash the upper part of one window? Why isn't she questioned regarding every second as Lizzie Borden was? Yet, according to her story, it was three-quarters of an hour. She didn't wash in all but three windows and a half. Yet the prosecution thinks nothing of this. If Miss Lizzie cannot escape being tripped up by one officer and another, she must be guilty. Now, to commit a crime there must be opportunity. I submit that unless she alone had an opportunity to commit the crime there is no ground for holding her. Bridget Sullivan was out washing windows. Nobody saw her but Mrs. Churchill. Bridget was three-quarters of an hour washing windows. Mind you, I don't say Bridget Sullivan did it. I distinctly state she did not, but I call attention to these points, which the State haven't considered yet. Now in regard to the length of time which those two people had been dead. Prof. Wood testified under cross-examination that, providing the digestion had been normal, Mrs. Borden was killed an hour and a half or two hours before Mr. Borden. If she was killed at 9:30 or 10 o'clock, Mr. Borden was there in the house. He goes to the Union Savings Bank a few minutes before 9:30. Surely Lizzie never killed her mother while her father was in the house. Surely she did not get her father out of the house to kill the mother. Now, in regard to this, it is perfectly clear to me why the answers to the questions of her whereabouts at the time of the killing of her mother and later that morning should be inconsistent. I have stated before that I considered the inquisition of the girl an outrage. Here was a girl they had been suspecting for days. She was virtually under arrest, and yet for the purpose of extracting a confession from her to support their theory, they brought her here and put her upon the rack, a thing they knew they would have no right to do if they placed her under arrest. As in the days of the rack and thumb screws, so she was racked mentally again and again. Day after day the same questions were repeated to her in the hope to elicit some information that would criminate her. Is it a wonder there are conflicting statements? Here is an intelligent lady, Mrs. Churchill, who went into the house with Bridget Sullivan and can't tell what became of the servant. Bridget Sullivan could not melt into thin air, but this intelligent lady can't tell whether she went upstairs or down. Here is Lizzie Borden, who has been under surveillance for days, who has been compelled to take preparations to induce sleep. She is brought here, and because she couldn't remember the minutest details, that is a sign of guilt. Now she tells that she got up that morning, goes down stairs about 9 o'clock, not feeling very well. Bridget Sullivan saw her, but can't say if she was reading an old magazine. She goes upstairs and then comes down again. She irons some handkerchiefs. I don't know but the State is going to say those handkerchiefs were being cleaned of blood. It wouldn't be more presumptuous than several other ideas they have tried. How about that fire? I am surprised the State hasn't taken up that. Perhaps he has not found out that it is hard to start a fire. Now about her whereabouts at the time her father came in. She first says she is upstairs. Then she says she is down stairs, and sticks to that. I submit that, if she was on the stairs when Bridget opened the door to let Mr. Borden in and laughed, as Bridget says she did, she must have been insane, and was insane at the time of the commission of the crime. No human being could do a deed like that and then stand and laugh at a remark like that made by Bridget Sullivan. It is beyond the bounds of human belief. Then she says she went out in the yard and stayed there, and then went into the barn. I don't believe she can tell how long she was in the barn. Look at the testimony in this case and see if you ascribe guilt to Lizzie Borden because she couldn't tell whether she was in the barn twenty minutes or half an hour. She goes into the barn and looks for this lead. Is there anything improbable or unreasonable in this? If one theory is correct, she couldn't have been there twenty minutes or half an hour. It is simply a guess. Then

INSPECTOR ADELARD PERRON.

she comes in and finds her father. It is said that she is guilty because she didn't call for her mother. She knew Bridget was in the house, and she hollered and called her down. Is she the calm, collected being who hasn't been moved by this? Mrs. Churchill looks over and sees a sign of distress. She says ' What's the matter?' and Lizzie says, ' Come over quick, my father is killed. ' Then her emotion is such that she requires the attention of her two friends. The testimony of everybody else in the case is that this girl had received a terrible shock. She asks her friends to search for her mother. She tells them her mother had said that she was going out to see a sick friend and that she thought she had heard her come in. Was it unnatural that, being unable to find Mrs. Borden, she should think she had been killed. Now Lizzie's story conflicts with Bridget's.

Lizzie says she thinks her mother went out. Bridget says no. Bridget don't see Mr. Borden go out. Why should she see Mr. Borden? Now the Government is bound to show that there is a motive for this crime. In the absence of it, unless there is direct evidence, their case has got to fall. What was the motive? The papers all over the country have published it as it was given out to them. Has there been a motive shown here? No, only that five years ago something happened. It was as a result of Mr. Borden's giving his wife's stepsister a residence, and the girls said they thought their father ought to have done as much as that for them. After that Lizzie called her Mrs. Borden. But now what kind of a motive would it have required to commit this crime. A man sometimes when pressed for money will commit crime, and in the case of Mrs. Robinson we know there was murder to get insurance money. I beg you to remember if crimes of this sort are committed unless there is a pressing want of money. And yet to get the motive they've got to say that without hatred, bitterness or previous quarrel, she murders him to get possession of the money which, in the natural course of events would be hers within a few years. I say that this is beyond the bounds of human credibility. They say the attempted purchase of prussic acid by Lizzie Borden shows she was going to do some deadly deed. If there is one thing which is weakest in criminal cases it is the matter of mistaken identity. The books are full of such references. These three persons say it was Lizzie Borden who went into that store and attempted to buy prussic acid. Neither of them knows her, but all three assert it is she. One of them, Bence, is taken to her house and he says he recognized her by her voice. He says he recognized it because it was tremulous. Kilroy says her voice was clear and distinct, yet Bence, with the life and liberty of this girl hanging upon his words, says he identified her by her voice. If it pleases Your Honor, Lizzie Borden did not attempt to purchase prussic acid, and she has asked to have her testimony taken upon this point. She declares that she never left her home Wednesday morning, and by a special providence, which seems to have watched over us in parts of this case, her words are corroborated by the dead woman who told John Morse that Lizzie had been sick in her room all day and had not left the house, and later, when Mrs. Bowen comes to the house and asks for Lizzie, Mr. Borden says: she was in the house all day and only went out at night, when she called on Miss Russell. I ask you, Your Honor, taking the testimony of Prof. Wood that no prussic acid was found in the stomachs of the murdered couple, who told the truth ? I don't mean to say that these young men meant to tell anything untrue, but in the light of these facts was it Lizzie Borden who entered that drug store and attempted to purchase prussic acid, or was it some person who looked like her ? Now, if they had proved a motive, if the motive they have given satisfies you, let us look at other evidence in the case. This girl has got at the most ten to fifteen minutes to commit the crime and conceal the weapon. Why didn't she wait before she called Bridget Sullivan downstairs ? What is her condition just afterwards ? Is there anything on her when the neighbors come to show that she committed the crime ? If she did have time to kill her mother and clear the blood stains from her garments, she did not have time to clear up the evidence of her work down stairs. If she had on an apron, where is the apron ? Officer Doherty attempted to describe the dress he saw her have on. Mrs. Churchill thinks it was of another color. The lighter the dress the better to find out if she did it, and, if she did it with the white skirt on, where are the blood spots ? Where did she get rid of the weapons ? The dress, the shoes she had on that morning. Are there any shoe buttons found in the fire ? Is there any smell of burnt clothing ? No. Why, at the time of the arrest of this girl we were enveloped in an atmosphere of poison, gore, hatchets and bloody hairs. Why, until Prof. Wood stepped on the stand, it had been given out, whether by the police I do not know, that the hatchet Prof. Wood had was the weapon with which the crime was committed, and that it bore signs of having been used to commit it. I confess that until Prof. Wood went upon the stand my heart almost stood still with anxiety. The Government is in this position. The more closely they hold Lizzie Borden in that house, the more they show she couldn't get out, they shut that bloody hatchet up there with her. Day after day, hour after hour they have searched and examined, and the only thing they produced was the hatchet, which Prof. Wood says contained no blood. I don't believe Dr. Dolan would willingly harm a hair of this defendant's head, and yet his description of this hatchet was one of the most terrible things of this trial. It would be such a hatchet as would commit this deed, he said, and it appeared to have upon it what seemed to him was a blood spot. The end he said was such as to cause the crushing wound in the head. But then comes Prof. Draper, who says there was no such crushing wound. You can imagine, Your Honor, the feelings of the counsel, who sat here almost heart sick day after day, waiting for that report and guarding the interests of a client whom they believe to be innocent, and who insist she is

innocent. I have no doubt that every person with a feeling of
sympathy for that girl felt their hearts leap with joy as Prof. Wood
gave his testimony. If I could have had my way I would have
shouted for joy. That was the deliverance of Lizzie Borden. If that
hatchet had been lost on the way by a railroad accident, Lizzie Borden
would have been a condemned woman upon the testimony of Dr.
Dolan, regarding the description of that hatchet. Lizzie Borden's
life was in Dr. Dolan's hands and by the goodness of God's providence
Prof. Wood came, and, like that shot at Concord, which rang round
the world, his story went like a song of joy from Maine to Mexico
and from the Atlantic to the Pacific. They haven't proved that this
girl had anything to do with the murder. They can't find any blood
on her dress, on her hair, on her shoes. They can't find any motive.
They can't find the axes, and couldn't clean the axe, and so I say I
demand the woman's release. The grand jury, if they meet more
evidence, can indict her. She is here—she can't flee. She isn't
going to flee. The great public is going to take your decision as they
took the arrest upon the strength of Mr. Knowlton's experience.
They can't find a motive, no blood, no poison, and so I say that this
woman shan't be sent to prison on such evidence as this, shan't be
sent to jail for three months, shan't be deprived of her liberty and her
good name. Don't, Your Honor, when they don't show an
incriminating circumstance, don't put the stigma of guilt upon this
woman, reared as she has been and with a past character beyond
reproach. Don't let it go out in the world as the decision of a just
judge that she is probably guilty. God grant Your Honor wisdom to
decide, and, while you do your duty, do it as God tells you to do it,
giving to the accused the benefit of the doubt. ''

As Mr. Jennings concluded, there were tears in the eyes of a
majority of those present. Col. Adams, the associate counsel, was
deeply affected, and Mr. Phillips, Mr. Jenning's assistant, was weep-
ing. The prisoner's lips were trembling, and the tears in her eyes
were hidden from view by her hands, which were placed there. As
Mayor Coughlin, Dr. Dolan and other prominent persons stepped
forward to grasp the hand of the attorney, a ripple of applause started,
which rapidly swelled into a loud expression of admiration and
sympathy, and with the echo of this applause, which there was no
attempt to suppress, the Court was adjourned till the afternoon.

CHAPTER XIX.

DISTRICT ATTORNEY KNOWLTON'S ARGUMENT.

K NOWLEDGE of the splendid presentation of the case of the defence by Mr. Jennings reached the streets almost in advance of its conclusion, and the effect was apparent at the opening of the afternoon session. The court room was crowded to excess, and there were larger throngs at the entrances on the square than had been noticed since the opening of the hearing. Everybody expected an interesting answer from the District Attorney, and the gathering assembled to listen to it included the leading professional men of the city. Attorney General Pillsbury arrived at noon, and was seated beside the District Attorney, as the latter began to speak. Lizzie Borden was pale as she entered, but she flushed a vivid crimson as the District Attorney arose to speak. He said: "I can fully appreciate Your Honor's feelings, now that the end of this hearing is about to be reached. The crime of murder touches the deepest sensibilities of feeling. There is the deepest feeling of horror about it, and above all in the unnaturalness that brings the thrill of horror to every mind. The man who is accustomed even to conflicts of arms may not be expected to be free from horror at the thought of the assassin. While it was not a pleasant summons that came to me, the almost despairing cry that came to me to come over here, I should not have been true to duty if I had not undertaken to ferret out the criminal. It was so causeless a crime. The people interested in it were so free from ordinary bickerings or strife that of all cases that transcend the ideas of men, this case was that case. The murdered man's daughter was arrested. I perfectly understood the surprise and indignation that started up. I am sorry that Your Honor was criticised. Does not Your Honor believe my own soul is filled with anguish that I must go on and believe the prisoner guilty, and yet the path of duty is not always the path of pleasure. The straight and narrow path is often full of anguish, and does not have the popular voice behind it. What is it we have done? There are three stages, yes, four, which are junctions of the law in a case like this. First, the stage of simple inquiry. I am sworn on

that book before Your Honor that an inquest shall be held, which is
necessarily private. That step has been taken. There then comes
another stage, when by the laws of inquiry it finally sees the evidence
points to any particular person and such an occasion as this follows.
That is the present state. To that tribunal it is Your Honor's duty
to direct such cases as seem too grave for Your Honor to decide.
Then the evidence appears to indicate that the balance of probabilities is in favor of finding the accursed guilty of the act. The
Commonwealth advances no statements as to probable guilt. Your
Honor's duty is before you. Let us go back to the pictures. They
are before you. Such was the scene presented four weeks ago this
morning. What are they? One is a man retired from business, of
simple and frugal habits, and so far as we know without an enemy in
the world. If there was some friction between him and his wife's
relatives, that domestic and honorable lady was absolutely without
harsh feelings on the part of the world, yet she was murdered, and
there was a hand that dealt those blows, and a brain that directed
them. There was not a man, woman or child in the world of whom
we could not have said, they would have done it. But it was done.
The presumption that some enemy killed him and then killed her,
for I presume that Your Honor will prefer the evidence of the chemist, Prof. Wood, rather than the story of a Medical Examiner who
has not examined the stomachs, is that Mrs. Borden was dead fully
an hour and a half before the murder of Mr. Borden. Who could
have done it? As an eminent attorney once said, there is no motive
for murder. There is reason for it, but no motive. I never in all my
experience saw a man so utterly low as to believe him guilty of such
a deed. But it was done. By what? Obviously by a hatchet.
The blows were struck from behind. It was the act of a physical, if
not a moral coward. It was the act of a person who, while willing to
murder, was not willing to let the murdered people see who was doing
it. As you listened to the description of the blows, you are convinced
of the fact that no man could have struck them. You are struck with
the thought that it was an irresolute, imperfect feminine hand that
could strike, and yet not with the strength of a man, and we do not
know who did it. It was not the result of spite as first thought, but
the blows were fast, swift blows of somebody who had a reason for
doing it. The first obvious inquiry is, who is benefited by that
removal. God forbid I should impute that motive, but what have we
before us? I don't know what was the cause of it. I have discovered the fact that she has repudiated the relation of mother and

daughter. I knew once two boys who in growing to be men discovered that their father had committed a crime and called him Mr., but I never heard of another case of that sort. We've got the terrible fact. She has repudiated the name of mother. Has Your Honor, as I have, ever learned that no more lasting hatred ever springs up than between step-parents and their children? We have seen that he didn't provide the house with gas, that he hadn't in the house what those daughters very much wanted, a bath tub, and that they quarrelled about property. Do you suppose that was a sufficient motive? I grant that that is not an adequate motive for killing her. There is no adequate motive for killing her. But I have found the only person in the world with whom she was not in accord. Let us look around and it cannot be imagined how anybody could have got in or out. I listened to the eloquent remarks of my brother and failed to hear him tell how anybody could have got in there, remained an hour and a half, killed the two people and then have gone out

without being observed. Doors locked and windows closed. Here was a house with the front door locked, the windows closed, the cellar door locked and the screen door closed, with somebody on guard in the kitchen. Nay, Mr. Borden locked the barn every night, and you can't go from one part of the house to the other without keys. That makes us begin to think. Of course, this is negative evidence. Of course

OFFICER MICHAEL MULLALY. it is neither sufficient, reliable or conclu-

sive, but all evidence is made up of circumstances of more or less weight. Yet from this house, on a main street, near the centre of the city, passed by hundreds of people daily, no man could depart without being seen. And that isn't the most difficult part of it. I can't devise any way by which anybody could have avoided those locks. Tell me not about the barn which Mr. Borden always locked himself; the front door was locked when Mr. Borden came in; there was not a hiding place when they came in; they could not get upstairs to the front of the house by the back way; they must be seen passing through the house; and I haven't dwelt on the chances of anybody escaping the notice of these five people and the refusal of the human mind to accept such a possibility. I can conceive of a villain. I can't conceive of the villain who did this; and I can't also conceive of a villian who is a fool. All the movements of this family must have been known, and

so the mind, not the mind which is actuated by sympathy and which
I understand but cannot follow, because I am sworn to my duty, but
the impartial mind looks toward the house. There has been no idle
and unjust suspicion.   It was natural that suspicion should be
directed towards the inmates of that house.   Morse is out of the way
and then comes the servant girl, perhaps the next one thought of.
The discharge of my duties have found in my eyes no difference
between one class and another.   When I came to Fall River I knew
no difference between honest and reputable Lizzie Borden and honest
and reputable Bridget Sullivan, and so Bridget Sullivan was brought
here to what my learned friend calls a star chamber inquiry, and was
questioned as closely and minutely as any other member of the family.
The innocent do not need fear questioning.   In all my twenty-five
years experience will my learned brother say that he ever heard or
knew me to treat a female witness discourteously.   She sitting in one
chair and the inquirer in another, presumably as innocent as anybody;
and yet fault is found that she is suspected when she answers
questions in two ways.   I'm going to assume that Your Honor
believes Bridget Sullivan has told the exact truth.   What took place,
Bridget Sullivan ? Mr. Morse went off that morning and left Lizzie in
the kitchen alone.   The only time when Mrs. Borden could have
been killed.   Mrs. Borden told her to wash windows and she goes out
to do it.   Lizzie didn't go up the back way because she couldn't get
up that way.   In the lower part of the house there was no person left
and Lizzie and her mother were upstairs.   Then Lizzie comes to the
screen door.   Maggie says, don't lock the screen door.   Mr. Borden
was then alive.   Mrs. Churchill saw Mr. Borden go off and then saw
Bridget washing windows.   Then the hatchet was driven into the
brain of Abby Borden.   Many a man has been convicted because he
alone could have committed a crime.   Maggie finishes her work, and
then, until Mr. Borden comes in, Lizzie and Mrs. Borden are alone
upstairs, and this is not all; Mr. Borden comes to the front door.   I
don't care to comment on Lizzie's laughter at Bridget's exclamation,
but Lizzie was where, if Mrs. Borden fell to the floor, she could not
have been twenty feet away from her, and where, if the old lady
made any noise, she could have heard it.   Then Lizzie comes down
stairs and commences to iron.   Bridget leaves her alone with her
father.   Less than fifteen minutes later the death of Mr. Borden takes
place.   She could have but one alibi, she could not be down stairs;
she could not be anywhere except where she could not see any person
come from the house.   It is now more difficult in the cool of September

than it was at the inquest, to imagine the improbability of the story told by Miss Lizzie. Where he was she can't tell; where he came from she didn't know; where was she between the hours of nine and ten, when her mother was killed; whatever else I may not say of Lizzie Borden, I will say that for one to even suggest that from the time she found her father dead she was not in full control of all her faculties, is to confess that they do not know the facts. She has not shed a tear, and it is idle for any one to say she has been confused or dazed. I asked her where she was when her father came back, and we get this story: 'I was down in the kitchen.' That's the kind of thumbscrew I apply, and it was a most vital thing. Almost a moment after: 'Where were you when the bell rung?' 'I think I was upstairs in my room.' 'Were you upstairs when you heard the bell?' No thinking now, no daze: 'I think I was on the steps coming down.' Isn't it singular, isn't it a vital thing that upon this most important subject she should not tell the same story upon two pages of the testimony. I prefer to take the story of one who gives the same answer twice, for I am not affected by the heat and the turmoil which surrounds this case, and for which I have no hard feelings towards anybody. Then I asked her: 'What were you doing while your father was out?' and she said she was waiting for the irons to heat. Unsatisfactory explanations. Isn't it singular that I can't get a satisfactory explanation from her as to how she spent the hour and fifteen minutes while her father was out and her mother was being killed upstairs. Finally, however, she says after urging twice, she saw him take off his slippers, when the photographs show he did not take off his boots, and after speaking to her father she tells him that she thinks her mother has gone out; and then she tells us that she went to the barn. And when we asked her 'where was your mother?' She answers, 'she is not my mother, but my stepmother,' and her bosom friend, Miss Russell, is compelled to testify that Lizzie told her she went out to get a piece of something to fix her window. Then she tells Dr. Bowen it was to get a piece of iron; then she tells the story of the fish line and the sinker. I say to her, 'Where did you spend twenty minutes or half an hour on that hot morning?' She says she went to fix a curtain at the west end of the barn and ate pears there. Let me say I never saw an alibi labor as this one does; you can see by reading that testimony how she was away from home during the questioning. She was going to that barn on the hottest of days to get something unnecessary. I don't say this is enough to convict her, but with Maggie's story that she had been where she could have committed the crime, there is something to challenge our credulity. Relation of mother and daughter. There was so little in common between the daughter and the mother that it was to Bridget the mother gave notice of her intended movement, and not to the daughter. We have it from Lizzie that her mother received a note from sick friends. Who sent it? Where did it come from? It did not come in the screen door, because Bridget was in the kitchen. Mr. Borden knew nothing about it. Lizzie says she told him. Some laughter was heard when a witness said a reporter was found sitting on the steps when the first officer arrived. I am not one who joined in that laughter, for the reporter in this case represents the anxious and agonized public, who wish to know any fact in this matter and every point of evidence, true or false. If there was any person in the world who wrote that note would he not in the interest of humanity come forward. There never was a note sent. It was a part of the whole cunning scheme, and if there had been, and the writer of it had been in the remotest corner of the world, he would certainly have come forward. It's an easy thing to say, but it is one of those things that, when a matter becomes public property, cannot be concealed. Nobody, Your Honor, has said this family was poisoned with prussic acid. All that the Commonwealth says is that this was the first proposition. I intended to say at the outset that the crime was done as a matter of deliberate preparation. Those young men recognized her not by her voice, but recognized her and her voice. Is there any different point of view in Lizzie Borden from any other person who is accused of crime. We find here the suggestion of a motive which speaks volumes. The druggist told her plainly she couldn't have it. Then how could this thing be done? Not by the pistol, not by the knife, not by arsenical poisoning. There was but one way of removing that woman, and that was to attack her from behind. That is a dreadful thing. It makes one's heart bleed to think of it. But it is done. I'd rather resign my office than deal with it, but I will not flee from duty. I haven't alluded to and I think I will not comment upon the demeanor of the defendant. It is certainly singular. While everybody is dazed there is but one person who, throughout the whole business, has not been seen to express emotion. This somewhat removes from our minds the horror of the thing which we naturally come to. Atrocious and wicked crime is laid to the door of some women. The great poet makes murderesses, and I am somewhat relieved that these facts do not point to a woman who expressed any feminine feeling. When Fleet came there she was annoyed that any one should want to search her room for the murderer of her father and step-mother. I know there are things that have not been explained. It has been a source of immense disappointment that we have not been able to find the apron with which she must have covered her dress, and which must contain blood, just as surely as did the shoes. It is a source of regret that we have not been able to find the packet, but she had fifteen minutes in which to conceal it. This was not a crime of a moment. It was conceived in the head of a cunning, cool woman, and well has she concealed these things. If Your Honor yielded to the applause which spontaneously greeted the close of the remarks of my earnest, passionate brother, if Your Honor could but yield to the loyalty of his feelings, we would all be proud of it, and would be pleased to hear him say: ' We will let this woman go.' But that would be but temporary satisfaction. We are constrained to find that she has been deal-ing in poisonous things; that her story is absurd, and that hers and hers alone has been the opportunity for the commis-sion of the crime. Yielding to clamor is not to be compared to that only and greatest satisfac-tion that of a duty well done.''

ELI BENCE.

There was a deathly silence in the crowded court room as the District Attorney concluded, and every eye was upon Judge Blais-dell. The features of the kindly old magistrate were saddened, and he was visibly affected as he commenced his remarks. He said: '' The long examination is now concluded, and there remains but for the magistrate to perform what he believes to be his duty. It would be a pleasure for him, and he would doubtless receive much sympathy if he could say ' Lizzie, I judge you probably not guilty. You may go home.' But upon the character of the evidence presented through the witnesses who have been so closely and thoroughly examined, there is but one thing to be done. Suppose for a single moment a man was standing there. He was found close by that guest chamber which, to Mrs. Borden, was a chamber of death. Suppose a man had been found in the vicinity of Mr. Borden; was the first to find the body, and the only account he could give of himself was the unreasonable one that he was out in the barn looking for sinkers; then he was out in the yard; then he was out for something else; would there be any question in the minds of men what should be done with such a man?" There was a brief, painful pause, and the eyes of the Judge were wet with tears. Then he resumed: "So there is only one thing to do, painful as it may be—the judgment of the Court is that you are probably guilty, and you are ordered committed to await the action of the Supertor Court." The glance of every person in the room was on Lizzie as the finding of the Court was announced. She sat like a statue of stone, totally unmoved, and without the slightest evidence of emotion or interest in the proceedings. Her aged pastor beside her placed his hands over his ears. He knew what was coming, and could not hear the words. The white faces of all in the court room rendered the seance particularly impressive. Then the prisoner stood up, still with that same impassive countenance, and far-away look. She listened quietly while the clerk read the sentence of the Court, ordering her confinement in Taunton Jail until the session of the grand jury on the first Monday in November. At the conclusion of the words, she seated herself quietly, and after a few minutes left the court room escorted by the sorrowing old clergyman. After this there were a few formalities. The recognizances of Bridget Sullivan and John V. Morse were renewed, Marshal Hillard and Officer Seaver becoming bondsmen for the domestic and ex-Congressman Davis for Mr Morse. Col. Adams announced that the attorneys had agreed that the piece of blood-stained plaster should remain in the possession of the Clerk, and with that, the case came temporarily to an end.

The Grand Jury.

CHAPTER XX.

Lizzie A. Borden Indicted.

CONTRARY to the expectations of a great many people, Judge Blaisdell held that Lizzie Borden was "probably guilty" of the murder of her father. She was not tried nor accused of the murder of her stepmother; all that the State desired was to hold her to await the action of the grand jury of Bristol County. The prisoner was transferred to the county jail at Taunton and delivered into the keeping of Sheriff Wright and his wife. The latter, the matron of the institution, formerly lived in Fall River, where she knew the Bordens very well. The accused was therefore in the hands of the kindliest of persons who undoubtedly made her stay as pleasant as it was possible under the circumstances. She was allowed certain privileges, and for the most part occupied her cell as an ordinary prisoner. Her sister Emma, Rev. Mr. Buck, Rev. Mr. Jubb and her lawyers made frequent visits to the jail. Her life in the county bastile was that of the other inmates, and nothing happened until November, to attract to her more than passing interest. The newspapers made frequent reference to the case, but as she never read the daily papers she was not disturbed by them. One New York newspaper printed a magnificent "fake" interview which its representative was supposed to have had with the accused, and ever and anon there would appear something to awaken interest in the case. The grand jury, composed of twenty-four men, assembled on November 7th to consider the criminal cases in Bristol county. The Borden case was reserved for the last. The greater part of the week ending November 21st, was devoted to this case. The State submitted most of its evidence and the District Attorney established a precedent by notifying Attorney Jennings that he would be allowed to present to the jury the evidence for the defense. This meant that Mr. Knowlton was so manifestly fair in conducting the case in the grand jury room, that he was willing and anxious that the jury hear not only the evidence against Miss Borden, but the testimony in her behalf. If after hearing both sides the jury found her not guilty, he would be well satisfied, and if on the other hand she was found to be guilty he would be equally satisfied. On the 21st the news of the adjournment of the jury without action in the case was heralded throughout the land. No one seemed to know what it meant, but almost everybody had a theory. Very few of these theories were alike, and perhaps none of them were correct. The grand jury simply adjourned until December 1st, and that was all the public knew.

On the day set, it convened again and the State presented more evidence.

Miss Alice Russell, an important witness, reappeared voluntarily, and relieved her mind of a few facts which it is said, had been forgotten or overlooked at the time of her first appearance.

The next day, the 2d of December, the grand jury returned three indictments against Lizzie Borden. One charged her with the murder of her father, Andrew J. Borden, another charged her with the murder of her stepmother, Abbie D. Borden, and the third charged her jointly with the murder of both. At the time the vote was taken on the question of her indictment by the jury there were twenty-one members present. Of these, twenty voted "yes" and one voted "no." So it happened that twenty men had said upon their oaths, after having heard the evidence impartially given, that Lizzie Borden was guilty. There were thousands of people who had maintained all along that the Fall River police, the Medical Examiner, the Judge of the District Court and the District Attorney had labored in vain, and that the grand jury would fail to find a true bill; but alas for those good people who had traduced the City Marshal's character, yes, assailed his honesty of purpose and doubted his capabilities, and in some instances gone even further—his acts as well as those of his associates had been endorsed. It was an hour of triumph for them even if it was one of sadness for the prisoner's friends.

The criticism of the City Marshal assumed various and in many instances unique forms. One instance will suffice to show to what extremities a few foolhardy editors carried their prejudices. An afternoon newspaper published in Worcester, Mass., inflicted upon its readers a screed worthy the ablest efforts of a Chicago anarchist. It printed an editorial, at the time of the cholera scare in New York, in which it expressed a desire that the Asiatic pestilence would come up Narragansett Bay and destroy every man connected with the prosecution of Lizzie Borden. It drew a pen picture of the dread disease in the act of purging the city of Fall River of such men as would dare to insinuate that the young woman was guilty. Then it sat back on its haunches, that editorial, and chuckled with goulish glee at the prospect. Looking at this case in the light of the action of the grand jury it would seem that the author of that editorial was a trifle hasty. This was an extreme case, and yet there were many instances wherein a similar sentiment was expressed.

Miss Borden remained in Taunton Jail until the 8th of May, 1893, when she was taken to New Bedford, Mass., and arraigned before Judge J. W. Hammond of the Superior Court to plead to the indictments. Her plea on each charge was "not guilty." The date of her trial was set for June 5 following, to take place in New Bedford—and she was taken back to Taunton. Meanwhile, Ex-Governor George D. Robinson was retained to assist in her defense. Her arraignment created anew public interest in the case and a few days later the news was sent out from Taunton that she was very ill with a cold contracted on the journey to and from New Bedford. Still another story was circulated to the effect that her mind was weakening under the great strain and worry, but it was promptly denied the next day.

About this time Mrs. Mary A. Livermore paid the accused a visit and was accorded an interview at Taunton Jail. The next day New England people were treated to a very pathetic story over the name of Amy Robsart, which was contrary to the report of Miss Borden's mental condition. Mrs. Livermore had told Miss Robsart and the latter had painted the picture.

CHAPTER XXI.

THE TRICKEY–McHENRY AFFAIR.

THE history of the Borden murder would be incomplete without reference to the affair in which Henry G. Trickey, the talented reporter of the *Boston Globe*, and Detective Edwin D. McHenry figured so prominently. They were not alone in the deal which resulted in the *Boston Globe* publishing on the 12th of October, 1892, a story which has since became famous as the most gigantic " fake " ever laid before the reading public. A dozen people, a majority of whom rank high in the estimation of the public were directly connected with this matter and while the writer of this book would be justified in giving each and every man's connection therewith, circumstances have arisen which would seem to indicate that by the publication of these names, an unfortunate occurrence would be stirred into action again, and perhaps no particular good would result. So delicate in fact has the matter become that no newspaper has attempted to publish anything more than an occasional reference to it; although more than one great daily is in possession of the main facts. It is a delicate matter because it has many sides to be presented, and each participant maintains that he was right in his actions and that the others were wrong. After hearing the story from many sources, each of which is apparently authentic, it becomes more confusing and treacherous. There are somethings however upon which all parties agree, and they will be discussed in this chapter.

Henry G. Trickey bargained with Detective McHenry for an exclusive story of the Borden case and the price to be paid was $500, according to Mr. Trickey. The story was delivered, paid for and published in the *Boston Globe*. It was false in every particular, and the *Globe* discovered its mistake ten hours after it had been made. Mr. Trickey left Boston soon afterward and was accidentally killed by a railroad train in Canada in the latter part of November. His friends insisted that he was unjustly dealt with by McHenry, and that his death was the indirect result of the transaction. They claim also that he represented a great newspaper and that his efforts in getting the story for publication were honest, praiseworthy, and done in a manner which is to be expected of the live newspaper man of the day. But the State represented in this matter by McHenry, makes a different claim, and it submitted evidence to the grand jury whereby Mr. Trickey was indicted for his connection with the affair. Had the unfortunate Mr. Trickey lived to meet his accusers the result would no doubt have been as interesting and quite as sensational as the killing of the Bordens. As the Fall River police in connection with McHenry secured the evidence upon which Mr. Trickey was indicted, it is but natural to expect that they had reasons for so doing. To offset this, the friends of the reporter claim that he was the victim of a plot of which McHenry was the moving spirit and they shoulder most of the blame on the detective. He, however, appears to be able to bear the burden, as Marshal Hilliard has repeatedly said that he found McHenry a capable, reliable and trustworthy officer so far as his connection with him had been. Thus it will be seen that if Mr. Trickey was innocent of the charges preferred against him he was at a disadvantage, for the Fall River police, as well as the District Attorney and the Attorney-General were kept thoroughly posted on what was taking place between the reporter and the detective. In order that both sides may be presented to the public the story of the transaction as told by McHenry as well as that of Trickey is given and can be taken for what it is worth. The detective has been unmercifully criticised by almost every newspaper in the country. Perhaps he deserved it richly and perhaps he did not. The following is his statement made to the writer. He said :—

"I was in New York the day of the Borden murders, and left that night for Fall River. Upon arriving on Friday morning, I, in company with State Officer Seaver, went to the Borden house to make a survey of the premises. This trip I took upon my own responsibility, as it were, prompted merely by a desire to look over the ground where so terrible a tragedy had been enacted. While in the yard I learned the story of the man who was said to have jumped over the back fence, and out of curiosity searched that part of the premises for a trace which the escaping man might have left. I was engaged in this work about three hours. I talked with John Cunningham who was the first man on the premises, and from him learned that the back cellar door was locked when he made an effort to open it shortly after the murders were reported. I then went to the door and counted eleven weekly cobwebs, that is cobwebs which had been in place a week or more. Assistant Marshal Fleet and I opened the door and concluded that no one had passed through it for a week at least. We then went to the barn and made further search. We were told that the place had been locked. After that, we made search of the Chagnon fence, and I measured it and took other observations. From the house, I went to the City Marshal's office and there met Mr. Hilliard and Mayor Coughlin. The two men were discussing the case. It was then that the Marshal employed me on the case, and the Mayor authorized his action. I was engaged in various work until Saturday afternoon or evening, when the Marshal said to me, 'Mr. McHenry, I understand that there is a Pinkerton man in the city. I want you to take care of him.' The Mayor was also present at this interview, and gave his sanction to the order. I learned afterward that the Marshal referred to the fact that Assistant Superintendent O. M. Hanscom of the Boston Agency was in the city, and believed that he was in the employ of Attorney Jennings

DETECTIVE EDWIN D. MCHENRY.

and the Borden family. But the same night I found Mr. Hanscom, and watched him according to orders. It happened that the Marshal, Officer Seaver and myself were at the Marshal's residence during the early part of the night in consultation on the case. Mr. Hilliard was at supper, and I took occasion to go out and look around the premises. As I did so, I saw two Pinkerton men at the back window evidently in the act of eavesdropping. I very quickly told them to get out, as we did not want any such cattle around. I did not mention the incident to the Marshal at the time, but later, as we walked up to the city, I informed him of what I had seen. He was naturally angry at the audacity of the men whom I had seen around his house. On the way to the police station we met Henry G. Trickey, and he immediately entered into conversation with the Marshal. I heard Mr. Hilliard say, 'I am making no special mark

of anybody in this investigation, but I do intend to probe this affair
to the bottom, no matter who it hits. I want you to convey this
information to your friend. Outside detectives must not interfere
with the work of my men.' Right here I want to state, by way of
parenthesis, that I did not go to the post office in Providence and
offer to sell the evidence in the Graves-Barnaby case to Mr. Trickey,
although he said that I did. And the reason that I state that, is that
this very night, of which I am speaking, saw the beginning of the
Trickey-McHenry affair, and it was but three nights after the
Borden murders. It did not have its origin in me at all, as you will
see as we progress. You will remember that yesterday I told you of
an alleged truce which was said by the newspapers, in fact by Mr.
Trickey himself, to have been patched up between us. The fact is
that three months before the Bordens were murdered, I, in company
with two friends, were in the Adams House, Boston, when Mr.
Trickey came up. We had not been on friendly terms, as you know,
since the Graves trial in Denver, and at that time we did shake hands,
and apparently the hatchet was buried. In Mr. Trickey's·own
statement of this affair, which was printed over his signature in the
Boston Globe of October 11th, 1892, appears this sentence, '' I went to
Providence to see about the lawyer story. '' Now that was manifestly
incorrect, as you know yourself that the *Boston Globe* published the
whole story ten days before, and I know that Mr. Trickey got it from
State Officer Seaver. I merely mention this to show to you some of the
glaring inconsistencies which are prominent in the story of the affair
from which that sentence was read. But that is not the point for
discussion now. On the night to which I referred awhile ago, which
was the 7th of August, Mr. Trickey, before meeting us as before
stated, had left Superintendent Hanscom across the street and Mayor
Coughlin had joined the party, which then consisted of Marshal Hilliard,
the Mayor, Officer Seaver, Mr. Trickey and myself. After the short
conversation with the Marshal, Mr. Trickey then turned to the Mayor
and commenced to abuse the Attorney-General for his course in the
then pending Trefethen-Davis case. Mr. Trickey said, 'Hanscom
had prevented the conviction of Trefethen so far, and he will lead
Pillsbury yet ; more than that, he will prevent the Fall River police
from hanging Lizzie Borden.' This thread of conversation was
kept up for awhile, and then Mr. Trickey, tnrning to me said, ' Just
a minute, Ned, I want to speak to you. ' I stepped aside with him.
The Mayor and Officer Seaver walked along ; the Marshal heeled up
a few feet away. Then Mr. Trickey delivered himself as follows :—

'Ned, you are a big chump if you don't throw that big clam digger, (meaning the Marshal) and deal to me. There is just 5000 bobs in this job for us.' The Marshal overhead this statement. I replied, 'What do you mean, Trickey?' Then he said, 'You know how I stood with Hanscom in the Graves matter, don't you? I just about own that Pinkerton Agency, and the men do just about as I say in these matters. Now, I am in a position to give you a chance to get square with the Pinkertons and at the same time catch 5000 nice juicy bobs.'

"This was a tempting offer, I must say, for a poor man to hear made, and I said, 'Well, Henry, I will consider your proposition awhile and see you again later.' Hardly had the words been uttered than he grabbed me with both hands, and at the same time spoke in a loud voice to the Marshal, who still remained near by, saying, 'I'll let Mack go in a minute, Marshal; I want to speak to him about a lady we knew in Denver.' Then lowering his voice he continued, 'Has Lizzie Borden got a lover? Can't I allege that she has in my story to-morrow morning? I want something big to scoop this gang of newspaper fellows who are in the town.' My reply to this was, 'Great God, Henry, no.' He talked on, saying, 'Judging from what I heard to-day, somebody is in love with Lizzie.' 'No, sir,' said I, 'the utmost consideration is and has been shown to Miss Borden, and I never heard that she had a lover.' The suggestion which Mr. Trickey made then was used in the great story which he bought some months afterward, and you can begin to see now, perhaps, why I was suspicious of the honesty of Mr. Trickey's intentions. He continued, however, saying, "I know a great deal more about this case than the Fall River police, and right here I want to give you a straight tip, and you take it to Hilliard. It will give him a valuable clue to work on. If my friend Hanscom, on his return from the next interview with Lizzie Borden, is satisfied that she is guilty, he is going to pull up stakes and leave the town.' This very statement, Mr. Trickey made again in the police office the next day in the presence of the Marshal and others. 'So,' said Mr. Trickey, 'if he leaves the town, you can jump Lizzie immediately.' Then in parting from me, he said, 'Don't forget to consider my proposition, and connect with me to-morrow. Then I will square myself with you for the dirty deal I gave you in the Graves case.' I would have smashed him in the nose right there, had not the Marshal been in hearing distance. I promised him to think the matter over and see him again. I walked up to the Marshal, and we entered my room at the Wilbur House. Then and there I related what I have just told you, and also told of Mr. Trickey's conduct in the Graves case. Went through it all from end to end. The Marshal said that he had overheard a part of the conversation, and that Mr. Trickey was up to just what he suspected. The Marshal said to me in the course of the talk, ' Ned, if this man is what he represents himself to be, in connection with these people, you watch him, and look to me personally for help. Take plenty of time and use good judgment. Have everything in black and white.' As I stated to you before, I had told him of my connection with the Graves case, and I suggested the advisability of my keeping in the background and under cover as much as possible, in the work before us. Dr. Graves was then under conviction of murder, and the Supreme Court had not passed upon his motion for a new trial. Until this was settled, I did not feel that I should be prominently mentioned in the Borden case, as there were many men, enemies to me, who would antagonize me at every step if they knew that I was a factor in the investigation. He told me to go ahead and follow these people to the end, and to spare no pains or expense to do the job well.

"Next morning I was given a great many anonymous letters which the Marshal had read, and in company with Inspector Medley, ran them down. That is, established a clue for work which was afterward carried out by Captains Harrington and Doherty. This was part of the work which I did for the police, and secrecy of it kept me in the background. I kept my eye on the movements of the people I have mentioned before, and at the end of the first month, made out my bill to the City of Fall River. It was allowed by the Board of Aldermen, but the *Fall River Herald*, in an alleged editorial, severely criticised the Marshal for allowing me to work on the case, and objected to me being paid for what I had done. I never rendered another bill to the City of Fall River, although I worked night and day for months. In view of the *Herald's* criticism, I concluded not to bring the editor's unjust ravings onto the heads of my friends, and so ever after that I paid my own expenses. I spent every cent of money I could rake and scrape to carry out the work assigned to me, until my family were all but destitute. I gave up all my time to this work, and stood still under the fierce and unjust thrusts of every editorial pen, with few exceptions, in New England. It made me a poor man, and eventually brought on an attack of nervous prostration, when I fell exhausted, penniless and perhaps friendless, in the streets of New York, and was carried into the Cosmopolitan

Hotel, where I lay among perfect strangers, while my wife and child fought alone the battle for life in Providence. Yes, I did this rather than have such learned men as the editor of the *Fall River Herald* spill his gall over the magnanimous sum of $106.00, which I claimed for work and expenses, while upholding in my humble way the dignity of, and straining every nerve to assist, the Fall River police. I took a solemn vow that no act of Ned McHenry should ever again compromise my friends Rufus B. Hilliard and His Honor John W. Coughlin. Therefore I plodded through in silence, and where is my reward? A few dollars for six months work of myself and wife, and half a dozen men whom I paid regularly. But I would not have you understand that I am complaining. Perhaps the City of Fall River will reimburse me when the end of the Borden murder case is reached. Now, in regard to all this bosh about my attempting to rob and defame newspaper men as a rule. I refer you to the *Boston Post* of October 11th, and there you will see how I saved a paper which has been friendly to me. You may ask the managing editor how I treated him and his men in this case, and I think it only fair that he give you an answer.''

At this point the writer asked Mr. McHenry if he furnished Mr. Trickey with a list of the witnesses for the government. He replied, '' The only living evidence that I furnished Mr. Trickey with the names of living witnesses, is that I did tell him that I, my wife and Bridget Sullivan were witnesses for the prosecution, and that he knew before I told him. I defy contradiction of this statement.''

'' Did you furnish him with that list of names which it is alleged that he showed the managing editor of the *Globe*, in order to convince him that the story which he had bought from you was true?'' Mr. McHenry answered, '' That list of names is in Mr. Trickey's own handwriting, and if you or anybody else want further evidence of the truth of this statement, examine the affidavits of those persons who were present when he wrote the list, and which are now locked up in the Attorney-General's office, Commonwealth Building, Boston.''

'' Who made these affidavits?'' I asked, and he answered, '' Several persons, but all of them were not summoned to the Grand Jury to testify. For instance, there are two Providence policemen, two Providence lawyers, two of my men, and Captain Desmond of Fall River, who know about this case, but were not called. All this documentary evidence against Mr. Trickey is in his own handwriting and laid away in the same place, and marked exhibit No. 1. I want to say here and now that Andrew J. Jennings has been clean and free in this whole business. In justice to the man I do not believe that he did in any way give his sanction to the action of other friends of the accused woman. I say this through no fear of Mr. Jennings, but because he would not countenance any such actions as Trickey represented to have come from those friends. As to the story I furnished Mr. Trickey, he had the gist of it in his pocket three weeks before it was printed in the *Globe*. I gave him a skeleton of what the alleged witnesses would testify to, and he carried that around with him, I suppose. The Attorney-General has the affidavits of eight witnesses to this transaction, all of whom heard what was said at the time I gave him the story. In an editorial of the *Globe* of October 12th, this statement appears : ' Reports are examined at short notice, and sometimes under great hurry and excitement, etc.' Now, that was no excuse for printing the stuff I sold Mr. Trickey, for he had the skeleton of the story for three weeks at least, and if he had wanted it primarily for the *Globe*, there was no reason why he could not have examined it at his leisure. The editorial goes on to say the story was so well written and on the face of it appeared to be so plausible, that it was used without attempt at verification. Now, I never read stronger language than that, and I consider it a great compliment to me from the editor of the *Boston Globe*. After Mr. Trickey had made the proposition to buy the State's case from me, I lay in bed that day and thought the matter over, and formed some idea of the story which I would give out. That night Trickey came down and he and I worked on the story, writing it out from

MRS. NELLIE MCHENRY.

the skeleton. He wrote and I dictated. We were at it until three o'clock in the morning. This was on Thursday before the Monday on which the story appeared in print. Mind you, I had not given the bogus witnesses names to him until that night. In the skeleton there appeared no names. But the separate statement of each witness was numbered, from 1 to 25, and it read something like this: Witness No. 1 will testify to so-and-so ; Witness No. 2 will testify to so-and-so ; and in this manner through the whole list. That night I told him who the witnesses were and he used their names instead of the numbers. After this was completed he showed me a draft made out by a certain gentleman payable to me in the sum of $5000. It was drawn on Andrew J. Jennings, and was in payment for the government's case. That draft was never honored. With it was a letter authorizing the expenditure of any sum of money to get at the whole case of the prosecution. That letter was laid in a convenient place, and I got Trickey out of my office long enough to afford other people a chance to get a good look at it and to read it. I consider that movement a nice piece of detective work. During the evening, Captains Harrington and Desmond sat behind the curtain in my office and heard Mr. Trickey say to me that he had bribed them and that they had told him many of the State's secrets. Why, Trickey went so far as to accuse the Mayor of the city of accepting a bribe and selling out to him, the representative of the defense."

At this point the writer asked McHenry, "How on earth did Mr. Trickey escape, in the face of such accusations as this?" McHenry replied at once, "He never met his match before." Continuing, McHenry said, "Trickey did agree in the hearing of the usual number of witnesses to give me twenty-four hours notice before he published the story.

"In his published statement of October 11th, he says I asked him two questions on the night of the 10th. This, mind you, was at the time of his first and last visit to my office after the alleged evidence had been published. The first question he quoted correctly, except he did not use the word "skeleton" as he should have done. The second is entirely wrong. I did ask him this question, "Trickey, did you not promise to come down to my office with the balance of that $5000?" and he replied, 'Yes.'

"I did inveigle Trickey into Massachusetts, for I wanted him to commit that crime in that State. By agreement I was in Attleboro and waiting to hear from Trickey. He telephoned to me from Boston that he would be in Attleboro on the 3 o'clock train, and he kept his engagement. I met him in front of the Park Hotel. The message was received by the proprietor of the Park Hotel, and he has a record of it. In Mr. Trickey's published account of this matter, he says that he has eight affidavits of parties to the effect that the alleged evidence was true and that they were sworn to before me as a notary in Providence. If he has, why don't they show them? I defy any man to produce such affidavits.

"On Monday night after the *Globe* published its story, I was in Fall River and started for home. I expected that there would be trouble, and so Captains Desmond and Harrington went up on a late train to get behind the curtain and watch the fun which was sure to come. I left on an afternoon train by way of Mansfield. Mr.

Carberry, a *Globe* reporter, followed me on the train and harrassed me until forbearance ceased to be a virtue. Arriving in Providence, I was met by about four newspaper men, including Charley Kirby and Mr. Trickey. They surrounded me at the entrance to the station, and demanded an audience. I eluded them, and was on my way home when they again caught sight of me, and when near Engine Company No. 4, matters almost came to a crisis. Mr. Trickey had his hand thrust into his pocket as if to draw a pistol, and he wore on his face the most aggravated look of desperation that it has ever been my misfortune to behold. I felt that he was in a state of mind which would lead him to do something rash. I feared he might attempt to take my life. I was not armed at the time, but I deter-

mined to make a bold stand, and so I told him that if he made a move I would kill him on the spot. Before leaving Fall River, I had telephoned to my wife that I would arrive home at a certain hour, and she had already made preparations for receiving me. Hardly had I made this threat to Mr. Trickey, than one of my men from the office rushed up and handed me a pistol. With this I ordered Mr. Kirby to stand aside, and told Mr. Trickey that if he wanted to speak with me, to proceed to my house, where I would hear

REPORTER HENRY G. TRICKEY.

what he had to say. Before moving from his tracks, he said, 'McHenry, I ought to kill you instantly.' I learned afterward that he had made the statement in Boston that there would be a funeral in Providence if he ever laid his eyes on me. In his published statement before referred to, he says that he was instructed before leaving Boston to treat me with the 'utmost consideration.' You can judge for yourself whether he did or not. I believe that he had been instructed to shoot me on the spot, and he would have done so had he the courage. We moved toward the house, and he marched in front. We entered, and left Kirby on the outside. We had a more rational talk about the publication and authenticity of the story, and he finally withdrew. As he backed down the steps, I told him I would shoot him dead in his tracks if he ever entered my house again. The next time I saw Trickey was on Broadway, New York, after he had left Boston. I was sent to this city to shadow and watch his movements, and I had kept track of him all the time up to the meeting of the Grand Jury. At the session of that body he was indicted on six counts. In the preparation and attempt at service of these warrants, there was some queer work, and I know that Trickey would have been arrested, had he not received a tip and skipped to Canada. He was in Boston when the warrants were issued, and had been for three days. I had him located, and was at the Attorney-General's office to get instructions as to how to proceed. He gave me a sealed letter of instructions to the clerk of the District Court in Taunton, and this I delivered in person. Instead of making out the warrant according to his orders, the clerk made them out to the Sheriff Constable, etc., of Bristol County. I did not know this at the time. There was in the room at the time the warrants were made out, State Officer Seaver, and he demanded that the clerk deliver the warrants to him for service. To this I most strenuously objected, and then there was a clash as to who was entitled to possession of the papers. I told Mr. Seaver that I was sorry to quarrel with a man whom I had always looked upon as a friend, but that I had been into this transaction from the start, and I proposed to stay in it until the finish. Without more ado I laid hands on the warrants and took them to Deputy Sheriff Brown of Attleboro, who in turn, delivered them into the hands of the Boston police. At police headquarters in Boston it was soon learned that the warrants were defective, inasmuch as they were made out in such a manner as not to be serviceable in any County except Bristol County. They had to be returned to the District Court in Taunton and rectified. This necessitated a delay of about twenty-eight hours, and gave somebody an opportunity to get Trickey out of the State. That is why he was not arrested. Mr. Seaver was especially desirous that I allow him to make the arrest of Mr. Trickey, but to this, as I said before, I successfully objected. There were some very strange things done in connection with these warrants, and if you doubt what I have said, I refer you to the records of the Boston police on the 15th of last October. This, briefly, is my connection with the Trickey-McHenry affair.''

In closing the interview I asked Mr. McHenry how many times Mr. Trickey visited his office in Providence during the carrying out of this work, and to this he replied, "Twelve." "My wife," said Mr. McHenry, "did a great deal of work in this case, and was of much service to the Fall River police. She was, I believe, the only woman who could and did succeed in getting the confidence of Bridget Sullivan. She was also of much assistance as a shadow, and was the famous veiled lady who was so mystifying to the newspaper men. She shadowed Trickey to Boston time and again, and on each occasion found that he went to the Pinkerton Detective Agency. Mr. Trickey always, after leaving my office, went to this place before he went to the office of the *Globe*."

Such is the statement of McHenry and it is but fair to say that the Fall River police admit that Captain Harrington was sent to Providence several times to overhear the conversation between Trickey and McHenry, and that Captain Desmond went one or more times. The police also admit that Mr. Trickey was indicted for tampering with a government witness.

There is, however, another side to this case, and that is the explanation made by Mr. Trickey of his conduct. It is conceded that he was one of the ablest and at the same time most brilliant man in his profession in the State, and there is no attempt made here to reflect discredit upon his methods or to question his honesty of purpose. Thus it is justice to him in giving his version of the affair. Before his departure from Boston and after the *Globe* had published its big story he made a written statement of connection with it, telling plainly of every move he made and of all the talk he had had with McHenry before and after the purchase of the story. This written statement was delivered into the hands of Superintendent John Cornish of the Pinkerton Detective Agency, and served as a basis for an extended investigation which the Pinkerton's carried on for months in Fall River, Providence, New York and Boston, with the intention of sifting the entire matter to its foundation. Mr. Trickey alleged, and his friends believe him, that McHenry was responsible for the injustice done the *Boston Globe* and that the detective actuated by motives of personal gain and revenge not only sacrificed Mr. Trickey and the *Globe* but deliberately misled the Fall River police and secured their sanction and co-operation in the deal. He startes out by saying that he was in Providence the early part of September on the lookout for the "lawyer story" and that he saw McHenry on the street. That the detective called him across and the two men entered into conversation, during which McHenry said that he had a good story to sell. "Well Mack" said Trickey "the *Globe* will pay as much for it as any other paper. '' '' Yes '' said the detective, '' but it's worth a great deal more to somebody else. '' '' who?'' asked Trickey. '' The defense '' replied McHenry. Then Trickey was given to understand that he could have the entire evidence in the Borden case for $1200. He says that McHenry gave him to understand that the matter would be sold only for the use of the defense and not for publication. Trickey didn't care anything about the defense, all he wanted was a story for his paper and with a view of getting it he humored McHenry by agreeing to call upon Col. Adams and ask him if he wanted to hire a good detective, one who could get at all the state's evidence against Miss Borden. Trickey did call upon Col. Adams and had a conversation about this matter with the result according to Trickey's statement that the lawyer didn't have any use for a detective and didn't care anything about investing his client's money in the purchase of the Commonwealth's case. In other words, Col. Adams refused to have anything to do with the proposed deal. But the reporter, knowing that his chances of securing the '' stuff '' for publication would be very materially lessened if he made known the result of his visit, concluded to act the part of an agent for the defense and represent to McHenry that Col. Adams did in reality desire to buy the story. With this conclusion in mind he again visited the detective and reported, (but wrongfully as he says) that the Colonel would buy if the price was lowered. McHenry then agreed to sell for $1000 and divide the money with Trickey. This was the reporter's opportunity. He knew that the *Globe* would give $500 and that sum he intended to pay over to the detective, representing that it came from Col. Adams, and that he had kept the other $500 as his share, according to agreement.

It might be said here that if any such deal as this was made the supporters of Mr. Trickey have failed to find a witness who overheard the bargain, while on the other hand the police deny that such a conversation ever took place and claim that Captain Harrington and others were in a position to hear all that was said upon the subject by Mr. Trickey and the detective. But this chapter is not an argument either for or against Mr. Trickey. His declaration goes on to say that after the 15th of September, or thereabout, he made numberless visits to the detective, and in this particular he agrees with the police version of the affair. He admits receiving the '' skeleton '' story first and later the names of the alleged witnesses, and that he did play the part of an agent for the defense prompted purely by a desire to get the story for publication. The fact that he hastened to print the story without further attempt to verify it, is due to two causes. First, he feared that McHenry would sell it to the *Boston Herald*. Second, that he had given a Fall River police officer (one whose name does not appear in this chapter,) the sum of $100 for a list of the witnesses in the case and they agreed with the names furnished by McHenry in the latter part of the transaction. The fact that it did agree convinced him that the story was all right and he did not want to take the chances of McHenry selling out to the *Herald*, so the agreement about the twenty-four hours notice was violated.

The writer has been assured by the police that if Mr. Trickey had given the twenty-four hours notice before publication the *Boston Globe* would have been spared the trouble of printing the "fake." In Justice to the *Boston Globe* it must be said that its editors made the most humble and abject apology for the wrong done Miss Borden by the publication of the " thirteen columns of lies " which Detective McHenry had sold to Mr. Trickey. The apology was made as prominent as the story had been and the Globe's position, although not an enviable one, appeared to be as graceful as the circumstances would admit.

It has been stated by persons who are in a position to know whereof they speak, that not only Mr. Trickey, but others were indicted for their apparent connection with this affair.

CHAPTER XXII.

BEGINNING OF THE SUPERIOR COURT TRIAL.

According to the arrangments already made, the trial of Miss Lizzie Borden commenced in New Bedford on the morning of the 5th of June, 1893. It was conducted before three Superior Court Judges. They were Chief Justice Albert Mason and Associate Justices Caleb Blodgett and Justin Dewey.

No spectators were allowed in the court room the first day of the trial, but this rule was not observed later. The only persons present at the opening were the 150 jurors from which twelve were to be selected, the court officers, a few of the intimate friends of the prisoner and thirty-five newspaper correspondents. Miss Borden was escorted to the court-house by Deputy Sheriff Kirby and to all appearances had not changed in the least during her ten months of confinement in Taunton jail. The court was opened by prayer by Rev. M. C. Julien, who spoke as follows:

"Almighty and all-wise God, our Father, we look to Thee as the only source of wisdom, as the only source of courage. We pray Thee that Thou wouldst grant that in entering on the solemn duties of this court, we shall have not only such help as comes from the experience of the past, through the history of the world, but such help as Thou, by Thy providence, wilt and canst give to Thy earthly children. We pray Thee that so innocence may be revealed and guilt exposed, to the glory of Thy own great name and the well being of the world. We ask it all for Thy name's sake. Amen."

The first day was devoted entirely to the selection of the Jury which was made up of the following named gentlemen.

Charles I. Richards, foreman, of North Attleboro; George Potter of Westport; William F. Deane of Taunton; John Wilbur of Somerset; Frederick C. Wilbar, of Raynham; Lemuel K. Wilber of Easton; Louis D. Hodges of Taunton; Augustus Swift of New Bedford; Frank G. Cole of Attleboro; John C. Finn of Taunton; William Wescott of Seekonk; and Allen H. Wordell of Dartmouth.

The second day of the trial was devoted to the opening of the case by the government's representative, Mr. William H. Moody, District Attorney of Essex County and assistant to District Attorney Knowlton of Bristol County.

During the afternoon of that day the Jury visited the scenes of the murder in Fall River. Mr. Moody spoke as follows:

May it please Your Honors, Mr. Foreman and Gentlemen of the Jury:

Upon the fourth day of August of the last year, an old man and woman, husband and wife, each without a known enemy in the world, in their own home, upon a frequented street in the most populous city in this county, under the light of day and in the midst of its activities, were, first one, then, after an interval of an hour, another, severally killed by unlawful human agency. To-day, a woman of good social position, of hitherto unquestioned character, a member of a Christian church and active in its good works, the own daughter of one of the victims, is at the bar of this court accused by the Grand Jury of this county of these crimes. There is no language, gentlemen, at my command, which can better measure the solemn importance of the inquiry which you are about to begin than this simple statement of facts. For the sake of these crimes and for the sake of these accusations, every man may well pause at the threshold of this trial and carefully search his understanding and conscience for any vestige of prejudice, and, finding it, cast it aside as an unclean thing. It is my purpose, gentlemen, and it is my duty to state to you at this time so much of the history of the cause and so much of the evidence which is to be introduced upon this trial as shall best enable you to understand the claim of the Government and to appreciate the force and application of the testimony as it comes from the witnesses on the stand. It is my purpose to do that in the plainest, simplest and most direct manner. And it is not my purpose to weary you with a recital of all the details of the evidence which is to come before you. Andrew Jackson Borden, the person named in the second part of the indictment, was at the time of his death a man of considerable property—somewhere, I believe, between $250,000 and $300,000. He had been retired from business for a number of years. He was a man who had obtained his fortune by earning and saving, and he retained the habit of saving up to the time of his death; and it will appear in the course of this trial that the family establishment was upon what might well be called, for a person in his circumstances, a narrow scale. He had been twice married. The first wife died some twenty-seven or twenty-eight years before he died, leaving two children, now alive—the prisoner at the bar, Lizzie

Andrew Borden, the younger, and then somewhere between two and three years of age, a sister, Miss Emma Borden, being a woman at the present time in the neighborhood of ten years older than the prisoner.   Not long after the death of the first wife Andrew Borden married again a woman whose maiden name, I believe, was Abby Durfee Gray.   The marriage, I believe, was something over twenty-five years before the time of their deaths, and there was no issue of the second marriage, at least none living and none that I have been informed of at any time.   Abby Durfee Borden, at the time of her death, was about six years younger than her husband, and that would make her, of course, sixty-four years of age.   Mr. Borden, I may say here, was a spare, thin man and somewhat tall.   Mrs. Borden was a short, fat woman, weighing, I believe, in the neighborhood of two hundred pounds.   The house in which these homicides were committed had been occupied by the Borden family for some twenty years. I shall have occasion to consider its construction and its relation to other buildings and streets later on in the course of this opening. There was, or came to be, between the prisoner and her stepmother, an unkindly feeling.   From the nature of the case, from the fact that those who know the most about that feeling, except the prisoner at the bar, are dead, it will be impossible for us at this hearing to get anything more than suggestive glimpses of that feeling.   It will appear that some five years before the death of Mr. and Mrs. Borden some controversy had arisen about some property, not important in itself.   Mr. Borden had seen fit to do some benefaction for a relative of Mrs. Borden, and in consequence of that fact the daughters thought that something should be done for them by way of pecuniary provision as an offset.   The details of what happened at that time are, as I have said, by no means important.   It is significant, however, that enough of feeling has been created by the discussion which arose to cause a change in the relations between the prisoner and Mrs. Borden.   Up to that time she had addressed her step-mother as " mother."   From that time she substantially ceased to do so.   We shall show to you that the spring before these homicides, upon some occasion where a talk arose between the prisoner and a person who did the cloak making for the family, the latter spoke of Mrs. Borden as "mother."   The prisoner at once repudiated that relation and said, "Don't call her mother.   She is a mean thing, and we hate her.   We have as little to do with her as possible." " Well, don't you have your meals with her?"   "Yes, we do some-times ; but we try not to, and a great many times we wait until they are over with their meals, and we stay in our own rooms as much as possible." I know of nothing that will appear in this case more significant of the feeling that existed between Mrs. Borden and the prisoner than a little incident which occurred not long after the discovery of these homicides. When one of the officers of the law, while the father and the step-mother lay at the very place where they had fallen under the blows of the assassin, was seeking information from the prisoner, he said, "When did you last see your mother?" "She is not my mother. My mother is dead." You cannot fail, I think, to be impressed in this respect with what will appear as to the method of living of this family. It will appear later on in the evidence that, although they occupied the same household, there was built up between them by locks and bolts and bars almost an impassable wall. In the early part of August of last year the older daughter, Miss Emma, was away, I believe at Fairhaven at the time. When Miss Emma was away the household that was left consisted of Mr. and Mrs. Borden and a servant, who had been in the service of the family nearly three years, Bridget Sullivan, and the prisoner. Upon the day preceding the homicides, John V. Morse, a brother of Mr. Borden's first wife, and, therefore, the uncle of his daughters, came upon a visit, or a passing visit, to the Bordens. The homicides, I may say now, were upon a Thursday, and the visit of Mr. Morse was on Wednesday. He came a little after the completion of the dinner; went away, I think, during the afternoon, returned in the evening and slept at the house upon the Wednesday night. Upon Tuesday night, Tuesday, August 2, an illness occurred in the household. Mr. and Mrs. Borden were taken suddenly ill with a violent retching and vomiting sickness, and it is said to a less degree the prisoner herself was affected by this illness. Bridget Sullivan was not. Upon the Wednesday morning Mr. and Mrs. Borden rose, feeling, of course, in the condition that people would be in after a night of that character, and Mrs. Borden consulted a physician with reference to her condition. Upon the noon of Wednesday, which you will keep in mind was the very day before these homicides, the prisoner went to a drug store in Fall River, the situation of which will be pointed out to you, and there asked the clerk for ten cents worth of prussic acid for the purpose of cleaning a sealskin cape. She was told that that was a poison which was not sold except on the prescription of a physician, and after some little talk went away. I think, gentlemen, you will be satisfied that there can be no question that the person who made this application for this deadly poison was the prisoner. There were three persons in the drug store, two of whom knew her by name and sight ; one of these, too, knew her as the daughter of Andrew J. Borden, and the third recognized her at once as he saw her.

On the evening of the Wednesday the prisoner made a call, not in itself unusual or peculiar, upon a friend of hers, Miss Alice Russell, and we shall commend to your careful attention what occurred during that interview. It will appear that the prisoner had been intending fo spend a vacation with a party of her friends at Marion, and had made some arrangements about going to Marion, and the talk between the two friends started upon that topic. The prisoner said : "I have made up my mind, Alice, to take your advice and go to Marion, and I have written there to them that I shall go, but I cannot help feeling depressed ; I cannot help feeling that something is going to happen to me ; I cannot shake it off. Last night, " she said, "we were all sick ; Mr. and Mrs. Borden were quite sick and vomited ; I did not vomit, and we are afraid that we have been poisoned ; the girl did not eat the baker's bread and we did, and we think it may have been the baker's bread. " " No. " said Miss Russell. "If it had been that some other people would have been sick in the same way. " " Well, it might have been the milk ; our milk is left outside upon the steps. " " What time is your milk left? " " At 4 o'clock in the morning. " " It is light then, and no one would dare to come in and touch it at that time. " " Well, " said the prisoner, probably that is so. But father has been having so much trouble with those with whom he has dealings that I am afraid some of them will do something to him. I expect nothing but that the building will be burned down over our heads. The barn has been broken into twice. " " That, " said Miss Russell "was merely boys after pigeons. " " Well, the house has been broken into in broad daylight when Maggie and Emma and I were the only ones in the house. I saw a man the other night when I went home lurking about the buildings, and as I came he jumped and ran away. Father had trouble with a man the other day about a store. There were angry words, and he turned him out of the house. " And so the talk went. That, I beg you to keep in your minds, was with Miss Russell—Alice M. Russell. There comes now the most difficult duty which I have in this opening. I am consoled, Mr. Foreman and gentlemen, by the fact that you will be aided beyond any explanation that I give you by a view of these premises that I am about to explain. . I hope I shall be able, even without the view, to

make myself entirely intelligible to you, because no one can understand this testimony that is to come and rightly reason upon it without an exact knowledge of the interior and exterior of that house.
In the first place, I may say that the house occupied by this family
was a common type of house in this community and in this State, a
house with the end to the street and the front door upon the end.
It was a rectangular house. It was situated upon Second street in
Fall River, which is one of the most frequented streets outside of the
main thoroughfares in the city, and is within, as all probably know,
a very short distance of the City Hall. It may fairly be called a
thoroughfare as well for foot passengers as for carriages. It is a
street used partly for residences and partly for business purposes.
Second Street runs substantially north and south. It is a street
which ascends toward the south. The higher part is south, the
lower part is north, and upon the east side of Second Street this
house is situated. At the south of the house is the residence of Dr.
Kelly, and also very near the house. To the north of the house, and
also near it, is the residence occupied by Mrs. Churchill, and diagonally in the rear of the house is the residence occupied by Dr.
Chagnon. The house is separated from the sidewalk by a wooden
fence, a picket fence, with two gates and in the rear of the yard, in
which is situated a barn, there is a high board fence, on the top and
the bottom of which there was at the time, and is, I believe, now, a
line of barbed wire. There are three exterior doors, three entrances
to these premises, and only three, excepting of course, the windows.
There is the front door leading directly from the sidewalk up a pair
of steps into the hall. There is a side door upon the north side,
facing Mrs. Churchill's house, leading into a small entryway which
leads into the kitchen. There is a third door exactly in the rear of
the house, which leads down to the cellar. There is what might be
called a porch, and a door leading into it, as you will see. As you
enter the front door you enter a hall, from which lead two doors, a
door into a parlor, which is the front room in the house, making the
northwest corner of the first story, a door leading into the sitting
room, and a stairway leading upstairs. Let us, in the first place, go
upstairs and see the arrangements there. It will aid us in considering this arrangement to remember that this house was originally a
double tenement house, and with the slight exception that I shall
refer to later on, the arrangement as it is upstairs is as it is upon the
first story. As you are about to see the premises, gentlemen, I do
not deem it wise to detain you at the present time by explaining this

plan in detail. I will try to make it as clear as I can by stating it to
you. As you turn and go upstairs from the front entry, you come
into a hallway. From that hallway lead three doors : first, a door
which leads into a large closet, used at this time for the keeping of
dresses, and which is almost large enongh to be a small bedroom ;
another door, which leads into the guest chamber, which is directly
over the parlor below, and corresponds to it in every respect. The
guest chamber is the chamber in which you will subsequently hear
that Mrs. Borden was found dead. It is a matter which is to be
carefully considered, that as you turn upon the journey upstairs, as
the stairs wind about, and to begin to face into the hall toward the
north, you can look directly into the door of the guest chamber. The
other door which leads from the hall is a door which leads into a
bedroom, and leads toward the rear of the house. Following, then,
my direction, gentlemen, as you come up the stairs, turn to your left.
As you approach the entry in front of you is the door leading into
the guest chamber, and to your right is the door leading into
a chamber which at that time was occupied by the prisoner. Between
the guest chamber and the bedroom of the prisoner there was a door.
I may as well dispose of it now for good. It was a door which always,
including the day of this homicide, was kept locked upon both sides,
and upon the side toward the prisoner's room there was against the
door a desk which she used. In other words it was not a practicable
opening. When you have got up into this part of the house, gentlemen, you can go nowhere except into this clothes closet, into this
guest chamber and into the room occupied by the prisoner. It is
important to remember that. All access to the other part of the
house is cut off not by the natural construction of the house but by
the way in which the house was kept. Follow me, if you please,
then, into the prisoner's bedroom. As you enter the bedroom a door
leads to the left into a room which has no other entrance than that
door. That is the room that was occupied by Miss Emma when she
was at home. The only access to it was through the prisoner's room.
There is another door at the rear of the prisoner's room,
and directly opposite the door of entrance which leads into the room
occupied by Mr. and Mrs. Borden, which is over the kitchen. The
prisoner's room was exactly over the sitting-room. The room in the
rear of the prisoner's room was exactly over the kitchen, and was
occupied as the bedroom of Mr. and Mrs. Borden. That door leading
into that room was kept always locked upon both sides. It was locked
upon the front toward the prisoner's room by a hook. It was locked

New Bedford Court House (outside).

NEW BEDFORD COURT HOUSE (INSIDE).

in the rear toward Mr. and Mrs. Borden's room by a bolt, and I may
as well say here as at any time that the proof that that door was
locked upon both sides upon this morning, from the morning down to
the time of the arrival of those who came alarmed by this homicide,
will be ample and complete. But as we go further, passing to the
rear into Mr. and Mrs. Borden's room, we find a door, and only a
single door, leading out into the entryway, which is over the entry-
way leading into the kitchen. That door, it will be clearly, amply
and satisfactorily proved, was locked all through this day up to and
beyond the time of the homicide. Now then, gentlemen, if I have
made myself clear upon this description, which is wearisome, I know,
but it is one of the wearisome duties that we must undertake in this
cause. I have made it clear to you that as you go up the hallway
you get access to but four rooms, the hallway itself, if you call that
a room, the closet, the guest chamber in which Mrs. Borden was
found, and the room of the prisoner and the room leading out of that,
the blind room, so to speak, that was occupied by Miss Emma when
she was at home, and there is no other access whatever to the rear of
the house. Now, gentlemen, let me, at the expense of being tedious,
go below. As you enter the hallway below, it is, I believe, exactly
as above, except, of course, there is no clothes closet there as there
is above. There are two small closets, very small ones, as you will
see. To your left as you enter is the door which leads into the
parlor under the room where Mrs. Borden was found dead. Going
straight ahead you enter into the sitting room, which is a room in the
rear of the hall at the south of the house, and directly under and
corresponding to the prisoner's bed room. Now you come to a
difference of construction in the two stories. You turn to
the left from the sitting room as you enter and you enter
the dining room, which is upon the north side of the house and is
directly under Miss Emma's room, and a large room, which was used
as a closet by Mr. Borden and which joined his room, another blind
room. That difference is made either by the taking down or putting
up of a partition. You enter the dining room and there is a door of
exit which goes into the kitchen. Above, that arrangement is varied
by a partition directly down through the room, which would
correspond to the door leading from the sitting room to the dining
room, leads from Miss Emma's room to the bedroom of the prisoner,
and the door corresponding to the door leading from the dining room
to the kitchen leads from the room which adjoins the blind room,
which adjoin the bedroom of Mr. and Mrs. Borden, so that the effect

of that partition is that while there is free communication two ways from the kitchen to the front part of the house downstairs, upstairs this partition reduces those ways of communication to one, and that one, you will recall, always and upon the day of the homicide was barred by two doors, locked. Again, gentlemen, I say that the difficulty of understanding this is great, but I am confronted by the fact that you will be aided by a view of these premises. Mr. Morse returned upon a Wednesday night. It is important to show who occupied the house on Wednesday night. Let us go first to the front part of the house. The prisoner came in the last one that night and locked the front door. Upon that front door were three fastenings, a spring latch, a bolt and a lock which operated by key. Those three fastenings were closed, by the way, when she came in, the last person that night by the front way of the house. The door leading into the cellar, the other exterior door, had been closed since Tuesday, the washing day, and by complete and ample evidence will be proved to you to have been closed all through Wednesday night and on Thursday morning including up to and beyond the time of those homicides. Bridget came in through the back door that night, found the back door locked when she came, unlocked it, locked it as she went in, went upstairs and went to bed. So, when Bridget and the prisoner had come in at their respective doors, every exterior approach to this house was closed.

Now, in the front part of the house that night the prisoner slept in one room, Mr. Morse slept in the guest chamber. There was no other room in that part of the house, except Miss Emma's room, which led out, as you still remember, of Miss Lizzie's room. Mr. and Mrs. Borden slept in the room over the kitchen, and Bridget slept in some room above in the third story of the house. Now, then, it becomes my duty to relate in considerable detail all that occurred in that household down to the time of the discovery of these homicides. In the morning Bridget was the first person up. We may safely assume that upon the proof the only human beings who were in that house at the time were Bridget, Mr. and Mrs. Borden, John V. Morse and the prisoner at the bar. Bridget comes down stairs first, the back way, goes down cellar and gets her fuel, builds up a fire in the stove; then she went to the door, took in the milk, unlocking the door, locked it after she got through. The rear door, I may explain here, was a double door; it was an ordinary wooden panel door which was used at night, and a screen door, which was used, at least, in hot weather, during the day time and was fastened by a hook on the inside. When the outside door was opened by Bridget at that time it was opened for good for the day, and the method of security was keeping the screen door locked from that time on. The next person who came down was Mrs. Borden. Bridget came down a little after 6; Mrs. Borden came down a little before 7. Next Mr. Borden comes down, and after coming down goes out into the yard and empties his slop pail and unlocks the door to the barn. Bridget saw him do that. Bridget did not see Mr. Morse until they all met at breakfast, a little after 7. Mr. and Mrs. Borden and Mr. Morse taking breakfast together. It will appear what the material of their breakfast was, but it is not important at all for me to state it at this time. After breakfast the first one to depart is Mr. Morse. He goes away at a quarter of 8, and Mr. Borden lets him out and locks the screen door behind him. Soon after Mr. Morse went away the prisoner came down stairs and began eating her breakfast, or what took the place of a breakfast, in the kitchen. While she was there Mr. Borden went upstairs, and while Mr. Borden was upstairs Bridget went out into the yard, because she was sick and desired to vomit. She was gone some minutes, just how long I cannot tell. When she came back, Mr. Borden had apparently gone down town. The prisoner was in the kitchen and Mrs. Borden was in the dining room dusting. There was some talk then between Mrs. Borden and Bridget about washing the windows on the inside and the outside, and Bridget received the directions from Mrs. Borden to do that service. Mrs. Borden disappeared at this time, and it will appear that she told the prisoner that, having made the bed in the spare room, she was going upstairs to put two pillow cases upon two pillows that were there—a trifling duty, a duty which would take less than a minute. You will be satisfied, gentlemen, that that was not far from half-past nine o'clock, and upon the evidence you will be satisfied that she never left that room alive, and that she was killed within a very few moments after she left the room, because no living person saw Mrs. Borden from that time until her death, except the assailant. In the course of beginning the duty of washing these windows Bridget had to go to the barn and down cellar to get some of the implements for doing the work. As she was at the screen door, about to go out, the prisoner appeared at that back door, and Bridget said to her. "You needn't lock that door, because I am coming in to get my water to wash the windows; but you may," she said, "if you wish, and I will get my water from the barn," as she did. The prisoner said nothing, and I believe it to be the fact, as the evidence will disclose it, that the door was not locked at that time. Then Bridget went into the kitchen and dining room and sitting room to close the windows in the sitting room and the dining room, and there was nobody there—neither the prisoner nor Mrs. Borden, who were the only two human beings in the house at that time except Bridget. In washing these windows there were two of the sitting room windows upon the south side of the house which were out of sight of the screen door, because they were on the other side of the house. Those two windows were washed first on the outside. Then Bridget came to the front of the house, washed two windows facing the street ; then she came to the south side of the house, the Mrs. Churchill side, and washed the parlor window and the two dining room windows. During all the time that Bridget was washing those windows she saw neither Mrs. Borden nor the prisoner in any part of the lower part of the house or anywhere else. When she finished washing the windows on the outside she came in at the screen door and hooked it behind her, and began to wash the windows upon the inside of the same windows that she had washed upon the outside. First, she went into the sitting room, which is upon the Kelly side, the south side of the house. She had partly washed one of the two sitting room windows when somebody was heard at the front door.

Now, gentlemen, let us pause a moment and find out, as well as we can, what time that somebody came to the front door, because it was Mr. Borden. Mr. Borden, it will appear, left the house some time between 9 and 9:30 o'clock in the morning. He was at two banks, two or three banks, between 9:30 or at twenty-nine minutes of 11—I am not quite sure which—he was at the store of a Mr. Clegg, who fixes the exact time. The next place we find him is at another store, which belonged to him, upon South Main street, near the corner of Spring and not far from his own home. He left there, apparently in the direction of his home, at twenty minutes of 11. That was a moment or two's walk from there to his house. The next we see of him is that he is seen by Mrs. Kelly, who lived upon one side of his house, and who was going down town, coming around, apparently, from the screen door, where he had attempted to get in, out upon the sidewalk and toward his own front door, taking out his key to open it. Mrs. Kelly will fix that time at twenty-seven or twenty-eight minutes of 11, which cannot be reconciled with the other time that I have stated here. There will be some explanation of that, and we think you will be satisfied that the clock by which she obtained this time was not one that could be depended upon, and that the real fact is that at twenty minutes of 11 Mr. Borden started to his home, which was but a moment or two's walk away. Now, then, we fix that as well as we can. When Mr. Borden came home, contrary to the usual custom in that house, Bridget found the front door locked with the key and bolted, as well as secured by the spring lock. Mr. Borden had not rung the bell. He had put his key in and made the noise which people usually do who expect to get in the house by the use of a latch key. But the door was locked and bolted. He came into the house, and as Bridget let him in made some talk or explanation about the difficulty of unloosening the locks. The prisoner from the hall above made some laugh or exclamation. At that time, gentlemen, Mrs. Borden's body lay within plain view of that hall, dead, probably, more than an hour. Mr. Borden came in, went first into the dining room. There the prisoner came to him, asked him if there was any mail and said to him, " Mrs. Borden has gone out; she had a note from somebody who was sick." That, gentlemen, we put to you as a lie, intended for no purpose except to stifle inquiry as to the whereabouts of Mrs. Borden. Mr. Borden then took his key, went upstairs, came down again, and, as he came down, Bridget had finished the other window and a half in the sitting room and was just going into the dining room to finish those windows. As she was washing the windows in the dining room the prisoner again appeared from the front part of the house, went to the kitchen, got an ironing board and began to iron her handkerchiefs. While there she told Bridget this falsehood about the note. She said, " Are you going out, Bridget, by and by ? " Bridget said : " I don't know ; I am not feeling very well to-day." " Well," she said, " if you do I want you to be careful about the locks ; I may go out myself. Mrs. Borden has gone out." " Where is she ? " said Bridget. " I don't know ; it must be somewhere in town, because she received a note to go to a sick friend." Bridget finished the washing of the windows in the dining room and her work was done. She went out into the kitchen, put her cloth away, emptied the water and was about to go upstairs, when the prisoner said to her : " There is a cheap sale of goods down town, Bridget, where they are selling some kind of cloth for eight cents a yard." Bridget says : " Well, I guess I will have some." And Bridget went upstairs. Now, gentlemen, probably all that occurred after Mr. Borden came in occurred in less time than perhaps it has taken me to tell it. We can measure time better by seeing what is done in the time than by the estimate of any witness of the time. After Bridget went upstairs there is nothing more that happened

until the alarm is given to her. Now, pursuing the same course, let
me so far as possible fix the time of that alarm. I shall have to
anticipate somewhat in doing it. Bridget, upon the alarm, came
down stairs, was immediately sent diagonally across the street for Dr.
Bowen ; returned rapidly, and was sent away for Miss Russell. As
Bridget went away Mrs. Churchill by accident came to the
house, or got the alarm and came to the house. There was
a moment's conversation between the prisoner and Mrs. Churchill.
Mrs. Churchill ran out, ran diagonally across the street to a
stable, there gave some sort of alarm, was seen by a man named
Cunningham, who heard what she said and went to a telephone in a
paint shop near by, telephoned to the Marshal of Fall River, who
gave directions to an officer to go to the spot. The officer, having a
duty which called his attention to the time, looked at his watch and
found it was quarter-past eleven. Now, then, gentlemen, stopping a
moment, let us try to find out as well as we can these times. It could
not have been, upon the evidence, far from quarter of 11 o'clock
when Mr. Borden returned. It could not, upon this evidence, have
been far from quarter-past 11 when the alarm reached the station.
Therefore the time between Bridget's going upstairs and down again
must be diminished on the one side by the time consumed by the
washing of a window and a half in the sitting room and two windows
in the dining room and the putting away of the cloth and water. On
the other side, the half hour between 11 o'clock and half-past 11 must
be diminished by the acts of Bridget and the acts of Mrs. Churchill
and the acts of Cunningham, which I have described. I shall not
attempt to fix that time ; you can fix it better and measure it better
yourself when you come to hear the evidence of what was done by
Bridget between the time Mr. Borden came and the noise was heard
upstairs and what was done between the time when the alarm took
place and the alarm reached the station house and the Marshal of
Fall River.

Now, gentlemen, you will be struck by the fact through the
evidence that is to come, that instinctively there leaped to the lips of
every inquiring person, of the prisoner, where were you before a
thought of the suspicion was over her head. She had been the last
person left with her father alive. When Bridget came down that
question arose, and she says: " Where were you, Miss Lizzie?" It
is not clear what the prisoner told Bridget, whether he was sick, or
killed, or dead. That is not important, but the moment the information was received arose the question: " Where were you?" She
said: " I was out in the back yard; I heard a groan, came in and

found the door open and found my father." Bridget was then sent to Dr. Bowen. She came down, found the prisoner somewhat agitated standing by the screen door and inside. There had been no screech, no alarm of any kind, and there was an attempt simply to secure the presence of Dr. Bowen. She came back unsuccessful from the search for Dr. Bowen. As she came back she was seen by Mrs. Churchill, who, looking out of her kitchen window, saw the prisoner standing inside the door, and something in her appearance attracted her and she called out to her. In the meantime the prisoner had said to Bridget, "You go down to Miss Russell's house." And gentlemen, it will in this connection occur to you that Miss Russell, though she lived a long distance away from this house, was the person to whom this prisoner was predicting disaster the very night before. Mrs. Churchill came there by accident, and she will testify in detail as to what had occurred after she came there. She, too, said, "Lizzie, where were you?" "I was out in the barn. I was going for a piece of iron when I heard a distressed noise, came in and found the door open, and found my father dead." Bridget returns from Miss Russell's, and, returning says: "Shall I not go down to Mrs. Whitehead's for Mrs. Borden?" "No," said the prisoner, "I am almost sure I heard her come in." Up to that time, by alarm, by screaming or by any attempt had there not been an effort on the part of the prisoner to communicate with Mrs. Borden. "I wish you would look," she said, "and see if you can't find Mrs. Borden." Mrs. Churchill and Bridget together went up this front stairway, turned, as they do turn, to their left, and as they turned Mrs. Churchill turned her head above the level of the floor. She looked in and saw Mrs. Borden's dead body as she looked under the bed. It is to be regretted that Dr. Bowen, a witness accustomed to observation, was the family physician and friend, and, therefore, affected, naturally, by this dreadful series of murders, for we might expect from him something of accurate observation, but Dr. Bowen thought Mrs. Borden had died of fright, and so expressed himself at the time. I do not and shall not attempt in detail to tell you all that occurred for an hour or two after the discovery of these homicides. Soon after people came in. The prisoner, who had never been in the room where her father lay dead, passed from the dining room diagonally through the corner of the sitting room, without stopping to look at her dead father, upstairs by the room where her step-mother lay dead, without an inquiry, without a thought; went into her own room, lay down; soon, without a suggestion from any one, changed her dressed and put on a loose pink wrapper. There are one or two things, however, in what she said that I ought to call your attention to at the present time. She told Dr. Bowen at that time that she was out in the barn for a piece of iron; she told Miss Russell that she went into the barn for a piece of iron or tin to fix a screen; she told Officer Mullaly that she went out into the barn, and upon being asked whether she heard anything or not, she said she heard a peculiar noise, something like a scraping noise, and came in and found the door open. There is, therefore, Bridget Sullivan, to whom she said she heard a groan, rushed in and found her father; Mrs. Churchill, to whom she said she heard a distressed noise, came in and found her father; Officer Mullaly, to whom she said she heard a peculiar noise like scraping, came in and found her father dead; and all these, gentlemen, you see in substance are stories which include the fact that while she was outside she heard some alarming noise which caused her to rush in and discover the homicide. Well, gentlemen, as inquiry begins to multiply upon her as to her whereabouts, another story comes into view, and she repeats it again and again, and finally repeats it under oath, that at the time Bridget went upstairs she went out into the barn, and into the loft of the barn to get lead to make sinkers. Now, gentlemen, having in view the character of her statements, that she heard the noise, you will find that when she gave a later and detailed account, she said that she went into the loft of the barn, opened the window, ate some pears up there, and looked over some lead for sinkers, came down, looked in the stove to see if the fire was hot enough that she might go on with her ironing, found it was not, put her hat down, started to go upstairs to await the fire which Bridget was to build for the noonday, and discovered her father. It is not, gentlemen, and I pray your attention to it, a difference of words here. In the one case the statement is that she was alarmed by the noise of the homicide. In the other side the statement is that she came coolly, deliberately about her business, looking after her ironing, putting down her hat, and accidentally discovered the homicide as she went upstairs. Gentlemen, upon this point it is my duty to point out to you a piece of testimony which will be for your consideration. This day, August 4, 1892, was one of the hottest days of the last summer in this vicinity. The loft of the barn was stifling in the intensity of its heat. Officer Medley, who came there quite early after the alarm, went to the barn and went up the stairs of the barn. He had, at that time heard of her going up into the loft, and as his head came up on a level with the floor of the barn he saw that it was thickly covered with dust. He stopped, put his hands upon the floor and drew them across, and saw the marks of them. He looked again, stepped up, counting his footsteps upon a part of the barn floor, came down into his position again and saw plainly every footstep which he made. I have said to you, gentlemen, that Mrs. Borden died some time before her husband, and it is my duty to open to you the proof upon that question. There will be many here who observed the two bodies as they lay. I shall not attempt to state their evidence in detail. It will tend to show that Mr. Borden's body showed freshly flowing blood ; was warm and was not rigid in death; that Mrs. Borden's body showed blood that was coagulated and hardened and dry ; that her body was cold, and that she was stiffened in death. There will be the judgments of some professional men who observed the two bodies soon after the discovery of the homicides. There will be other important testimony in this case. The stomachs of the two victims were taken to Prof. Edward S. Wood, who examined them and is prepared to state their exact contents. The stomach of Mrs. Borden contained eleven ounces of food in progress of digestion. One-fifth of that eleven ounces was water and four-fifths of it was this partially digested food. Mr. Borden's stomach—and you will remember that they ate breakfast at the same time—contained only six ounces of matter, and nine-tenths of that was water, and only one-tenth solid food ; so you will see there was a very marked difference in the contents of their stomachs. Upon the autopsy it appeared that the upper intestines, leading directly from the stomach—the intestine into which the contents of the stomach first pass—in Mrs. Borden's case was empty of food. Now, gentlemen, you will have the opinion of many who are competent to give an opinion upon all these facts, and they will say to you that upon those facts alone they are able to give a judgment that Mrs. Borden must have died at least an hour before her husband. And that, gentlemen, you will remember and take into view with the fact that anywhere between nine and half-past nine o'clock she went upstairs for a mere temporary purpose, and apparently never left the room that she went to.

Now, gentlemen, it will appear that about the two rooms in which the homicides were committed there was blood spattered in various directions, so that it would make it probable that one or more spatters of blood would be upon the person or upon the clothing of the assailant. And there has been produced for the inspection of the Commonwealth—it was produced a good many days after the homicide—the clothing said to have been worn by the prisoner on the morning of August 4—the shoes, stockings, dress, skirt.'' At this point the articles of clothing mentioned were produced and placed on the table, after which Mr. Moody continued as follows : ''The most rigid examination by the most competent expert in this country fails to disclose any marks of blood upon the dress which is produced as the one she wore on the morning of the homicide, and upon the skirt which she is said to have worn upon that morning is one minute spot of blood, which I do not think it worth while to call to your attention at the present time. I must go back a moment in this story. You have in mind, of course, the interval which elapsed between the two homicides. The prisoner has said—and it is important to consider, and we shall prove that she has said—that the reason she left her ironing was because she found the fire was low ; that she took a stick of wood, put it on top of the embers of the fire and went out to the barn to await its kindling; that when she went out it was smoking and smoldering, as if it was going to catch ; that when she came back the stick of wood was there and the fire had all gone out. It will appear—and it was pure accident that this observation was made—that soon after the alarm an officer of Fall River was attracted by something that Dr. Bowen was doing to the stove—I do not mean to suggest anything—but the fact that he was tearing up a note and was going to put it into the stove, and he looked in and saw what was there, and found a large roll of what appeared to be burnt paper. The prisoner had a calico, or cotton dress, perhaps I ought to say, which she was in the habit of wearing mornings. It was a light blue dress, with a fixed figure, a geometrical figure of some sort, and the figure was not white, but navy-blue—a darker blue. Dr. Bowen has said, and I have no doubt will say here now, that she had on a cheap calico dress, a sort of drab colored dress. Mrs. Churchill says she had on, that morning, a light blue ground with white in it—that is, white in the blue, not a white figure, but white in the blue, to make it lighter blue, I suppose, and a mixed figure of navy blue, without a white spot in it at all, a diamond figure of navy blue, as she will describe it. And upon being shown that dress (showing dress to the jury), she will say that it is not the dress that the prisoner at the bar had on when she came in upon the morning of the homicide. You will recall that soon after the homicide Miss Russell and the prisoner went to the bed room of the prisoner. While they were there the prisoner said, '' I think I had better have Winwood for undertaker, '' and Miss Russell went away upon the errand of getting Dr.

Bowen to see about the undertaker. And as Miss Russell came back she found the prisoner coming from Emma's room with the pink wrapper on that I have described to you before—the loose wrapper. Upon Saturday night the chief executive officer of the city of Fall River, Mayor Coughlin, informed Lizzie Andrew Borden that she was under suspicion for these murders. Saturday night Bridget Sullivan left the house. Alice Russell was staying with her friend, and of course Miss Emma was at home at that time.

On the morning of Sunday Miss Russell came into the kitchen. There were officers about on the outside of the house, but none in, and there was the prisoner with the skirt of her dress upon her arm, and what appeared to be its waist lying upon some shelf, and we will describe that dress. It was a dress which the prisoner had purchased in the spring of that year, a cotton dress and not a silk dress like this (holding a dark blue silk dress up to view). It was a light blue dress. You will recall Mrs. Churchill's description of that in this connection. It was a light blue dress with a fixed navy blue spot on it. The dress ordinarily worn in the morning corresponds to that description, and was also bought in the spring. As she saw the prisoner standing by the stove and as she approached her, Miss Emma turned round and said, "Lizzie, what are you going to do?" The prisoner replied, "I am going to burn this dress, it is all covered with paint." Miss Russell turned away. She came again into the room and she found the prisoner standing with the waist of the light blue dress, apparently tearing it in parts, and said, "Lizzie, I would not do that where people can see you." The only response which the prisoner made was to take a step or two further out of observation. Miss Russell turned again and went away. Upon the following day, in consequence of some talk with Mr. Hanscom, a Pinkerton detective not in the employ of the Government, Miss Russell went into the room where the prisoner and her sister Emma were sitting and said: "Lizzie, I am afraid the burning of that dress was the worst thing that you could have done." She said: "Oh, why did you let me do it then?" A considerable search had been made by the officers for clothing and for weapons, and they will say that no clothing unconcealed covered with paint could have escaped their observation. You have noticed, Mr. Foreman and gentlemen, this indictment, a more particular description of which is to the jurors unknown. It is the duty of the Government to bring forward all its information upon this subject, and I propose to open it all to you at the present time. Upon the premises that day were found two

hatchets and two axes. Upon one of those hatchets spots were discovered, which, upon view, were thought to be blood.   It is
extremely difficult, impossible, in fact, Dr. Wood, the highest authority on this subject in this country, if not in the world, will say, to
distinguish between blood and some other substances.   Attention
upon the view then was directed to one of these hatchets, it is not
important which (holding both hatchets in hand before the jury.)
It is said to be the one I hold in my right hand.   These axes, gentlemen, are so far out of the question that I need not waste any time
on them.   They could not have been the weapons with which these
homicides were committed.   Upon careful examination neither of
these hatchets is seen to contain the slightest evidence of blood stain.
The appearances which were thought to be blood turned out to be
something else.   You will observe, gentlemen, that there are ragged
pieces near and about the entrance of the handle to the blade of this
hatchet, that the same appearances exist there in that weapon, also
on the outside of the handle, and Dr. Wood will say to you that
those weapons could not in all probability have been used for these
homicides, and have been washed so as to have prevented the traces
of blood from being caught on those ragged surfaces.   In that view
of the fact we may well lay those weapons aside as entirely
innocent.   Upon the day of the homicide another weapon, or part of
a weapon, that was thought to be a bloody hatchet, had been discovered and attracted little attention.   It was seen by one officer, and
left where it was.   At that time this fragment of the handle was in
its appropriate place in the helve, if that is the proper name, of the
hatchet, in the place fitted in the head.   It was covered with an
adhesion of ashes, not the fine dust which floats about the room
where ashes are emptied, but a coarse dust of ashes adhering more
or less to all sides of the hatchet.   Upon the Monday morning this
hatchet was taken away, and its custody from that time to the
present will be traced.

You will observe, gentlemen, that both hatchets are rusty, the
hatchet which is innocent, the handless hatchet now under discussion,
but the rust in the case of the handless hatchet is uniform upon both
sides and upon all parts of its surface, such rust, for instance, as
might be the result of exposure upon wet grass to the night's dew,
such rust as must result from an exposure uniform in its extent upon
all parts of the hatchet.   Prof. Wood will say to you—he saw this
hatchet soon after it was found—that while there were ragged
fragments of wood which would detain absolutely no indications of

the blood in these weapons, that if that weapon had had upon it the remainder of the hatchet, and was as smooth as he saw, by the application of water soon after the homicide, blood could be readily, effectually and completely removed. Dr. Wood will also tell you that that break which had not the color then which it has now—it has been subjected to some acid process—was a new break and was a fresh break. By that I do not mean to be understood as a break which had necessarily occurred within twenty-four hours, within forty-eight hours, or within a week, but perhaps a break which might have been a day or might have been a month old. It was a fresh break. In accordance, Mr. Foreman and gentlemen, with the unbroken practice of the authorities in this Commonwealth, such parts of the mortal remains of the victims as would tend to throw light either in the protection of innocence or the detection of guilt, have been preserved and must be presented here before you for your consideration. I do not think it is necessary for me to allude to them at this time. There is one story that is unmistakably told by those skulls and by the chipping blows that are upon them, and that is that the weapon which produced them was a sharp weapon. There is another thing that is unmistakably told by one of the skulls—I think that of Mr. Borden—and that is that the weapon which brought him to his death was just three and one half inches on its blade, no more, no less. That is the exact measurement of the blade of that hatchet. Let there be no mistake, Mr. Foreman and gentlemen, about my meaning. The Government does not insist that these homicides were committed by this handleless hatchet. It may have been the weapon. It may well have been the weapon. The one significant fact which in this respect is emphasized is that the bloody weapon was not found by the sides of the victims, upon the premises, or near them. Doubtless you will consider that fact well when you come to consider whether these homicides were the acts of an intruder or stranger flying from his crimes with the bloody weapon in his possession, through the streets of Fall River at noonday, or the acts of an inmate of the house, familiar with its resources for destruction, obliteration and concealment. When these bodies were found it was discovered that not a thing in the house had been disturbed. No property had been taken. No drawers had been ransacked. Mr. Borden had upon his person a considerable sum of money as well as his watch and chain. We almost might hope that it was not necessary to exclude another motive, but sad experience tells us that age of a woman is no protection from an assault from lustful purpose, but I may say, gentlemen, there was nothing to indicate a motive of that sort.   In and about the rooms where these two homicides were committed there was not the slightest trace of a struggle.   The assailant, whoever he or she may have been, was able to approach each victim in broad daylight and without a struggle and without a murmur to lay them low before him.   Mrs. Borden was found prostrated between the bureau and the bed, her face upon the floor and the right side of her head hacked to pieces by blows, some of great force, some of uncertain and vacillating weakness.   Mr. Borden was found reclining on a sofa in the sitting room and apparently had passed from life to death without a struggle or a movement, and his head, too, bore the same marks as the head of his wife bore.   It will appear that no one, and it is confirmatory evidence, not in itself of the strongest character, but confirmatory of the conclusive evidence of the opportunity in the house—it will appear that no one was seen to escape from any side of that house nor to enter that house on the morning of August 4.

Gentlemen, let me stop a moment and see where we are.   The Commonwealth will prove that there was an unkindly feeling between the prisoner and her step-mother; that upon Wednesday, August 3, she was dwelling upon murder and preparing herself with a weapon which had no innocent use; that upon the evening of Wednesday, August 3, she was predicting disaster and cataloguing defences; that from the time when Mrs. Borden left the dining room to go upstairs for this momentary errand, up to the time when the prisoner came down stairs an hour later from this hallway which led only to her chamber and that in which Mrs. Borden was found, there was no other human being except the prisoner at the bar present; that these acts were the acts of a human being; that they were the acts of a person who, to have selected time and place as it was selected in this case, must have had a familiar knowledge of the interior of the premises and of the whereabouts and the habits of those who were in occupation of them at that time.   We shall prove that this prisoner made contradictory statements about her whereabouts, and, above all, gave a statement virtually different upon the manner in which she discovered these homicides.   We shall prove beyond all reasonable doubt that this death of Mrs. Borden was a prior death.   Then we shall ask you to say, if say you can, whether any other reasonable hypothesis except that of the guilt of this prisoner can account for the said occurrence which happened upon the morning of August 4.   Now, gentlemen, my present duty is drawing to its close. The time for idle rumor, for partial, insufficient information, for hasty and inexact reasoning, is past. We are to be guided from this time forth by the law and the evidence only. I conjure you to keep you minds in that same open and receptive condition in which you have sworn they were; I pray you to keep them so to the end. If, when that end comes, after you have heard the evidence upon both sides, the arguments of counsel, the instructions of the Court, the evidence fails, God forbid that you should move one step against the law or beyond the evidence to the injury of this prisoner. But if your minds, considering all these circumstances, are led irresistibly to the conclusion of her guilt, we ask you in your verdict to declare the truth : and by so doing, and only by so doing, shall you make true deliverance of the great issue which has been committed to your keeping.

CHAPTER XXIII.

Third Day of the Trial.

CIVIL Engineer Thomas Kieran gave an exhaustive statement of measurements he had made on the premises. James A. Walsh, photographer, of Fall River, testified as to the accuracy of the pictures he had made of the victims and the house on the day of the killing. John Vinnecum Morse was the third witness called. His examination was conducted by District Attorney Moody, and was not different in any manner from that at the preliminary trial. Abram G. Hart, treasurer of the Union Savings Bank, testified as to Mr. Borden's movements on the morning of the 4th of August. As also did John T. Burrill, cashier of the Union National Bank, Everett M. Cook, cashier of the First National Bank, Jonathan Clegg, a hat dealer, Joseph Shortsleeves, a carpenter, and John Maher a carpenter.

The afternoon of Wednesday, the third day of the trial was devoted entirely to the examination of Bridget Sullivan. Bridget's testimony did not differ materially from that given in the lower courts. Her direct examination was the same as appears heretofore. On cross examination by Mr. Robinson these facts were disclosed.

She had lived with the Bordens nearly three years and it was a pleasant family to live with so far as she knew. She never saw any quarrelling but she didn't see the family all this time. It was customary for Lizzie and Emma to eat alone; sometimes, however, they ate with the family. They usually slept later than the others. Lizzie spoke to Mrs. Borden and Mrs. Borden spoke to her. Lizzie gave her a civil answer on the morning of the murder. Going back to the house with his questioning Mr. Robinson asked her if she locked the screen door when she returned from the yard, and told her that she had testified before that she did not know whether she had hooked it or not. This confused the witness and she finally said she didn't know whether she hooked it or not. She did not remember what was asked her about the family eating together, when she was questioned at the inquest, but she was ready to say now that they

always ate together so far as she knew. Bridget had nothing to do
with the front part of the house and seldom went in those rooms ; she
could not got go into those rooms unless she got a key, which was
kept on the mantel in the sitting room ; there was a door bell for
upstairs, but she knew nothing about it ; nobody else occupied the
attic with the witness the night before the murder. She got up at
6:15 by her bedroom clock. There was a clock in every room. Mr.
Robinson required her to tell again what was on the breakfast table.
Bridget added that they had butter, which occasioned some little
merriment. He tried Bridget's memory by asking her what Mrs.
Borden did on Wednesday morning. He got an answer. She was
positive that Lizzie had on a blue wrapper Wednesday morning, but
she could not tell the kind of dress she wore Thursday morning. In
the afternoon she had on a pink wrapper. There was a kitchen closet
in the back corner of the north side of the house which she had
occasion to enter; it had a window in it, but she did not know how
it was—open or shut; all the time she was washing windows the
screen door was unhooked ; she did not anticipate that there would
be any trouble, and she went to the barn six or seven times to get
water; this was while the door was unhooked. She went to the
corner of the yard on the south side of the house and talked to Mrs.
Kelly's girl, and anybody could have entered the side door and not be
seen by her. " Well, " said Robinson, "the coast was clear while
you stood talking to the Kelly girl!" " Yes, " said Bridget, " I
could see the front door but I conld not see the side door. " Bridget
did not enter the front part of the house that morning until she heard
a noise at the front door ; the last time she saw Mr. Borden before he
went out was when he took his pitcher and key and went up the back
stairs ; while she was drawing water in the barn, she saw no one and
did not look for any one. She might have seen them if they came
and might not; witness could not tell anything about the parlor or
its windows; if any one was in that room she would not have known
it ; after she had finished work she came into the house and locked
the door on the inside; as she let Mr. Borden in the front door
she heard Lizzie laugh, but did not see her; Lizzie was afterward
talking with her father about the mail; she did not pay any attention
to what was said, but the talk was pleasant.

Didn't pay any attention to the fire and didn't know whether it was
out or not ; the flats were on the stove ; thinks Lizzie had them there;
while Lizzie ate her cookies and coffee witness was out in the back
yard ; thinks she got upstairs about three minutes before 11 o'clock

and had seen nothing wrong about the house; Lizzie said to her, "Maggie, come down quick; father is killed," or words which meant the same; then she went right off to get Dr. Bowen; she could not tell whether the door was locked or not; in fact, she was confused and cannot remember just what did happen for awhile. When she returned from Alice Russell's house, Dr. Bowen was in the house and so was Mrs. Churchill; she did not see any blood on Lizzie; after awhile Lizzie went upstairs. "I did not see anybody come with a note; I think I would have seen them had they entered the back door," said Bridget. When she went to go upstairs with Mrs. Churchill she passed through the dining room, and Lizzie was then left in the kitchen. Mr. Borden was then on the sofa covered up with a sheet, and when Lizzie went upstairs she passed through the sitting room also. Witness thought it was about 10:30 o'clock when Mr. Borden entered the front door. On Wednesday morning she learned that all of the family had been ill the night before. That is the day she had on the light blue wrapper. Mr. Moody asked her if this dress she had on Wednesday was the same one referred to as made in the spring, and the answer was "yes." There was a time when Mrs. Borden was sick, and neither of the girls went into the room.

CHAPTER XXIV.

FOURTH DAY OF THE TRIAL.

DR. S. W. BOWEN, the family physician, was the first witness called. After telling of his arrival at home he said: "I saw Miss Lizzie Borden and Mrs. Churchill in the side hall, just at the end of it, the kitchen door; I said, ' Lizzie, what's the matter?' she said, ' Father has been killed or stabbed'; I asked, ' Where is your father?' she said, ' In the sitting room.' That was all she said in that conversation at that time. In consequence of what she said I went into the dining room and then into the sitting room; I saw the form of Mr. Borden lying on the sofa at the left of the sitting room door; I found upon inspection that his face was badly cut, apparently with a sharp instrument; felt of his pulse and was satisfied that he was dead; I glanced about the room and saw that nothing was disturbed; he was lying on his right side with his face toward the south ; the face was hardly recognizable. I don't think the photograph shows the case of a person asleep ; in this the form has sunk down from where I first saw it; by sinking I mean the general collapse." During the showing of the picture Lizzie kept her eyes riveted on the floor, never once glancing up. Witness said, in explaining the picture to the jury— " The head is lower than it was; the sofa has been moved; it was, when I saw it, even with the door. With reference to the back of the sofa the head is substantially as when I saw it. As I went into the sitting room Lizzie followed me part. way, and as I turned to go out after finding he was dead I asked her if she had seen anyone and she said no; I asked her where she had been and she said, ' In the barn to get some iron,' then she said she was afraid her father had had trouble with some of his tenants; then I asked her to get something to cover Mr. Borden. Bridget brought me a sheet ; the sheet was brought from Mr. Borden's

C. C. RUSSELL.

room and the key was taken from the mantel, I believe, where it was usually kept. After the sheet was used, Lizzie asked me if I would telegraph to Emma, and in consequence of that request I did so; up to that time nothing had been said of Mrs. Borden, but just before I went to the telegraph office somebody asked where Mrs. Borden was and Lizzie said she had received a note to visit a sick friend and had gone out. As I was going out I met Officer Allen. On my return from the telegraph office I met in the kitchen hallway Mrs. Churchill, and she said they had found Mrs. Borden up stairs in the front room; she said I had better go upstairs and see her; I went through the dining room and sitting room and up the front stairs, stopping a moment at the door of the guest chamber; at that point I looked over the bed and saw the prostrate form of Mrs. Borden; then I was standing in the doorway; I went around at the foot of the bed, placed my hand on her head, and found a wound in her head; then I felt her pulse and found she was dead. I never said to any one that she died of fright or in a faint; but I will say this, my first thought was that she had fainted; I went down stairs and told the people Mrs. Borden was dead; that I thought she was killed by the same instrument with which Mr. Borden was killed and that I considered it fortunate that Lizzie was out of the way.

When I went downstairs first Lizzie was in the kitchen; Lizzie, Mrs. Churchill, Miss Russell and my wife and Bridget were in the kitchen; they were fanning her and working over her; she afterwards went in the dining room and I told her then that she had better go to her room, where I saw her that day; between 1 and 2 Miss Russell came to me about some medicine for her and I gave her bromo caffeine to allay the nervous excitement. I left directions and a second dose and carried a bottle there for her; I ordered morphine for her on Friday, and on Saturday I doubled the dose, continuing it on Saturday and Sunday; at the inquest I know Lizzie testified before I did; on Friday I gave her one-eighth grain, on Saturday I doubled it and continued the treatment all the time up to her arrest and while she was in the station; there is no question about the effect of morphine on the mind; by changing and allaying their views and gives them hallucinations. I saw her take the medicine on Thursday; that was bromo-caffeine, which will not create hallucinations."

Miss Adelaide B. Churchill was called and said: "On the morning of Aug. 4, I saw Mr. Borden first about nine o'clock; I was then in the kitchen; he was by his steps but don't know where he went; he was standing there; it was on the barn side of the steps; that morning

I went out and purchased something for dinner; returning I walked southward and upwards towards my house; in going that way I had to pass the Borden house first; when I reached my house I saw Bridget Sullivan going across the street from Dr. Bowen's to her house. She was white and going rapidly; I went in the side door of my house and into the kitchen, laying my bundles on a long table, and looking out of the window saw Lizzie inside of the screen door leaning against the east side of the door casing. I opened the window and asked Lizzie, what is the matter? She said: 'Oh, Mrs. Churchill, come over; some one has killed father. I went right out the front door over to their house; when I stepped inside the screen door, she was sitting on the second step; I put my hand in her right arm and said: 'Oh, Lizzie, how did it happen?' She said: 'I don't know.' 'Where were you?' 'I was in the barn to get a piece of iron, and when I came back I found the screen door open.' She said they must have some enemies, and she thought they had all been poisoned, as they were all sick in the night. I offered to go for a doctor and returned, after going to where my brother worked and getting him to telephone. Dr. Bowen was there and wanted me to go in and see the body of Mr. Borden, but I refused to go in; he asked for a sheet and someone handed Bridget a key. She and I went up in Mrs. Borden's room, where Bridget unlocked the door for us; we got a sheet and brought it down; Lizzie asked Dr. Bowen to send a telegram to Emma; then Miss Russell came in and Lizzie said she wished somebody would try to find Mrs. Borden as she thought she heard her come in; I volunteered to go with Bridget, and as we went up the stairs and when my head was on a level with the floor, I saw the body, then I turned about and went back.

"Miss Russell said 'Is there another,' and I said 'Yes, she is up there.' On the day of the tragedy the agitation of Lizzie wasn't manifested by tears; I don't remember whether Lizzie said to me that the reason she came in from the barn was because she heard a distressed noise; the dress she had while I was there was a light blue calico or cambric with a dark navy blue diamond, printed. The whole dress was alike; I don't remember how often I saw her wearing this dress, and I don't know how long she had owned it."

Miss Alice M. Russell was the next witness called, and when her name was mentioned, Lizzie straightened up in her chair and began to watch the door. When Miss Russell came in, she looked everywhere but where Lizzie was seated. "About two years ago I lived in Dr. Kelly's house," said Miss Russell; I knew all of the family well.

On Aug. 4, 1892, I lived on Borden street, between Third and Fourth streets, and near by a baker shop; occasionally Lizzie and I visited each other; when I went to her home she received me, generally, in the guests' room. On Wednesday night, Aug. 3, Lizzie came to see me; she came alone, and stayed till about 9 o'clock. We conversed and during the evening we spoke about going to Marion. I think when she came in she said, ' I have taken your advice, and am going to Marion. ' I said 'I'm glad you're going '; I spoke about her having a good time, but she said, ' I don't know; I feel distressed; when I was at Marion the other day the girls were laughing and they asked me what was the matter with me. ' Then she spoke of her father and mother and her being sick the night before, but Maggie wasn't sick; she (Lizzie) wasn't sick enough to vomit; she heard the others vomiting and stepped to the door to help them; she spoke of the bread and the milk and we talked about that, and I said it couldn't possibly be the bread, because others would have been sick. Lizzie spoke about believing her father had enemies and spoke of the man who came there and wanted to hire a place, and of the quarrel; then she spoke of seeing a man about the place at night; about the barn being broken into, and about the burglary in the houses. I said that I never heard of the burglary before, and Lizzie said her father had forbidden them to speak of it ; she described the robbery to me and said it was done in Mrs. Borden's room ; she was afraid somebody would burn the house down, and that she was afraid to go to sleep at night. Lizzie also spoke about the manner of her father treating his friends and how badly he used Dr. Bowen at one time. On the morning of August 4th, while I was at work, Bridget Sullivan came to me; I changed my dress and went at once to the Borden house and saw Lizzie down stairs; she was standing up when I went there and I asked her to sit down, which she did. She told me when I asked her, about going to the barn and her reason, that she went to the barn to get a piece of iron to fix her screen; I don't remember that she spoke about the note, but I heard it talked over. While I was downstairs she looked faint and I started to loosen her dress, but she said she wasn't faint; I only unloosened it a little at the lower part. When she went upstairs I was with her ; she spoke about getting an undertaker and I went down and spoke to Dr. Bowen; when I went back, met her coming out of Emma's room tying the strings of her wrapper ; at one time when I was in the room I saw her going to the closet door, unlock it and go in; I don't know whether Mr. Fleet went in that closet or not. Saturday and

Sunday nights I occupied Miss Emma's room ; on Sunday I got the breakfast ; after breakfast I left the lower part of the house and returned before noon ; when I came back, I went in the kitchen and saw Lizzie standing by the stove, Emma by the sink ; Lizzie had a dress and I asked her what she was going to do with it and Lizzie said she was going to burn it, it was all covered with paint.   I said nothing and went out.   When I came in the room again, Lizzie was tearing the dress, I said : ' I wouldn't let anybody see me doing that, ' and she stepped one step back ; it was the waist she was tearing ; I didn't remember about the skirt ; there were no officers in the house at that time, though there were some about the premises ; Bridget had left before that.   I saw Mr. Hanscom and saw him at the Borden house on Monday and conversed with him in the parlor ; in consequence of that talk I saw Miss Lizzie and Emma in the dining room and I said—' I'm afraid the worst thing you could have done was to burn that dress ; I have been asked about your dresses, and she said, ' why did you let me do it ?' ''

John Cunningham told the story of how he had telephoned news of the horror to the Central police station; and Deputy Sheriff Francis H. Wixon related that he was in the station when the message was received.

Officer George W. Allen said he was sent to the Borden house at 11 :15 on the morning of the 4th.   He described the manner in which he went and about enlisting Mr. Sawyer for an outside guard.   He saw Lizzie at the table in the kitchen and he also saw the body of Mr. Borden.   He saw that the front door was locked with a night lock and a bolt.   When he went to the station and reported to the Marshall he hadn't heard of Mrs. Borden's death.   He detailed his coming again and his searches through the house and his finding the cellar door locked on the inside, or bolted.   Witness said that when he saw the body of Mrs. Borden, there was a small stand upon which were two books and a small oil lamp about three feet away, but there were no marks of blood on the books or the stand.   He noticed a bloody handkerchief on the guest chamber floor, lying about midway between the body and the wall.

Assistant City Marshal John Fleet, when sworn, testified that he went to the house arriving at 11 :35.   Saw several persons and went into the house and saw the bodies.   Came out and found the door at the head of the stairs locked ; it leads into a closet ; then went into Lizzie's bedroom upstairs ; she sat with Mr. Buck ; told her that he was an officer and asked her if she knew anything about the killing ; she said she did not ; all that she knew was that she was ironing when her father came home and saw him sit on the sofa; he was feeble and she assisted him to lay down; then she went out and up to the barn and remained about half an hour upstairs in the barn. She came back and found her father on the sofa in the position she had left him, except that he was dead; she then called Maggie; asked her who Maggie was, and she said the servant girl; said she sent her after Dr. Bowen and Miss Russell; told me there was no one else in the house beside the family and her uncle, John Morse; said Morse could not have killed the people because he left the house and did not return till nearly 12; said Maggie could not have done it, because she had gone upstairs after her father came in. I then asked her if she knew who could have killed her father and mother. She answered: "She is not my mother; she is my stepmother; my own mother died when I was a child." Witness said that on the way up he tried the door of Mr. Borden's bedroom and found it locked; all the rooms except Bridget's was locked; the witness went into the cellar and found a lot of officers; Mr. Mullaly had two axes and hatchets on the floor; searched the cellar for any instrument, but found none at the time. A few days before, her father had some angry talk with a man in the back yard about a storeroom. Mr. Fleet then went down stairs through the rooms on the lower floor and then up to Bridget's room. The weapons which Mullaly had were placed behind some boxes in the cellar. At this point Mr. Moody brought out his collection of axes and hatchets which Mr. Fleet identified as the ones he had seen in the cellar. The red stain which he had seen on the handle of one hatchet had disappeared. Then Mr. Fleet went to Lizzie's door and rapped; Dr. Bowen came, and holding the door eight inches open, asked, 'what is wanted.' I told him we came to search. He said, 'Wait a a moment,' shut the door and talked with Lizzie, opened it and asked if it was absolutely necessary to search it, and I said, 'Yes;' I said again to Lizzie, 'You said this morning that you were up in the barn half an hour; what do you say now?' She replied, 'I say from twenty minutes to half an hour.' Asked her when she saw Mrs. Borden last and she said, 'In the guest room, about nine o'clock,' and that some one brought a letter or note to Mrs. Borden and that she supposed Mrs. Borden had gone out. Then went to a door leading into another bedroom and found it was hooked; opened it and went in; saw a bed standing in the middle of the room; Lizzie told him that she hoped he would get through as soon as possible, as

she was getting tired of it and he told her that he would; she also
said there was no use in searching her own room, because she always
locked it and no one could get into it or throw anything into it.   He
then came down stairs; saw Dr. Dolan and the officers in the cellar;
spoke to them and then found in the middle cellar, on a shelf near
the chimney, the head of a hatchet; the shelf was about six feet from
the ground; at the time he found the hatchet there was a small piece
of wood sticking in the head, it was a part of the handle.   The
hatchet was covered with a heavy coat of white ashes upon both
sides of the blade; in fact all over the hatchet; the substance, as he
thought, was fine ashes; there were other tools on the box at the
time, they were covered with a light dust but not ashes; the dust on
the other tools was lighter and finer than the ashes on the hatchet;
he saw that the piece of the handle was a new break; the break
was also covered with ashes; he put it back into the box with the
other tools.   He then went outside.

CHAPTER XXV.

FIFTH DAY OF THE TRIAL.

THE forenoon was devoted to an exhaustive cross examination of Mr. Fleet by Mr. Robinson. Captain Philip Harrington was the next witness. "I was at dinner on the day of the tragedy, and it was 12 o'clock when my attention was first called; I went in by the front gate, along the north side, and went in at the north door; I saw Mr. Sawyer at the door; I didn't see Lizzie there, but there were some ladies and some officers. I asked a question or two, and was directed to the sitting room, where Mr. Borden's body was on the lounge, covered with a sheet; I looked at the face, but could not recognize it; some of the blood was very dark, some very bright; it all had a fresh appearance, and as I stood there a small drop came down the side of his face; when I was there one or two persons stood beside me; then I went up to the room where Mrs. Borden's body lay; I saw the body when I was on the stairs, my head being just on a level with the floor. I went in, looked at the body, saw blood on her dress, on the pillow sham, and some on the spread. The blood was quite dark; then I went out and met two officers in the doorway; in the doorway on the east I looked and saw Miss Russell and Lizzie; I had a conversation with Miss Borden, asking her to tell me all she knew, but she said 'I can tell you nothing at all;' she said her father came home from the post office with a small package in his hand; 'I asked him if he had any mail for me; then I went out in the yard, and into the barn,' saying she had heard nobody in the meantime; she said she was up in the loft. I asked her if the motive was robbery and she said no; everything was all right, even to the watch in his pocket and the ring on his finger; I asked her if she had any reason to suspect anybody. 'No-o-o, I have not.' Said I, 'Why hesitate?' 'Well,' she said, 'a few weeks ago father had angry words with a man about something.' 'What was it?' 'I don't know, but they were very angry at the time, and the stranger went away.' 'Did you see him at all?' 'No, sir: they were in another room—but from the tone of their voices I knew everything wasn't pleasant between them.' ' Did you hear your father say anything about him?' ' No, sir. About two weeks ago he came again. They had a very animated conversation, during which they got angry again, and I heard father say, ' No, sir, I will not let my store for any such business.' But before they separated I heard father say, ' When you are in town, come again, and I will let you know about it.' She was dressed in a plain—or in a house wrap, striped in pattern, a pink and light stripe alternating—pink the most prominent color or shade. On the light stripe was a diamond figure formed by small bars or stripes, some of which ran parallel with the stripe and others biased to it, or diagonally. It was fitted to the form on the sides, standup collar, plaited on the sides and closely shirred in front."

Captain Harrington's testimony was a comprehensive story of what he had seen and heard at the house on that day.

Captain Patrick H. Doherty said that he heard of the murder at 11:39, and went direct to the house, overtaking Deputy Sheriff Wixon on the way ; both went in together ; witness described going into the house and his wanderings about it ; he was asked to state what Dr. Bowen had said about the body before he (witness) examined it, but the court ruled the question out as being incompetent. " Mrs. Borden, when I saw her, was lying face down with her hands up over her head ; the head was close to the wall, six or seven inches away ; I lifted the head and looked at it ; the furniture in the room wasn't disturbed, that I remember; on the floor was a bunch of hair, as big as my fist, which appeared to have been cut off ; the first time I went there I didn't see Miss Borden, Miss Russell or Mrs. Churchill. During the afternoon I saw Miss Borden in the kitchen ; I asked her where she was when this was done; she said it must have been done while she was in the barn; she said she heard no outcry or screams, but she did hear some noise like scraping ; then I had some talk with Bridget and Mr. Mullaly and I went about the house and looked it over pretty thoroughly, going into a room we found open, and then we went down cellar where Mullaly and I found a hatchet. I think it was a claw-headed one. Then I went out in the yard and then to the office ; I saw Miss Borden in her room that day before I went away ; I went to her room and she came to the door and said ' One minute,' and went in and shut the door ; It was a minute before she opened it ; we looked about the room ; when she was down stairs I thought she had on a light blue dress, with a small spot, and there was a ' bosom ' to the dress. On Friday morning Lizzie had a talk with Bridget about the back cellar door; she asked ' Maggie ' if she was sure the cellar door was fastened, and ' Maggie' said she was."

Officer Michael Mullaly said he was sent to the Borden house and arrived there at 11: 37; he looked at his watch and fixed the time thus; "I saw Miss Borden and she told me she was in the yard and when she came in he was dead on the sofa; she told me what property her father had on his person. I asked if there were any hatchets or axes on the premises, and she said Bridget Sullivan would show me where they were; Officer Doherty searched the body and found things as Lizzie had said they were." Witness described at length his search of the premises. On cross-examination he testified to finding a hatchet handle in the cellar box. District Attorney Knowlton, on being asked for this extra piece of handle, said he did not have it, and this was the first time he had ever heard of it. Mr. Fleet was recalled and asked about the broken handled hatchet, where he found it and what else he found. He said he found nothing in the nature of a piece of wood with a new break in it. This created a decided sensation. Charles H. Wilson, a police officer, testified that he went to the house about 1 o'clock on the afternoon of the 4th; heard the talk between Miss Borden and Mr. Fleet; Mr. Fleet asked her where her mother was, and she answered that she saw her last in the guest chamber about 9 o'clock; that she had received a note and gone out; witness described the search of the house.

Annie M. White, the court stenographer of Bristol County, was called to tell her story of what took place at the inquest in Fall River. Gov. Robinson arose and asked that the further examination of this witness be dispensed with until a full explanation could be made of the important question which the testimony proposed to be submitted, brought up.

CHAPTER XXVI.

Seventh Day of the Trial.

ON Monday morning the Court came in and Mr. Moody argued at length in support of his claim that the testimony given by Lizzie Borden at the inquest be allowed to go before the jury. It was a verbatim report of this testimony which Miss White would have testified to. Mr. Robinson made an extensive reply and in the afternoon it was decided that the testimony was incompetent, and therefore ruled out. Thus the strongest prop of the State's case was broken down. Officer Joseph Hyde told the story of a search of the premises.

Medical Examiner Dr. William A. Dolan said he had been a practising physician for eleven years; '' I first went to the Borden house at 11: 45 a. m.; I was passing by the house; I was in there ten or fifteen minutes when the City Hall clock struck 12 ; I first saw Mr. Sawyer, then Dr. Bowen, Bridget Sullivan and Mr. Morse, also Miss Russell and Mrs. Churchill, Officers Allen, Mullaly and Doherty were there. I had a little talk with Lizzie Borden that morning ; she was in her room; I asked her about that note and she said Mrs. Borden had received a note to go and see somebody who was sick ; I asked her what had become of it, and she said she supposed she had thrown it in the stove ; when I first went in I saw a form lying on a sofa ; the end of the sofa was flush with the jamb of the dining room door; the body was covered with a sheet. Dr. Bowen and I went together ; I looked at the body, touched it and saw the body was warm and that blood was still oozing from the wounds in the head ; the head was resting on a small sofa cushion ; a coat was under that and an afghan under that ; I made no particular examination of the wounds ; I then went upstairs to see Mrs. Borden. I got Mr. Kieran to take some measurements for me; some time after I noticed the blood was coagulated ; Mrs. Borden was lying more on the left side of her face, so as to expose the rear of the right back of the head ; there I found a handkerchief, it was an old one, of silk, and was bloody ; it was near her head ; I did not take the handkerchief, but it was buried with the rest of the clothes. I was only there two or three minutes at that time ; I had a thermometer with me, but I didn't use it ; I found the temperature of Mr. Borden to be very high ; I learned this from the hands ; at that time the blood was dripping in two places down the head of the sofa ; there was no blood on top of the carpet, but it had soaked in ; I saw no coagulated blood on Mr. Borden ; I touched the body of Mrs. Borden, and it was much colder than Mr. Borden's. I made an examination of Mr. Borden's wounds, and found there what seemed to be from eight to ten." In his pocket book witness found eighty-one dollars and sixty-five cents in money ; his watch and chain were in their usual place ; there was a ring on his finger ; witness collected a sample of the morning's milk, in consequence of what was told him, and afterwards analyzed it. Continuing he said : " Then I went into the cellar and found some axes and hatchets ; I saw one a claw hammer, which appeared to have been scraped. It was 12: 30 or thereabouts that first day when I first saw those axes ; I went away and went back again about 3 or 3: 30 ; then I had the bodies photographed ; the bodies were in the same position as when I first saw them except that I think Mrs. Borden's hands were moved."

CHAPTER XXVII.

Eighth and Ninth Days of the Trial.

THE greater part of the forenoon of the eighth day was devoted to the examination of Dr. Dolan and he told a comprehensive story of what he had seen and done in his official capacity.

Prof. Edward S. Wood of Harvard College, had received the stomachs of the murdered Bordens and had tested them for prussic acid poisoning with negative results. He then said "afterwards they were analyzed in the regular way for other poisonous substances, with a negative result. There was nothing abnormal or irregular in the condition of the stomachs; assuming that they both ate at the same time and of the same kind of food, the difference in the time of death, from the condition of the stomachs, would be about one and one-half hours; digestion stops at death; I have heard all the evidence thus far, and taking all these facts and the examination I made myself, the most important facts to show the time of death are the condition of the blood and the condition of the stomachs and the heat of the bodies." In this opinion he agreed with Dr. Dolan. He had examined all the hatchets and found no blood. All of the prisoner's clothes, shoes and stockings were found to be bloodless, except a white skirt. This had one drop of blood less than the size of a pin's head and on the back part eight inches above the hem. Dr. Frank W. Draper of Boston, medical examiner of Suffolk county, testified to the condition of the bodies and wounds at the time he assisted Dr. Dolan at the Oak Grove autopsy. He talked at length upon the kind of weapon which could have made the wounds and told of the way in which the blood might have scattered. Dr. R. W. Chever of Boston, had examined the skulls of the Bordens and testified as to the kind of weapon which made the wounds.

CHAPTER XXVIII.

TENTH DAY OF THE TRIAL.

CITY Marshal Rufus B. Hilliard was the witness called. He testified as had the other officers about his search at the house. He said: "On Saturday evening following the killing, I went to the house in company with Dr. Coughlin; there was a large crowd of people present, perhaps two or three hundred people; I sent for officers and had the crowd removed to the street; then I went into the house, where I saw the prisoner, her sister and Mr. Morse; there was a conversation between Dr. Coughlin and the others; after we entered the parlor Dr. Coughlin asked that the family remain in the house for a few days; that there was much excitement and he thought it would be better they should remain there and not go on the street. I think he told them if they were annoyed by the people to send word to the city marshal or himself and they should be protected; Mr. Morse asked about the mail and he was told they had better send for it; then Miss Lizzie asked, 'What, is there anybody in this house suspected?' the Mayor said, 'Perhaps Mr. Morse could answer that from what occurred last night;' Lizzie then said, 'I want to know the truth,' and the Mayor said he was sorry to say it, but that she was suspected; then Emma spoke up and said, 'We have tried to keep it from you as long as we could.' Then the Mayor asked Lizzie where she was when the affair happened, and she said in the barn for twenty minutes, looking for lead sinkers; Lizzie said, after Emma spoke, 'Well, I am ready to go any time.' " The witness was cross-examined at great length and told of all his connections with the case.

Dr. John W. Coughlin, Mayor of Fall River, said that on Saturday evening following the Borden murder he went to the house with the marshal; there was a large crowd present and he instructed the marshal to disperse the crowd; it was done; in the house the first person he saw was Miss Emma; then he saw Lizzie and Mr. Morse. "We all went into the parlor where I said, 'I have a request to make of the family, and that is that you remain in the house for a few days, since I think it would be best for you all.' Lizzie asked, 'Why, is there anybody in this house suspected?' and I said, ' Well, perhaps Mr. Morse can awswer better, as his experience of last even- ing might tend to convince him that somebody in the house was suspected;' then Emma said, ' We have tried to keep it from her the best we could,' and Lizzie said, 'Well, if I am suspected I am ready to go at any time;' then Miss Lizzie, in answer to my questions, told where she was when the murders occurred; Miss Emma then said she wanted us to do everything we could for them, after I had told them to call on me for any protection needed.''

Mrs. Hannah H. Gifford said: "I am a cloak maker and did work for the Bordens. I made a sack for Lizzie in March, 1892, and had a talk with her about her stepmother. "I spoke, and called Mrs. Borden, 'mother.' She said, 'Don't call her mother, she is only my stepmother, and she is a mean, hateful old thing;' I said 'Oh Lizzie, don't say that,' and then she said she always kept apart from her, and ate her meals alone.''

The evidence which Miss Anna H. Borden (not a relative) was about to give in relation to something she had heard the prisoner say about her stepmother was excluded.

Miss Lucy Collett who sat on the veranda of Dr. Chagnon's residence most of the forenoon testified that she saw no one pass out across the Chagnon yard. Thomas Bolles was washing a carriage in Mrs. Churchill's yard and saw no one. Patrick McGowan, Joseph Desrosiers and John Denny, stone cutters, were at work all the fore- noon in John Crowe's stone yard adjoining and back of the Borden premises, and they each swore that they saw no one pass out that way. Mrs. Hannah Reagan, matron of the Central Police Station and who had the care of Miss Borden at the time of the preliminary trial said: " On the 24th of August Emma came in to see Lizzie in the morning; I was in the room, cleaning up; she spoke with her sister and I went into a toilet room and hearing loud talk, looked out and saw Lizzie lying on her side and Emma bending down over her. Lizzie said: ' You have given me away, Emma, but I don't care, I won't give in one inch,' measuring on her finger. Emma said: ' Oh, Lizzie, I didn't;' at the same time sitting down; they sat there until 11 o'clock, when Mr. Jennings came, but Lizzie made no talk at all with her sister after; never opened her mouth to her; when I first heard the noise of loud talking I was about four feet away, in a closet; when Emma left that morning there was nothing said by either and no good-bye ' exchanged.'' This testimony created a decided sensation.

Cross-examined by Mr. Jennings—"Emma remained there in that room until you came, and when you came you said to Emma, 'Have you told her all?' and Emma said she had told her all she had to tell; Emma came back again in the afternoon, but I can't tell just when; Mr. Buck was there, I am quite sure; he came every day. When Miss Emma came in the afternoon I can't tell; there was no one there in the morning but her sister and you; I don't remember whether Mrs. Holmes, Miss Annie Holmes or Mrs. Brigham were there or not; I know that Miss Borden looked more excited when you (Mr. Jennings) left the room than she did before. I do remember something about an egg one afternoon; it was over the fact that I said an egg could be broken one way and not another, and I made a bet with Mrs. Brigham about it; Lizzie took the egg and tried to break it her way, and failing, said this was the first time she ever attempted to do anything and didn't succeed; when I spoke of the affair between the sisters I spoke of it as a quarrel; this was before the first hearing. I don't know whether the story of the quarrel was published in the morning papers; I was asked about it by reporters; it was that very afternoon, and a so in the morning; I never told any reporter that it was all a lie, that there wasn't a word of truth in it; Mr. Buck spoke to me about it in my room, but I never told him it wasn't true; I never said a word to Mrs. Holmes about it. There was a paper drawn up subsequently, in relation to this story; it was brought to me by Mr. Buck." (Statement was here read, in which it was set forth that there had not been a quarrel between the sisters, and that she had never said so.) She said she never expressed a willingness to sign the paper, and that Marshal Hilliard never said a word to her about signing the paper; he never said, to her remembrance, "If you sign that paper you sign it against my express orders." Mr. Buck never asked her about signing the paper if the marshal was willing. "The marshal told me to go to my room; there was no one in the room when I went back for I had the door locked and the key in my pocket; I never said to the marshal that I'd rather leave my place than have such lies told about me; I never had any conversation with Mrs. Holmes about this paper; I never said to Mrs. Holmes in referring to the story, 'You know they didn't quarrel because you were here and we were talking about the egg.' The reporter to whom I told the story in the afternoon was Mr. Porter of the *Fall River Globe*; I never saw the contents of any paper, but Mr. Buck came to me and said he had heard of such a report, that he had seen it in a paper, and I said, 'You can't always believe all you see in the papers;' he wanted me to sign the paper; said that if I did it would be all right between the sisters; I said I would go and see the marshal about it. We went down to the marshal's office and he told me to go to my room, told Mr. Buck to mind his own business, and he would attend to his; the marshal said then what story I had to tell I would tell in court; I do not remember your (Mr. Jennings) being in the marshal's room and I don't remember your conversation with him; I never heard you say to the marshal 'If you refuse to let this woman sign this paper, I'll publish you to the world.'"

Eli Berce, a drug clerk, was then called. He was prepared to tell the story of how the prisoner attempted to buy ten cents worth of hydrocianic acid from him on the day before the murders, but Gov. Robinson objected. The Jury was sent out and counsel argued the question of the admissibility of the testimony. The State claimed that it would show the state of Miss Borden's mind the day before the homicides. The Judges decided that it was incompetent and therefore must be ruled out. This was the second prop knocked from under the Government's case. This ended the testimony for the prosecution and the case rested.

CHAPTER XXIX.

ELEVENTH DAY OF THE TRIAL.

DURING the forenoon of the eleventh day, Andrew J. Jennings Esq., presented the defendant's case as follows: "May it please your honors, Mr. Foreman and gentlemen of the jury,—I want to make a personal allusion before referring directly to the case. One of the victims of the murder charged in this indictment was for many years my client and my personal friend. I had known him since my boyhood. I had known his oldest daughter for the same length of time; and I want to say right here and now, if I manifest more feeling than perhaps you think necessary in making an opening statement for the defence in this case you will ascribe it to that cause. The counsel, Mr. Foreman and gentlemen, does not cease to be a man when he becomes a lawyer. Fact and fiction have furnished many extraordinary examples of crime that have shocked the feelings and staggered the reason of men, but I think no one has ever surpassed in its mystery the case that you are now considering. The brutal character of the wounds is only equalled by the audacity, by the time and the place chosen here : and, Mr. Foreman and gentlemen, it needed but the accusation of the youngest daughter of one of the victims to make this the act, as it would seem to most men, of an insane person or a fiend. I do not propose to go into details about the character of those wounds or the appearance that was presented. I think you have heard sufficiently about that already. But, Mr. Foreman and gentlemen, knowing what they were, the person who is arrested for doing the deed which I have characterized as I have was the youngest daughter of one of the victims themselves. A young woman, thirty-two years of age, up to that time of spotless character and reputation, who had spent her life nearly in that immediate neighborhood, who had moved in and out of that old house for twenty or twenty-one years, living there with her father and with her stepmother and with her sister—this crime that shocked the whole civilized world, Mr. Foreman and gentlemen, seemed from the very first to be laid at her door by those who represented the government in the investigation of the case. We shall show you that this young woman as I have said had apparently led an honorable, spotless life : she was a member of the church: she was interested in the church matters : she was connected with various organizations for charitable work : she was ever ready to help in any good thing, in any good deed, and yet for some reason or other the government in its investigation seemed to fasten the crime upon her. Now a crime like this naturally awakens at its first result a sort of a selfish fear in men. There is really an outcry of human hearts to have somebody punished for the crime. But, Mr. Foreman and gentlemen, no matter how much you may want somebody punished for the crime, it is the guilty and not the innocent that you want. The law of blood for blood and life for life, Mr. Foreman and gentlemen, even in its most stringent form in the past, never, except in barbarous and uncivilized nations, called for the blood of the innocent in return for the blood or life of the murdered one. Our law—and it is the law that you have sworn to apply to the evidence in this case—presumes every man innocent until he is proved guilty, not guilty until he is proved innocent. I know you may say it is the duty of the State to vindicate the death of one of its citizens. Mr. Foreman and gentlemen, it is a higher duty, and one recognized by the law of this State, that it shall protect the lives of its living citizens. The law of Massachusetts to-day draws about every person accused of this crime or any other the circle of the presumption of his or her innocence, and allows no juryman or jury to cross it until they have fulfilled the conditions required : until they show that it has been proved beyond a reasonable doubt that he or she is the guilty party, they are not allowed to cross the line and take the life of the party who is accused. The commonwealth here has charged that Lizzie Andrew Borden, in a certain way, at a certain time, killed Andrew Jackson Borden and Abby Durfee Borden with malice aforethought. And that alone is the question that you are to answer : Did she on that day commit that deed? Did she commit it in the way alleged, or to put it in its other form, have they satisfied you beyond a reasonable doubt that she did it? And what is a reasonable doubt? Well, I saw a definition, and it struck me it was a very good one. A reasonable doubt is a doubt for which you can give a reason. If you can conceive of any other hypothesis that will exclude the guilt of this prisoner and make it possible or probable that somebody else might have done this deed, then you have got a reasonable doubt in your mind. Now, Mr. Foreman and gentlemen, I want to say a word about the kind of evidence. There are two kinds of evidence, direct evidence and circumstantial evidence. Direct evidence is the testimony of persons who have seen, heard or felt the thing or things about which they are testifying. They are telling you something which they have observed or perceived by their senses. For instance, if this was a case of murder by stabbing, and a man should come before you and testify that he saw the prisoner strike the murdered person with a knife, that is direct evidence; that tends directly to connect the prisoner with the crime itself. Circumstantial evidence is entirely different and I want to say right here, Mr. Foreman and gentlemen—I call your attention to it now, and I do not think that the commonwealth will question the statement when I make it—that there is not one particle of direct evidence in this case from beginning to end against Lizzie Andrew Borden. There is not a spot of blood, there is not a weapon that they have connected with her in any way, shape or fashion. They have not had her hand touch it, or her eye see it, or her ear hear it. There is not, I say, a particle of direct testimony in the case connecting her with this crime. It is wholly and absolutely circumstantial. In proving a murder it is necessary for the government to prove that all of the facts existed which to your minds make you morally certain that the murder must have followed from it. In other words, in circumstantial evidence it is simply an opinion on your part, it is simply an inference drawn by you as to the facts that are proved as to whether the essential issue has been proved or not." Here Mr. Jennings cited several cases intended to show how uncertain is circumstantial evidence. Continuing he said: "It is not then, as I said before I started upon this long talk about circumstantial evidence, and I hope you will pardon me, for I think it is very important that you get this point in your mind, it is not for you to unravel the mystery of how he died. It is not for you to withhold your decision until you have satisfied your mind as to how it was done, and just who did it. It is, have they furnished the proof, the proof that the law requires, that Lizzie Andrew Borden did it, and that there is absolutely no opportunity for anybody else. Now, Mr. Foreman and gentlemen, I have taken a little more time than I intended to in discussing the question of circumstantial evidence. I have said that it was necessary for them to prove beyond a reasonable doubt the allegation of the indictment. Circumstantial evidence has often been likened to a chain. These facts which have to be proven in order to allow you to draw the inference as to her guilt or innocence have been called links in the chain, and every essential fact, Mr. Foreman and gentlemen, every essential fact in that chain must be proved beyond a reasonable doubt—every one of them. You cannot have it tied together with weak links and strong links. You cannot have certain facts in there which you believe and tie them to some other facts of which you have a reasonable doubt. You cannot put them together. You must throw aside every fact about which you have any reasonable doubt, and unless with the lines which you have left you can tie this defendant to the body of Andrew J. Borden and Abby Durfee Borden, you must acquit her. That is the law, and that is the law you have sworn to apply to the evidence. Now Mr. Foreman, we contend that with the evidence that has already appeared in this case, and what will be shown to you, there is absolutely no motive whatever for the commission of this crime by this defendant. They have not a scrap of evidence in the case but that which was given by Mrs. Gifford, and you have heard also the evidence of Bridget Sullivan. But it may be said that it is not necessary to prove the motive. Somebody killed them; what motive did somebody else have? We cannot tell, Mr. Foreman and gentlemen. One of these persons that is killed is this girl's own father. And while in direct evidence, where the person was seen to kill, where they have been directly connected with the killing, it is of little or no importance whether a motive is shown or not, (if you kill, the law infers a motive, the law infers a motive there, direct evidence connects you with the crime,) yet, where, Mr. Foreman and gentlemen, you want the motive in order to have it as one of the links in the chain which connects the crime with its defendant, it becomes of tremendous importance. Tremendous importance; and we shall show you, if not already shown that this defendant lived quietly with her father; that the relations between them were the relations that ordinarily exist between parent and daughter. We shall show you by various little things, perhaps, that there was nothing whatever between this father and his daughter that would cause her to do such a wicked, wicked act as this. And I want to say right here, Mr. Foreman and gentlemen, that the goverment's testimony and claim, so far as I have been able to understand it, is that whoever killed Abby Durfee Borden killed Andrew J. Borden; and even if they furnish you with a motive on her part to kill the step-mother, they have shown you absolutely none to kill the father. Absolutely none; unless they advance what seems to me the ridiculous proposition that she, instead of leaving the house after killing the mother, waits there an hour or an hour and a half for the express purpose of killing her own father, between whom and herself there is shown not the slightest trouble or disagreement whatsoever. In measuring the question of motive you have got to measure it in this case as applied between the defendant and her father, because, as I understand it, the government claims that whoever killed one killed both. Now as to the weapon, Mr. Foreman and gentlemen, I do not know as it is necessary for me to say much about that. The blood that was shown upon the axes, which was guarded so carefully at first in this case, as shown by the evidence, has disappeared like mist in the morning sun. The claw-headed hatchet that Dr. Dolan was so sure committed the deed at the Fall River hearing, so sure that he could even see the print which the claw head of the hatchet made in the head of Mr. Borden has disappeared from the case. And I would like to remark in passing, Mr. Foreman and gentlemen, that it didn't disappear until after Prof. Wood had testified so absolutely on that, to the counsel for the defense, glorious morning in Fall River, that there was not a particle of blood upon either one of those hatchets, and that they could not be cleaned in any reasonable time from blood if they had been used in killing those persons.

"And Mr. Foreman and gentlemen, I want to call your attention right here that there has not been a living soul put upon the stand here to testify that they saw Andrew J. Borden come down street from his house. From his house to the Union Savings Bank he was actually invisible. Was it any easier for him to be than it would be for somebody escaping from this house if they walked quietly away? But we shall show you, in addition to that, there were other strange people about that house; people who have not been located or identified. We shall show you that the government's claim here about Miss Lizzie's not having been out to the barn is false, and that this— well, if it was not for the tremendous importance, I should be tempted to call it cake walk of Officer Medley in the barn, exists in his imagination alone. We shall show you by evidence which I think will convince you—as we are not bound to convince you, beyond a reasonable doubt, that people were up and around and in that barn and all over it before Officer Medley opened the door. And I think we shall satisfy you that Miss Lizzie did go out to that barn, as she stated in those conversations, and was out there when this deed was committed, so far as Mr. Borden was concerned. As to the burning of this dress, we shall show you that it did have paint on it, according to the statement which was made by Miss Lizzie in the testimony of Alice Russell; that it was made some time in May; that soon after it was made this was got upon it; that the dress was soiled and useless, and that it was burned there right in the broad light of day in the presence of witnesses, with windows open, with the inside door open, with offices on every side of that house. And so, Mr. Foreman and gentlemen, without spending further time, we shall ask you, if you believe this testimony which has been offered or drawn out, rather, from the government witnesses by the cross-examination of the defense, supplemented as it will be by the evidence which I have suggested, we shall ask you to say in view of the presumption in favor of human nature, in view of the feelings which exist between a father and a daughter who stand here, so far as the evidence to-day is concerned, just as every other father and child stood, from the presumption of innocence which the law says you shall consider, from the fact that there is no blood, not a spot upon her hand, her head, her dress or any part of her, no connection with any weapon whatever shown by any direct evidence in this case, with an opportunity for others to do the deed, with herself in the barn when the deed was done, we shall ask you to say, Mr. Foreman and gentlemen, whether the government has satisfied you, beyond a reasonable doubt, that she did kill not only her stepmother, Abby Durfee Borden, but her loved and loving father, Andrew Jackson Borden, on the fourth day of August last.''

The first witness for the defense was Sarah R. Hart, of Tiverton, and she said: ''I knew Andrew J. Borden by sight, and knew where he lived; I had a sister who lived in the Dr. Kelly house some fifteen years, and I was in the habit of going there frequently; on the day of the murders I passed by Mr. Borden's house with my sister-in-law, Mrs. Manley; it was about 9 :50; we passed by the north gate and stopped there to speak to my nephew, who was there in a carriage, and went up to the back of his carriage. While I was there I saw a young man standing in the gateway; it was not Mr. Borden; he was resting his head on his left hand, his elbow being on the gatepost; I was there five minutes and he was there when I went away.''

Charles S. Sawyer was then called: ''I was in No. 61 Second street, Mr. Rich's shop, when I heard that a man had been stabbed, and I went out on to the street; I saw Mr. Hall and Miss Russell; she was going up on the other side of the street and I went over to talk with her; I walked along with her until I got to the gate of the Borden house, when I turned around and walked away; when I

turned away, I met Officer Allen at Mrs. Churchill's gate ; I went
back with him and he put me on guard at the side door, after we had
been in the house. When I was in there Miss Russell, Mrs.
Churchill, Miss Lizzie and Miss Bridget Sullivan were in the kitchen ;
Miss Lizzie was sitting in a rocking chair and the others seemed to
be working over her, fanning her and rubbing her hands ; I was close
to her all the time ; she appeared to be somewhat distressed ; I saw
no signs of blood on her head, hair, hands, or dress ; I cannot tell
what kind of a dress she had on, whether it was dark or light ; after
that I was back and forward in the entry, and when people came I
let them in ; sometimes I was out on the steps. ''

Mark Chace testified to having seen a strange man in a buggy in
front of the Borden house that forenoon.

Dr. Benjamin J. Handy. '' I went by the house on the morning
of the murder at 9 and 10 :30 ; saw a medium-sized young man very
pale in complexion, with eyes fixed on the sidewalk passing slowly
towards the south ; he was acting strangely : in consequence of his
appearance I turned in my carriage to watch him ; he was acting
different from any person I ever saw on the street in my life ; he was
agitated and seemed to be weak ; he half stopped at times and then
walked on ; he seemed to be mentally agitated, by the intensely
agitated expression on his face ; I think I had seen him before, some
other day ; there was nobody else on the sidewalk. ''

John J. Manning, reporter. '' I first heard of the Borden murder
some time before 11 :30 ; Mr. O'Neil, city editor of the *Fall River
Globe*, told me to go up Second street as there had been a stabbing
affray there, and I ran most of the way ; when I was going there I
saw Mr. Cunningham, Bolles and one or two others ; I went into the
yard and up to the house, and found Mr. Sawyer at the door ; he
wouldn't allow me to go in, and I sat down on the steps. Dr. Bowen
came, but I wasn't allowed to go in ; then Officer Doherty and Mr.
Wixon came and I was allowed to go in with them ; I went into the
kitchen and found Miss Borden, Miss Russell and Mrs. Churchill
near her, fanning her ; went into the sitting room and Dr. Bowen
showed me the body of Mr. Borden and described the wounds ; then
I went up in the guest chamber with Dr. Bowen ; my recollection as
to this room is that it was not very light ; Officer Doherty pulled the
bed away so a better view could be obtained of the body ; then I
went down stairs and into the kitchen, but the people had gone from
there ; Bridget Sullivan was sitting on the back stairs ; I can't say
how long I had been in the house ; but when I came out I think I

saw Mr. Fleet on the north side of the house ; then I went around on the east side, walked along the Kelly fence, walked along a pile of lumber and then came to the barn, where I think there were two or three persons inside ; there were other people about the yard, but I don't recall any boys there. Coming out of the barn, Walter Stevens and I went around the house looking for footprints ; we tried the cellar door, but found it fast; I never saw Medley there ; I got back to the office at 11 :50 ; I remember the story of the publication of Mrs. Reagan's story, and I had an interview with her ; I think it was the same night of the publication; in answer to a question from me, she said there was nothing in it ; I wanted to know whether it was true or not, and I wanted a negative or affirmative statement.''

Thomas F. Hickey,reporter, of the *Fall River Globe.* ''As reporter I saw Mrs. Reagan on Friday about the story referred to above ; I said : ' I see you're getting yourself in the paper, Mrs. Reagan ;' she said: ' Yes, but they have got to take that all back;' I asked her about the quarrel and she said there had been no quarrel; I asked her if she had repeated any of the words of the sisters; asked her if there was any truth in the report, and she said absolutely none.'' Cross-examined— '' I represent the *Boston Herald,* and the *Boston Globe* published the story. The *Globe* had what is called a ' scoop,' although I understood that morning that the *Herald* had published the story; I went into her room where she was on duty and was alone; I knew her ; I was sent by Mr. Billings and was after something to offset the *Globe's* ' scoop.' ''

Mrs. Mary R. Holmes, Fall River, wife of Charles J. Holmes. '' I know Miss Borden and have known who she was from childhood; she is a member of the church I attend, the Central Congregational ; she has been a member five years and has taken part in much of the church work ; I was engaged with her in some of the special work of the church ; she was on the hospital board with me, but she was engaged in the Chinese work while I was in the Bible class ; I am considerably older than she. I was but little acquainted with Mrs. Abbie D. Borden, although she was a member of the same church; I have seen Miss Lizzie Borden and her stepmother at church together; I first heard of the Borden murder at 11:45; I went to the house about 1 o'clock and sat down in the kitchen; someone told me soon after that Lizzie would like to see me; she was in her room and some men were talking with her; I don't think Officer Fleet was there then; I think Dr. Bowen came up a few minutes after, and before Officer Fleet came; we locked the door because there were so many men about that we didn't want them to come in the room. I had a talk with Mrs. Reagan about the quarrel story, and she said, 'Mrs. Holmes, you know it is not so.'"

Charles J. Holmes, Fall River, banker, testified that he had lived in Fall River fifty years; "I know Miss Lizzie Borden; I was present at the hearing on the first day in the Fall River court house; I know about the paper given Mrs. Reagan to sign; it was read to Mrs. Reagan; I heard it read; I have a copy of the original paper in my pocket; I have a copy of the newspaper in which it was published also." Here witness produced a copy of the *Fall River Herald* saying, when he saw it, that he supposed it was a copy of the *Daily News* of that city, but after diligent search the article was found and vouched for by Mr. Jennings. Witness was shown a type written copy of the same, identified it and read it; it was essentially a denial of the story. "It was read to Mrs. Reagan and she said it was true and that she would sign it, if the marshal would allow her; then Mr. Buck and she went down to the marshal's office; then they came back and went into the matron's room, and I don't know personally what happened there; down stairs, after the marshal refused to allow her to sign, I had a part in the altercation which ensued."

Cross-examined—"I heard Mr. Jenning's voice and a reporter whom I think was Mr. Porter; there was a very heated conversation, and I had an idea that he was connected with a Fall River paper; I attended the trial all through as a friend of Miss Borden; I don't think that Mrs. Reagan had ever been summoned as a witness, and the only reference to the taking back of anything was as to what was published in a newspaper; the day was one of a great deal of excitement; I was trying to get a denial from Mrs. Reagan of the story over her own signature, and it had no bearing upon the case then going on in court; it was simply to correct one newspaper story; she never signed it."

John R. Caldwell, reporter, New York. "I reported the trial in Fall River; I recall the date when Mrs. Reagan was asked to sign the paper, and saw it read to her, but was too far off to hear what was said; Mrs. Reagan took the paper to Marshal Hilliard and he said if she signed it, it would be against his orders; then she went out and he ordered me out." Cross-examined—"I don't know that Hilliard said she would say what she had to say in court; there was quite a crowd in the corridors when Mrs. Reagan went down, most of it being reporters; Mr. Percy, another reporter and I were the only ones who went into the office; Mr. Percy is now in Italy."

Mrs. Mary E. Brigham, Fall River. "I know Lizzie Borden, and have known her all my life; we were life-long friends, and attended the same church; I visited her quite frequently; Mrs. Reagan told me one day, after court, when we were in the matron's room, about a quarrel between the sisters; I saw Mr. Buck with a paper in his hand, which he read to her; they both went out, and she came back mad; she said she was willing to sign the papers, but the marshal wouldn't let her; that she would rather leave her place than to stay where she had been lied about; that it was all a lie and there had been no quarrel."

Miss Emma L. Borden, sister of Lizzie Borden. "We have lived in the house we now live in twenty-one years last May; at the time of the murder Lizzie was possessed of property as follows: $170 in the B. M. C. Durfee Safe Deposit and Trust Co., $2000 in the Massasoit National Bank, $500 in the Union Savings Bank, $141 in the Fall River Five Cents Savings Bank, two shares of the Fall River National Bank stock, four shares of the Merchants Mfg. Co. stock and five shares of same, another date. My father wore a ring on his finger," said witness, after the property list had been read; "it was given him by Lizzie; she had worn it herself before; he constantly wore it after, and it was buried with him; I have an inventory of the clothes in the closet on the afternoon it was searched, made up about a week ago, from recollection; there were eighteen or nineteen dresses in there; only one belonged to Mrs. Borden; the others were Lizzie's and mine; there were ten dresses there in which blue was a marked color; eight were Lizzie's, two were mine; I was there when the search was going on. Lizzie and I both went to the attic to assist them in opening a trunk; we never made the slightest objection to their searches and told them to come as often as they could and make as thorough searches as they could; the Bedford cord dress was made the first week in May at our home; it was a very cheap dress, twelve and a half or fifteen cents a yard, and about eight or nine yards in it; plainly trimmed; not more than two days were used in making the dress; Lizzie and I assisted, as we always did; the work was done in the guest room where it was always done; the dressmaker made several for us at the same time. The painters began work after the dress was made; Lizzie got some paint on this dress within two weeks after it was made; she got the paint on the front breadth and on the side; that dress was hanging in the front closet on the day I came home; I know because I went in to hang up a dress and found there was no nail. I said, 'You have not destroyed that old dress yet; why don't you do so?' It was very dirty, badly faded, and I don't remember having seen her use it for some time; it couldn't have been made over because, besides being badly soiled, the material and collar were such as to render it impossible; it was a very long dress, an inch and a half longer than her pink wrapper; the sleeves were full and the waist was a blouse; the back skirt was longer than any other dress except those cut en train. She had no other dress which she could have got on over that dress, because they were too snug; she could not have had it on under the pink wrapper, because it would have shown; the next I saw of the Bedford cord dress was in the kitchen on Saturday, when I heard my sister's voice; I looked around and saw her with the dress on her; she said, ' I'm going to burn this old dress,' and I said, ' I would,' or ' Why don't you,' and turned away; I didn't see her burn the dress; Miss Russell was there at the time. On Monday Miss Russell came to us in the dining room and said she had told Mr. Hanscom a falsehood, and I asked her what that was for; she said he asked her if all the dresses were in the house that were there at the time of the murder, and she had said yes; and then it was decided between us all that she should go and tell Mr. Hanscom she had told a falsehood; my sister said at the time, ' Why didn't you tell him about it; why did you let me do it?' I remember the story about the quarrel between my sister and I; it was told me by you (Mr. Jennings) the morning the story was published; I never had any such conversation

with my sister as was reported; there was never any trouble or quarrel in the matron's room between us while she was there or anything that could be construed into a quarrel; Lizzie never did put up her finger and say anything about giving in; there was no conversation about you (Mr. Jennings) telling her (Lizzie) all.''

W. T. BILLINGS.

Mrs. Mary Raymond, dressmaker. '' I have done dressmaking for Lizzie Borden at her home; I also worked for Mrs. Borden; I made some dresses for Lizzie last spring (1892); I went to the house the first week in May and was there three weeks; the Bedford cord dress I made, the first one because she needed it; it took about three weeks and the sisters helped me; it was a light blue dress with a dark figure; it was made with a blouse waist and full skirt; the skirt was longer by half a finger than she had been in the habit of wearing; it was a cheap cotton dress with little trimming. The painters were painting the house when Lizzie was wearing the dress; she put it on as soon as it was done; I saw the dress after it was 'painted'; the paint was on the front and back; she had an old wrapper which this was to take the place of; she cut some pieces out of the old wrapper while I was there and took it down stairs; she couldn't get that dress on under any other dress."

Hyman Lubinsky was called, and there was a show of interest manifested in the audience. "I am a pedler, and remember the time of the Borden murder, but I did not know where the house was until afterwards; I keep my horse at Gardner's stable; that morning I went by the Borden house in my team, leaving the stable a few minutes after. When I got to the Borden house I saw a lady come out of the barn and walk to the side door steps; she had on a dark colored dress and nothing on her dress; I don't remember whether she went into the house; I was in my team; I know the servant and have delivered her ice cream; I am sure she was not the lady I saw approaching the house." This ended the testimony for the defense and the court adjourned until Monday.

CHAPTER XXX.

Twelfth Day of the Trial.

ON Monday morning Ex-Governor George D. Robinson made
his plea for the prisoner which was as follows :

May it Please Your Honors, Mr. Foreman and Gentlemen—One
of the most dastardly and diabolical of crimes that was ever committed
in Massachusetts was perpetrated 'in August, 1892, in the city of
Fall River. The enormity of it startled everybody, and set all into
diligent inquiry as to the perpetrator of such terrible acts. Our
society is so constituted, gentlemen, that every man feels that the
right must be done and the wrong punished and the wicked doer
brought to his account as promptly as due procedure of law will
permit. Here, then, was a crime with all its horrors, and well may
those who stood first to look at the victims have felt sickened and
distressed at heart, and human nature be broken so that the experience of a lifetime will never bring other such pictures. '' Who could
have done such an act ?'' says everybody. In the quiet of home, in the
broad light of an August day, upon a street of a populous city, with
houses within a stone's throw, nay, almost within touch, who could
have done it ? Inspection of the victims disclosed that Mrs. Borden
had been slain by the use of some sharp and terrible instrument,
inflicting upon her head eighteen blows, thirteen of them crushing
through the skull; and below, lying upon the sofa, was Mr. Borden's
dead and mutilated body, with eleven strokes upon the head, four of
them crushing the skull. The terrors of those scenes no language
can portray. The horrors of that moment we can all fail to describe.
And so we are charged at once, at the outset, to find somebody that
is equal to that enormity, whose heart is blackened with depravity,
whose whole life is a tissue of crime, whose past is a prophecy of
that present. A maniac or fiend we say. Not a man in his senses
and who has heart right, but one of those abnormal productions that
deity creates or suffers, a lunatic or a devil. So do we measure the
degree of character or want of it, that could possibly prompt a human
being to such acts. They were well-directed blows. They were not

the result of blundering. They were aimed steadily and constantly for a purpose, each one finding its place where it was aimed, and none going amiss on the one side or the other. Surely we are prompted to say at the outset that the perpetrator of that act knew how to handle the instrument, was experienced in its control, had directed it before or others like it, and it was not the sudden, untrained doing of somebody who had been unfamiliar with such implements. Now, suspicion began to fall here and there. Everybody about there was called to account so far as could be. That is proper. That is right and necessary. Investigation proceeds. The police intervene. They form their theories. They proceed to act. They concern this one and that one. They follow out this and that clew. They are human only. When once a theory possesses our minds you know how tenaciously it holds the place, and how slow the mind is to find lodgment in something else. Now, no decent man complains of investigation. No one says there ought not to have been anything done. Everything ought to have been done. Nay, more, we say everything was not done and that the proper pursuit was not taken. Now, proceed with this matter a little and let us see how it stands. A person is charged with a crime, like this defendant, suspicions surround her, investigations in regard to her proceed, and inevitably, naturally, if the matter is deemed of consequence, she is brought before the court, the district court in that instance, to have an examination preliminary into the probabilities of the crime on her part. Then if she, having nothing to do with it, having no control of it, having no opportunity to accept, to be heard, be bound and compelled to answer to this court, what then? Then the grand jury of the county is called together and sits by itself under the direction of the district attorney, to investigate and see whether it ought to come before a jury like yourselves. Now remember that at that time, and when this indictment of last December was framed, this defendant had no voice, it was purely one sided. They said, "We make this charge, serious as it is, against the defendant. We will ask her to come to the Bristol county court house and meet that charge, and if we cannot prove it against her in the ordinary way she shall go free : she is not guilty."

Now, that is one sided up to that point, practically, and so you are to draw no inference whatever, and I know you will not ; you will draw no inference whatever as against this defendant until you have heard the evidence in this case, in this court room, at this time. You have nothing to do with what was done in Fall River any more than you have with what is now proceeding in Australia. The finding of Judge Blaisdell of the district court in Fall River, worthy man as he may be, is of no sort of consequence here, and has no sort of influence or obligation over you. We would not be safe if in these great crises our lives hung upon the decision of a single man in a prejudiced and excited community. No, we walk away from Fall River, we come down to the broad seashore, we sniff the breezes of the sea, and here is freedom, here is right, here are you, gentlemen. I say, then, at the outset, as you begin to contemplate this crime and its possible perpetration by the defendant, you must conclude at the outset that such acts as those are morally and physically impossible for this young woman defendant. To foully murder her stepmother, and then go straightway and slay her own father is a wreck of human morals; it is a contradiction of her physical capacity and her character. Now, before I pass, let me say that this defendant complains of no prosecution on the part of the district attorney of this district. He has only one duty, and that is, as a gentleman and lawyer, to conduct this investigation so that the truth as to her may be elicited. With his well-earned reputation and his high standing at the bar he would have no need to search for laurels for his fame, and he is one of the last men that would demean himself so as even to think of it. He stands above the miserable assertions that unthinking people will make, and he walks into this court room only as the representative of the commonwealth of Massachusetts, that is, yours and mine and his, and says : " Gentlemen, all I have to show you is the case we have against this woman. And if the case I have brought to me by the Fall River police is not sufficient, or you have any doubt about it, he will say, if he speaks what his heart prompts him to utter, he will say, " For God's sake, say so, like men, and Bristol county will be the happier and the securer afterward. " He is not here for blood, neither is he helped to such dishonorable work, if it were attempted, by our excellent friend, the district attorney from the great county of Essex, one of our best and most reliable lawyers. So you will see no small play, you will see no mean tactics on the part of the commonwealth here, but only a presentation not overstrained in one jot or one tittle, a presentation of what has been proven here, and only that. So merciful is our provision of the law that a defendant shall have a decent chance that she becomes convinced how faithfully that is carried out when she recalls the numerous kindnesses and considerations on the part of the sheriff of this county. He has done with her, not as a convicted criminal, but as a young woman of his county,.

entitled to her rights, guaranteed to her in the constitution and laws of our State. And so she comes into this court, presided over by our best of the judiciary, clean, able, honorable gentlemen, who sit vigilantly upon the bench to guard against any possible wrong, who want the commonwealth's case tried, but the defendant to pass without abuse or wrong, and taking the law into your hands as they will give it to you, you have only to deal with the facts. I said the case was brought to the district attorney by the Fall River police. I have not time to go into sarcasm or denunciation of those gentlemen. They are like a great many bodies of police that you find in all communities. Policemen are human, made out of men, and nothing else, and the blue coat and the brass buttons only cover the kind of a man that is inside. And you do not get the greatest ability in the world inside a policeman's coat. You may perhaps get what you want, and what is sufficient, but you must only call upon him for such services as he can render. Now, when a police officer undertakes to investigate a crime, he is possessed and saturated with the thoughts and experiences he has with bad people. He is drifting and turning in the way of finding a criminal, magnifying this, minimizing that, throwing himself on this side in order to catch somebody, standing before a community that demands the detection and punishment of the criminal, blamed if he does not get somebody into the lockup before morning. "What are the police doing?" says the newspaper, and the newspapers, you know, are not always right, mostly. Saying to him: "Look here, Mr. Marshal, these murders were committed yesterday and we haven't a murderer in the lockup. Get somebody in." Now they are sensitive to all those expressions. Naturally policemen, feeling the responsibility of their office, must go there and do just such work as that, in that way. That can only be expected of them. And when they come upon the witness stand they reveal their weakness, do they not? They knock their own heads together. They make themselves, as a body of men, ridiculous, insisting that a defendant shall know everything that was done on a particular time, shall account for every moment of that time, shall tell it three or four times alike, shall never waver or quiver, shall have tears, or not have tears, shall make no mistakes. But they, stripped of their blue clothes, and in their citizens' garb, show themselves to be only men here, and liable to human infirmities and errors. Now I dismiss them without any unpleasant reflection. I will talk about them a little later on : but I have nothing to say now, any more than this, that you must not ask of them more than they ought to give, you must not be

surprised that they fail even of the standard that they set up for everybody else.   So I say to you, as a distinguished advocate in a similar
cause expressed himself to the jury : "This defendant comes before
you perfectly satisfied that the jury is the most refreshing prospect in
the eye of accused innocence ever met in human tribunal.   Who are
you twelve men, and how came you here ? Selected out of one
hundred and fifty men that were drawn from the body of this county,
passing the gauntlet of criticism and objections put upon you by the
court or the attorneys, you are sworn here in this cause.   Who are you ?
Men : Bristol county men.   Men with hearts and men with heads,
with souls, and men with rights.   You come here in obedience to the
laws that we prescribe for the orderly administration of our courts.
You come here because, in answer to the demand, you feel that you
must render this great service, unpleasant and trying as it may be,
exhaustive as are its labors ; you come here because you are loyal men to
the State. Nay, more. You are out of families, you come from firesides,
you are members of households, you have wives and daughters and
sisters and you have had mothers, you recognize the bond that unites
and the flash that plays throughout the households.   Now bring your
hearts and your homes and your intellects here and let us talk to you
as men, not as unmeaning things.

The clerk swore you to your duty, and perhaps you did not hear
that oath so closely as I did.   But I heard him say, " You shall well
and truly try and true deliverance make between the commonwealth
and the defendant, whom you shall have in charge. "   In no case
except a capital case is the oath offered in that way—"whom you
shall have in charge. "   And Lizzie Andrew Borden from the days
when we opened this trial until this hour, has been in your charge,
gentlemen. That is the oath you took. And not alone with you,
Mr. Foreman, or any one of you, but with each and all of you.   You
have her in charge.   Now has come the time when not alone her
lawyers are to speak for her, not alone the judges are to watch for
protection, not alone is the learned attorney of the commonwealth to
ask no more than he ought to have, but the twelve men who sit here
to try this question take the woman in this charge, and the commonwealth says, " We intrust her to you. "   Now that is your duty.   She
is not a horse, she is not a house, she is not a parcel of land, she is
not the property of anybody, but she is a free, intelligent, thinking,
innocent woman, in your charge.   I noticed one day as we were proceeding with this trial, a little scene that struck me forcibly.   It was
one morning as the court was about to open, when you were coming

into your seats and standing there and the judges were passing to the bench to take their positions and the defendant was asked to pass around from the place where she now sits in order that she might come in so as to be near her counsel, and right at that moment of transition she stood here waiting between the court and the jury ; and waited in her quietness and calmness until it was time for her properly to come forward. It flashed through my mind in a minute ; there she stands protected, watched over, kept in charge by the judges of this court and by the jury who have her in charge.

If the little sparrow does not fall unnoticed to the ground, indeed, in God's great providence this woman has not been alone in this court room, but ever shielded by his providence from above and by the sympathy and watchful care of those who have her to look after. You are trying a capital case, a case that involves a human life, a verdict in which against her calls for the imposition of but one penalty, and that is that she shall walk to her death. You are then to say, '' I will critically consider this question, and I will make no mistake, because if I do, no power on earth or in heaven can right the wrong.'' You come here without prejudice or bias, I take it. You said you did. I believed you. I believe you now. You said that though you might have read about this transaction, you might have formed an opinion, might have expressed an opinion, as I think some of you with perfect honesty said, because in this intelligent age people do think and read and talk, and it is all right they should, but when a man is big enough to walk up and say in answer to the questions the chief justice put to him, '' I have read and thought and judged about it, and I stand up here now, and before my God and my people, say I will find a true verdict on the evidence under the law.'' That is a man we all want to see in the jury box. I would rather see him there than to have one of these miserable pieces of putty on whom the last man who stuck his finger into him can make an impression. You will need at the outset, gentlemen, to dismiss from your minds entirely everything that the press ever said about the case, anything that your neighbors have ever said about it, anything that you have ever heard about it except in this court room at this time. Every rumor, every idle tale or every true tale that has been told you must banish from your minds absolutely and forever. Why, gentlemen, if we were to try the case on the street we need not have spent these days and you would have been enjoying your entire freedom like the rest of us, you would not have been prisoners yourselves. But we are not trying the case in this way. And so certainly, I believe, does the court guard it, that you are shut off from reading the newspapers, from having communications, from indulging in conversation about the case during the progress of the trial. What use in taking these precautions if you are all coming in with your heads brim full of what you have heard before and will not give that up? Now every man of you is man enough to say, when you go to the jury room to delib- erate on this thing, and somebody presents an idea. "Well, that is not in this case. You have no right to consider any such thing. You have no more right to do it than you have to take a knife and cut this woman's throat"—I mean under your duties as prescribed by the law. Then you come here patiently day after day, and you will sit here again and again until this case is concluded, and then proceed with your deliberation with that calmness and fidelity that is guaranteed in the expression of your countenance.

> When the life of man is in debate
> No time can be too long, no care too great.

Hear all, weigh all with caution. Now, gentlemen, it is not your business to unravel the mystery. You are not here to find out the solution of that problem. You are not here to find out the murderer. You are not here to pursue anything else. You are simply and solely here to say, is this woman defendant guilty? That is all, and though the real criminal shall never be found, better a million times that than you find a verdict against this woman upon insufficient evidence and against your human experience and contrary to the law, so that an unhealthy appetite may be satisfied, and blood be given that belongs to the owner of it beyond anybody's taking. Not who is it? Not how could it have been done? Did she do it? That is all. Reflect if you have not yet been able to bring that evidence with a certainty and a reasonable construction to a conclu- sion, so that you, as decent gentlemen, can go to your homes and sit down and say, "We have done our whole duty. We have brought in a verdict against her," although perhaps, within a week we wish we had not, when we think of it. Nor must you think for a moment that this defendant is set to the business of finding out who did it. If she cannot find out and tell you who perpetrated these acts, somebody says, "Go hang her." She is not a detective, and the commonwealth has put her in a place for the last ten months so she could not be very vigilant or active if she had all the ability in the world. She has been in jail in this county; she has been under control of the police from the very time, from Thursday, August 4, as you know from all these facts, and do not expect her to do things that are impossible. Pray, do not load upon her the responsibility of setting her to go when she cannot go, or do what she cannot do, or else hold her to account for it with the severest penalty known in the law. The commonwealth does not want any victim, either. In the old days they had sacrifices of lambs and goats, and even human beings were offered in expiation and in sacrifice. But we have got over all that. We do not even burn witches now in Massachusetts. The commonwealth wants no victim, and so, gentlemen, I have attempted in this way to array before you what I consider, in my own manner, the duties that lie upon you and the limitations under which you act. And what is the call upon you? Why, simply to be true to yourselves. "To thine own self be true, and it must follow, as the night the day, thou canst not then be false to any man." Now there always goes with any person the presumption of innocence of crime. I stand here at this moment addressing you, and I am clad all over with that presumption of innocence of every crime; so is each one of you. That is your bulwark; that is born with you, nay, rather is given to you out of the great consent of all the people, and you say "guilty?" Why I think not. I am innocent, and the court will tell you that that presumption started with this prisoner on August 4, and has been with her by night and by day. When you had her in charge that presumption of innocence has been in her favor and it never leaves her until by the verdict of a jury that presumption is overcome and she is declared guilty.

It is true that people who have heretofore been innocent commit crime, and so the law says, "We will not demand the unreasonable and impossible thing, but you, the defendant, shall have that presumption go with you until it is entirely overturned and it says that you are of a criminal heart and criminal act." Now, bear that in mind, if it comes to any question in the discussion of the evidence of a doubtful consideration, then that presumption is all the time in the scale. The beam of the scale does not stand level to start with. We say the scales of justice hang even, but there is always with the defendant the presumption of innocence that tips the scale in her favor, and the commonwealth must begin and load in on the other side facts until they shall overcome the presumption—nay, more, and overbalance the facts that the defendant shall produce.

I shall not attempt to talk to you at length about the different kinds of evidence, direct evidence and circumstantial evidence. The learned court will explain those different features to you, and the lines have been drawn so clearly in the many cases that have been tried that it is wholly unnecessary for me to take your time and your patience. You know, or will know, when his honor has uttered to you the charge in the best way what we mean by direct evidence, and what we mean by circumstantial evidence. Direct evidence, testimony from actual observation and actual knowledge, is what we very frequently rely upon. But that is not always certain. I am bound to say to you, not always sure, because the man who gives the direct evidence may be a miserable liar and you would not believe him under oath unless you kept your hand on him. Now, that is direct evidence and then sometimes facts are found out by circumstances. You reason from hearing a noise or from seeing a person in a given place. You see a man going somewhere and you say he has gone in there for that particular business there, whether it is banking or insurance or grocery. Well, you may be right or you may be wrong. You have been given different circumstances to try to draw out a reasonable conclusion, but I am not going to enlarge upon that because I deem it unnecessary and because I have other things in my mind which are more important. You do not start in here to try to convict anybody—other people may, but you do not. If you are asked to convict upon any evidence, whether that is direct or circumstantial, you will, of course, bring it your clearest perception and strict honesty, and look to see whether it fits in, whether it is all right, and whether it has not run against this corner and also knocked itself to pieces, whether the circumstances are all in and whether something has not been left out, whether the chain is not broken with which it is sought to bind the defendant. Look it over, search it through and through, as I will in the argument as I proceed, and discover whether there is any claim that is insufficiently proved. Then, too, the court will tell you that by whichever method you proceed as to this defendant, the proof must come up in your mind as a moral certainty—not a mathematical certainty, but a moral certainty. It must be beyond a reasonable doubt.

Now, you saw in criminal cases before—very likely you have had a man before you on trial who had stolen five dollars or something of that kind, and the same rule applies. And you are told that you must not convict him unless you are satisfied beyond a reasonable doubt. It is not different in this case. In the one case you are perhaps dealing with a man who will be subjected to a penalty of a fine, or a brief imprisonment at the most. Here the same rule applies, and you are dealing with a woman, whose life is at stake, and nothing else. Now, you will see that while the rule of law is the same in the one case as in the other, the magnitude of a mistake about it is not to be lightly considered. So that when you are asked to find these essential facts beyond a reasonable doubt of a curmudgeon who sits off in a corner and says, "I won't talk with anybody; I am an ugly fellow: I will make myself disagreeable in this jury room," that is not it. That is not a reasonable doubt, no matter which side he is on. He is not fit for service in the jury room. It is the doubt of such men as I take you to be, with your home influences, with your church belongings, with your business associations, with your social relations, with all that binds you up to each of us.

It is the reasonable doubt of a reasonable man, confronted with the greatest crisis he has ever met in the world. Yes, the greatest crisis ; because, though I doubt not some of you have worn the blue and faced the cannon shot, though you may have heard and felt the thunders of war, and you may have seen blood flow in streams, yet that is one thing; this—to sit here and to have in charge this young woman and to say upon your oaths you are satisfied that she is guilty or not guilty, is a duty to which very likely none of you have ever been called, and which probably you will never be asked to perform again. You will go to your graves thinking of how you performed this task, and it ought not to be that you can have any compunctions that you made a mistake which nobody could retrieve. Then again, under the laws of this State, the defendant in a criminal case is permitted to testify upon the stand as she desires to, but if she does not desire to she can refrain from testifying, and then the statute says, specifically and directly, no inference shall be drawn against her from the fact that she has not testified. And so the learned district attorney in his closing argument will not by the slightest suggestion or insinuation insult this court and jury by intimating that the defendant ought to have testified. That law was born under two considerations. Formerly the defendant could not testify. Later it seemed to be wise to give a defendant an opportunity to testify, but it says at once, although he does not come to the stand, you shall not take that against him in any way. And again, too, as if in the charity of human nature our law givers felt that it was too great a strain oftentimes to put upon a defendant to place him in such a position that he must either go upon the stand or have that argument laid against him, that he ought to have done it, the law which I have cited to you—not in its exact term, but in its essential features and expressions—was framed in the way I have stated. And I dismiss that again. The court will tell you in emphatic and clear language, and it will look you in the eye, and touching your sense of justice, say to you : Gentlemen, you must not consider that, and you will not as you go to yonder room under your oath depart from that, because if you do so what is the use in having scales for justice to hold or courts for the apparent administration of it either. Now I said you must leave out rumors, reports, statements which you have heard before the trial commenced. That is true. I repeat it ; but more, you must leave out of your minds absolutely every single thing that the learned gentleman who opened this case, Mr. Moody, said that he was going to prove, unless he has actually proven it. Now I would not like to say that about him in private affairs. I would not be pleased to intimate to you that he would say anything that he was not going to do, because he is the soul of honor. But he speaks for the commonwealth, that is all, and the commonwealth tells him : " You must not say anything but what you are going to do and you must tell them that and that only. " And I shall expect the learned district attorney to withdraw the things that brother Moody said he was going to prove, because he has rot proved them. The court room ought not to echo still with the utterances of the gentleman who opened this case, because they tend to create a prejudice against the defendant. Now let us tell you about that so that you will understand it. Mr. Moody said that the government was going to claim and prove that this defendant was preparing a dangerous weapon on August 3, the day before the murder. You heard him say that. I did. He said it. They have not proved it, have they? Was there a thing about it in the evidence ? You have heard some discussion that we have had at the bar because, in order that there should be no prejudice, you have been asked to stop. Many of those things which have been offered in good faith have not been proved, because the court has said that they are not proper to be proved in this case. They have nothing to do with it. They will only mislead the jury, and the jury shall not hear them in this case. Whenever another case arises, if these things are pertinent and proper they shall be heard, but not now. No, the commonwealth came with the idea of putting these things before you, I say, with good intention, but the court says, " No, though your intention is good, it is not proper, and we will not complicate this thing. It will create a bias against the prisoner which may divert the course of justice, and that shall not be introduced here : it has no right here though you mean to be right. " Now, there is no proof at all, gentlemen, about any dangerous weapon having been prepared upon the 3d of August. And to make it more specific, Mr. Moody said in his opening that they would prove that this young woman went out to buy a poison on August 3. You have not heard any such evidence. It is not proved : the court did not allow it to be proved, and it is not in the case. Now you will not go to the jury room with the thought that if it had been allowed you would have considered that it was proven. But it is not allowed : no such evidence came before you, and I shall expect the district attorney, man fashion, to get up and say so, and I think you will, and I shall be disappointed in him if he does not. He will tell you that upon that subject, and that the case is not touched at all. Then he said that they were going to show you that the defendant had contradicted herself under oath about these occurrences. Well, there is another question which went to the court, and the court said : " That is not proper in this case. You cannot show that. " And so there is nothing of the kind. Now, are you not going to sit back there and say, " Well, I rather think Mr. Knowlton and Mr. Moody would not have offered it unless there is something behind it." That is not the way to try cases. That is not the way you hold this defendant in charge. You might just as well have got your verdict before you started, and said, "Guilty, because she is here." You might as well say, "We don't want to hear any evidence. " You do not want to say that you do not care whether you hang her right or wrong,—" give us somebody. " Now, the court sits here to guard you and all of us against any such mistake. That will not do. The court says : " Here, gentlemen, decide this case on the evidence given right here from the witness stand and on nothing else. " When you stand there in the box ready to answer, and somebody says to you, " O, don't mind what they put in about particular evidence, whether competent or incompetent, " you say, " No, I want my rights. I am here under the protection of the law, and I call upon these twelve men, decent men, under their oaths, to stand by me and see that I am not wronged. " So you will leave those things out, gentlemen. No prussic acid, no preparation of a weapon by this woman, no statement made by her under oath in this trial, or anywhere that you know anything about or have a right to consider—I do not care what you have read. Now, we shall agree in the consideration of this case very largely upon many things. My position in this case, in speaking for the defendant, is not to misrepresent or distort facts, but to take the proofs as they are, put them against each other and find out what is right. This defendant wants nothing but justice, and she desires to have it in the proper administration of the law.   Things that are not in dispute I hope I shall not contest.   I hope I shall array before you the facts altogether in an intelligent and clear way, and then ask you to give me your judgment on them by and by, and I just as sincerely trust that I will not, even by a single letter, step over the line of the proof or deal unjustly, even with the commonwealth that is really so dear to us all.   Now, let us see if we cannot get at these things in a fair way without prejudice.

Mr. Andrew J. Borden left his house and went down street that morning, Thursday, August 4, about 9 :30 o'clock, so that he arrived at the Savings Bank, upon the evidence, about 9 :30.   He went into several places along the street, not material now to consider, walked back along South Main street toward his house, stopped at a store of his that was being repaired, talked with Shortsleeves and Mr. Mather, and after picking up an old block, which he wrapped up in paper and took home, he started to go to his house.   You recollect something was said that it is not material to consider in this connection, but he walked along up toward his house, arriving there, the defendant thinks, about 10 :45.   It did not vary, probably, more than two, or possibly three minutes from that time.   It must have been as much as that because you recollect how Mr. Mather put it, his looking at the clock and the time that Mr. Borden lingered at the store, went upstairs, came down, went out into the middle of the street, went back and talked with Mather and Shortsleeves a minute or two and then went on.   It was 10 :40, twenty minutes of 11, as he came up to the store.   Now he probably consumed two or three or four minutes in doing those things that they have spoken of, and so you may well, perhaps, infer that he reached his house about 10 :45.   We have learned of several things that he did, that he came into the house, sat down, went upstairs to his room, laid down his little package, and so on, was occupied with a few things that would consume a short space of time, so that we can say that he was murdered somewhere within a given fifteen or twenty minutes of time which may be between five minutes of 11 and ten minutes past 11.   I presume that the commonwealth will not differ with me about this.   At any rate, if there is a clearer statement of it to be made, the defendant has no objection if it lies within the proofs.   That is the way I propose to argue, to take that as a fact.   Mrs. Borden had died earlier.   On the testimony of the physicians, inspecting the character of the wounds, the condition of the blood, the state of the stomachs and the intestines, they put it from an hour to an hour and a half earlier than he died. That is probably correct. At any rate, no issue is made about it; and so, if I may be permitted to state it, she would seem to have died between 9:45 o'clock and 10:15, somewhere within that half hour, taking all the evidence into account. That answers the demands of the physicians, and seems to me, if I may be permitted to say it, to accord to the facts. Now you have those tragedies within that short space of time in that place, and it is for us to see whether the defendant is connected with them: whether the defendant alone or the defendant with any confederate, if there is any proof about it, did the deed. I am at a loss to know where there is any evidence about any accomplice or anybody else connected with it at all, and so it is only my inquiry to find out if there is any truth as to this defendant. Of course, I need only suggest to you that until there is some sort of evidence that connects somebody with it, it is not well to assume that she must have had somebody, because you cannot think of anything else. That is not the way to try this case. Now it will be my endeavor in discussion of these questions to be very guarded about giving my opinion of the evidence. I have no right to put in whatever personal weight I may have in my construction of the evidence. That is bad practice, and I should expect, if I get over the line, for the learned court to call me to order, because I trust I know my place.

I have no right to tell you that I believe so and so about this case. I may believe all I want to, but my duty is to keep it inside of me, that is all. And so the district attorney will do the same: carrying his great weight and the strength of his convictions every way into this case, he is not so to demean himself as to tell you that he believes so and so. You do not want our beliefs, we want yours and your judgment. Now there sits the defendant. In yonder city were the crimes. Those crimes were the foulest and the darkest kind. She comes here under this presumption of innocence. It must be overcome absolutely and you must bind her up to the acts before you can say she is guilty. What is the cord that holds her to those terrible criminal acts? Let us see where it is to be found. It is not in the charge that is read in the indictment; it is not in the procedure of the court, but it must be in that chain of circumstances or in that line of direct proof that shall show you that she is tied up to this thing, that she is the one, and that it is not reasonable that anybody else did it or could have done it; that there is no reasonable way of accounting for the things that are proved except that she did it. That is the kind of bond that you must frame in order to hold her or to permit you even to think of holding her.

If a person commits a murder like this and we know it, we have
no occasion to inquire for what reason he did it. If he did it then it
does not make any difference whether he had any motive or not. He
might have done it for pure deviltry, without a motive. He may have
done it in insanity, and then the law comes in, in another way, to
intervene in his behalf. But if it is proved—proved, I say, not
guessed, but proved—that he did it, it is not of the slightest
importance whether he had a motive or not. If he did it, that
is all there is about it. Now, why is the commonwealth bound
in this case to attempt to show a motive for doing? merely this, gentlemen, because they say here are the crimes—there are the crimes, there
sits the defendent, you see her over there? Now, in order to hold her
responsible for the crimes we have got to bind her up to the crimes. We
have no direct evidence that puts her there, we have some circumstances
that look as if she might get there: and so in order to bring her to it,
we must show a reason why she would do it. What moved her to do
it, that is the motive, that is to say the motive in this case, is only to
explain the evidence. You get my idea I think. It is only to tell you
how you can explain her acts or her words. If you can explain them
in a reasonable and honorable way she is entitled to that. But if they
cannot explain except that you find a criminal thought running
through them, then that motive operates against her. Not to make
her commit the crime, but to show you that what is said about it is a
reasonable construction, that she was led to do it. That is it, if I
understand the case properly, and I state it just as I believe it to be
—the court will correct me if I am wrong—and I believe I state it
about as the commonwealth attorneys would state it, intentionally I
do; and so that motive is only to be inquired into to help out about
the circumstances, and I think I can explain it to you—and I am
guarding myself against saying anything I ought not to. Suppose
the crime were committed in another place, and a man was suspected
of it, and he proved that he were in the state of Georgia at the time,
at the very instant, and everybody knew it. Well, now, you could
not bind him for doing the crime anyway, no matter if he stood down
there and swore profanely that if he could only get home he would
have killed that man. That would not be anything, because the
circumstances do not come up to it, they are not connected. So you
do not want his motive to explain his acts. He hasn't any acts to
explain. Now, the government says that Miss Lizzie Borden has
some acts to explain, therefore they will find out whether there is
anything in her motives that will put a color on it. I think you see

that, and they are inseparable from the conditions. Now, I say that the argument will be only this, that you are to look at the motive to see what effect you shall give to the evidence. It will not do to say that no adequate motive is shown and none is necessary. That is true when the crime is proved. That is true when you have the facts. But that is not true when you are trying to show the motive in order to explain the facts. Now there is absolutely (and I think the commonwealth will say it) no direct evidence against Miss Borden, the defendant. You know what I mean. Nobody saw or heard anything or experienced anything that connects her with the tragedies. No weapon whatever, and no knowledge of the use of one, as to her, has been shown. You know if you had found her with some weapon of that kind in her control, or in her room, or with her belongings, that would be direct evidence. But there is nothing of that kind. It is not claimed. It is not shown that she ever used an implement of the character that must have produced these murders. It is not shown that she ever touched one, or knew of one, or bought one, or had one. In fact, the evidence is that she did not know where the ordinary things in the house of that kind were.

And the murders did not tell any tales on her either. There was no blood on her, and blood speaks out, although it is voiceless; it speaks out against the criminal. Not a spot on her from her hair to her feet, on her dress or person anywhere. Think of it. Think of it for an instant. Yes, there was one drop of blood on the white skirt as big as the head of the smallest pin, says Prof. Wood. Less than a sixteenth of an inch in diameter; and that is every particle of blood that was found upon her clothing. And that was not where you could expect it to be ; not in the front of the skirt that must, if she had it on and had done these foul deeds, have first come in contact, but around back down toward the bottom near the placket, as I believe the women call it, out of the way. I do not know but the government are going to say that she turned her skirt round hind side before, before she began, in order to get at it in a practical way. I don't know what they are going to say yet. I shall have occasion to speak of that by and by. But Prof. Wood does not claim now— I don't know as there is a Fall River policeman, from the top down, that claims now—that that little fly speck, as it were, of blood tells any tale here. I forbear to allude to what is proved in this case— Miss Borden's illness, monthly illness, at that time—and to tell you or remind you that Prof. Wood said he would not undertake to say that that blood was not the menstrual blood. You know the facts.

I need not give them in detail. You know enough in your own households ; you know all about it. You are men and human. You have your feelings about it. I am not going to drag them up, but you must not lose sight of these things. Then there was some talk about a roll of burned paper in the stove, where Mr. Philip Harrington, I believe, was the officer. He took off the cover and saw what he said looked like the embers of a rolled up piece of paper, burned, that is all. And there was some sort of dark insinuations here floating around that didn't clothe themselves in words, but there was something in the manner that meanly intimated that Dr. Bowen was doing something about it—Dr. Bowen—I suppose they don't make any allegation that he committed these murders, or helped to cover up, or assisted in doing anything about it. When the evidence is heard, it seems that Mr. Philip Harrington says that Dr. Bowen was throwing in some pieces of an old letter that had nothing to do with these transactions, something about his own family matters of no account. And Mr. Harrington, I think I am right in the name of the officer, when they were thrown in, saw some little piece of paper, rolled up paper, about an inch in diameter, that had been rolled up and was lying there, the embers of it, and there was a small, low fire. Well, we thought the handle was in there. We thought that was the plan that the government possessed itself with the idea that that handle was rolled up by the defendant in a piece of paper and put down in there to burn; and it had all burned up except the envelope of paper. Did you ever see such a funny fire in the world? What a funny fire that was. A hard stick inside a newspaper and the hardwood stick would go out beyond recall, and the newspaper that lives forever would stay there. What a funny idea; what a theory that is. And we wrestled with that proposition here, on the part of the defense, through weary nights, troubled about it, until Fleet and Mullaly got here together, and then we were relieved from every doubt. For the handle is in it, and it is out of it. Fleet did not see it ; Mullaly did see it. Fleet did not take it out of the box, and Mullaly saw him do it. And it is in the box now, and they run over to Fall River to get it, or they wanted to, and can't get into our house, and explain about it. So we rather think that the handle is still flying in the air, a poor orphan handle without a hatchet, flying around somewhere. For heaven's sake get the one hundred and twenty-five policemen of Fall River and chase it till they can drive it in somewhere and hitch it up to its family belongings. Then, too, upon the best testimony of the experts, and probably in your own common sense, whoever committed that murder of Mrs. Borden stood astride her body. She was a large, stout, fleshy woman, weighing two hundred pounds. Conceive of the situation. You looked at the place. You saw the little gap between the bureau and the bed, stated to be about thirty to thirty-four inches, and you are to conceive of the murderer standing over the body in this way. Here she lies, there, and the murderer standing over her and literally chopping her head to pieces. I shall have more to say about that by and by, but I call it to your attention. And they all agreed that Mr. Borden was butchered by somebody who stood at the head of the sofa and between that and the parlor door. You know how it is placed and we make no question about it. That looks reasonable, we will say, and so we take the things as they are. Now, what reason is there for saying that this defendant is guilty? The commonwealth asks you to come up here and hear all this evidence and point out whether you think she is guilty or not. If you do not think she is, why, you say, " Not guilty;" and the commonwealth is satisfied, and the district attorney goes away, having done his whole duty, satisfied to let it alone. He does not find any fault about it, he is relieved of it. It is a great relief to him to get rid of the case. He does not enjoy it. He says, come up and hear all we have got against her and let the jury say she is not guilty and that will stop this matter, or if you come up and hear it and you say she is guilty, then that relieves me about it. I put this responsibility on you. And the court says, "I put this woman into your charge." Now you have got it all. Now what right have they to say anything about it? Well, I want to run it through, which I have done with some care, and tell you why they claim that she did it.

In the first place, they say she was in the house in the forenoon. Well, that may look to you like a very wrong place for her to be in. But it is her home. I suspect you have kind of an impression that it would be a little better for her than it would be out traveling the streets. I don't know where I would want my danghter to be, at home ordinarily, or where it would speak more for her honor and care, and reflect somewhat of credit upon me and her mother (who is my wife, I want to say), than to say that she was at home, attending to the ordinary vocations of life, as a dutiful member of the household, as belonging there. So I don't think there is any criminal look about that. She was at home. She is shown to have been upstairs to her room, the government says, about ten minutes before ten, and she must have seen, as they claim, the dead body of Mrs. Borden, as she, the defendant, went up and down the stairs. Now, let us look at that, because that is an important feature in the case, important for the commonwealth, important for the defendant. You went there and saw the situation. You know how the stairs go up, turning around as you go up, and at the top of the landing you are right there at Miss Lizzie's door. When you stand at the top of the landing you cannot see into the guest chamber, you know. It is as if you stood over there where the officer stands, or a little further. You are not looking into the door at all. It is not like a good many houses where you come up at the top and are looking in at both doors at the same time. Then it is said that at a certain point on the staircase, right on one tread of one stair, if you look in under the bed across the floor of the guest chamber you could see any object that was over between the bed and bureau. And you were all asked to do that by traveling up and traveling down—you remember the experience you had—and looking. And therefore they say that, although Miss Lizzie, when she was at her door as she undertook to pass down, could not see Mrs. Borden over there behind the bed, that if she went downstairs she could have seen Mrs. Borden lying there behind the bed, and, therefore, that she must have seen her. Now if we had marched up and down the stairs and told you nothing of what we wanted you to look at, there is not one of you that would have squinted under that bed on that particular tread of the stairs. You would not have thought of it. But you were going to see if you could see, and you were told to look all you could, and see if you could see. So you got ready to see, and made up your minds that you were going to see if there was anything to see. You have not been home for the last two weeks. But when you get home, and after you get over this in two or three weeks from now, and I meet you, I want you to tell me where you looked when you came down stairs that morning, and whether you looked to see what you could see at any particular stair. How was it the last day you were at home? Do you remember anything about it? What time in the morning did you come down? At what stair did you look to see what you could see? Right in your own house where nothing had happened. Now we are talking of a time with regard to Miss Lizzie when nothing had happened, when everything was all right. It was so at that time as to her. Now people do not go searching and squinting and playing the detective and all that to begin with. I do not. If I did I should think I was a rascal some way or other, and that something was happening to me. If she did that thing, if she was looking to see if anybody could see it, if she walked down and looked under and not said anything about it—there goes the murderess, see her ; she didn't see it, and she might. Therefore she is the criminal. She did see it because she could, and, therefore, she is the criminal. No, no. You and I, until we get to be too old, run up and down stairs just as we have a mind to. They are our stairs. We do not ask anybody's pardon or qualify our act a particle. Then there is not the slightest evidence that that door was open at that time. Remember that there is evidence that it was open later but no evidence that it was open before Mr. Borden came in. I am right about that, and that is very important. So that if, when Miss Lizzie was down stairs and went upstairs, as she undoubtedly did during that forenoon, to her room, if she went up and down stairs and the door was closed or nearly closed or stood ajar, then, of course, she could not see. She had no occasion to go into that spare room. Wouldn't go in there. As you know about the habits of the family in which she lived, the spare room was closed up practically. Mrs. Borden had gone there to make the beds, and after she had left it all right, undoubtedly she would push to the door. The door was pushed to, at any rate. There is no evidence that it was wide open. Now the government starts out with the idea that the door was standing wide open, and, therefore, that she could see : and I have told you how you can reason it very plainly out in your own common experience you wouldn't look. If she had been lying right in front of the bed, outside, why I should have said it would be very improbable that a passer up and down the stairs would not have seen her, and yet that is not impossible. You walk along the streets sometimes, possibly—I do not want to say anything wrong about you—and you meet your own wife and don't see her, go right along. They used to tell a story about Prof. Peirce over at Cambridge who didn't know his own wife when he met her, and he had been spoken to about it so much that finally he thought to make amends, he would speak to the first thing he met, and that was a cow. He said " Good morning. " He didn't make any more mistakes. People are not looking for everything at every minute, especially if they are innocent. It is the guilty man that is always looking around to see when there is somebody round going to catch him, lay hand on him. Now do not ask her to do things that nobody else does. Besides, you remember the testimony from Dr. Bowen and Mr. Manning and some others—it is not necessary to state them—that the upper hall was dark when they went up there, and that the guest chamber was dark. You remember that in that guest chamber there are these tight board shutters that shut up. And you know the New England housewife does not like to have her carpet fade, and the more they live in the old style the more careful they are.

I remember with some reflections about my old mother, how she looked after the carpet and the boys, and they did not get the light in. The boys wanted to live out in the sunlight, and she did not want her carpets there. And so the natural thing in that room in the Borden house was to keep the shutters shut, those tight shutters. And the doctors say, they all of them say, that when they went in it was dark and they had to open them so they could see something. Now you recollect that we tried that on you over there. You marched up and down in the first place, with the shutters all flung open, so that that room was as light as this, or more so. Then we shut the shutters and asked you to go up. You know the instance. You can see across the street, but it is always difficult to look down into a well and see what is at the bottom. Now, they say further, as a reason, that she is guilty, or they claim it, that Mr. Fleet tells you that Lizzie said she saw Mrs. Borden about 9 o'clock, when she, meaning Mrs. Borden, was making the bed. Now, taking that as true, there is no contradiction of it, I am bound to say, however, in fairness to the defendant, that it is possible that Mr. Fleet was mistaken. But it is of no great account, as the defense looks at this case. Admit that, then, for the time being, for this discussion, to be true, I do not say it is, but just assume it. See what it comes to, then : that is, Miss Lizzie said to Mr. Fleet—assume that it is a fact —that as she went down stairs or went upstairs she saw Mrs. Borden making the bed in the spare room. Well, what of it ? what of it ? True, you say. Your daughter goes upstairs this morning to her room and she sees her mother in the spare room making the bed. Well, what of it ? Well, they say she was upstairs when Mrs. Borden was making the bed. That is true. But she was upstairs in her own house, in her own room, at a time when the orderly woman of a house goes to look after the morning work. It does not appear one way or the other whether they were in conversation or not, and it does not appear whether she went up and down stairs that morning two or three or more times or not. Why, you would naturally infer, I should say, that it would be the commonest thing in the world for this young woman to pass up and down stairs to her room in the ordinary way of living ? Why not ? Do you suppose that your wives and daughters can tell the number of times they went up and down stairs six months ago on a given day? Not at all, or even the day before, unless they were very careful about something. Now, there is no doubt at all in my mind that she did go up and down stairs. Mrs. Borden was making the bed. That was before she had been killed, of course. And while she was there, pursuing that work, nothing whatever except the passing up and down is what is claimed here. Now, grant it all. Grant that she did go up and down stairs that morning about 9 o'clock. Mrs. Borden was alive. It is not claimed that she killed them at that time. But the commonwealth undertakes to tell you without any evidence, gentlemen, without any evidence that she stayed up there that forenoon, practically, until her father came in. I say there is no evidence of it, and I will show you that later. That she went up and down I do not care to question. I should expect it. That she stayed up, no; or that she was there, having stayed all the time until her father came, no. Now, she told about the note, they say, and that is evidence of guilt. She told about Mrs. Borden having a note. Now, there is considerable interest in that question, and I ask your attention to it. You know that after the tragedies, when Miss Lizzie was asked about where Mrs. Borden was, she told Bridget, so Bridget tells us, that Mrs. Borden had a note and had gone out. I said: " Who is sick?" " I don't know ; she had a note this morning ; it must be in town." Now, that is what Bridget said to Mrs. Churchill and she says : "I said," meaning herself, "I said, ' where is your mother?' She said, 'I don't know : she's just had a note to see some one who is sick.' !" Next question : listen to it. "What did Bridget tell about Mrs. Borden having a note?" and, "She said Mrs. Borden had a note to go and see some one that was sick, and she was dusting the sitting room, and she hurried off and said she didn't tell me where she was going : she generally does." Now, that is what Bridget told Mrs. Churchill. You get the idea. Both Bridget and Lizzie had learned from Mrs. Borden that she had had a note. Mrs. Borden had told Lizzie. Mrs. Borden had told Bridget. She had given Bridget the work to do, washing the windows. She says to her: " I have got a note to go out and see some one that was sick." That was when she was dusting in the sitting room. That is when Bridget says it was to Mrs. Churchill: that was at the first, when there was no mistake about it. And Bridget says: " She didn't tell me. She hurried off." No, Lizzie didn't say anything about her hurrying off; nobody says that. Bridget told it to Mrs. Churchill. She hurried off, and " She, Mrs. Borden, didn't tell me, Bridget, where she was going; she generally does.'' Now have you the slightest doubt about that Mrs. Churchill you saw? She was called upon three times to tell that and she told it very clearly and I think convincingly. Now notice the questioning that follows: ''That was what Bridget told you?'' ''Yes, sir.'' ''That was not what Lizzie told you?'' ''No, sir.'' ''Bridget said Mrs. Borden had a note?'' ''Yes.'' ''And she hurried off?'' ''Yes, sir.'' ''She was dusting the sitting room?'' ''Yes, sir.'' ''And Bridget says, 'she didn't tell me where she was going; she generally does,' Bridget says.'' ''Bridget said that?'' ''Yes, sir.'' ''That was not what Lizzie said?'' '' No, sir.'' ''Now, you have got that right, haven't you; no doubt about that?'' ''Bridget said that Mrs. Borden had a note to go and see some one who was sick. 'She was dusting in the sitting room; she hurried off. She didn't tell me where she was going: she generally does.' '' Now, my friend who opened this case for the commonwealth said that Lizzie told a lie about that note. He used that word. I submit that that will hardly stand upon his evidence. If he had heard the evidence fully through

EX-GOVERNOR ROBINSON.

he would not have uttered that expression, because here you have proved that Bridget gave the clearest and fullest statement about this matter, and you will probably infer from this that Lizzie learned from Bridget that Mrs. Borden had gone out, and she had a note to go because Bridget tells it with exact detail and holds it down herself. That is not criminal on the part of Bridget at all. I am only calling your attention to the directness of the testimony at the time, right on the very moment. Now, there is not anything in the testimony that really qualifies that at all. Miss Russell says that she heard the talk about the note, but she did not know who told it. Now notice that, and Bridget was there, Lizzie there, Mrs. Churchill there, and Miss Russell says she heard the talk about the note, but she does not know who told it, so that you see that you are uncertain there. Then Miss Russell tells about the conversation with Dr. Bowen, and with Lizzie about the note. Listen to it : "Lizzie, do you know anything about the note your mother had?" And she hesitated and said, well, no, she didn't. Said Dr. Bowen, "I had looked in the waste basket," and Miss Russell said "have you looked in your pocket?" and I think I said, "Well, then, she must have put it in the fire." And Lizzie said, "Yes, she must have put it in the fire." You see that the suggestion of putting it in the fire came from Miss Russell, not from Lizzie. Dr. Bowen had been searching the waste basket. He had looked around to see if he could find the note. He did not succeed, he calls their attention to it in this way I have stated, and they all assent to it and very likely that was true. It was not of any account. The woman had got the note and had tossed it away, very likely threw it in the kitchen stove and burned it, but we do not know anything about it. But they all seemed satisfied right there on the spot.

Then he said that he had searched for it, Dr. Bowen ; it is Miss Russell telling it, and at any rate she says what was said about that was said in the presence of Lizzie and "the same person said she must have burned it?" "I think I answered that question." That is Miss Russell. Well now you get nothing from the officers, merely that Mr. Fleet learned from Miss Lizzie that Mrs. Borden had a note and had gone out. Officer Wilson says the same thing, that she said she had received a note and that she thought she had gone out. That was after the murder, and she said that Mrs. Borden had a note and she thought she had gone out, that is during the forenoon she thought she had gone out. Dr. Dolan says the same thing, so that when you come to consider it you see that the evidence in regard to the note comes from what was told at the very first. If you believe that Mrs. Borden told both Lizzie and Bridget about the note it all looks plain. And why should it not ? They were all in the family there together, and she receives a note to go out, and she did have the note, or else they both tell something that Mrs. Borden told that was not true, and we are not going to believe that. Taking the evidence that comes from the living and that drops from the lips of

the dead, you must find that Mrs. Borden did have the note and that
she told the two women about it and hurried off, as they thought,
and did not tell Bridget or either one of them where she was going.
It was not of any great account probably. She got a note to go out,
and see a woman, and did go out, as far as we learn to the contrary.
It was a natural and ordinary thing, and the note was thrown away
and tossed into the fire. It was not a bank note to be kept, but a
little scrap of paper probably indicating what was wanted. Now, a
person may say " Where is the note?" Well, we would be very glad
to see it, very glad. They looked after it and they could not find it.
The construction of Miss Russell was that she had burned it up. Very
likely that was it. They say that nobody has come forward to say
that she has sent it. That is true. You will find men now, perhaps
living in this county, who do not know that this trial is going on.
They do not know anything about it, don't pay much attention to it,
they are about their own business : do not consider it of any
consequence. And after a lawsuit, it very often happens in every
court room that some one will come forward and say, "Well, if I had
really known that that question was in dispute, I could have told you
all about it. " Bless his dear heart, why didn't he come out of the
cellar so we could see him? Well, sometimes people don't want to
have anything to do with it. They don't want to get into the court
room, even if a life is in danger—women especially; they have a
dread of all sorts of things. The note may have been a part of the
scheme in regard to Mrs. Borden. It may have got there through
foul means and with a criminal purpose. We don't know anything
about it. But that a note came there on this evidence you cannot
question. That Lizzie lied about it is a wrongful aspersion, born out
of the ignorance of the facts as they were to be developed in this case,
not with a purpose to wrong her but mis-stating the evidence as we
all do when we do not know quite what is coming, really anticipating
something that is not proven. So I say that it is not true that Lizzie
told a lie about it. If she did Bridget did the same. I would not
say that for a minute. There is nothing to connect Bridget with this
transaction. See how quickly you would suspect anybody because
you get them under pressure. Now look at it. Suppose that Bridget
were suspected of this crime, and Mrs. Churchill came forward and
told that Bridget said these words that I read, how quick some people
would be to say, "O, Bridget!" "She did it. She did it because
she told a lie about that note. " Do you see it? It is plain, it is a
demonstration. Now I dismiss it with the remark that nobody thinks

that Bridget Sullivan had anything to do with this crime at all. Lizzie does not think so, because she has said so openly. Now she told about her visit out to the barn they say. She told the officers that she went out to the barn; went out in the yard, some twenty or thirty minutes. Now remember that we get this information in regard to the time from the police officers. The others tell us that she said she went to the yard and the barn. It takes assistant marshal Fleet here to tell us about the thirty minutes. You see him. You see the set of that moustache and the firmness of those lips and the distinction he wrought in the court room telling that story.

And there he was, up in this young woman's room in the afternoon, attended with some other officers, plying her with all sorts of questions in a pretty direct and peremptory way, saying to her: "You said thirty minutes, and now you say twenty minutes : which way will you have it?" Is that the way for an officer of the law to deal with a woman in her own house? What would you do with a man— I don't care if he had blue on him—that got into your house and was talking to your wife or daughter in that way? You would do just what Marshal Hilliard did with Caldwell, get him out. That is the way to do. Recollect that this was after the tragedies, this was when the terrible pall was over that house and the neighborhood, and an officer should be pretty careful. Recollect that the air was full of policemen at that time; they were running all over that house, putting her to every possible strain, asking her in her loneliness, her absence from any friend, her sister gone—following her up in this way, insinuating in that way and talking to her as if she were a liar. Well I can tell the truth and behave pretty well, if a man treats me decently, but I want to get him out if he talks to me as a liar to begin with. Now she told about her visit to the barn, and they undertake to tell you that she did not go out to the barn. Now let us see about it. They say that it's another lie. We have got so we know what the small words in the English language mean in the idea of the commonwealth. We can get rid of three letters pretty quick, but you cannot dispose of the facts. Now, let's see about that. Did she go to the yard or the barn? She told them she did, and they bring it in here, and they say she could not have gone to the yard or the barn. Now let us see whether she did or not. If she did not go out to the yard or the barn then she was there upon her own showing at the time when the murder of her father was committed. You see that. That will end the case if you see it. Now, Bridget Sullivan said: " I went right over to Dr. Bowen's and when I came back I asked her, 'Miss Lizzie, where was you?' I says '**Didn't I leave** the screen door hooked?' She says, 'I was out in the back yard and heard a groan and came in and the screen door was open.'"

I am going to talk about going to the barn, and by and by talk about the groan—take them separately. Now, she says that she went into the yard. You understand? What did they have in the yard? Pear trees. That is the evidence, and the evidence that in the partially digested contents of the stomachs pear skins were found. Bridget says Mr. Borden had been out and had brought in a basket of pears and they had these in abundance. You saw the trees; the neighbors saw the trees; Patrick McGowan saw them and got in one of them and helped himself. We know that there is no lie about it. This was an August morning, and it appeared that before this time Lizzie had been ironing, had been around the kitchen trying to iron some handkerchiefs. No doubt about that. She had been in and out about her work. She tells us she has been out in the yard. That was true, we will say, upon that statement. Now, Dr. Bowen said, "where have you been?" Her reply was, "in the barn, looking for some irons," or "iron." Both can be reasonably true, can't they? She could not get into the barn unless she went into the yard, naturally, and that she should stop there by the trees five or ten minutes is perfectly consistent. Does that look unreasonable? Do you not see families out in the yard, strolling about in your own yards, stopping under the trees, sitting under the trees, especially when they have a right to have a little leisure. Mrs. Churchill says, "I stepped inside the screen door, and she was sitting on the second stair, at the right of the door. I put my right hand on her arm, and said, 'O Lizzie.' I then said: 'Where is your father?' She said, 'In the sitting room,' and I said, 'Where were you when it happened?' and said she, 'I went to the barn to get a piece of iron.'" Miss Russell says, "she told about going to the barn, she says she went to the barn, she told us when she came in she saw her father, and he was killed." "Did she say anything about why she went to the barn?" "Not until I asked her." "State what you asked her and what she replied?" "I said 'What did you go to the barn for, Lizzie?' and she said, 'I went to get a piece of tin or iron to fix my screen." "Did she refer to any screen in particular, or simply 'my screen?'" "My screen."

Now, Mr. Fleet told us that she went into the dining room, she said that her father lay down and that she went out into the barn: and he brings in the half-hour—he is the only one that does. And then he goes there and talks to her about it, as to whether she means a half-hour or twenty minutes. Now just listen to this man. Recollect when this was, Thursday afternoon. Recollect he is the same man that said ''Dr Bowen was holding the door on him—holding the fort.'' Think of it. And Mrs. Holmes and Dr. Bowen and Miss Russell tell you, and Wilson, the officer who went with him, comes right up here and says there was not the slightest resistance, that he knocked at the door, and just as soon as Dr. Bowen could ask them if they were ready to have the officers come in, and I am sure that was perfectly proper—they were admitted without any trouble. Now this man Fleet was troubled, and he was ascent for a job. He was ferreting out a crime. He had a theory. He was a detective. And so he says, '' You said this morning you were up in the barn for half an hour. Will you say that now?'' I think the man impertinent. I beg your pardon, the defendant thinks he was : thinks he was impertinent. She said, '' I do not say half an hour ; I say twenty minutes to half an hour.'' ''Well, we will call it twenty minutes then.'' Much obliged to him. He was ready to call it twenty minutes, was he? What a favor that was ; now Lizzie has some sense of her own, and she says, '' I say from twenty minutes to half an hour, sir?'' He had not awed her into silence. She still breathed although he was there. Think about a woman saying something, ordering something in the presence of a man who talks that way to her, under such circumstances. Mr. Harrington states that she said to him that she was there about twenty minutes. He asks her whether she would not have heard the opening or closing of the door. Why not? ''You were but a short distance away, and you would have heard the noise if any was made.'' But Bridget said she did not hear the screen door shut at all and she said she would not hear it in her room, and never heard it when it shut unless somebody slammed it or was careless about it. You remember that.

Now you see there is no inference to be drawn from the fact that Miss Lizzie did not hear it when she was in the barn or in the yard for that matter. And you recollect how the side door stands with reference to the yard. That when a person is out around the corner, under the pear tree, or even under the first pear tree that stood from the south door to the barn, he cannot see up to that door because of that jog. So that if she was even out under that pear tree anybody could have passed in or out that side door without her hearing him, much more if she were in the barn, either upstairs or down stairs. Wilson has told us that she said, ''twenty minutes to half an hour.'' He was there with Fleet. Medley says, ''She says she was upstairs in the barn—I am not positive as to the stairs part, she was up in the barn." Now take that, is there anything unnatural or improbable in her going to the barn for anything she wanted? She was, you will say, a person who was free to go about, and did go about, and went in the natural call of things that she was going to do. You have heard talk of the party at Marion, and you know where it is better than I do, but I suspect from what has been said about it that it is somewhere near the water and where the fish swim, and it would not be strange if a party of women were going there, they would try to catch something—I mean fish ; and when they got there they would want something to catch fish with. Perhaps they do ; that is the way we bob around for fish up in the country. We don't have much to do with seafish, but isn't that common? She said she wanted some lead for sinkers. She also said she wanted something to fix the screen. Perhaps she had both things in her mind. It is perfectly natural. She wanted a piece of tin or iron to fix the screen. If she had set out to be this arch criminal that they claim, she would have had it all set down in her mind so that she would tell it every time just the same, line for line and dot for dot. He had to stay in the court room until the other fellow was heard to hold him. We had twins here ; they didn't look alike. We kept them here ; that is Mr. Mullaly.

Now you are going to say, gentlemen, whether you believe Mr. Lobinsky, who stands uncontradicted and undisputed, or believe another man who is fully contradicted by a man with him who was his own associate in the police court. Now, Mr. Foreman and gentlemen, the government knew where Mr. Lobinsky was, and that was at the tinshop of Mr. Wilkinson. They knew where he was. And they knew, too, that Lobinsky's horse was kept at Mr. Gardner's stable on Second street, corner of Rodman, and they could have found whether Lobinsky had left the stable at 11 o'clock or 10:30. But we have not troubled them to do that. Mr. Gardner, who owns the stable has told his own story, and has he not told you that Lobinsky's statement is correct, that he did not leave the stable until after 11 o'clock ? He testified that that was because other teams were to be hitched up to go ahead of Lobinsky, and he was late, so that he did not get away until 11 or five minutes past 11 o'clock. My friend Knowlton in cross-examining him wanted to know whether he told the time on his watch by the long hand or the short hand. But that is all right. Its good practice, but it is no test. Gardner remembers it, and gives it, even, but Lobinsky did not have the watch. He told us what time he left and the time he was passing by the yard on Second street. And then we have Mr. Newhall, a man from Worcester, who happened to be there; he comes here and tells you he went along the street, and he fixes the time by the hour that he went to the bank, and the places where he was that morning, and you have these three men that hold it down to the time I refer to, that is 10 : 30 o'clock. Is it not fair to say Mr. Mullaly is mistaken, to say the least ? Then if they want to find anything more about it, we land Mr. Douglass in this case, who was there at the time, in Fall River. They knew about it and they could have proved about it and they know it was as we say, and yet they did not try to prove it. They say a story is true because told all times alike, but those of us that have dealings with witnesses in court know that witnesses that tell the truth often have slight variations in their stories and we have learned to suspect the ones that get off their testimony like parrots, as if they had learned it by heart. Honest people are not particular about punctuation and prepositions all the time. Now did she go to the barn ? She says she did and her statement is entitled to credit as she gave it on the spot the moment when Bridget was upstairs and might know about it. Did she go to the barn ? Well, we find she did, find it by independent, outside witnesses, thanks to somebody who saw her. Possibly this life of hers is saved by the observation of a passenger on the street. There comes along a pedler, an ice cream man, known to everybody in Fall River. He is not a distinguished lawyer or a great minister or a successful doctor. He is only an ice cream pedler, but he knows what an oath is, and he tells the truth about it, and he says he passed down that street that morning, and as he passed right along it was at a time when, he says, he saw a woman, not Bridget Sullivan whom he knew, coming along, walking slowly round the corner just before she would ascend those side steps. Now there was no other woman alive in the house except Bridget and Lizzie at that time. He knew it was not Bridget by the best instinct, because he had sold her ice cream and he knew her. He says "it was the other woman whom I had never sold ice cream." Recollect, that was Lizzie or some stranger in the yard. You will say undoubtedly it was Lizzie as she comes back from the barn. It may be asked why did he look in. I say because anyone might do so. They say Lizzie must have looked under the bed. I say Lubinsky must have looked into the yard. He was an enterprising young man, he was looking for business because he has sold ice cream there before, and therefore, he noticed the yard. Now is that something he remembers today and comes up here to tell about or anybody has brought him to tell about? Nobody will make that insinuation in regard to the defendant. Was he got to tell it? Let us see. He told it on the 8th of August to the police, and they had it all in their possession. Now, that is not a yarn made up for the occasion at all, and the only sort of conflict about it is attempted in this way, not to dispute it but to admit or say that Mr. Lubinsky is mistaken about a half-hour of time.

Mr. Mullally is one of the knights of the handle, you know. You know who he is—Mr. Mullaly. Mr. Mullaly comes with a book, and it is thrown down here on the table with a great display to us, for us to pick it up, and with something written in it. It is not competent evidence and has no business on the table, because it might be lost and carried away, and it should be, but Mr. Mullaly says that on the 8th of August he had a talk with Mr. Lubinsky and Mr. Lubinsky told him it was half-past ten o'clock. Now, if Mr. Lubinsky went by that yard at half-past ten he did not see Miss Lizzie go to the barn. Is Mr. Mullaly mistaken? Gentlemen, as you take cases in court, carefully weighing the evidence, would not you say that Lubinsky went there at the time he states and that the two others passed along that street and that he saw Miss Lizzie going into the house? If that is true, then the commonwealth must take back the charge that she lied about going to the barn. She was out of the house at the very time when the slayer murdered Mr. Borden. I will stop at this time for a moment.

Chief Justice Mason: "The jury may withdraw with the officers for a recess of five minutes."

One other thought, as you remember, that Lubinsky saw Manning as he was going down and I think Gardner and Newhall also and you know when Manning got there to the house all about it, so that you see it is confirmed again in another way. Then they have an opportunity to find out by Mr. Wilkinson whether this man was really late that day or not, and as they have not told anything to the contrary, we will assume that that is proved. Now the district attorney brought out the fact from Mrs. Bowen that when Lizzie sat there in the kitchen her hands were white and she was pale and distressed, as you know from other witnesses. And I suppose from that he is going to argue to you that she was not all covered with rust and dust that she got in the barn. Well, you will see the strength of that argument, and think what it amounts to. Think whether she could not go up there and look; whether she picked up anything there or not nobody knows. I don't know how he can tell whether she was fumbling around with dusty iron and lead. There is no evidence here about it, and I have seen many a young woman, and I presume most of them, who could walk out into the barn and come back without getting their hands dirty. So I will not stop long about that. Bridget told about the groan and Mullaly told about the scraping, speaking of her statements, but there is nothing else. Whether she said that or not, we don't know. If she did, it was nothing more than the statement that all of us are likely to make. When anything happens we imagine that we heard something; if it had not happened we should not have heard anything. How common that is. Then there were noises not connected with this tragedy which might actually have been heard. There are noises in that street; you were there long enough to find out about that; such noises are a common occurrence. Then it may be that the people in their excitement—Bridget in great excitement because she was running about breathless to find something and Mullaly in the breathlessness of his search may have got it wrong—may not have got it just right. It is not a serious matter. They may argue it for all it is worth on the part of the commonwealth. She thought she heard Mrs. Borden come in. They undoubtedly will make something out of that, so I want your attention there to see about that. This comes now in the first place from Bridget Sullivan. She is asked, after detailing the circumstances to a certain point, "What happened then?" You recollect that Bridget had told Mrs. Churchill that Mrs. Borden had a note and had gone out—"hurried off, did not tell me where she was going." So you see anything from Bridget about that note and about Mrs. Borden coming in is all sustained. Now Bridget Sullivan says, in answer to the question, "What happened then?" "O, I says, Lizzie, if I knew where Mrs. Whitehead's was I would go and see if Mrs. Borden was there, and tell her that Mr. Borden was very sick." You see the confirmation about that note business right there right off. What should she say that she should go and see Mrs. Whitehead for if Mrs. Borden was there, unless she (Bridget) knew that Mrs. Borden had a note and supposed she had gone out as they both did. Then Lizzie said, "Maggie, I am almost positive I heard her coming in, and won't you go up stairs and see." Bridget said: "I am not going up stairs alone." Now, following the testimony down, the very next question is: "Before that time that she said that, had you been up stairs?" "No, sir: I had been upstairs after sheets for Dr. Bowen."

Now remember how that occurred. When Dr. Bowen came he
wanted a sheet to cover up the body of Mr. Borden and he called
upon Bridget and Mrs. Churchill to get one. They went into the
sitting room and took the key off the mantel and went up the back
stairs (where you went) unlocked the door to Mrs. Borden's room,
got the sheets and came down the back. So Bridget had been up the
back stairs to that room, but she had not been up the front stairs.
Therefore when they got down stairs with the sheets Bridget and Mrs.
Churchill knew that Mrs. Borden was not in her own room, because
they had been up there. Therefore they knew that she was not in
the back of the house, and Lizzie knew that she was not in the back
part of the house, because they went up to get the sheets into Mrs.
Borden's room. See how plain that is when you look at the testimony,
and it is brought out plainly in the testimony in the questions that
are asked by the commonwealth. So you see that when Lizzie spoke
about going upstairs to see if Mrs. Borden was in, Lizzie meant the
front stairs, because they all knew, the three of them, that Mrs.
Borden was not in her own room, and that if she was anywhere in the
house she must be in the front part of the house. So Lizzie knew
that Mrs. Borden had had a note and had gone out, and Bridget
knew that she had a note and had gone out, as they both believed ;
that Lizzie had seen her up in the room making the beds and finishing
up before 9 o'clock, and she had not seen her since, believing that
she had gone out, and she recalled that she might have heard
her come in before her father came back, before Mr. Borden did,
and she said at once, ''Go up at once and see if Mrs. Borden is
not up in her room. Mrs. Borden is not here. I heard a noise as
though she came in, and she must be upstairs in the front room
somewhere. Go and see.'' Now, that is natural. They thought
she was in the upper and back part of the house, and there can be no
doubt about that, because Miss Russell testifies to the same thing
Mrs. Churchill does, Bridget Sullivan does, and then, after they came
down, there it was that conversation about going to Mrs. Whitehead's
occurred. '' What happened then ? '' ''Oh, '' I says, '' Lizzie, if I
knew where Mrs. Whitehead's was, I would go and see if Mrs.
Borden was there. '' These two women acting in perfect good faith
about it, relying upon the truth of that note story, which Mrs. Borden
had told them. Then Bridget would not go up the front stairs,
because in order to go up the front stairs they must necessarily pass
through the room where Mr. Borden's dead body was lying, or else
they must pass through the dining room way and go by the corner

the room. They went that way, and found Mrs. Borden killed. Mrs. Churchill and Miss Russell tell precisely the same thing in substance about going up and finding Mrs. Borden. Now the suggestion on the part of the commonwealth would be, if this evidence was not so clear, that Lizzie knew that she was up there, and if you assume Lizzie had killed her, then, of course, it would be quite plain that she knew where she was, but if you do not presume the defendant guilty to begin with, it shows nothing until she is proved guilty. Then we have no difficulty with the statement of these three women. They define and make it very plain. Mr. Borden, you will remember, came in, as I have said, about 10 :45 o'clock. Now the inference that Mrs. Borden had come in was the most natural thing in the world ; hearing some noise in the house, perhaps the shutting of a door. By and by we will say something about who might have shut it—perhaps the movement of somebody else in that house that she heard—she had no occasion to go to look and see, she was not called to, and her father came in, and as Mrs. Borden had not appeared in the sitting room, you understand, and as the two women going upstairs found she was not in the back room upstairs, they would undoubtedly think if she had come in she was in the front part of the house, and then she recalled as she thought she did the fact that she had heard a noise which indicated to her Mrs. Borden had come in. Now, I submit to you, gentlemen, that, taking the testimony as it is here, and there is no other that I know of, it exactly and clearly gives the situation as it was, and just as they acted. Then they said that she showed no feeling when her stepmother was lying dead on the guest-room floor ; that she laughed on the stairs.

Well, Bridget said something about opening the door. She said she said, '' O, pshaw,'' and she said it in such a way that Lizzie laughed, standing somewhere at her room door, a room where she could not see into the guest chamber, and the door of which, so far as we know, was closed. Nobody knows anything about it. What was there then why she shouldn't laugh? O, they say, she had murdered her step-mother. Oh, hold on. That is not proved yet. You might think that everything was all right in your house, and somebody track a joke on you and you laugh, but if the evidence should turn out that your son had fallen dead on the floor above, that does not warrant the conclusion that you were laughing when his dead body was lying on the floor, because you did not know it. They say she knew it. Well, then, I should agree if she knew it and was laughing and joking about what Bridget said that she should be blamed, and we would

criticize her and condemn her, but they have not any evidence of it.
They assume it, and the district attorney opened it, that while the
dead body of Mrs. Borden was lying in the guest chamber Lizzie
laughed. Well, the inference was that she had murdered her and then
laughed. But that is assuming what they have not proved. They say
she did not look at her dead father. Well, she had looked at him with
horror. She had come in from the outside into the back hallway and
come into the kitchen, and the door stood ajar, and she started to go
into the sitting room when this horrible sight met her gase. She had
seen her father. Did they ask her to go and wring her heart over the
remains that were mutilated beyond recognition? and because she
did not rush into the sitting room and stand over against that mutilated
body they say she is guilty. Why, Mrs. Churchill and Bridget
Sullivan and Miss Russell could not pass through there unless they
touched the corner after the body was covered. Let us ask of other
innocent people the same thing that you would ask of Lizzie. They
say that Miss Lizzie did not show any signs of fear, but that Dr.
Bowen and Mrs. Sawyer were afraid. They told you about it. Well,
how do they know she did not show any signs of fear? Why do they
make any such statement as that? Because she said to Bridget,
"You must go get somebody, for I can't stay in this house alone."
Look at things in a natural and easy way, in a common sense way,
assuming her innocence and not assuming her guilt. That is the
way you will meet these things and all of the facts. Then they start
off on another track, and they say she killed her stepmother and her
father because that was a house without any comforts in it. Well,
gentlemen, I hope you all live in a better way than the Borden family
lived, so far as having good furniture and conveniences. Are your
houses all warmed with steam? Do you have carpets on every one
of your floors, stairs and all? Do you have pictures and pianos and a
library and all conveniences and luxury? Do you? Well, I con-
gratulate you, if you do.

This is not a down-trodden people. There is lots of comfort in
our country homes. I know something of them, but I remember
back in my boyhood we did not have gas and running water in every
room. We were not brought up that way. We did not have such
things as you saw in the Borden house. It wasn't in poverty-stricken,
desolate quarters like a shanty, where the folks simply live and
breathe and do not eat anything. They paraded here the bill of fare
for breakfast. I do not know what they are going to talk about,
what sort of breakfast the ordinary country people have in the houses.
They do not live as well as we do in hotels, perhaps they live better.

I do not wish to say a word against the hotel, but perhaps a coarser fare is as good as the fixed-up notions that we get on the hotel table, but at any rate it is the way people live in our towns and cities, and no considerable number of people have come to harm.

Andrew Borden was a simple man, an old-fàshioned man. He did not dress himself up with jewelry. He carried a silver watch. He was a plain man of the every day sort of fifty years ago. He was living along in that way. His daughters were brought up with him. They had become connected with prominent things in Fall River, for they lived at home. They had the things which you saw upon them. You will know well enough they were not poorly supplied, and were not pinched and were not starved into doing this thing. Do you think it looked as if they were starved into the crime and pinched into wrong? Here was a young woman with property of her own. Starved to death, they say; pinched so that she could not live, wrought up to frenzy and madness, so that she would murder her own father for the want of things, and yet, as has been shown here worth in her own right of money and personal property from $4000 to $5000, owning also real estate in common with her sister there in Fall River. What is the use of talking about that? Did she want any more to live on in comfort? Do they say she wanted to get her father's property or a half of it? Do they reason that she went and killed the stepmother first so that when the property came by inheritance it would pass to herself and sister. They must say something. They say she killed her stepmother because of trouble. That is one of the arguments about which I will speak by and by, but then there is no trouble with her father, as they see, and then she had a change of purpose, or she had a double purpose, to kill Mrs. Borden because she did not like her, and to kill her father because she liked him,' but she wanted his money. What sort of a compound! Two motives are running through that argument inconsistent with each other, each directed independently to a specific end : Carried out as to one in the early part of the murder, and then she not only changed her dress and cleaned herself and became another woman, but found herself inhabited with a distinct motive and then slaughtered her father. Sometimes when a young man goes on a rig and becomes dissolute and a spendthrift he will do almost anything to retrieve what he calls the misfortune which he has brought upon himself, and many an old father has found the gray hairs in his head multiplied because of the waywardness of his boy. Sometimes these great crimes are committed in that way, but if you expect to find in this case that a young woman like her was slaughtering her father when she herself was moral and upright and christian and charitable and devoted to good things in this world, you will find something that the books have never recorded, and which will be a greater mystery than the murder itself. They tell us about the ill-feelings. Well, gentlemen, I am going to consider that in a very few words, because I say to you that the government has made a lamentable failure on that question. They say that is the motive that so qualifies the different acts that are testified to here that it puts this defendant in close connection with the murder of Mrs. Borden, and then they say that Mrs. Borden being murdered, Lizzie murdered Mr. Borden for his property, or possibly they may say, murdered him to conceal her crime—for that or some other reason, but it does not rest at all on this foundation of family relations. Let us see what there was in it. What have they proved? They have proved that from five or six years ago Lizzie did not call Mrs. Borden mother. Lizzie is now a woman of thirty-one or thirty-three years old, thirty-two when these crimes were committed. Mrs. Borden was her stepmother, and she was not her own mother. It is true that Mrs. Borden came there when Lizzie was a little child of two or three years, and sometimes we see that where a stepmother has come into a large family and has brought up a family the children know no difference and always call her mother just the same. That is true in a very large degree, happily so, too : but sometimes when the children get grown up, and when they are told about their mother that died long ago, somehow or other there springs up in the mind of the children a yearning or a longing to know of the parent that they really had ; and how many a man says, in speaking of the family from which he came, '' She is not my mother.''

He calls her mother, perhaps. He introduces her as '' my mother,'' but the first words after you engage him in conversation are, '' She is not my mother, she is my stepmother. My mother died long ago. She lies buried twenty-five years, but still she was my mother.'' I suspect that man never lets into the inner chambers of his heart the feeling that anybody else in the world can stand where his mother did. You may gloss it over, you may talk about it as much as you will, but happy is the man that remembers his mother, that pure mother that lived to see him grow up, and kind as anybody else may be, there never goes out of his heart the feeling for that dead one that is gone, that stood first and foremost to him, and nursed him in his babyhood. It does not require passion or ill will to hold that feeling, begotten in the heart. Show me the man that does not stand for the reputation and character of his mother, for nobody forgets that his own mother was the one he first was interested in, although he from a prattling child has never known her to remember her. Now, says Mr. Fleet, in his emphatic police manner, Miss Lizzie said to him, '' She is not my mother; she is my stepmother.'' Perhaps she did. We will assume she said it, but there is nothing criminal about it, or nothing that indicated it, or nothing savoring of a murderous purpose, is there? Why, Martha Chagnon, a very good looking little girl that was here a day or two ago, stepped on the stand and began to talk about Mrs. Chagnon as her stepmother. Well, I advise the city marshal to put a cordon around that house so that there will not be another murder there. Right here in your presence she spoke of her stepmother. And a good-looking woman came on the stand afterward, and I believe the blood of neither of them has been spilled since. Why, Lizzie, who undoubtedly speaks in just that positive way, when the police asked her about where she was and what she was doing, spoke positively. There are a good many people living in New England who would do the same. They know when they are insulted, and are free in expressing their minds, and sometimes do so too freely and talk too much, but we never think they are going to murder any one. Now you have got the whole thing right there in that statement, as they call it. Now, they say that Mrs. Gifford told us this. It was told on the stand. Let us have it for all it is worth. She is the cloakmaker, you remember. I do not discredit her. ''Don't say mother to me. She is a mean, good-for-nothing thing.'' ''I said, 'O.' She said, 'I don't have much to do with her. I stay in my room most of the time.' And I said, 'You come down to your meals, don't you?' and she said 'Yes, but we don't eat with them if we can help it.''' That is the whole of it. That was a year ago last March. Now, my learned friend who opened the case said that Mrs. Gifford would say that she hated her. My friend, the district attorney, who makes the argument, will take out that, will admit she did not say any such thing. You heard her story on the stand, and that was not so. Now I agree with you that Lizzie A. Borden is not a saint, and, saving your presence, I have some doubts whether all of you are saints; that is to say, whether you really never speak hurriedly or impatiently. I hope that is so for the peace of our families, but I do know good-looking men, just as good-looking as you, if you will allow me to say it, that speak sometimes in their households a little hastily and quickly, and sometimes the daughters, too, and sometimes their fathers and mothers do. It is to be regretted that they do, but they will. Yet you don't read of murders in those houses. There is nothing to indicate any deep-seated feeling. You will hear people speak to each other on the street in such a way that if you thought it really amounted to anything it would shock you. Now, is there anything bad about this case, where a woman like this defendant speaks openly and frankly, and says right out, "She is not my mother: she is my stepmother." She spoke so about the man who was called a Portuguese. What did she say? "He is not a Portuguese. He is a Swede," in just the same tone of voice. That is her way of speaking, you will find on this testimony, and she speaks right out. Now these people are not the ones who do the harm in this world. The ones who do harm are like the dog that does not make any noises about it. The dog that comes round your heels and barks is not the one that bites. It is the one that stays inside and looks serious, you will find. So it is with individuals. It is not the outspoken, blunt and hearty that do the injury. But now I do not want to trouble myself about that.

Bridget Sullivan, who lived in the family two years and nine months, who was nearer to all of them than anybody else, tells you the condition of the household. She says, though brought in constant contact with them, she never heard anything out of the way. There was no quarreling. Everything seemed cordial among them. The girls did not always go to the table. They were often out late, and I suppose they did not get down to breakfast as early as the old folks. The longer ago you were born the earlier you will probably rise now. If you were born seventy years ago, you will probably be up in the morning a 4 o'clock, and be disposed to find fault with the Creator that it cannot be summer all the time with more light and longer days. But the girls did not come until they wanted to. They had a right to do that. Bridget says she never heard a word of complaint. And mark you, that Thursday morning on which they tell you that Lizzie was entertaining that purpose or plan to murder both those people—that is, their theory is what they will undertake to satisfy you of—that Lizzie was talking to Mrs. Borden. Bridget Sullivan says: "I heard them talking together calmly, without the least trouble, everything all right." Mr. Borden talks about the meal, and the conversation goes on in the usual way without the slightest indication of any ill-feeling. That is the way my people do at home. That is the way your family greets you in ordinary conversation.

They are waiting for you to come back just now, and they will meet you in the same way I know, and there will be no suspicion about it. O, they say, just look at her, wretch and fiend and villain that she was, she could put all this on when she had terrors unimaginable in her heart and purposes that no language could describe. Well, gentlemen, you have to judge of people according to the ordinary things. There being no proof of such purposes on her part, you will not justify ,yourselves in ascribing them to her. You will remember that Mrs. Raymond, the dressmaker, a lady to all appearances, came and testified of their being together a few months before, four of them being dressmaking, sitting in the guest chamber sewing, a regular dressmaking party. Philip Harrington ought to have been there and had the whole style developed to him, to learn more than he knows, if it is possible to put anything into his head on the subject. There they are. Was that an angry family? Was that a murderous group? You take another thing. You have them there, as Bridget says, and there is no evidence to the contrary; they have told you the whole thing ; when Emma Borden comes on the stand to tell the inside condition of the family they will say to you that Miss Emma Borden, the sister who was away from home on a visit at this time, against whom they have not the slightest suspicion, but they will say that her sisterly affection carries her along to swing her from the truth. You'll judge of her. I will not apologize for her. She has a right to be where her sister is. It is creditable that she does stand by her and it will take a long time for a man in his heart to say she is untruthful for telling what she does here.

She went on to say that they had trouble five or six years ago in regard to property and there was no resentment so far as Lizzie was concerned; it was all adjusted. When we get the open and unrestrained testimony of Miss Emma we are told there was trouble. The father had put in Mrs. Borden's hands a piece of property, and she says : " we did not feel satisfied, and we told him so, and then came the word to us through another person, 'your father is all ready to give you a property for yourselves to make it even if you will only ask for it.' " They asked for it and got it. And Emma says she never felt right about it afterward. She says up to the day of the death of Mrs. Borden she had not overlooked it, but she says as to Lizzie there never was any trouble about it—never was after that time. There is a difference between the two girls. One blurts out exactly as she feels, the other bears what she is called upon to endure in silence. You will find the same separate and distinct dispositions often in the same family. From that time, five years, more than half of it covered by the residence of Bridget Sullivan, there is no word of any trouble or indication of anything except this remark made by Mrs. Gifford. If you take it all, what is there in it that signifies anything, enough to find the motive for these dastardly crimes?

But there is another thing: Here was an old man with two daughters, an elderly one and a younger one. They had gone on together. He was a man that wore nothing in the way of ornament or jewelry but one ring, and that ring was Lizzie's. It had been put on many years ago when Lizzie was a little girl, and the old man wore it and it lies buried with him in the cemetery. He liked Lizzie, did he not? He loved her as his child. And the ring that stands as the pledge of plighted faith and love, that typifies the dearest relationship that is ever created in life, that ring was the bond of union between the father and the daughter. No man should be heard to say that she murdered the man that so loved her. The old-fashioned man lived in a simple way, did not care anything about the frivolities of life, was not attractive, perhaps, to some of the younger and go-ahead people, but was one who lived in his own way, had worked himself up to what would be called a fortune, had taken care of it, was then superintending its use and the income, and for all that on his little finger was that ring which belonged to his little girl. You may tell me, if you want, that the relation between that parent and child was such that alienation was complete, and wrong was the purpose of her heart, but you will not ask me to believe it. Mind you that on this question of the relations of these people there is not a word that comes from Mr. Morse of any ill-feeling, or from Miss Russell or any other living person, and so I think you will agree with me that there is not anything whatever in this assumption that the feelings were such that the defendant could have had guilty intent and worked out this guilty act. I pass. The learned district attorney, in his opening, said that there was an impassable wall built up through that house. But the moment we got at the wall, down it went, doors flew open and instead of showing a line in the house shut in and hedged in by locks, we find that Mr. Borden's room was doubly and trebly locked, Bridget's room was locked and Mrs. Borden's door was locked, and you find Miss Lizzie's room locked, as well as Emma's, the guest chamber is locked, the parlor and sitting room—I don't know but what everything, and that was all because there had been a burglary in the house and barn, and Mr. Borden, old-fashioned, in that he was, thought they wanted to lock the house pretty securely. He kept a safe in that back room which kept valuables. This was locked day and night, and not a little care was given to the fastening of the doors and all parts of the house. But you see the impassable wall was not as against the two girls, but was simply a matter of protection to keep people out. If it was an impassable wall, and not to keep people out, why did they have a lock on the door to the back stairs, and why did they lock up the attics? They say she rushed in from the outside and discovered the homicide. There is no proof of that. In another place they say she did not go out of the house. They claim in one breath that she did not go to the barn and then say that she ran in and discovered the homicide. Rushed in from where, if she did not go out? But if after she discovered it, she passed in and saw the horrid sight, the testimony shows that she retreated to the side room, and got as far from it as she could. She undoubtedly dreaded an attack from the murderer who had killed her father, and she stood at the closed screen door with the open wood door behind it and shouted to Bridget. Bridget was the quickest to respond. She could not go to the front part of the house without passing the horrible sight, her dead father. Where could she go? Where would you go under the circumstances? She called for Bridget to run and get some one as quickly as she could. If she had murdered those two people do you think she would have called for Bridget as quick as that? Wouldn't she have gone down the street or done something of that kind where she would not have been in such close proximity to the scene of this tragedy? But she went and shouted for Bridget and asked her to come down, all in the trepidation and alarm, to find Mr. Borden killed. You cannot faint away, you cannot look pale when you try to, and so when Bridget had gone this woman stood pale and trembling by that open door on that August morning. Looking over she saw Mrs. Churchill; Mrs. Churchill, too, saw her, and noticed the distress she was in, and as she stood by the closed window where she could not speak to her she hurried at once to the open window and called out, " O, Lizzie, what is the matter ? "

Have you any patience with any man who will tell you that Lizzie stood at that door that morning like a marble statue, without any feeling ? I have told you about Mrs. Borden. All those three people were sick in the house on Tuesday, including Lizzie. It was in August weather, and whether they had eaten something or the weather had caused it, we do not know, but the government seems

to be floundering around with the idea that because Bridget was not
sick, they had been poisoned. There was talk about poison, and
poison was feared in the family, because all had been made sick.
Then they say for some reason, I do not know what, that Miss
Lizzie went downstairs in the cellar that Thursday night. There
had been people there examining the rooms and looking over the
bodies, and there was water in the pitcher up in her room, and people
had been washing there during the day, that Mrs. Holmes said, "If
I should stay there all night I should want the slop-pail emptied."

But that house was surrounded by policemen, and Officer Hyde
was there, and Miss Lizzie had a full-grown kerosene lamp in her
hand and the windows were all open with ample opportunity for
observers outside to see in and those within the house knew that
policemen were all around so that there was nothing concealed.
Now, a person who is going to do anything to cover up crime will
not carry an electric light with him. The criminal goes into the
dark to do his dark deed. Miss Lizzie did not see anybody, though
they say Officer Ferguson was in front, but he is not brought forward,
and if he were he could not see through two high board partitions.
That would tax the energy and perspicacity of even a Fall River
policeman. Then they say she burned a dress. Well, the
general thought in the mind of everybody is that if a person
burns up anything in connection with some important transaction, he
does it to get it out of the way for the purpose of avoiding observation. That is natural. The government stakes its case on that dress.

The government says: "You gave us up the blue dress that lies
before me. That is not the dress. You practically commit a falsehood by giving us that. The defendant says that this is the dress.
The government says we want that bedford cord, and if we had that
bedford cord we should know all about it, and you burned the bedford
cord. Now, let us look at it. There is a dispute here, a disagreement, not intentional, but unavoidable, among the persons who saw
what Lizzie had on that morning, some of them saying that she had
on this very dress, or a dark blue dress and another, and Mrs.
Churchill speaking of it as a light blue coming almost up to a bay
blue, or something a good deal lighter than this.

Now between the two there is a difference of recollection; just
as good people on one side say it was a dark blue as those on the
other who say it was a light blue. But you will remember that at
that time there were several ladies and Bridget was there with a
lighter-colored dress, and that those who speak of a lighter-colored

dress may have had in mind what Bridget had on. It was not a time for examining colors, and afterward they recollected as well as they could. They are good, honest people, but some of them are mistaken, and of course are not wilfully stating what they do not believe to be the fact. So that there is a conflict of testimony about that. That dark blue dress lying here is given as the one that Lizzie had on. They say, "You had a light blue dress on." We say it is not so, but we say to you when we produced the dark blue dress you took it and put into the hands of Dr. Dolan, the medical examiner, and you went away with it and used it in framing your indictment, and now you find through Prof. Wood, a man who knows something, instructing Dr. Dolan, that there is not and never was any blood on it.

CHIEF JUSTICE MASON.

Then the government does not want that dress, but another. They want the bedford cord. We will talk about it, then. Let us look at it. Suppose they had this bedford cord. Lizzie had it on this morning, you say. This is the present theory. The government said she had it on up to 12 o'clock, so that she did not change to the pink wrapper until that time. The witnesses all say and every single person who has testified that while she was there and about with them, including Mrs. Churchill, Bridget and Dr. Bowen, Mrs. Bowen and others, there was not a particular spot of blood on it. They say there was no blood on her hands, her face or hair. I am talking now of the dress principally. Now recollect that she had that on. Policemen were coming in all about there. She was lying on the lounge. They tell you that that dress was covered or had blood spots on it and

not a living person saw or suggested it.   Suppose she did burn it up
—the time that had elapsed for observation would be long enough.
They had all had it to look at at that time.   They had all seen her
and every one says there was not a spot of blood on it.   So you see
you start with a dress that every one of the witnesses they produced
says did not have blood upon it.   Now, you have removed from
that all idea that that dress was burned with a wrongful intent,
because all the witnesses say it was perfectly clear of blood.   Now,
what more ?   That dress was in that closet.   You, gentlemen, saw
it over the front door, and there it remained.   In that closet were
eighteen or twenty dresses, and the government witnesses claimed
that they did not see any such dress, notwithstanding that Miss
Lizzie had eight blue dresses of different shades in that hall closet.
They examined and did not see any that had a particle of blood upon
them, and so the pretense of the government is that the dress was
not in there, but Miss Emma says that when she came home on
Thursday night she went to the closet room to put away her clothes
and that on Saturday night she was there again and that dress was
hanging on the second row of the nails that were driven into the
edge of the shelf.   She says she discovered that old dress hanging
there that had been covered with paint ever since May, and by
covered with paint I mean stained and daubed with it.   She spoke
to Lizzie about it, saying, ''Why don't you get rid of that thing.
I can't find a place to hang my dress on?''   It had been in there,
and on Saturday night they ransacked this place and found the dress
which they supposed had blood upon it.   They carried it to Dr.
Dolan, who made the discovery, certain to their mind, that would
convict this woman, and so they did not want anything else.   They
went through the form of looking over everything else, but had got
the damning evidence here; but when Dr. Dolan conversed with a
man who knew something, they were told it was not blood at all,
and then they said : ''Get another dress.''

   Now, is it true? Was there grease or paint on it? We have
brought you the painter here that painted that house a week earlier
in May, and we have brought a dressmaker who made the dress,
and the painter has told us that Lizzie did the superintending of the
painting, and got up at 6 o'clock in the morning to see that the
paint was of the proper color, and says that she tried it upon the
side of the house.   You have heard Mr. Grouard, who testified that
that dress had got soiled, and said that it was not fit to wear.   And
then it was not worn of any account except on the days when she

had dirty work to do, and Emma knew about it, Mrs. Raymond knew about it, and it is the indisputable fact that it was besmeared with paint and it was not fit for anything else. Why, we are talking about a dress that did not cost but twelve-and-a-half or fifteen cents a yard and took eight or nine yards to make it, and did not cost altogether when it was commenced probably over two dollars, and was not good for anything after they got it done, because the material was so poor, wearing out and fading out. And then it got dirty, got paint on it, and what more did they want of it? As Emma said, " Put it out of the way. Why do you keep the old thing?" This morning, you remember, was after the police had searched everything in the house so completely that there was nothing more to be found unless they took the paper off the walls and the carpets off floors, and we will take their word for it. Unless that, there was nothing more to be seen and nothing more to be found, and they had all they wanted, and had got her clothes and her stockings, and even an unmade dress pattern, and wanted to see if that had not been made up into some sort of a mantle to wrap her up in. They had got the whole thing, and had looked over everything, and had taken all they could find and all they wanted, and notified them they had all got through. Then, in obedience to Emma's injunction, Lizzie walks down into the kitchen with it that Sunday morning, the windows all open, no blinds shut, policemen in the yard looking right in at everything, that was going on, and deliberately and in the presence of Emma—Emma saying to her " Well, I think you had better do it "—put it into the fire and burned it up. Had not she time enough Thursday morning down to that time to burn it up without anybody knowing it, if it was covered with blood? Had not she time enough to get it out of the way, and if she had that purpose to cover up this crime, if she had committed it, would she have burned it in the presence of her sister and Miss Russell and said she was going to do it? That is not humanly probable. Now, you have got the whole thing about the dress. There is no concealment about it. And when Miss Russell, in her trepidation, and having been advised by somebody about it, came to her and said: "I think you have done the worst thing you could in burning that dress," Lizzie spoke up in her prompt and honest way, saying, "O, why did you let me do it, then?" reproaching them for not advising her against it. And, truthful as they are, when they knew Miss Russell had been questioned about the matter, they said tell all you know about it. And Miss Russell walks to the man Hanscom and says she has come to tell him because they said go and tell about it. Lizzie said: "Go and tell all about it." It does not hurt people, sometimes, to tell the truth, to tell all about it. "But, gentlemen, hang upon that one blue dress. They have it in the testimony now; they know all about it. Their own witnesses that they bring do not help them at all in this theory. But I ask them this: If Lizzie Borden killed her mother at 9:45 o'clock that morning and then was ready to come down stairs and greet her father and meet him, having on the blue dress, do you think that is probable, besmeared and bedaubed as she would have been with the blood of the first victim, standing astride and chopping her head into pieces by these numerous blows, blood flying all over the walls and furniture, on the bed and everywhere, and she wasn't touched at all with blood? Then, of course, they are going to say: "O, but she changed her dress, and then, when she killed her father she either had that back again or put on another." Did she have it back again? Then she had to put that on over her clothes again, and over her person, exposing herself to have her underclothing soiled in that way, a thing not probable in any way. And then, if she put on another dress, then there were two dresses to burn instead of one. The government only wants one; they have all the rest. Think of it. She walked right into that sea of blood, and stood there, slashing it over herself in the first murder; then went and took off that dress and laid it away until her father came in, and then dressed herself for the second slaughter. Then they say that she murdered these two people because Mrs. Reagan, I forbear almost to mention her name, came up here and told you that those sisters had a quarrel, and that Lizzie said to Emma, "You have given me away." Gentlemen, if there is anybody given away in this case, it is Mrs. Hannah Reagan.

We have got right over among the reporters for the solid truth, now, and we have got John R. Caldwell and Thomas F. Hickey, and John J. Manning. They came from different papers and different cities, and these gentlemen tell you they went to Mrs. Reagan and she said there was not a word of truth in it, and while Mr. Caldwell was trying to find out the facts from Marshal Hilliard, that official, in the abundance of his politeness, told him to get out. My learned friend asked Hickey if it was not a "scoop" between the *Boston Globe* and the *Boston Herald*.

And they say that possibly she contradicted herself on some little things, and you noticed the humor there was about it when Philip Harrington said, "I advised her not to submit to another interview that day. '' I thank him. But in walked the rest of the score, and they proceeded to interview, not asking Harrington's leave, and Harrington himself went there that night again to try his search over with her. That is the way they dealt with her. Now, gentlemen, there is not one of them that, interpreted in the light of the common every-day transactions in the household, is entitled to your credit. And if not, then you cannot group them so as to make them strong or of any influence. She did not try to get Bridget out of the house. If she had undertaken to do these deeds, think you not that she would not have sent Bridget down street to buy something, to go for the market-ing, to go to the store, one thing and another? Or send her on some errand, and then have had time undisturbed. You know that she would. But instead of that, everything goes on as usual, and Bridget was about the work. Lizzie happens to walk out to the door, and Bridget says to her, '' You need not lock the door, I will be around here. '' Bridget knew what the habit of that house was, and so she said, '' You need not lock that door, I will be around here. '' So Lizzie did not lock it. Lizzie called her attention later after she got the work done, and that they say, after Mrs. Borden was killed, she called her attention to locking the doors if she went out, because she herself might go out. And she spoke to her about the cheap sale at Sargent's, and there is no doubt about that being true, because they could readily find out in Fall River whether there was any cheap sale at Sargent's at that time. Now, these are the grounds on which the government will claim or has claimed, and I don't know what other theories they have claimed, the guilt of the prisoner.

Who did it, and what did it? You see last year they had the theory about these other things, and if they could have tried the case at that time they would have sought to convict this woman on those first four. They now do not dare to say that they would ask to convict her even upon these. They say it may have been. Is the government trying a case of may-have-beens? Will the judges tell you, as they charge you, that you can convict this defendant upon a theory that it may have been. I think not. Never. And, if they cannot tell you that that is the implement that committed the crimes, where is it. Fall River seems to be prolific of hatchets. Perhaps if we wait awhile there will be another one born. Possibly the district attorney, or the officers over there—not the district attorney, for I don't think he has anything to do with it, to do justice to him, or possibly some officer, will find some other hatchet and want to bring it in. Well, we are thankful, gentlemen, that this woman was not tried last August or September, because then, if she had gone to trial on the things that are now declared to be innocent, and they had convicted her with the cow's hair and the appearances of blood, she possibly would now have been beyond their recall, although they had actually put her to death wrongfully. So much for the theory of experts. And now we are asked at this time to take up another one that they do not vouch for and that they did not dare to stand on, and we are asked to submit this defendant to that incriminating evidence which they say they are not sure about or may have been, and they want to convict her now on things they do not know anything about and do not claim to know anything about, and put it out of their power, six months hence, to tell them if she knows anything about somebody else committing these murders. They have had her for ten months in close control. It has been irksome and wearisome and wearing. Bad as the government would represent her home to be, and falsely so ; bad as they would picture it, it is a paradise compared with a jail, and they have transferred her, such is the process of the law, from her home into the custody of the State. And they thought that Tuesday's sickness and Wednesday morning's sickness was caused by some irritant poison. But Mr. Wood said : " No, everything is all right; no blood, no poison, nothing whatever." He has practically said to these men : " Hold on, you are going too far; you cannot go this way." Now failing in that, as I argue to you, they have unmistakably, they proceed upon the theory, who did it? Now we are not obliged to resort to that, as I told you at the outset. The question is, is this defendant a guilty person, and that is all. But they say, and they said they would prove to you, that there is exclusive opportunity. Well, gentlemen, I meet it right squarely. I say that if they can lock into that house Bridget and Lizzie alone and without having any other way for any other person to get in, and no other person does get in, and two persons are found dead, I am ready to say that Mr. Borden did not kill his wife in that way and then afterward kill himself. I am sure about that. But the exclusive opportunity is nothing but an anticipation that was not realized, as I think we have shown you.

They said nobody else could have done it. Emma was gone. Morse was gone. There is no doubt about that. Bridget was out doors, they said, and later in her room. They said that the defendant was really shut up in the house with the two victims and that everybody else was actually and absolutely shut out. Now I think you and I will agree about the evidence. The cellar door was undoubtedly locked ; I mean the one outside. I have no doubt of that. The front door in the usual course, so says the evidence, was bolted up by Lizzie Wednesday night and unbolted by her Thursday morning. Now they assume she bolted it Wednesday night, but they are not going to assume, I suppose, that in the usual course she unbolted it Thursday morning, but I do, because that is the evidence, leaving only the spring lock on when she unbolted it. They say you do not know that. Well, I say, you do not know it, and you have got the burden of proof, not I. It was fastened by the bolt when Bridget let Mr. Borden in, that is true—the bolt and the key.

The side screen door, gentlemen, was unfastened from about 9 o'clock to 10:45 or 11. That is when Bridget was washing windows and about the house and around the premises in the way she said she was. Now, if that door wasn't locked, gentlemen, Lizzie wasn't locked in and everybody else wasn't locked out. Was it so, the screen door unfastened? You know Bridget said to Lizzie, "You needn't lock the door, I am going to be around here." There is no doubt about it. Bridget says she didn't lock it. Then there was a perfect entrance to that house by that rear screen door, wasn't there ? And when the person got in all he had to do was to avoid meeting Bridget and Lizzie. Bridget was outdoors, she wasn't in the way, and therefore there was but one person in the house so far as appears, one person below, against whom the intruder could run. Now, look at it. Bridget was outside talking with the Kelly girl, over there on the south side, away off at the corner. She said plainly and decidedly there was nothing to hinder anybody going right in. Mr. Borden had gone down street and there was nobody there on the outside but Bridget, and she was everywhere on the outside. She washed the parlor windows. You know how those are. She couldn't see the side door when she was there. She went to the barn seven or eight times for water, she says : it may have been more. She was at the dining room windows on the north side of the house ; and she said that when she was there she couldn't even see into the dining room, because the windows are so high that unless a person stood up close to the window they couldn't see in.

Now, see the significance of that. The government will be going to claim that she stood there and she could have seen way across into the sitting room. But she could not. She was washing the windows with a pole and brush, she wasn't up on the steps on the outside. And then Lizzie was about the house as usual. She was in the house and about the house. Doing just the same as any decent woman does, attending to her work. Ironing handkerchiefs, going up and down stairs, going down to the cellar, to the closet. You say these things are not all proved? No, but I am taking you into the house just as I would go into the house, for instance, and say, what are your wives doing now? Well, doing the ordinary work around the house, getting dinner. Well, where do they go? Undoubtedly they are going down stairs for potatoes, going out into the kitchen, to the sink room, here and there. You can see the whole thing. It is photographed in your mind. It is just the same there. She was ironing, she was in the dining room. Bridget says she don't know but she had the dining room door shut to keep the heat out, and she would have occasion to go down cellar for reasons stated. Might she have gone into the parlor for anything? There was a clock there. There are various things you might think about. Now, suppose the assassin came there, and I have shown you he could without question, the house was all open on the north side, and suppose he came there and passed through. Suppose Lizzie was upstairs, suppose she were downstairs in the cellar. He passed through. Where could he go? Plenty of places. He could go upstairs into the spare room, right up the front stairs, and go in there; he could go into that hall closet where you opened it and looked in, and where two men can go in and stand; he could go into the sitting room closet; he could go into the pantry there in the kitchen; you saw that. He could go into various places. He could go into just such places in that house as all these thieves run into if they can find a door open. So it was easy enough for a man to do that. It was easy enough for him to go up into that bed chamber and secrete himself. Now, what is going to be done? He is there for the murder; not to murder Mrs. Borden, but to murder Mr. Borden. And he is confronted and surprised by the former. And he knows—possibly he is somebody that she knew— you do not know, she cannot tell us—somebody that would be recognized and identified, and he must strike her down; and his purpose to kill Mr. Borden would not stop at the intervention of another person, and Lizzie and Bridget and Mrs. Borden, any or all of them, would be slaughtered if they came in that fellow's way.

Now, at that time in the morning, with the opportunity to go in there and go up into all the house, and when he went in there and had murdered Mrs. Borden in that front chamber, Lizzie could pass up and down stairs, and could go to her room, and know nothing about it, see nothing about it, because of course he did not have the door open and disclose himself. She could pass up and down stairs.

There is no trouble about that, closed door or open door. And when he had done his work, and Mr. Borden had come in, as he could hear him, he made ready then to come down at the first opportunity, and when he came down he would very naturally leave the door open, and so they found it afterward, the door, I mean, to the spare chamber. He could come down, and he was right at the scene ready. Bridget was outdoors, Lizzie outdoors, on all the evidence, which you certainly believe. And then he could do his work quickly and securely, and pass out the same door, if you please, that he came in at, the side door. Now, that is not all. It is well enough to see that a person could come in at the front door. The bolt slid back in the morning, the latch locked, a man can open that door, they all say, by giving it a pressure and trying to come in. And when he gets in what does he do? He doesn't want to be surprised. He locks the door himself, he takes care of himself, and then when Mr. Borden comes it is slid back by Bridget and left in that way. It is easy to see all these things. You can see then how everything in this idea of exclusive opportunity falls to the ground, because there was no exclusive opportunity.

Now, it is not for us to maintain a theory. It is for the government to prove theirs. You may adopt a theory just as well as I. You may find other theories, as I have no doubt you will as you look at this evidence. You will see other ways in which persons could enter that house by which the exclusive opportunity theory is overturned. It is not a matter for you to sit down in the jury room and criticise the theory that I have advanced to you, because you are going to sit down in the jury room and criticise the theory that the government advances, and you will see that it is vulnerable, and when you see that a person can take one of those theories as well as another, you will hear from the court that you cannot convict upon such evidence, because all the essential facts must be in harmony with this charge against the prisoner, and must not be in harmony with any other theory or any other reasonable explanation. Now, there are two or three things which in the hurry of speaking this morning—perhaps you thought I had not hurried, but speaking rapidly, they were inadvertently passed by—little things, but I want to speak of them before I pass on. Miss Lizzie was ironing downstairs, and there cannot be any question about that. Bridget says so, and you recollect the testimony of Miss Russell and Mrs. Holmes, that that morning when they were clearing up they found the handkerchiefs that she had ironed in part, and the sprinkled ones were carried upstairs and put away separately by themselves, a dozen or more. You see that it is genuine; it is not a fiction. It is really one of those little things that help to establish the truth. I must also in this connection speak of Mr. Medley's testimony, because the commonwealth relied upon Mr. Medley to make the examination, as he said, of the dust in the barn, to show you that Miss Lizzie could not have walked on the upper floor. Now, if you could be sure of that there would be some test in it. If you did not see a track through freshly fallen snow you would say no person had passed there. It would be a little more doubtful about walking on a floor, but when you find a detective looking after this thing, you begin to suspect that he may be in error, and when you find as you do by the testimony, a half a dozen or more people up there in that barn walking around before Mr. Medley got there at all, as it was proved upon the testimony there had been when he got there, and when he met Mr. Fleet and where he met him, between the gateway and the back steps, and then went directly into the house, Sawyer being at the door, you see how unreliable his testimony is. Well, then, you have the testimony of Mr. Clarkson and you have that of Mr. Manning and Mr. Stevens and the two boys that called themselves "Me and Brown," Barlowe and Brown. Now, those boys, like all boys, just the same as you and I when we were boys, wanted to go upstairs, to look at things about there and stay as long as they could, and it appears they went there and were out in that barn before Mr. Medley came there. He went into the house and talked with Miss Lizzie and was some minutes in the house before he went to the barn. So when he got there there had been people all about there, and those people give their testimony in such a way as to carry the conviction of truth in their statement, so that you find them up there and walking around in the very place where Mr. Medley went to look, and it shows you that Mr. Medley must have been in error. His detection was not so sure as he thought. He was mistaken about it, consequently while he may have honestly meant what he said, I do not call that in question for the time being, but I want to say that that is not anything which you can depend upon under these circumstances, and when you find him confronted with three or four other witnesses, John Donnelly and the boys and Clarkson, there can be no question that Mr. Medley is mistaken, so that we have in addition to the positive proof that Miss Lizzie went to the barn, to which I called your attention this morning, the affirmation of these other witnesses that they were there, and Mr. Medley finds nobody to support him.

Why, do you not all think with me of what a blessed Providence it was that interfered with that girl, so that as she walked about that house, passing from the sitting room into the dining room and hall, she did not step on some of the blood and have it on her shoes? Anybody else, according to the theory of the government, could have stepped on that blood and have bloody shoes, but if Lizzie had walked there just the same as any other person innocently, and there had been so much as a pin head stain upon one of her shoes, it would have led her to the severest penalty on their theory. See within what close limitation we walk in commonest things and see how close we come to precipitate of danger when we find any part in the wrong. Why, upon the theory of the government—no, it isn't the theory of the government, for I really do not know what it is, but the handleless hatchet down there in the box, the theory being for the time, if it is a theory and is indulged, that she ran down and put that through a course of washing, scraping with ashes, etc., and threw it up in the box after breaking the handle off, as claimed, and then got rid of the handle; they say that they found it there, and put it right up into the box to which she directed Bridget to go with the officers and find the hatchets and axes. Why gentlemen, she is not a lunatic or an idiot. She is a great colossal contriver of wrong and murder, shrewd, discriminating, far-seeing, with premeditated malice aforethought, and planned all this thing. Well, she did not plan so foolishly as that. She would not send officers to find the very thing and in the very place where she had put it. She burned no clothing that day. She put none away. They tell us nothing about that with all the vigilance of their searches, and you know that the officers say that when they went there first, and looked in that box down cellar, they took out the two smaller hatchets that were on top. Now, whatever the theory, or any theory of the government in regard to that hatchet, you have got to assume she was down there and washed it up and got it all clean beyond what science can do, and got the blood out of it, and then broke off the handle, and went herself and took out the other two hatchets so as to get this old one under-neath, and then she had it all covered with ashes, too. And when they found it that Thursday afternoon it was all dry and covered with dust like the other. They undertake to tell you it was coarser dust. Just see into what a labyrinth of impossibilities and improbabilities they try to lead this woman. Then she had to run upstairs, run up to her own room and make a change, run down cellar and take care of herself, and take care of the hatchets, upon their theory, run back again and get up there and call Bridget—all in that short space of time. I said it was morally and physically impossible. You may find her not guilty, if that be your judgment, for two reasons. One because you know that it has not been proven. And the court will tell you that if, when you reach that point in your decision, you are not satisfied and convinced as reasonable men, beyond a reasonable doubt, no matter what your suspicions may be and what you may think about it otherwise, you have but one duty to perform and one that is safe to you to render in this case.

You may have heretofore thought things looked dark for her. You may have said, "If they can come into the court and show all the things I have seen in the newspapers, gossip and rumor and report, I might feel that I ought to, but now that I find the government's case only the thing that it is, insufficient, weak, contradictory, critical, lame, why, I have nothing else to do in my conscience but to say to Massachusetts, we have this woman in charge, you have not proved it against her, we still keep charge of her, and we say to you, you have not proven this against her and she is not guilty." But there is another ground. If, when you see through this evidence, you are satisfied again, convinced—which is more—you are convinced affirmatively that the woman is innocent, that you are entitled to say, "Not guilty," and you are bound so to speak. It is rare that the defendant goes so far as to prove her innocence. It is not a task that is set before her. But I dare to speak to you upon that branch in this case with full confidence. Look at it for a period. Take the facts as they are, and I would not misrepresent or belittle any of them. I have not knowingly omitted any of them, for a purpose of benefit to the defendant. Take them as they are. What is there to prove to you absolutely, as sensible men, the innocence of this defendant? You go and search some other man's house and let me alone. Search somebody else, I think he had some trouble with my father: that would be the policy of such a defendant. What was her conduct? Uniformly, openly frank every time, shutting all the doors against any person that might be put under this foul suspicion. Why, you say, shutting them against herself. Yes, it was the impulse, the outcome of an honest woman. Were she a villian and a rascal, she would have done as villians and rascals do. There was her uncle, John Morse, suspected as you heard, followed up, inquired about, and she is asked and she said, no, he did not do it. He went away from the house this morning at nine o'clock. Some one said Bridget did it. Now there were but two persons around that house as we now find out, so far as we can locate anybody, and the busy finger was pointed at Bridget Sullivan—Bridget Sullivan, only an Irish girl, working in the family, working for her weekly pay, been faithful to them, been there two years and nine months, lived happily and peacefully with them and they have had no trouble, and Lizzie spoke. out right determinedly, as you know, and promptly: Why, Bridget did not do it. Then somebody said : Why, the Portuguese on the farm. No, says Lizzie, he is not a Portuguese ; he is a Swede, and my father has not any men that ever worked for him that would do that to him. Not Alfred Johnson that worked for them, not Mr. Eddy, another farmer that worked for them, no assistant—I cannot believe it of any of them.

How do you account for that except in one way ? She was virtually, if she was a criminal, virtually putting everybody away from suspicion and leaving herself to stand as the only one to whom all would turn their eyes. Suppose she had been wicked and designing and Bridget as innocent as Bridget is to-day. Suppose Lizzie had undertaken to tell something that would involve Bridget, would it not have been easy ? And it might have been. Then if she had led the way in treachery and repeated crime Lizzie might have led Bridget right into the toils in which she herself became involved to the relief of Bridget by her statement that Bridget is not to be suspected. It is not every human being who can stand that strain. It is not every man that has strength of purpose and purity of mind.

Did she ever stand in the way, or her sister likewise ? Go, search everything, we will come and help you open everything. We will join you ; find out all you can. Do all you want to here. Never a sign of reluctance. Never an intimation of objection is the unanimous testimony of everybody that went there. They say she was cool. Thank the Lord there was enough left of her so that she could be cool under the visitations of gentlemen who flocked there by the score. Her clothes, her dress, her unmade dress, her shoes, her stockings, everything, her absolute freedom from the marks of the crime, her readiness to do anything that was wanted, and then that scene of Saturday night which transcends all in exhibition of innocence. There has been that woman shut up in that house, the premises crowded by the police. She was virtually under arrest. She could almost feel the pressure of a hand upon her arm, and in that house on that Saturday night were the mayor and city marshal of Fall River, and in the parlor they called her, her sister and uncle together, and then they began that advising them—now notice how it was done, for this is an essential part of their case, they advised them that the family had better remain in the house.

Miss Lizzie says, why? Well, the mayor says, Mr. Morse, perhaps, can tell you. It was something that occurred down street last night, and then comes the question that from there Morse went down street and had some trouble. Now, that seemed to indicate that Mr. Morse was probably under suspicion, and Lizzie spoke at once as they spoke of putting officers around the house and said, "Why, is there anybody in this house suspected?" and the mayor says, "I regret to say, Miss Borden, that you are suspected." Then she says, "I am ready to go now, or at any time."

Gentlemen, murderers do not talk that way. Criminals are not so situated as to have committed this great and monstrous wrong and then have had that superb quietness of spirit and that confident feeling that wrong had been done her in the charge that is made, and the assurance within herself that, God knowing it, she is free and pure. Gentlemen, as you look upon her you will pass your judgment that she is not insane. To find her guilty you must believe she is a fiend. Does she look it? As she sat here these long, weary days and moved in and out before you have you seen anything that shows the lack of human feeling and womanly bearing. A word more. There must be no mistake, gentlemen. That would be irreparable. There can be but one mistake which nobody can ever right, and for which there can never be any atonement to her. If you make a mistake as against the commonwealth that is something which the future may correct, but if you go wrong as to this woman now, and go to the length of saying that she is guilty, and you have done it upon insufficient grounds and the improper findings, the case and the woman have gone beyond your control, and, so far as you can know, beyond the power of man. To condemn her as guilty of the diabolical crimes that have been described to you, when there remains any reasonable doubt in the minds of any one of you of the true verdict, would be so deplorable an evil that the tongue can never speak its wickedness. We say, the crier utters it, God save the commonwealth of Massachusetts, and the prayer is heard in the prosperity of the old bay state, but little it amounts to if we hear some one pray to God for his guidance of the old commonwealth that when we have a prisoner in charge we forget that we can do a good deal toward saving the commonwealth and all her people. It will be little worth preserving if the innocent are to be executed and one calamity and wrong step fast upon the heels of another, and that, too, under the forms of law made as well to shield the innocent as to punish the guilty. Do I plead for her sister? No. Do I plead for Lizzie Andrew Borden herself? Yes. I ask you to consider her, to put her into the scale as a woman among us all, to say as you have her in charge to the commonwealth which you represent, it is not just to hold her a minute longer, and pleading for her I plead for you and myself and all of us that the verdict you shall register in this most important case shall not only command your approval now, unqualified and beyond reasonable doubt, but shall stand sanctioned and commended by the people everywhere in the world, who are listening by the telegraphic wire to know what is the outcome as to her.

She is not without sympathy in this world. She is not having people by day and by night thinking it is not to be found out in Massachusetts that so great a wrong against her can be committed as to condemn her upon the evidence that has been offered. Gentlemen, with great weariness on your part, but with abundant patience and intelligence and care, you have listened to what I have had to offer. So far as you are concerned, it is the last word of the defendant to you. Take it: take care of her as you have, and give us promptly your verdict not guilty, that she may go home and be Lizzie Andrew Borden of Fall River in that blood-stained and wrecked home where she has passed her life so many years.

CHAPTER XXXI.

DISTRICT ATTORNEY KNOWLTON'S PLEA.

HOSEA M. KNOWLTON, attorney for the State, spoke as follows: May it please your honors, Mr. Foreman and you, gentlemen of the jury—Upon one common ground in this case all human men can stand together. However we may differ about many of the issues in this trial, there can be no doubt, and I do not disguise my full appreciation of the fact, that it is a most heartrending case. Whether we consider the tragedy that we are trying and the circumstances that surround it, the charge that followed it, the necessary course of the trial that has been had before you, the difficult and painful duty of the counsel upon both sides of the case, or the duty that shall finally be committed to your charge, there is that in it all which lacerates the heart strings of humanity. It was an incredible crime, incredible but for the cold and merciful facts which confront and defeat that incredulity.

There is that in the tidings of a murder that thrills the human heart to its depths. When the word passes from lip to lip and from mouth to mouth that a human life has been taken by an assassin, the stoutest hearts stop beating, lips pale and cheeks blanch, strong men grow pale with the terror of the unknown and mysterious, and if that be so with what I may, perhaps, by comparison call an ordinary assassination, what were the feelings that overpowered the community when the news of this tragedy was spread by the lightning to the ends of the world? Nay, gentlemen, I need not ask you to imagine it. You were a part of the community. It came to you in your daily avocations, it sent a thrill through your beings and you felt that life was not secure. Every man turned detective. Every act and fact and thought that occurred to the thousand, to the million men all over the United States, was spread abroad and furnished and given for the identification of the criminal, and still it remained an impenetrable mystery. My distinguished friend says, Who could have done it? The answer would have been, nobody could have done it. If you had read the account of these cold and heartless facts in any tale of fiction before this thing had happened, would you not have said, Mr. Foreman—you would have said, That will do for a story, but such things never happen.

In the midst of the largest city of this county, in the midst of his household, surrounded by people and houses and teams and civilization, in the midst of the day, right in that household, while they were attending to their household duties in the midst of their families, an aged man and an aged woman are suddenly and brutally assassinated. It was a terrible crime. It is an impossible crime. But it was committed. And very much, very much, Mr. Foreman, of the difficulty of solving this awful tragedy starts from the very impossibility of the thing itself. Set any human being you can think of, put any degraded man or woman you ever heard of at the bar, and say to them, "You did this thing," and it would seem incredible. And yet it was done; it was done. And I am bound to say, Mr. Foreman, and I say it out of a full heart, that it is scarcely more credible to believe the charge that followed the crime. I would not for one moment lose sight of the incredibility of that charge, nor ask you to believe it, unless you find it supported by facts that you cannot explain or deny. The prisoner at the bar is a woman, and a christian woman, as the expression is used. It is no ordinary criminal that we are trying to-day. It is one of the rank of lady, the equal of your wife and mine, of your friends and mine, of whom such things had never been suspected or dreamed before. I hope I may never forget nor in anything that I say here to-day lose sight of the terrible significance of that fact. We are trying a crime that would have been deemed impossible but for the fact that it was, and are charging with the commission of it a woman whom we would have believed incapable of doing it but for the evidence that it is my duty, my painful duty, to call to your attention. But I beg you to observe, Mr. Foreman and gentlemen, that you cannot dispose of the case upon that consideration. Alas, that it is so! But no station in life is a pledge or a security against the commission of crime, and we all know it. Those who are intrusted with the most precious savings of the widow and the orphan, who stand in the community as towers of strength and fidelity, suddenly fall, and their wreck involves the ruin of many happy homes. They were christian men, they were devout men, they were members of some christian church, they had every inducement around them to preserve the lives that they were supposed to be living, and yet, when the crash came, it was found that they were rotten to the core. Nay, Mr. Foreman, those who are installed with the sacred robes of the church are not exempt from the lot of humanity. Time and again have we been grieved to learn, pained to find, that those who are set up to teach us the way of correct life have been found themselves to be foul as hell inside. Is youth a protection against crime. It is a matter of the history of the commonwealth that a boy of tender years was the most brutal, the most unrelenting, the most cruel, the most fiendish murderer that the commonwealth ever knew. Is sex a protection to crime? Is it not a matter of common knowledge that within the remembrance of every man I am talking to, a woman has been found who murdered a whole cart load of relatives for the sake of obtaining a miserable pittance of a fortune. Ah, gentlemen, I do not underestimate, I do not speak lightly of the strength of a christian character. Far be it from me to join in the sneers which are sometimes thoughtlessly indulged in that a man who is a good Christian is not therefore a good man. Most of them are. Many times all of them are. But they are all sons of Adam and Eve. They fall because they are human. They fall all at once because they have never been shown to the light, and their fall is all the greater because their outward lives have been pure before. I do not forget what a bulwark it is to you and me, Mr. Foreman, that we have heretofore borne a reputation that is above the suspicion of crimes and felonies. It is sometimes the only refuge of a man put in straits. But nobody is beyond the rank of men. Else would it not have been said even by the disciples themselves, "Lead not thy servant into presumptuous sins." It was not ordained by the Saviour that the weak and the trembling and the wicked and the easily turned only should utter the prayer, lead us not into temptation. We are none of us secure. Have you led, sir, an honorable, an upright life? Thank your Heavenly Father that the temptations have not been too strong for you. Have you, sir, never been guilty of heinous crime? Is it your strength of character or is it your fortune that you have been able to resist what has been brought against you? Mr. Foreman, let me not be misunderstood. Not for one moment would I urge that because a man or a woman has led an upright and devout life that therefore there should be any reason for suspecting him or her of a crime. On the contrary, it is a buttress to the foundation, to the presumption of innocence with which we start to try anybody. I am obliged to tread now upon a more delicate ground. The prisoner is a woman, one of that sex that all high-minded men revere, that all generous men love, that all wise men acknowledge their indebtedness to. It is hard, it

HOSEA M. KNOWLTON.

is hard, Mr. Foreman and gentlemen, to conceive that woman can be guilty of crime.   It is not a pleasant thing to reflect upon.   But I am obliged to say what strikes the justice of every man to whom I am talking, that while we revere the sex, while we show our courtesies to them, they are human like unto us.   They are no better than we; they are no worse than we.   If they lack in strength and coarseness and vigor, they make up for it in cunning, in dispatch, in celerity, in ferocity.   If their loves are stronger and more enduring than those of men, am I saying too much that, on the other hand, their hates are more undying, more unyielding, more persistent?   We must face this case as men, not as gallants.   You will be slow to believe it is within the capacity of a man to have done it.   But it was done.   You will be slower to believe that it was within the capacity of a woman to have done it, and I should not count you men if you did not, but it was done.   It was done for a purpose.   It was done by hatred.   But who did it?   You have been educated to believe, you are proud to recognize your loyalty, your fealty to the sex.   Gentlemen, that consideration has no place under the oath you have taken.   We are to find the facts.   I am said to be impervious to criticism, but those who have said one thing of me may have the consolation of knowing that the shaft has struck home.   When it has been said of me that in the trial of this cause, in the prosecution of this case, there entered into it anything but the spirit of duty, anything like a spirit of revenge, any unworthy motives like ambition or personal glory, if they had known how I shrank from this horrible duty, those slanderous tongues would never have uttered those words.   Gentlemen, it is the saddest duty of my life—it is the saddest duty of my life.   Gladly would I have shrunk from it if I could have done so and been a man.   Gladly would I have yielded the office with which I have been intrusted by the votes of this district if I could have done so honorably.   And if now any word I say, any evidence I state, any inference I draw, shall be done with any purpose or intent to do that woman an injustice, may my right hand wither and my tongue cleave to the roof of my mouth.   With that spirit, gentlemen, let me ask you to enter upon this case.   It was a crime that may well challenge your most sober and sacred attention.   That aged man, that aged woman, had gone by the noonday of their lives.   They had borne the burden and heat of the day.   They had accumulated a competency which they felt would carry them through the waning years of their lives, and hand and hand they expected to go down to the sunset of their days in quiet and happiness.

But for that crime they would be enjoying the air of this day. But for that assassin many years of their life, like yours, I hope, sir, would have been before them, when the cares of life were past, when the anxieties of their daily avocation had ceased to trouble them, and together they would have gone down the hill of life serene in an old age that was happy because the happiness had been earned by a life of fidelity and toil. Over those bodies we stand, Mr. Foreman. We sometimes forget the past. Over those bodies we stand, and we say to ourselves, is it possible that this crime cannot be discovered. You are standing, as has been suggested, in the presence of death itself. It is only what comes hereafter, but it is the double death that comes before. There is a place—it is the chamber of death—where all these personal animosities, passions and prejudices have no room, where all matters of sentiment are one side, where nothing but the truth, the naked truth, finds room and lodgment. In that spirit I adjure you to enter upon the trial of this case. It is the most solemn duty of your lives. We have brought before you as fully and frankly as we could, every witness whom we thought had any knowledge of any surrounding of this transaction, I do not know of one that has been kept back.

They were not merely the officers of the police. They were the domestic of that establishment, the tried and faithful servant, and, for aught that I know or have heard, the friend of these girls to-day. They were the physician who was the first one called on the discovery of the tragedy. They are the faithful friends and companions of this defendant. And we have called them all before you and listened to what they had to say, whether it was for her or against her. Nay, we called the relative himself and had his story of what he knew in the matter, and all the people who by any possibility could have known anything about this thing we have tried to produce to you to tell all that they could tell. Then there came another class of witnesses, if I may classify them. As soon as this crime was discovered it became, Mr. Foreman, did it not, the duty of those who are intrusted with the detection of crime to take such measures as they thought were proper for the discovery of the criminal. They are officers of the police. When you go home, sir, to your family, after this long agony is over, and a crime has been committed that approaches this in magnitude, or any crime whatever, where will you go? to whom will you appeal? on whom will you rely? Upon the very men that my distinguished friend has seen fit by direction to criticise as interested in this case. He put a question the other day which I forgave him for because it came in heat, but it illustrates what I am saying—saying to one of these officers, "speaking to you not as a police officer but as a man." It is true they are police officers, but they are men, too. They are to find out what the truth of it is. They made many mistakes. The crime was beyond the experience of any man in this country or in this world ; what wonder that they did ? They left many things undone that they might have done ; what wonder that they did ? It was beyond the scope of any men to grasp in its entirety at that time. But honestly, faithfully, as thoroughly as God had given them ability, they pursued the various avenues by which they thought they might find the criminal. My distinguished friend has not charged in words, and it is not true that their energies have been bent to this unfortunate prisoner. It was in evidence that many things were followed up, that many trails were pursued, and I am not permitted even to tell you how many men were followed with the thought that perhaps they had something to do with this crime, how many towns and cities were investigated, and how many people were watched and followed, how many trails have been pursued. Don't you suppose, Mr. Foreman, they would be glad to-day if it could be found that this woman did not do this thing ? Is there a man so base in all this world that hopes she did it, that wants to believe she did it, that tries to believe she did it ? Nay, nay, Mr. Foreman. All the evidence in this case that is entitled to great weight from the police officers came before (as I shall show you by and by) any suspicion came to them that she was connected with it. And it was only after they had investigated the facts, had gotten her stories and put them together, that the conviction forced itself upon them, as perhaps it may upon you, that there is no better explanation which will answer the facts that cannot be denied.

A blue coat does not make a man any better ; it ought not to make him any worse. They are men ; Mr. Fleet is a man, Mr. Mullaly is a man, Mr. Medley is a man, and they are not to be stood up in a row and characterized as good or bad because they are officers, but upon what you think of them as men. There is another thing that troubles my friends—I now include the learned advocate who opened this case as well as the distinguished counsel who closed it— and which perhaps from your ordinary and accustomed channel of thought may have troubled you. I speak of it frankly, for many honest men have been heard to say—I have heard many an honest man say, that he could not believe circumstantial evidence. And I respect the honesty of the man who says it: But, gentlemen, the crime we are trying is a crime of an assassin. It is the work of one who does his foul deeds beyond the sight and hearing of men. All it means is this: That when one sees the crime committed or one hears the crime committed then the testimony of him that sees or hears is the testimony of a witness who saw it or heard it and is direct evidence. All other evidence is circumstantial evidence. That is the exact distinction. Did you ever hear of a murderer getting a witness to his work who could see it or hear it? Murder is the work of stealth and craft in which there are not only no witnesses, but the traces are attempted to be obliterated. What is called sometimes circumstantial evidence is nothing in the world but that presumption of circumstances, it may be one or fifty. There isn't any chain about it: the word "chain" is a misnomer as applied to it; it is the presentation of circumstances from which one is irresistibly driven to the conclusion that crime has been committed. Talk about a chain of circumstances! When that solitary man had lived on this island for twenty years and believed that he was the only human being there and that the cannibals and savages that lived around him had not found him nor had not come to his island, he walked out one day on the beach, and there he saw the fresh print in the sand of a naked foot.

He had no lawyer to tell him that was nothing but a circumstance. He had no distinguished counsel to urge upon his fears that there was no chain about that thing which led him to a conclusion. His heart beat fast, his knees shook beneath him, he fell to the ground in fright, because Robinson Crusoe knew when he saw that circumstance that man had been there that was not himself. It was circumstantial evidence; it was nothing but circumstantial evidence, but it satisfied him. It is not a question of circumstantial evidence, Mr. Foreman; it is a question of the sufficiency of circumstantial evidence. It is like the refuse that floats upon the surface of the stream. You stand upon the banks of the river and you see a chip go by; that is only a circumstance. You see another chip go by. That is another circumstance. You see another chip in front of you going the other way. That is only another circumstance. By and by you see a hundred in the great body of the stream, all moving one way, and a dozen or two in this little eddy in front of you going the other way. The chain is not complete, some of the chips go up the stream; but you would not have any doubt, you would not hesitate for a moment, Mr. Foreman, to say that you knew which way the current of that river was, and yet you have not put your hand in the water, and yet have only seen things from which you inferred it, and even the things themselves did not go the same way. But you had the wit and the sense and the human and common experience to observe that those that went the other way could be explained, and the great body of them went that way. Mr. Foreman, there have been very few cases of assassination in which there was direct testimony. My learned friend, the counsel, who opened this case, has culled out from the billion of cases that have been tried by juries in English-speaking countries—I think I do not exaggerate—from the thousand million of cases which have been tried upon circumstantial evidence in English-speaking countries, an instance here and an instance there where it was found, perhaps, that there was a mistake ; and even those cases, with one single exception (and in that case the man never got hanged) are open to great doubt and discredit. But every lawyer knows, every man who is accustomed to the trying of cases is familiar with the fact that the testimony of men is wrong a hundred times where facts are wrong once. What impresses one as the remarkable and distinguishing feature of this case is the gradual discovery of the surprising fact that these two people did not come to their death at the same time. I have no doubt that each one of you, as you heard the stories as they came flashed over the wires, had the idea that was common to everybody who did not know anything about it, and there was nobody that did, that some man had come in, rushed through the house, killed the old gentleman, rushed upstairs and killed the old lady, and then had made his escape. But it was found that that was not so. It has been proved so conclusively that counsel do not dispute the proposition. It is scarcely worth while for me to recapitulate the evidence. I will not do it. Mr. Wixon, Mr. Pettee, who is not in any way connected with the government and holds no government office— came in there and made their explanation, and as Dr. Dedrick put it, it appeared to him—for he is a physician of experience, that the deaths were several hours apart. Dr. Dolan examined more carefully the blood and the wounds and the head, and he thought there was a difference of from an hour to an hour and a half.

But, Gentlemen, there is within us, provided by the Almighty, a clock by which the eye of science can tell the time. When a man falls into the water and drowns, his watch stops and fixes the time when he drowns ; anybody can tell that. But when the human life stops, if precautionary measures are taken, as were taken in this case, a man who is skilled in the examination of these things can tell as accurately the relative time of the deatn of that man as we can tell the time by that clock up there. And so we proved—ah, it was a suspicion born of consciousness and not of anything we said in this case when it was suggested that we were trying to show the poverty of the mode of her life here ; there never has been a word of that on our side of the case; my learned associate did not even hint that we were going to claim there was anything mean or poverty-stricken in this family, and it never was said until my distinguished friend saw fit to defend that family from what never was charged. But for the purpose of scientific investigation which was necessary, we proved—and for no other purpose whatever—what was the breakfast of that family that morning, and that the members of it sat down and partook together. It was a good breakfast, it was the ordinary New England breakfast, and nobody has said the contrary. Do not let me be misunderstood for one single moment in this case. And for that purpose we showed you that these people sat down to breakfast at from seven to quarter past seven, and finished from half past seven to quarter of eight, and ate together and ate at the same time. They lived their lives out prematurely cut off by the hand of the assassin : their bodies lay upon the floor. Their stomachs were taken out, digestion stopped when they stopped, and were sent to the eminent, that scientific, that honest, that utterly fair man, Prof Wood, whom my learned friends will join with me in saying is the most honest expert there is in Massachusetts to-day. He alone was able to determine accurately the time of their death, assuming that digestion went on normally within them, and he says that in all human probability the time of her death preceded his by an hour and a half ; it might possibly have been a half hour less ; it might possibly have been a half hour more : Singularly enough, science is corroborated by the facts. Singularly enough, everything fits into that proposition. Andrew Jackson Borden probably never heard the clock strike 11 as it pealed forth from the tower of city hall ; and she was found dead with the implement with which she had been engaged in dusting the rooms at her head and close by her death. She was stricken down while she was in that morning work in which she was engaged the last time anybody saw her. And all the evidence in the case points to the irresistible conviction that when Andrew Borden was down at his accustomed place in the bank of Mr. Abraham Hart, the faithful wife he had left at home was prone in death in the chamber of the house he had left her in. At half-past nine, if we are to believe the consensus of all this testimony, the assassin met her in that room and put an end to her innocent old life.

Gentlemen, that is a tremendous fact. It is a controlling fact in this case. It is the key of the case. Why do I say that? Because the murderer of this man was the murderer of Mrs. Borden. It was the malice against Mrs. Borden that inspired the assassin. It was Mrs. Borden whose life that wicked person sought, and all the motive that we have to consider, all we have to say about this case, bears on her. It is a tremendous fact for another thing, a significant fact for another thing. We are driven to the alternative of finding that there was a human being who had the unparalleled audacity to penetrate that house when the entire family were in and about it, so far as he knew, to pursue his murderers with a deadly weapon in his hand, to the furthest corner of the house, and there to select an innocent and unoffending old lady for his first victim, and then lie in wait until the family should all get together an hour and a half later that he might kill the other one.

This murderer was no fool: he was obedient to craft and cunning. He could not forsee that Bridget would go upstairs. He could not forsee that Lizzie would go to the barn. He might have known from the habits of Andrew Borden that he would come back, but it would be back to a house full of people—Morse might come at any time : he knew not when Emma might come. He was waiting for the family to assemble, this man who committed this deed. It was no sudden act of a man coming in and out. It was the act of a person who spent the fore-noon in this domestic establishment, killing the woman at her early work and waiting till the man returned for his noon-day meal in order that he could be killed when everybody would be likely to be around him. It is a tremendous fact, Mr. Foreman. It appears in this case from the beginning to end. She had not an enemy in the world. You and I sometimes have our jars and discords. Andrew J. Borden had had his little petty quarrels with his tenants, nothing out of the ordinary, but Mrs. Abby Durfee Borden had not an enemy in all the world. There she lay bleeding, dead, prone by the hand of an assassin. Somebody went up there to kill her. In all this universe there could not be found a person who could have had any motive to do it.

We must now go into this establishment and see what manner of family this was. It is said that there is a skeleton in the household of every man, but the Borden skeleton—if there was one—was fairly well locked up from view. They were a close-mouthed family. They did not parade their difficulties. Last of all would you expect they would tell the domestic in the kitchen, which is the whole tower of strength of the defense, and yet, Mr. Foreman, there was a skeleton in the closet of that house which was not adequate to this matter—O, no, not adequate to this thing. There is not anything in human nature that is adequate to this thing—remember that. But there was a skeleton of which we have seen the grinning eyeballs and the dangling limbs. It is useless to tell you that there was peace and harmony in that family. We know better. We know better. The remark that was made to Mrs. Gifford, the cloakmaker, was not a petulant outburst, such as might come and go. That correction of Mr. Fleet, at the very moment the poor woman who had reared that girl lay dead within ten feet of her voice, was not merely accidental. It went down deep into the springs of human nature. Lizzie Borden had never known her mother. She was not three years old when that woman passed away, and her youthful lips had scarcely learned to pronounce the tender word mamma, and no picture of her lay in the girl's mind. And yet she had a mother—she had a mother. Before she was old enough to go to school, before she arrived at the age of five years, this woman, the choice of her father, the companion of her father, who had lost and mourned and loved again, had come in and had done her duty by that girl and had reared her, had stood in all the attitudes which characterize the tenderest of all human relations. Through all her childhood's sicknesses that woman had cared for her. When she came in weary with her sports, feeble and tired, it was on her breast that girl had sunk as have our children on the breast of their mothers. She had been her mother, faithful persevering, and had brought her up to be at least an honorable and worthy woman in appearance and manner.

This girl owed everything to her. Mrs. Borden was the only mother she had ever known, and she had given to this girl her mother's love and had given her this love when a child when it was not her own and she had not gone through the pains of childbirth, because it was her husband's daughter. And then a quarrel ; what a quarrel. What a quarrel, Mr. Foreman. A man worth more than a quarter of a million of dollars, wants to give his wife, his faithful wife who has served him thirty years for her board and clothes, who has done his work, who has kept his house, who has reared his children, wants to buy and get with her the interest in a little homestead where her sister lives.

How wicked to have found fault with it. How petty to have found fault with it. Nay, if it was a man sitting in that dock instead of a woman, I would characterize it in more opprobrious terms than those. I trust that in none of the discussion that I engage in to-day shall I forget the courtesy due from a man to a woman; and although it is my horrible and painful duty to point to the fact of this woman being a murderess, I trust I shall not forget that she is a woman, and I hope I never have. And she repudiated the title that that woman should have had from her. Did you ever hear of such a case as that? It was a living insult to that woman, a living expression of contempt, and that woman repeated it day in and day out, saying to her, as Emma has said, you are not interested in us. You have worked round our father and have got a little miserable pittance of $1,500 out of him, and you shall be my mother no more. Am I exaggerating this thing? She kept her own counsel. Bridget did not know anything about it. She was in the kitchen. This woman never betrayed her feelings except when some one else tried to make her call her mother, and then her temper broke forth. Living or dead, no person should use that word mother to that poor woman unchallenged by Lizzie Borden. She had left it off herself; all through her childhood days, all through her young life Mrs. Borden had been a mother to her as is the mother of every other child to its offspring, and the time comes when they still live in the same house and this child will no longer call her by that name. Mr. Foreman, it means much. It means much. Why does it mean much? They did not eat together. Bridget says so. My distinguished friend tried to get her to take it back, and she did partly. The woman would have taken most anything back under that cross-examination, but this is her testimony: "That is so, they always ate together." "Yes, they always ate in the same dining-room." Bridget is going to have her own way yet. But I do not put it on Bridget. I put it on Lizzie herself. When Mrs. Gifford spoke to her, talking about her mother, she said, "Don't say mother to me."—that mother who had reared her and was her father's companion under the roof with whom she was then living, whose household she shared, to whom every debt of gratitude was due and whom she had repudiated as her mother, she could not find the heart to say to this cloakmaker was her mother, for I believe that you believe this story is true—"she is a mean, good for nothing old thing." Nay, that is not all—"We do not have much to do with her. I stay in my room most of the time."

Is not that so? Uncle John Morse came to visit them, stayed over night, and during the afternoon and evening, and next morning, and never saw Lizzie at all—her own uncle. "Why, you come down to your meals?" said Mrs. Gifford, and Lizzie said, "Yes, but we don't eat with them if we can help it." I heard what Miss Emma said Friday, and I could but admire the loyalty and fidelity of that unfortunate girl to her still more unfortunate sister. I could not find it in my heart to ask her many questions. She was in the most desperate strait that any innocent woman could be in, her next of kin, her only sister, stood in peril, and she must come to the rescue. She faintly tells us the relations in the family were peaceful, but we sadly know they were not. But you will say, you will fairly say, Mr. Foreman—let me not underrate this thing one atom—you will fairly say, what is that? I don't know. I don't know how deep this cancer had eaten in. It makes but little show on the surface. A woman can preserve her appearance of health and strength even when the roots of this foul disease have gone and wound clear around her heart and vital organs. This was a cancer. It was an interruption of what should have been the natural agreeable relations between mother and daughter, a quarrel about property, not her property, but her father's, and property that he alone had the right to dispose of. A man does not surrender his rights to his own until he is dead, and not even then if he chooses to make a will. She could not brook that that woman should have influence enough over her father to let him procure the little remnant of her own property that had fallen to her from her own folks. She had repudiated the title of mother. She had lived with her in hatred. She had gone on increasing in that hatred until we do not know, we can only guess, how far that sore had festered, how far the blood in that family had been poisoned by the misfortune of these unfortunate relations between them. I come back to that poor woman lying prone, as has been described, in the parlor. It is wicked to have to say it, it is wicked to have to say it, but, gentlemen, there is no escape from the truth. Had she an enemy in all the world? She had one. Was anybody in the world to be benefitted by her taking away? There was one. There was one. It is hard to believe that mere property would have influenced this belief. We are not obliged to, although it appears that property was that which made or broke the relations of that family, and a small amount of property, too. But there was one woman in the world who believed that that dead woman stood between her and her father, and was the enemy of her and the friend of her father, and between whom there had grown up that feeling that prevented her from giving her the title that the ordinary instincts of decency would have entitled her to. Let us examine the wounds upon that woman. So we look at the skull and we look at these wounds, and what do

we read there? We know afterwards, by another examination downstairs, that no thief did this thing; there was no object of plunder.
We are spared the suspicion that any base animal purposes had to do
with this crime. No, Mr. Foreman, there was nothing in these blows
but hatred, but hatred, and a desire to kill. What sort of blows were
they? Some struck here at an angle, badly aimed; some struck here
in the neck, badly directed; some pattered on top of the head and
didn't go through; some, where the skull was weaker, went through.
A great strong man would have taken a blow of that hatchet and
made an end of it. The hand that held the weapon was not the hand
of masculine strength. It was the hand of a person strong only in
hate and desire to kill. We have not proved anything yet, but we
must take things as they come, no matter where they lead us. It
was not the work of a man who, with a blow of that hatchet, could
have smashed any part of that skull, and whose unerring aim would
have made no false blow or false work. In was the indecisive blow
of hatred, the weak, puttering, badly aimed, nerveless blows—I
forbear for the present to bring that sentence to a conclusion, for I
won't do it until I am obliged to. I won't ask you, until I am
obliged to, to listen to it. Now we must go back and see what the
circumstances of that crime were, for that is the crime we are trying.
We will come at the other one by and by, and see how and when and
why they happened. But now we are trying that crime, the motive
of that crime, the probable author of that crime, who could have
committed that crime, what sort of person committed that crime, and
why it was done. We find, Mr. Foreman, perhaps the most remarkable house that you ever heard of. My distinguished friend has
admitted so many things that I am saved the necessity of arguing
very much about the circumstances surrounding the house. Everything was locked up. Why, did you notice there was even the
barbed wire at the bottom of the fence as well as on the top and on
the stringers? Everything was shut up. It was the most zealously
guarded house I ever heard of. The cellar door was found locked
by all the witnesses that examined it. The barn door was locked at
night and was kept locked all night and opened in the morning, by
the undisputed testimony of Bridget, whom nobody has suggested or
ventured to suggest has told anything more than she knows in the
case. The closet door, up to the head of the stairs, was found locked
by Mr. Fleet, and every time that he wanted to go in there, or anybody else wanted to go in there, or Lizzie herself, she furnished the
keys that unlocked it. So that door was locked up. The front door

was a door which had been kept by a spring lock until that day. The day before, when Dr. Bowen called, Bridget let him in by the spring lock. That night, when Lizzie came home from her call on Miss Russell, she let herself in by the spring lock. There isn't an atom of evidence that up to the time of this tragedy and when people began to come in and out and upset the ordinary arrangements of that house, but that the front door had always been kept by a spring lock and opened in the morning. That morning it was not opened. It was that woman's business to open it, and she did not open it. She came down stairs and went into the kitchen and went about her ordinary avocations, and by and by, when Mr. Borden came home, he expected to find it unlocked, because he tried his key to it and it wouldn't fit, and he had to call her attention to get in. And it was not only with the spring lock, but with the bolt and with the lower lock (all three put together) as people lock their door when they go to bed. Not the shutting in of an assassin, as my distinguished friend has suggested, who was trying to lock himself into the house, wild and improbable as that suggestion is. Then the screen door. It may be, perhaps, as good a way to do as any to refresh your memories about it as well as my own. I will go back to the night before. That afternoon at 5 o'clock that screen door was locked. That night when Bridget went out she locked the back door after her. That night when she came back she found it locked, and she locked up the screen door and the outside door and went upstairs to bed. No chance for anybody to get in that day. The cellar was never unlocked except on the Tuesday before—and I get this right from the testimony because I do not want to argue anything but what is strictly correct. The next morning Bridget got up at 6.15 and took in the milk and hooked the screen door, unlocked the big door. A little while afterwards Mrs. Borden came down, some time between 6:30 and 6:45, and went into the sitting room. Mr. Borden came a little while afterwards, put his key on the shelf, and unhooked the screen door and went into the yard, Bridget remaining in the kitchen all the time. When he came back Bridget was out of view of the screen door and don't know whether he hooked it or not.

But the next person that went out was Morse, and Mr. Morse tells us—for he fills all that cavity up—Mr. Morse tells us that he unhooked the screen door when he went out and Mr. Borden hooked it after him, so that Mr. Borden must have hooked it when he came in. Then, when Mr. Borden came in he hooked the screen door again, Bridget being on guard in the kitchen all the time. Then

Bridget went about her work, eating her breakfast, clearing off the dining room dishes, right there on guard in the kitchen all the time. By and by Lizzie came down. Lizzie came into the kitchen, and her father had not then gone and Bridget went out into the yard a few minutes, because she was sick, too. She remained there in the yard for a moment or two, and when she came to, Lizzie had got through her breakfast and had got back into the other part of the house, she didn't know where, and Mr. Borden had gone off down town. When she came in she hooked the screen door. Up to that time, Mr. Foreman, no human being could have got into that house. We go further than that. By and by Bridget goes into the dining room to clear off her dining room things, and sees Mrs. Borden dusting in and out of the sitting room and the dining room, and Mrs. Borden directs her, when she gets through her work, to wash the windows. Bridget goes on about her work and Mrs. Borden disappears upstairs and Lizzie is out of sight. She gets through with her work—and I call your particular attention to this. She gets through with her work, Bridget does, goes down cellar and gets her pail, comes back into the house, goes through the house and puts down the windows and there isn't anybody below the stairs. Mr. Borden has long since gone down town. It must have been about half past nine when Bridget went out to wash the windows, or possibly a little later. She goes out of the screen door, which up to that time no human being could have gone through. She has no more than got out of doors than Lizzie, who had not been down stairs up to that time, who had not gone away from the house, and, as she herself says, saw her mother up there making the bed, or working in that guest chamber, Lizzie comes to the back door to see if Bridget is fairly out of doors, goes back into the house, and the murder is then done, as Prof. Wood's clock tells us.

Never mind the impossibility—I won't argue that now, Mr. Foreman—never mind the impossibility for the present of imagining a person who was so familiar with the habits of that family, who was so familiar with the interior of that house, who could forsee the things that the family themselves could not see, who was so lost to all human reason, who was so utterly criminal as to set out without any motive whatever, as to have gone to that house that morning, to have penetrated through the cordon of Bridget and Lizzie, and pursued that poor woman up the stairs to her death, and then waited, weapon in hand until the house should be filled up with people again that he might complete his work.

I wont discuss with you the impossibility of that thing for the present. I will come back to the facts in this case and ask you whether or not, at that time when the murder was done—up to that time there had been no room for the assassin to come in, and after that time the house was there alone with Lizzie and her murdered victim. The dead body tells us another thing. It is a circumstance, but it is one of those circumstances that cannot be cross-examined nor made fun of nor talked out of court. The poor woman was standing when she was struck, and fell with all the force of that two hundred pounds of flesh, flat and prone dead on the floor. That jar could not have failed to have been heard all over that house. They talk about its being a noisy street. Why, Bridget tells us that she could hear the screen door from her room when it slammed. She did hear Andrew Borden trying the lock of the front door and went to let him in without the bell being rung. Lizzie heard her down there letting her father in. Nothing happened in one part of the house that wasn't heard in the other. My friend has spent some time in demonstrating, as he believes, to you, the unlikelihood of her seeing her murdered mother as she went up and down the stairs. But Lizzie Borden has ears as well as eyes. If she was downstairs she was in the passageway of the assassin. If she was upstairs there was nothing to separate her from the murder but the thinness of that deal door that you saw. And do you believe for a moment, Mr. Foreman and gentlemen, do you believe for a moment that those blows could have been struck—that woman was struck in a way that did not make her insensible—that she could have been struck without groaning or screaming; that she could have fallen without a jar, a woman as heavy as I am (I just use that by way of illustration), on that floor, nearer than I am to you, sir, from Lizzie, and she know nothing of it? If the facts I have put to you, Mr. Foreman, are true, at the very instant when the murders were committed we leave Lizzie and Mrs. Borden in the house together. Was she in the passageway when this assassin came in? She alone knows. Was she in her room when that heavy body fell to the floor? She alone knows. But we know, alas, we know, Mr. Foreman, that when Bridget opened that screen door and went out to wash the windows, after Mr. Borden had met his half-past nine appointment at the bank, that she left in the house this poor woman and the only enemy she had in the world. And there had been no more chance, if there was any conceivable possibility existing to mankind that anybody else got in than there would be of getting into this room and you and I not seeing them. But that is not all.

It is provided, as I humbly and devoutly believe, by the divine justice itself, that no matter how craftily murder is planned, there is always some point where the skill and cunning of the assassin fails him. It failed her. It failed her at a vital point, a point which my distinguished friend has attempted to answer, if I may be permitted to say so, and has utterly failed. She was alone in that house with that murdered woman. She could not have fallen without her knowledge. The assassin could not have come in without her knowledge. She was out of sight and Mrs. Borden was out of sight, and by and by there was coming into the house a stern and just man, who knew all the bitterness there was between them. There came into that house a stern and just man who would have noticed the absence of his wife, and who would have said to her, as the Almighty said to Cain. "Where is Abel, thy brother?" And that question must be answered. He came in; he sat down; she came to him, and she said to him: " Mrs. Borden"—she would not even call her "mother" then—"Mrs. Borden has had a note and gone out." That stilled his fears; that quieted any apprehensions he might have felt or reason of her absence either from the sitting room or the kitchen, or her own room upstairs, where he was sure to go with his key, as he did. When Bridget went to her room, and I call your attention to this as being the first information that Bridget had of it—it will appear by and by by the evidence itself—before Bridget went upstairs to her room Lizzie says to her, " If you go out, be sure and lock the door, for Mrs. Borden has gone out on a sick call and I might go out, too. " Bridget says, " Miss Lizzie, who is sick?" naturally enough. She said. " I don't know, but she had a note this morning and it must be in town."

Mrs. Churchill came over. " Where is mother, Lizzie?" She said: " I don't know. She had a note to go to see some one who was sick, but I don't know but she is killed, too, for I think I heard her come in." I will talk about that by and by, if I don't weary you too much. Then she said something to Fleet. Although she told Fleet that the last time she saw her stepmother was 9 o'clock, and she was then making her bed in the room where she was found dead, she said, "some one brought a letter or a note to Mrs. Borden," and she thought she had gone out, and had not known of her return. Then when Bridget came back she wanted to find her. She knew that one of the mother's only relatives was Mrs. Whitehead, the sister of her husband, as it turned out, because it turned out by Miss Emma's cross-examination and she said: " Oh, Lizzie, if I knew where Mrs. Whitehead lived I would go and see if Mrs. Borden is there and tell her that Mr. Borden is very sick.'' Mr. Foreman, charged with the responsibility of the solemn trust imposed upon him, my learned associate said in opening this case that that statement was a lie. Conscious as I am, Mr. Foreman, that any unjust or harsh word of mine might do injury that I never could recover my peace of conscience for, I reaffirm that serious charge. No note came; no note was written; nobody brought a note; nobody was sick. Mrs. Borden had not had a note. My learned friend said, '' I would stake the case on the hatchet.'' I will stake it on your belief or disbelie in the truth or falsity of that proposition. Afterwards, after Lizzie had told Bridget that Mrs. Borden had had a note to go out and see some one, that Mrs. Borden had gone out on a sick call and had had the note come that morning, she told her before she went to the room and that murder was discovered, and after it was a matter of common talk, and when Mrs. Churchill was asking Bridget not as a source of original information but for all the news there could be had about it, Bridget then said to her, not '' to my own knowledge Mrs. Borden had a note to go out to see some one who was sick,'' but repeated it as the story of the original and only author, Lizzie Borden. Obviously that is so, because when my learned and distinguished friend comes to the cross-examination of Bridget, this is what Bridget said, that she never had any knowledge of a note at all, except what Lizzie told her. Pardon me for reading it, because this is vital to the case. '' You simply say that you didn't see anybody come with a note?'' '' No, sir; I did not.'' '' Easy enough for anybody to come with a note to the house and you not know it, wasn't it?'' '' Well, I don't know if a note came to the back door that I wouldn't know. The door bell never rang that morning at all.'' '' But they wouldn't necessarily go to the back door, would they?'' '' No. I never heard anything about a note; whether they got it or not, I don't know. I never heard anything about a note.'' She was obviously telling the story as Lizzie had told it to her. Bridget had last seen Mrs. Borden dusting in the sitting room. She had been told by Lizzie that she had got a note and gone out.

No, gentlemen. In the first place, Bridget was on guard at that back door until she had washed the windows, and no note came that way. She testifies, and you can easily believe her testimony, because the front door was locked with three locks all the time, that nobody came to the front door and rang the bell with a note. I said that Almighty providence directed the course of this world to bring murderers to grief and justice. Little did it occur to Lizzie Borden when she told that lie to her father that there would be manifold witnesses of the fatality of it. They have advertised for the writer of the note, which was never written and which never came. Gentlemen, incredulity sometimes can be dismissed by evidence, but I am not looking in the face of one single man that will believe for an instant that the writer of that note would not months ago have come forward and cleared that thing up. There never was one. Ah, but my distinguished friend is pleased to suggest—he hardly dares to argue it, such is his insight and fairness—he is pleased to suggest that it was part of the scheme of assassination. How! To write a note to get a woman away when he was going there to assassinate her? What earthly use was there in writing a note to get rid of Mrs. Borden, when there would still be left Lizzie and Bridget in the house? O, no, that is too wild and absurd. The whole false-hood of that note came from the woman in whose keeping Mrs. Borden was left by Andrew Borden, and it was as false as was the answer that Cain gave to his Maker when he said to him, "Where is thy brother Abel?" I regret to ask you so to believe, gentlemen. It pains me beyond expression to be compelled to state these things. God forbid that anybody should have committed this murder, but somebody did, and when I have found that she was killed, not by the strong hand of man, but by the weak and ineffectual blows of woman, when I find that those are the blows of hatred rather than of strength, when I find that she is left alone at the very moment of murder, shut up in that house where every sound went from one end to the other, with the only person in all God's universe who could say she was not her friend, with the only person in the universe who could be benefited by her taking away, and when I find, as I found, and as you must find, if you answer your consciences in this case, that the story told about a note coming is as false as the crime itself, I am not responsible, Mr. Foreman, you are not responsible for the conclusion to which you are driven. Bridget finished the washing of her windows, came into the house, no one being below the stairs, took her step ladder and began the work upon the inside of the windows. Meanwhile the old gentleman was finishing the last walk of his life. You find him leaving his house by the back door, where Mrs. Churchill saw him, probably, although it may not have been the occasion of his leaving. We certainly find him down at his accustomed place in the bank that had honored him by making him its president, at his usual hour of 9:30. We find him going on from this to the other bank that honored him by making him a trustee, a little later in the day. The malice was all before this fact. The wickedness was all before the fourth day of August. The ingratitude, the poisoning, the hate, the stabbing of the mind, which is worse than the stabbing of the body, had gone on under that roof for many, many moons. All we know is that there was a jealousy which was unworthy of that woman. All we know is that, as Emma expressed it herself, they felt that he was not interested in them and no step could be taken by that poor man, no suggestion could be made by that poor man, that would not fan the embers of that discontent into the active fires of hatred that we have seen, alas, too many times manifested in many an unhappy home. I speak of these things, Mr. Foreman, at this time because I have left the dead body of that aged woman lying upon the guest chamber floor, in the room where she was last at work, and am asking you to come down with me to a far sadder tragedy, to the most horrible word that the English language knows, to a parricide. I do not undertake, far be it from me to seek to detract one iota from the terrible significance of that word ; and when I am asked to fight and prove and declare and explain a motive for that act, well may my feeble powers quail at the undertaking.

There may be that in this case which saves us from the idea that Lizzie Borden planned to kill her father. I hope she did not. But Lizzie Andrew Borden, the daughter of Andrew Jackson Borden, never came down those stairs. It was not Lizzie Andrew Borden, the daughter of Andrew Jackson Borden, that came down those stairs, but a murderess, transformed from all the thirty-three years of an honest life, transformed from the daughter, transformed from the ties of affections to the most consummate criminal we have read of in all our history or works of fiction. She came down to meet that stern old man. His picture shows that, if nothing more, even in death. That just old man, of the stern puritan stock, that most of you are from, gentlemen, that man who loved his daughters, but who also loved his wife, as the Bible commanded him to, And, above all, the one man in all this universe who would know who killed his wife. She had not thought of that. She had gone on. There is cunning in crime, but there is blindness in crime, too. She had gone on with stealth and cunning, but she had forgotten the hereafter. They alway do. And when the deed was done she was coming downstairs to face Nemesis. There wouldn't be any question of what he would know of the reason why that woman lay in death. He knew who disliked her. He knew who could not tolerate her presence under the roof. He knew the discussion which had led up to the pitch of frenzy which resulted in her death, and she didn't dare to let him live, father though he was, and bound to her by every tie of affection. It is the melancholy, the inevitable attribute of crime that it is the necessary and fruitful parent of crime. He moved slowly. He went to the back door, as was his custom, but nobody was there to open it, and so he went around to the front door, as very likely he often did, supposing, of course, that he could gain entrance, as any man does into his own house in the day time, by the use of a spring lock. We have heard something about the noise and confusion of

that street, but Bridget's ears, which are no quicker than Lizzie's, heard him as he put the key into the lock, and came to the door and let him in. He came in and passed into the dining room, because she was, I presume, working in the sitting room, took off his coat and sat down and replaced it with a cardigan jacket and down came Lizzie from the very place where Mrs. Borden lay dead and told him what we

ATTORNEY GENERAL PILLSBURY.

cannot believe to be true about where his wife was. I am told, gentlemen, that circumstances are to be regarded with suspicion. Mr. Foreman, a falsehood that goes right to the very vitals of crime not a circumstance; it is proof. Where was that mother? She knew. She told what never was true. That would pass off for awhile; that would keep the old man quiet for a time, but it would not last.

She took out her ironing-board. Why had she not been ironing in the cellar part of the house. Mr. Foreman, we do not know. She had no duties around the household, so Emma tells us. There was nothing for her to do. Bridget goes into the dining room. Having finished her windows in the sitting room, it took only a moment to go inside. Comes into the dining room to wash the windows and the old gentleman comes down from his room and goes into the sitting room and sits down. She suggests to him, with the spirit in which Judas kissed his master, that, as he is weary with his day's work, it would be well for him to lie down upon the sofa and rest. Then she goes into the dining room again, gets her ironing board, and proceeds to iron her handkerchiefs. Bridget finishes her work. She tells Bridget, and that is the first time that Bridget heard it directly, as I stated to you yesterday, that if she goes out that afternoon to be sure to lock the doors, because Mrs. Borden had gone out on a sick call. And she says: "Miss Lizzie, who is sick?" Miss Lizzie replies: "I don't know, but it must be in town, for she had a note this morning." She never did, and Bridget goes upstairs to take her little rest and leaves this woman ironing those handkerchiefs nearer to her father as he lay on that sofa than my distinguished friend is to me, at this moment. Again she was alone with her victim. O, unfortunate combination of circumstances, always. Again she is alone in the house with the man who was found murdered. It may be safely said to be less than twenty minutes from that time she calls Bridget down stairs and tells her that her father is killed. There is another straw, Mr. Foreman, another chip on the surface, not floating in an eddy, but always out in the middle of the currant, that tells us with irresistible distinctness of what happened after Bridget went upstairs. She had a good fire to iron the clothes with. Why do I say that? I will not speak without the evidence if I can help it. Officer Harrington comes along, takes a car that reaches city hall at 12:15, goes along Main street, goes to the house, talks with Lizzie, and, last of all, takes the cover off the stove and sees there, and I will read his own words: "The fire was near extinguished; on the end there was a little fire, I should judge about as large as the palm of my hand. The embers were about dying." That was as early as 12:30. I need not say to you that if there was fire enough to be seen at 12:30 there was fire enough to work with an hour and a half before 11 o'clock. There was fire enough. There is no trouble on that account. It was a little job she had to do, nine handkerchiefs at the outside, perhaps eight or seven, and when this thing is over Miss Russell gets the handkerchiefs and takes them upstairs, where we find a fatal thing, we find that four or five, I give the exact words of those handkerchiefs: "Are ironed and two or three are sprinkled ready to iron.'' Whatever else is true, she had begun her work before Bridget went upstairs, she was engaged in it when Bridget left her. It was a job that could not have taken her any more than ten minutes at the outside, if I may use the common expression of mankind in that sort of work, and the clock of Lizzie's course of life stopped the instant Bridget left the room. What for? What for, gentlemen? It would have taken but a minute or so to finish them. The day was well gone, the dinner hour was approaching. There were four or five to take away and but two or three to finish, and in less time than I am speaking it would have been done.

It is terribly significant. There is that in this case which is far deeper than these accidental variations. She says to Bridget, not to an officer, ''I was out in the back yard and heard a groan, and came in and the screen door was wide open, I may have occasion to say that that story was not true either, and was not consistent with any other story that she told. Dr. Bowen came next, I believe. He says, '' Where have you been?'' O, pregnant question that nobody could fail to ask. ''In the barn looking for some irons or iron,'' she answers. Mrs. Churchill came next—I may not have the order right —and that honest woman asked it the first thing, ''Where were you when it happened, Lizzie?'' '' I went to the barn to get a piece of iron.'' Miss Russell heard the remark. She does not distinctly remember asking it, and she is her friend : ''What did you go to the barn for, Lizzie?'' ''I went to get a piece of tin or iron to fix my screen.'' And Mr. Fleet came in, and politely, as you may believe, courteously, as you are glad to think, he talked to her about that important question of where she was when this thing happened. Let me read it word for word, for it is vital and significant and Mr. Buck will not say that one word of it is misconstrued or misremembered or falsely stated. He asked her if she knew anything about the murders. '' She said that she did not, all she knew was that her father came home about 10 :30 or 10 :45, went into the sitting room, sat down in a large chair, took out some papers and looked at them. She was ironing in the dining room some handkerchiefs, as she stated. She saw that her father was feeble, and she went to him and advised and assisted him to lie down upon the sofa. She then went into the dining room to her ironing, but left after her father was lain down, and went out into the yard and went up in the barn. I asked her how long she remained in the barn ; she said she remained in the barn about half an hour. I then asked her what she meant by ' up in the barn. '

She said, 'I mean up in the barn, upstairs, sir.' She said after she had been up there about half an hour she came down again, went into the house and found her father lying on the lounge." Mr. Foreman and gentlemen, we must judge all facts, all circumstances as they appeal to your common sense. There is no other test; there is no other duty; there is no other way of arriving at justice, and tried by that standard I assert that that story is simply incredible. I assert that that story is simply absurd. I assert that that story is not within the bounds of reasonable possibilities.

That is not all. Saturday again the mayor of the city, who I assume is a gentleman, whom I know you will believe to be one, and Marshal Hilliard, who has answered by his dignified and courteous and wholly respectable presence all the slanders you have heard about him in his simple and unaffected way of testifying in this case, which is refutation enough of all the wicked things that have been said of him—that men came there Saturday evening, and again incidentally that story was referred to. She told her friend Alice that she went to get a piece of iron to fix her screen. She told them that she went out into the barn to get some sinkers. It is not so much the contradiction I call your attention to, for I want to be entirely fair, for both errands might have been in her mind.

Why could we not have had somebody to have told us what was the screen that needed fixing, and to have corroborated that story by finding the piece of iron that was put into the screen when she was left alone and when she came back in her fright. Show us the fish line that these sinkers went on. It was easy to do if they were in existence, if there was any truth in the story. Show us something by which we can verify this ferocious fact, that the alibi she was driven to put for herself is a good one. I will spend a little time in the prosecution of this argument to discuss Mr. Lubinsky. What he saw and when he saw it are absolutely indefinite. Let me treat him with entire fairnesss and justice. To begin with, he is a discarded witness. He went with his story first to Wilkinson and then to Mr. Mullaly and then to Mr. Phillips before the hearing in the district court. Mr. Mullaly tells you just what he told him. He saw Mr. Mullaly and told him it was about half past 10 when he went by and saw somebody coming from the barn. That was on the 8th day of August. About two weeks after the time—I do not need the record, for I remember it as though it was yesterday—about two weeks after that time he told Mr. Phillips. Yes, it would be the 22d of August. This hearing ran through the 24th, 25th, 26th, 27th, and into the first day of September. He told a reporter, and I presume it was published, although I do not know about that. I won't say that, for I don't know. Mr. Phillips was present there in court; witnesses were called for the defense, and Lubinsky was not called. He had not got things patched up. And I want to know in this connection what was the necessity of having that line drawn so carefully by the surveyor across the plan of the first day. What has been the significance of that thing by which it was made to appear that a surveyor could find a line clear from a point on the street to the barn door? And you were asked to squint across there. You saw that you could not see the fraction of a rabbit that came out of that barn door. Has that any connection with the first attempt at Lubinsky? I do not know It is one of those things they have started and have flashed in the pan. Medley was the first one there. He got the news before 11 :30. He took a team that was coming up the street, and drove as fast as he could drive it. He went to the station house and got the men, started for the Borden house, and as he went by the city hall clock it was nineteen or twenty minutes before 12. He went there; he went into the house. He saw Miss Borden. He came out and went into the barn. Other men did the same thing. It occurred to many, he went there first because he was the one that found the door shut, and the others, excepting these wonderful boy detectives, found it open. All the contradiction of Medley is an attempt to contradict him about time. Something has been said, Mr. Foreman and gentlemen, as to the conduct of the defendant during this trying time. In my desire to say no word that is not borne out by the exact facts, I forbear to criticise or to ask you to consider against her her general demeanor after this tragedy. I quite agree for once with my distinguished friend in his suggestion that the absence of tears, that the icy demeanor may have either meant consciousness of guilt or consciousness of loss.

I would not lift the weight of my finger to urge that this woman remarkable though she is, nervy as she is, brave as she is, cool as she is, should be condemned because grief, it may have been, but for other things in the case, drove back the tears to their source and forbade her to show the emotions that belong to the sex. But there are some things that are pregnant. My distinguished friend tells of the frequency of presentiments. They are frequent in the storybooks, Mr. Foreman. If they occur in real life they are usually thought of afterward. Did you ever hear one expressed beforehand? Tell me that this woman was physically incapable of that deed? My

distinguished friend has not read female ·character enough to know
that when a woman dares she dares, and when she will she will, and
that given a woman that has that absolute command of herself who
told Mrs. Reagan even, that the failure to break that egg was the
first time she had ever failed in anything she undertook, a woman
whose courage surpassed that of any man I am talking to, I very
humbly believe—tell me that she is physically incapable of this act?
But those are trifles, Mr. Foreman. Those are trifles. Those are
little chips that do not perhaps directly indicate which way the
current flows. But there is more in the case than that. Of course the
question arises to one's lips. How could she have avoided the
spattering of her dress with blood if she was the author of these
crimes? As to the first crime, it is scarcely necessary to attempt to
answer the question. In the solitude of that house, with ample fire
in the stove, with ample wit of woman nobody has suggested that as
to the first crime there was not ample opportunity, ample means and
that nothing could be suggested as a reason why all the evidence of
that crime could not have been amply and successfully concealed.
But as to the second murder the question is one of more difficulty.
I cannot answer it. You cannot answer it. You are neither
murderers nor women. You have neither the craft of the assassin
nor the cunning and deftness of the sex. There are some things,
however, in the case that we know, and one of them is, and perhaps
one of the pregnant facts in the case is, that when the officers had
completed their search, and in good faith had asked her to produce
the dress she was wearing that morning, they were fooled with
that garment which lies on that trunk, which was not upon her when
any human being saw her. That is a pretty bold assertion. Let us
see what the evidence of it is, because as to that matter the evidence
is contradictory, and it is the first proposition, I believe that I have
addressed touching which there is even an attempt to show contradictory evidence. I have trod on ground on which no attempt has
been made to block the ordinary course of reasoning, and I now
approach the first subject in which there is any attempt to show
contradiction, and it turns out to be no contradiction whatever. This
dress has been described to you as a silk dress and dark blue evidently,
a dress with a figure which is not at all like a diamond, a dress which
is not cheap, a dress which would not be worn in ironing by any
prudent woman, of course not. It is an afternoon dress. Do your
wives dress in silk when they go down in the kitchen to work, and
in their household duties in the morning before dinner? But I am

not compelled to stay at suppositions of reasoning: I come to facts. There was one woman in this world who saw Lizzie Borden after these murders were done, and when she saw her did not suspect that murder had been done.

Who was that? It was that clear, intelligent, honest daughter of one of Fall River's most honored citizens, Adelaide Churchill. Everybody else saw her when they knew murder had been done. Addie Churchill saw her when the most she suspected was that somebody had become sick again. She describes the dress she had on that morning. I will read it, word for word, to you, because it is vital: "It looked like a light blue and white ground work; it seemed like calico or cambric, and it had a light blue and white ground work with a navy blue diamond printed on it. Was the whole dress alike, the skirt and waist? It looked so to me. Was that the dress she had on this morning (showing dark blue dress?) She did not wish to harm a hair of Lizzie's head. She was her neighbor and her friend, and she would avoid it if she could. But she answered, "It does not look like it." Mr. Moody puts it again: "Was it, was it?" Ah, Addie Churchill will have to give an answer which will convict this woman of putting up a dress which is not the one she wore. She is no police detective conspiring against her life, but her next door neighbor, her friend, and her friend to-day. When Mr. Moody puts the straight question to her: "Was it?" she answers: "That is not the dress I have described." Still it is not quite close enough. My learned friend wants it answered more closely, and asks, "Was it the dress she had on?" Mrs. Churchill can avoid answering no longer, and she says, "I did not see her with it on that morning." She further describes the dress as having the ground work of a color "like blue and white mixed." It is not the testimony of one who wants her convicted. I may well believe, I am glad to believe, although I know nothing of it, that it is the testimony of one who would rejoice if she were not convicted. Now comes another witness, who I believe would cut his heart strings before he would say a word against that woman if he could help it, and that is her physician and friend, Dr. Seabury W. Bowen, who away back in the early stages of this case gave testimony, and the testimony is all the more valuable because it comes from her intimate friend, and was given at a time when it was not supposed there was ever to be any discussion about it. He undertakes to describe the dress. Do you remember how Lizzie was dressed that morning? "It is pretty hard work for me. Probably if I could see a dress something like it I could guess, but I could not describe it; it was a sort of drab, not much color to it to attract my attention—a sort of morning calico dress, I should judge." That is not all. The morning dress she had worn many times, as Miss Emma is obliged to say, poor girl. She put it in her testimony (she wanted to help her sister) that it was very early in the morning. Oh, unfortunate expression. Did you ever know a girl to change her dress twice a morning, ever in the world? It was a morning dress, and the day before the tragedy happened Bridget tells us that that cheap morning dress, light blue with a dark figure, Wednesday morning the dress she had on was of that description, and it was this very bedford cord. Undoubtedly. She never wore it afterward. Friday she has on this dress. Saturday she has on this dress, mornings and afternoon. It is good enough for her to wear then. Perhaps there is not any distinction of morning and afternoon then in that house of the dead. We have had evidence of the character of the search that was made in the house. It can, perhaps, all be well summed up in the suggestion that the search of Thursday was perfunctory, insufficient and indecisive. It was with no particular definite aim in view. It was absolutely without any idea that the inmates of the house knew of this crime. It was that sort of a search which goes through and does not see what it ought to see. But it was enough to set them on their guard. There was in that house somewhere a bedford cord dress. That bedford cord dress had been stained with paint. I welcome that fact. My learned associate never said it had not been stained with paint. I believe it had. No, I ought not to say that. I hope, I may be corrected if I say that I believe it at any time. There is no assertion or pretence that it had not been stained with paint. It had not stopped the wearing of it, though.

It was good enough for a morning dress, good enough for an ironing dress, good enough for a chore dress around the house in the morning. But the Thursday's search had put them on their guard, and when, Saturday afternoon, the officers came there, they were prepared for the most absolutely thorough search that could be made in that house. Where was that paint stained bedford cord? Where was that dress with paint spots on it, so thickly covering it that it was not fit to wear any more? Where was it that the officers did not see it? Emma alone can tell us, and Emma tries to tell us that it was in that closet. Emma says that Saturday night she saw that dress upon the hook, and said to Lizzie "You'd better destroy this dress," and Lizzie said she would. Nobody heard that conversation

but Lizzie and Emma. So we cannot contradict their words excepting by what followed. Mark the exact use of language. Alice
Russell said that when she came down stairs that morning she went
into the kitchen and Lizzie stood by the stove with a dress skirt in
her hand and a waist on the shelf near by, and Emma turned round
and said to her, " Lizzie, what are you going to do ? " " I am going
to burn this old thing up. It is all covered with paint." There is
scarcely a fact that is not incriminating against Lizzie. Mrs. Reagan
has come on the stand and told upon her oath against a woman who
is her friend, with whom she had no difficulties and who is of her own
sex, against whom she can have no object of resentment or hatred,
as to induce her to commit the foulest of crimes, has told a story
which is extremely significant. I should have hesitated to express
myself as to its significance were it not for the attestation of that fact
by the agitation, the hurrying and scurrying, the extraordinary
efforts put forth by her friends as soon as it was unadvisedly published
to suppress and deny it. They saw its significance, they are unwilling
witnesses to the character of the story and the way it bears upon
the case. That thing took place. Mrs. Reagan has appeared before
you and you are to judge whether you like her looks or not. You
are to be judges of her evidence. Miss Emma, who knew what took
place, never came to Mrs. Reagan, and said, " You have told a lie ! "
They were the ones to have denied it. They were the ones to have
asked her to take it back. Miss Emma was in there the next day
after the publication, and she never found it out in her heart to say
to Mrs. Reagan : " Why, Mrs. Reagan, you have published an
infamous and wicked lie about us ! " It was these same self-constituted
friends who have filled the newspapers with denunciations of delay
in a trial of this cause because the appointed officer was lying sick at
his home and could not attend to it, when the courteous · and accomplished gentlemen, who had her interests in charge, my learned
friends never complained and do not to this day complain, to their
credit be it said.

I had intended, Mr. Foreman and gentlemen, at this point, to
attempt to recapitulate these things to you. I do not think I will do
it. If I have not made them plain they cannot be made plainer.
Every one of them excepting the incident of the burning of the dress
and the accuracy of the witnesses as to the dress that is produced,
depend upon facts that there is no denial of. We find a woman
murdered by blows which were struck with a weak and indecisive
hand. We find that that woman had no enemies in all the world

excepting the daughter that had repudiated her. We find that that woman was killed at half past nine, when it passes the bounds of human credulity to believe that it could have been done without her knowledge, her presence, her sight, her hearing. We find a house guarded by night and by day so that no assassin could find lodgment in it for a moment. We find that after that body had been murdered a falsehood of the very essence of this whole case is told by that girl to explain the story to the father, who would revenge it and delay him from looking for her. We find her then set in her purpose turned into a mania, so far as responsibility is concerned, considering the question of what to do with this witness who could tell everything of that skeleton if he saw fit. He had not always told all he knew. He had forbidden telling of that burglary of Mrs. Borden's things for reasons that I do not know anything about, but which I presume were satisfactory to him, but he would not have so suppressed or concealed this tragedy, and so the devil came to her as God grant it may never come to you or me, but it may. When the old man lay sleeping she was prompted to cover her person in some imperfect way and remove him from life and conceal the evidences, so far as she could in the hurried time that was left her. She did not call Maggie until she got ready. She had fifteen minutes, which is a long time, and then called her down, and without helping the officers in one single thing, but remonstrating with them for going into her room and asking her questions—those servants of the law who were trying to favor her, never opening her mouth except to tell the story of the barn, and then a story of the note, which is all she ever told in the world. We find that woman in a house where is found in the cellar a hatchet which answers every requirement of this case, where no outside assassin could have concealed it, and where she alone could have put it. We find in that house a dress which was concealed from the officers until it was found that the search was to be resumed and safety was not longer assured. The dress was hidden from public gaze by the most extraordinary act of burning that you ever heard of in all your lives by an innocent person.

We say these things float on the great current of our thought and tell just where the stream leads to. We get down now to the elements of ordinary crime. We get hatred, we get malice, we get falsehood about the position and disposition of the body. We get absurd and impossible alibis. We get contradictory stories that are not attempted to be verified. We get fraud upon the officers by the substitution of an afternoon silk dress as the one that she was wearing that morning ironing, and capping the climax by the production of evidence that is beyond all question, that there was a guilty destruction of the dress that she feared the eye of the microscope might find the blood upon. What is the defense, Mr. Foreman? What is the answer to this array of impregnable facts? Nothing, nothing. I stop and think, and I say again, nothing. Some dust thrown upon the story of Mrs. Reagan which is not of the essence of the case, some question about time put upon the acts of Mr. Medley which is not of the essence of the case; some absurd and trifling stories about drunken men the night before and dogs in the yard the night before. Of men standing quietly on the street the same day of the tragedy, exposing their bloody persons for the inspection of passersby, of a pale, irresolute man walking up the street in broad daylight. Nothing, nothing. The distinguished counsel, with all his eloquence,which I can't hope to match or approach, has attempted nothing but to say, "Not proven." But it is proven; it is proven. We cannot measure facts, Mr. Foreman. We cannot put a yardstick to them. We cannot determine the length and breadth and the thickness of them. There is only one test of facts. Do they lead us to firm belief? if they do they have done the only duty they are capable of. You cannot measure the light that shines about you; you cannot weigh it, but we know when it is light because it shines into our hearts and eyes. That is all there is to this question of reasonable doubt. Give the prisoner every vestige of benefit of it. The last question to be answered is taken from these facts together. Are you satisfied that it was done by her? I have attempted, Mr. Foreman, how imperfectly none but myself can say, to discharge the sad duty which has devolved upon me.

He who could have charmed and entertained and inspired you is still detained by sickness, and it has fallen to my lot to fill unworthily the place of the chief lawgiver of this commonwealth. But I submit these facts to you with the confidence that you are men of courage and truth. I have no other suggestion to make to you than that you shall deal with them with that courage that befits sons of Massachusetts. I do not put it on so low a ground as to ask you to avenge these horrid deaths. O, no, I do not put it even on the ground of asking you to do credit to the good old commonwealth of Massachusetts. I lift you higher than that, gentlemen. I advance you to the altitude of the conscience that must be the final master of us all. You are merciful men. The wells of mercy, I hope, are not dried up in any of us. But this is not the time nor the place for the exercise of it. That mighty prerogàtive of mercy is not absent from the jurisprudence of this glorious old common wealth. It is vested in magistrates, one of the most conspicuous of whom was the honored gentleman who has addressed you before me, and to whom no appeal for mercy ever fell upon harsh or unwllling ears. Let mercy be taken care of by those to whom you have intrusted the quallty of mercy. It is not strained in the commonwealth of Massachusetts. It is not for us to discuss that. It is for us to answer questions, the responsibility of which is not with you nor with me. We neither made these laws, nor do we execute them. We are responsible only for the justice, the courage, the ability with which we meet to find an answer to the truth. Rise, gentlemen, rise to the altitude of your duty. Act as as you would act when you stand before the great white throne at the last day. What shall be your reward? The ineffable consciousness of duty done. There is no strait so hard, there is no affliction so bitter, that it is not made light and easy by the consciousness that in times of trial you have done your duty and your whole duty. There is no applause of the world, there is no station of hight, there is no seduction of fame that can compensate for the gnawings of an outraged conscience. Only he who hears the voice of his inner consciousness, it is the voice of God himself saying to him ''Well done, good and faithful servant,'' can enter into the reward and lay hold of eternal life.

CHAPTER XXXII.

Judge Dewey's Charge to the Jury.

THE chief justice addressed the prisoner as follows: Lizzie Andrew Borden—Although you have now been fully heard by counsel, it is your privilege to add any word which you may desire to say in person to the jury. You now have that opportunity.

The prisoner arose and responded: "I am innocent. I leave it to my counsel to speak for me." The charge to the jury was then delivered by Mr. Justice Dewey, as follows:

Mr. Foreman and Gentlemen of the Jury—You have listened with attention to the evidence in this case, and to the arguments of the defendant's counsel and of the district attorney. It now remains for me, acting in behalf of the court, to give you such aid towards a proper performance of your duty as I may be able to give within the limits for judicial action prescribed by law; and, to prevent any erroneous impression, it may be well for me to bring to your attention, at the outset, that it is provided by a statute of this state that the court shall not charge juries with respect to matters of fact, but may state the testimony and the law.

I understand the government to concede that defendants' character has been good: that it has not been merely a negative and natural one that nobody had heard anything against, but one of positive, of active benevolence in religious and charitable work. The question is whether the defendant, being such as she was, did the acts charged upon her. You are not inquiring into the action of some imaginary being, but into the actions of a real person, the defendant, with her character, with her habits, with her education, with her ways of life, as they have been disclosed in the case. Judging of this subject as reasonable men, you have the right to take into consideration her character such as is admitted or apparent. In some cases it may not be esteemed of much importance. In other cases it may raise a reasonable doubt of a defendant's guilt even in the face of strongly criminating circumstances. What shall be its

THE JURY.

effect here rests in your reasonable discretion. I understand the counsel for the government to claim that defendant had towards her stepmother a strong feeling of illwill, nearly if not quite amounting to hatred. And Mrs. Gifford's testimony as to a conversation with defendant in the early spring of 1892 is relied upon largely as a basis for that claim, supplemented by whatever evidence there is as to defendant's conduct towards her stepmother. Now, gentlemen, in judging wisely of a case you need to keep all parts of it in their natural and proper proportion, and not put on any particular piece of evidence a greater weight than it will reasonably bear, and not to magnify or intensify or depreciate and belittle any piece of evidence to meet an emergency. I shall say something before I have done on the caution to be used in considering testimony as to conversations. But take Mrs. Gifford's just as she gave it, and consider whether or not it will fairly amount to the significance attached to it, remembering that it is the language of a young woman and not of a philosopher or a jurist.

What, according to common observation, is the habit of young women in the use of language? Is it not rather that of intense expression, whether that of admiration or dislike? Consider whether or not they do not often use words which, strictly taken, would go far beyond their real meaning. What you wish, of course, is a true conception of the state of the mind of the defendant towards her stepmother, not years ago, but later and nearer the time of the homicide, and to get such a true conception you must not separate Mrs. Gifford's testimony from all the rest, but consider also the evidence as to how they lived in the family, whether as Mrs. Raymond, I believe, said, they sewed together on each other's dresses, whether they went to church together, sat together, returned together, in a word, the general tenor of their life. You will particularly recall the testimony of Bridget Sullivan and of defendant's sister Emma bearing on the same subject. Weigh carefully all the testimony on the subject, in connection with the suggestions of counsel, and then judge whether or not there is clearly proved such a permanent state of mind on the part of defendant toward her stepmother as to justify you in drawing against her upon that ground inferences unfavorable to her innocence. The law requires that before a defendant can be found guilty upon either count in the indictment every material allegation in it shall be proved beyond a reasonable doubt.

Now you observe, gentlemen, that the government submits this case to you upon circumstantial evidence. No witness testifies to seeing the defendant in the act of doing the crime charged, but the government seeks to establish by proof a body of facts and circumstances from which you are asked to infer or conclude that the defendant killed Mr. and Mrs. Borden. This is a legal and not unusual way of proving a criminal case, and it is clearly competent for a jury to find a person guilty of murder upon circumstantial evidence alone. Then, after you have determined what specific facts are proved, you have remaining the important duty of deciding whether or not you are justified in drawing, and will draw, from those facts the conclusion of guilt. Here, therefore, is a two-fold liability to error, first, in deciding upon the evidence what facts are proved, and second, in deciding what inference or conclusion shall be drawn from the facts. This is often the critical or turning point in a case resting on circumstantial evidence. The law warrants you in acting firmly and with confidence on such evidence, but does require you to exercise a deliberate and sober judgment, and use great caution not to form a hasty or erroneous conclusion. You are allowed to deal with this matter with your minds untrammeled by any artificial or arbitrary rule of law. As a great judge has said: "The common law appeals to the plain dictates of common experience and sound judgment."

In other words, failure to prove a fact essential to the conclusion of guilt, and without which that conclusion would not be reached, is fatal to the government's case, but failure to prove a helpful but not an essential fact may not be fatal. Take an essential fact. All would admit that the necessity of establishing the presence of the defendant in the house, when, for instance, her father was killed, is a necessary fact. The government could not expect that you would find her guilty of the murder of her father by her own hand unless you are satisfied that she was where he was when he was murdered. And if the evidence left you in reasonable doubt as to that fact, so vital, so absolutely essential, the government must fail of its case, whatever may be the force and significance of other facts, that is, so far as it is claimed that she did the murder with her own hands. The question of the relation of this handleless hatchet to the murder. It may have an important bearing upon the case, upon your judgment of the relations of the defendant to these crimes, whether the crime was done by that particular hatchet or not, but it cannot be said, and is not claimed by the government, that it bears the same essential and necessary relation to the case that the matter of her presence in the house does. It is not claimed by the government but what that killing might have been done with some other instrument. I understand the government to claim substantially that the alleged fact that the defendant made a false statement in regard to her stepmother's having received a note or letter that morning bears an essential relation to the case, bears the relation of an essential fact, not merely the relation of a useful fact. And so the counsel, in his opening, referring to that matter, charged deliberately upon the defendant that she had told a falsehood in regard to that note. In other words, that she had made statements about it which she knew at the time of making them were untrue, and the learned district attorney, in his closing argument, adopts and reaffirms that charge against the defendant. Now what are the grounds on which the government claims that that charge is false, knowingly false? There are three, as I understand them. First, that the one who wrote it has not been found : second, that the party who brought it has not been found, and third, that no letter has been found. And substantially, if I understand the position correctly, upon those three grounds you are asked to find that an essential fact, a deliberate falsehood on the part of the defendant, has been established. Now what answer or reply is made to this charge? First, that the defendant had time to think of it; she was not put in a position upon the evidence where she was compelled to make that statement without an opportunity for reflection. If as the government claims, she had killed her stepmother some little time before, she had a period in which she could turn over the matter in her mind. She must naturally anticipate, if she knew the facts, that the question at no remote period would be asked her where Mrs. Borden was, or if she knew where she was. She might reasonably and naturally expect that that question would arise. Again, it would be urged in her behalf, what motive had she to invent a story like this? What motive? Would it not have answered every purpose to have her say, and would it not have been more natural for her to say simply that her stepmother had gone out on an errand or to make a call? What motive had she to take upon herself the responsibility of giving utterance to this distinct and independent fact of a letter or note received, with which she might be confronted and which she might afterwards find it difficult to explain, if she knew that no such thing was true? Was it a natural thing to say, situated as they were, living as they were, living as they did, taking the general tenor of their ordinary life, was it a natural thing for her to invent? But it is said no letter was found. Suppose you look at the case for a moment from her standpoint, contemplate the possibility of there being another assassin than herself, might it not be a part of the plan or scheme of such a person by such a document or paper to withdraw Mrs. Borden from the house? If he afterward came in there, came upon her, killed her, might he not have found the letter or note with her, if there was one already in the room. Might he not have a reasonable and natural wish to remove that as one possible link in tracing himself? Taking the suggestions on the one side and the other, judging the matter fairly, not assuming beforehand that the defendant is guilty does the evidence satisfy you as reasonable men, beyond any reasonable doubt, that these statements of the defendant in regard to that note must necessarily be false.

However numerous may be the facts in the government's process of proof tending to show defendant's guilt, yet if there is a fact established—whether in that line of proof or outside of it—which cannot reasonably be reconciled with her guilt, then guilt cannot be said to be established. In order to warrant a conviction on circumstantial evidence it is not necessary for the government to show that by no possibility was it in the power of any other person than the defendant to commit the crimes; but the evidence must be such as to produce a conviction amounting to a reasonable and moral certainty that the defendant and no one else did commit them. The government claims that you should be satisfied upon the evidence that the defendant was so situated that she had an opportunity to perpetrate both the crimes charged upon her. Whether this claim is sustained is for your judgment. By itself alone, the fact, if shown, that the defendant had the opportunity to commit the crimes, would not justify a conviction; but this fact, if established, becomes a matter for your consideration in connection with the other evidence. When was Mrs. Borden killed? At what time was Mr. Borden killed? Did the same person kill both of them? Was defendant in the house when Mrs. Borden was killed? Was she in the house when Mr. Borden was killed? Gentlemen, something has been said to you by counsel as to defendant's not testifying. I must speak to you on this subject. The constitution of our State, in its bill of rights, provides that: "No subject shall be compelled to secure or furnsih evidence against himself." By the common law persons on trial for crime have no right to testify in their own defense. We have now a statute in these words: "In the trial of all indictments, complaints and other proceedings against persons charged with the commission of crimes or offences, a person so charged shall, at his own request, but not otherwise, be deemed a competent witness; and his neglect

or refusal to testify shall not create any presumption against him."
You will notice that guarded language of the statute. It recognizes
and affirms the common law rule that the defendant in a criminal
prosecution is an incompetent witness for himself, but it provides
that on one condition only, namely, his own request, he shall be
deemed competent. Till that request is made he remains incompetent. In this case the defendant has made no such request, and she
stands before you, therefore, as a witness incompetent, and it is
clearly your duty to consider this case and form your judgment upon
it as if the defendant had no right whatever to testify. The Superior
Court, speaking of a defendant's right and protection under the
constitution and statutes, uses these words : " Nor can any inference
be drawn against him from his failure to testify." Therefore I say
to you, and I mean all that my words express, any argument, any
implication, any suggestion, any consideration in your minds unfavorable to defendant, based on her failure to testify, is unwarranted in
law. Nor is defendant called upon to offer any explanation of
her neglect to testify. If she were required to explain, others
might think the explanation insufficient. Then she would lose the
protection of the statute. It is a matter which the law submits to
her own discretion, and to that alone. The defendant may say : " I
have already told to the officers all that I know about this case, and
my statements have been put in evidence. Whatever is mysterious
to others is also a mystery to me. I have no knowledge more than
others have. I have never professed to be able to explain how or by
whom these homicides were committed." There is another reason
why defendant might not wish to testify. Now she is sacredly
guarded by the law from all unfavorable inferences drawn from her
silence. If she testifies she becomes a witness, with less than the
privileges of an ordinary witness. She is subject to cross-examination. She may be asked questions that are legally competent, which
she is not able to answer, or she may answer questions truly, and
yet it may be argued against her that her answers were untrue, and
her neglect to answer perverse. Being a party she is exposed to
peculiar danger of having her conduct on the stand and her testimony
severely scrutinized and perhaps misjudged, of having her evidence
claimed to be of little weight, if favorable to herself, and of great
weight so far as any part of it shall admit of an adverse construction.
She is left free, therefore, to avoid such risks.

If, proceeding with due caution, and observant of the principles
which have been stated, you are convinced beyond reasonable doubt

of the defendant's guilt, it will be your plain duty to declare that conviction by your verdict. If the evidence falls short of producing such conviction in your mind, although it may raise a suspicion of guilt, or even a strong probability of guilt, it would be your plain duty to return a verdict of not guilty. If not legally proved to be guilty, the defendant is entitled to a verdict of not guilty. Then take the matter of Mrs. Reagan's testimony. It is suggested that there has been no denial of that testimony, or, rather, that the persons who busied themselves about getting the certificate from Mrs. Reagan had no denial of it. Mr. Knowlton; "Not by me, sir. I admit it." Judge Dewey; "Admit what?" Mr. Knowlton; "That she did deny it." Judge Dewey; "Mrs. Reagan?" Mr. Knowlton; "Yes, sir." Judge Dewey; "O, no doubt about that. It is not claimed that Mrs. Reagan does not deny it. But I say it is suggested that the parties who represented the defendant in the matter, and who were seeking to get a certificate from Mrs. Reagan were proceeding without having received any authority to get the certificate, and without having had any assurance from anybody that the statement was false and one that ought to be denied. You have heard the statement of Miss Emma about it here; and it would be for you to judge as reasonable men, whether such men as Mr. Holmes and the clergymen and the other parties who were interesting themselves in that matter, started off attempting to get a certificate from Mrs. Reagan contradicting that report without first having taken any steps to satisfy themselves that it was a report that ought to be contradicted. Gentlemen, I know not what views you may take of the case, but it is the gravest importance that it should be decided. If decided at all, it must be decided by a jury. I know of no reason to expect that any other jury could be supplied with more evidence or be better assisted by the efforts of counsel. The case on both sides has been conducted by counsel with great fairness, industry and ability. The law requires that the jury shall be unanimous in their verdict, and it is their duty to agree if they can conscientiously do so. And now, gentlemen, the case is committed into your hands, the tragedy which has given to this investigation such widespread interest and deeply excited public attention and feeling. The press has ministered to this excitement by publishing, without moderation, rumors and reports of all kinds. This makes it difficult to secure a trial free from prejudice. You have doubtless read, previous to the trial, more or less of the accounts and discussions in the newspapers. You must guard, so far as possible, against all impressions derived from having read in the newspapers accounts relating to the question you have now to decide. You cannot, consistently with your duty, go into discussion of those accounts in any way. Use evidence only, for the discovery of the facts, and any other course would be contrary to your duty. And, entering on your deliberations with no pride of opinion, with impartial and thoughtful minds, seeking only for the truth, you will lift the case above the range of passion and prejudice and excited feeling, into the clear atmosphere of reason and law. If you shall be able to do this, we can hope that, in some high sense, this trial may be adopted into the order of providence, and may express in its results somewhat of that justice with which God governs the world.''

The jury retired to its room and remained one hour and ten minutes.

The jurors having answered to their names, the clerk said: Lizzie Andrew Borden, stand up.

The prisoner arose.

The clerk—Gentlemen of the jury, have you agreed upon your verdict?

The foreman—We have.

The clerk—Please return the papers to the court.

The officer returned the papers to the clerk.

The clerk—Lizzie Andrew Borden, hold up your right hand. Mr. Foreman, look upon the prisoner; prisoner, look upon the foreman. What say you, Mr. Foreman.

The foreman (interrupting)—NOT GUILTY.

There was an outburst of applause from the spectators which was at once checked by the officers. The prisoner dropped into her seat.

The clerk—Gentlemen of the jury, you upon your oaths do say that Lizzie Andrew Borden, the prisoner at the bar, is not guilty?

Several jurors—We do.

The clerk—So say you, Mr. Foreman; so say all of you, gentlemen?

The foreman—We do.

Mr. Knowlton—May it please the court. There are pending two indictments against the same defendant, one charging the murder which is charged in this indictment on the first count, and the other charging the murder which is charged in this indictment on the second count. An entry should be made in those cases of *nol prossed* by reason of the verdict in this case. Now, congratulating the defendant and the counsel for the defendant on the result of the trial, I believe the duties are concluded.

Judge Mason—The jurors may be seated.

The clerk—Lizzie Andrew Borden.   (The prisoner arose.)   The court order that you be discharged of this indictment and go thereof without delay.

Judge Mason—The court desires to express to the jury its appreciation of their faithful service, and recognize its performance under conditions imposing great hardship upon the members of the jury.   I trust it is not necessary to assure them that it is only in deference to the usages of the law and to what is deemed essential for the safety of rights that they have been subjected to the inconvenience in question.   I trust that they will have the satisfaction of having faithfully performed an important duty as their compensation for this inconvenience. You are now discharged from any further attendance.

Thus ended, on the thirteenth day, the famous trial of Lizzie Andrew Borden, and she returned guiltless to her friends and home in Fall River.

THE END.